Digital Demagogue

This book comes with a free eBook, *Nationalism 2.0: The Making of Brexit on Social Media*, by Christian Fuchs.

By analysing reactions on social media immediately after the results of the Brexit referendum were announced, Fuchs shows how Brexit deeply polarised British society. By using extensive empirical data drawn from the comments and reactions of users who posted on Nigel Farage's and Boris Johnson's Facebook profiles, a disturbing picture of a deepening nationalist sentiment appears. *Nationalism 2.0* reveals how the political fetishism of nationalist ideologies has displaced attention from the roles of capitalism and class as factors causing social problems today.

To download the eBook, go to bit.ly/nationalism20

Digital Demagogue

Authoritarian Capitalism in the Age of Trump and Twitter

Christian Fuchs

PLUTO PRESS

First published 2018 by Pluto Press
345 Archway Road, London N6 5AA

www.plutobooks.com

British Library Cataloguing in Publication Data
A catalogue record for this book is available from the British Library

ISBN   978 0 7453 3798 2   Hardback
ISBN   978 0 7453 3796 8   Paperback
ISBN   978 1 7868 0281 1   PDF eBook
ISBN   978 1 7868 0283 5   Kindle eBook
ISBN   978 1 7868 0282 8   EPUB eBook

This book is printed on paper suitable for recycling and made from fully
managed and sustained forest sources. Logging, pulping and manufacturing
processes are expected to conform to the environmental standards of the
country of origin.

Typeset by Stanford DTP Services, Northampton, England

Simultaneously printed in the United Kingdom and United States of America

Contents

List of Figures

List of Tables

1
Introduction

POLITICAL CONTEXT

We live in insecure political times, where the intensification of crises has turned into the emergence of authoritarian capitalism:

> 2016 saw the idea of human dignity and equality, the very notion of a human family, coming under vigorous and relentless assault from powerful narratives of blame, fear and scapegoating, propagated by those who sought to take or cling on to power at almost any cost. [...] Donald Trump's poisonous campaign rhetoric exemplifies a global trend towards angrier and more divisive politics. Across the world, leaders and politicians wagered their future power on narratives of fear and disunity, pinning blame on the 'other' for the real or manufactured grievances of the electorate. (Amnesty International 2017, 12)

Donald Trump: 'America First'

In the USA, Donald Trump won the 2016 presidential election with a nationalist campaign that promised to put 'America first' and to 'make America great again'. He used stereotypes, such as the one of immigrants as 'people coming through the border, that are from all over, and they are bad, they are really bad. [...] You have people coming in, and I am not just saying Mexicans. I am talking about people that are from all over that are killers, and rapists, I mean they are coming into this country' (Trump 2015c). 'On the political stage, perhaps the most prominent of many seismic events was the election of Donald Trump as President of the USA. His election followed a campaign during which he frequently made deeply divisive statements marked by misogyny and xenophobia, and pledged to roll back established civil liberties and introduce policies

1

which would be profoundly inimical to human rights' (Amnesty International 2017, 12).

India: Narendra Modi

In India, the Bharatiya Janata Party came to power in 2014. Hindu nationalism has proliferated under Prime Minster Narendra Modi. In 2016, 'authorities used repressive laws to curb freedom of expression and silence critics. Human rights defenders and organizations continued to face harassment and intimidation, and vigilante cow protection groups carried out several attacks. Thousands protested against discrimination and violence faced by Dalit communities' (Amnesty International 2017, 183). Sedition charges, among others, were brought against student leader Kanhaiya Kumar from Jawaharlal Nehru University in 2016 for allegedly shouting anti-Indian slogans. Kumar commented:

> This government has resorted to dictatorial and fascist ways. Those who speak against them and their ideology are being branded as anti-nationals. Laws like sedition are not needed in a liberal democratic state. It is being misused. It is being used as a political tool by this government. It's the same law drafted by the colonial power. No changes have ever been made. It's being used on the same pattern as the British used it. [...] The government is attacking educational institutions. It's a continuous attack against India's intelligentsia, which talks about protection of constitution, human rights and freedom. Voice of dissent arises from there. [...] The scope of freedom of expression has not shrunk but it is under continuous attack from the government. (Khalid 2016).

Turkey: Recep Tayyip Erdoğan

Turkey's state has, under President Recep Tayyip Erdoğan (Justice and Development Party), become increasingly authoritarian:

> On 15 July [2016], factions within the armed forces launched a violent coup attempt [in Turkey]. It was quickly suppressed [...] Freedom of expression deteriorated sharply during the year. After the declaration of a state of emergency, 118 journalists were remanded

in pre-trial detention and 184 media outlets were arbitrarily and permanently closed down under executive decrees, leaving opposition media severely restricted. People expressing dissent, especially in relation to the Kurdish issue, were subjected to threats of violence and criminal prosecution. Internet censorship increased. At least 375 NGOs, including women's rights groups, lawyers' associations and humanitarian organizations, were shut by executive decree in November. [...] Signatories to a January petition by Academics for Peace calling for a return to peace negotiations and recognition of the demands of the Kurdish political movement were subjected to threats of violence, administrative investigation and criminal prosecution. Four signatories were detained until a court hearing in April; they were released but not acquitted. By the end of the year, 490 of the academics were under administrative investigation and 142 had been dismissed. Since the coup, more than 1,100 of the signatories were formally under criminal investigation. (Amnesty International 2017, 367, 368)

The Academics for Peace petition demanded that the Turkish government create 'the conditions for negotiations and create a road map that would lead to a lasting peace which includes the demands of the Kurdish political movement' as well as 'an immediate end to the violence perpetrated by the state'.[1] President Erdoğan called the signatories 'so-called intellectuals' and 'a fifth column' (Weaver 2016). In the course of the crackdown against alleged supporters of Fethullah Gülen, many of the Academics for Peace lost their jobs. They also face an occupational ban from Turkish public services, and many journalists and opposition politicians face legal charges in Turkey. Noam Chomsky (2016a), who signed the petition, has argued that Erdoğan installed a 'deeply authoritarian regime'.

Philippines: Rodrigo Duterte

Philippine President Rodrigo Duterte said in 2016: 'Hitler massacred three million Jews. Now, there's three million drug addicts. I'd be happy to slaughter them' (Holmes 2016).

---

1. www.europe-solidaire.org/spip.php?article36944, accessed 14 October 2017.

The [Philippine] government [in 2016] launched a campaign to crackdown on drugs in which over 6,000 people were killed. Human rights defenders and journalists were also targeted and killed by unidentified gunmen and armed militia. In June [2016], the government launched a campaign to crackdown on drugs which led to a wave of unlawful killings across the country, many of which may have amounted to extrajudicial executions. These killings followed the election of President Duterte, who repeatedly and publicly endorsed the arrest and killing of those suspected of using or selling drugs. No police officers or private individuals were known to have faced charges for over 6,000 deaths during the year. (Amnesty International 2017, 295)

Europe: Viktor Orbán, Heinz Christian Strache, Norbert Hofer, Marine Le Pen, Geert Wilders and Nigel Farage

In 2016, Hungary continued its systematic crackdown on the rights of refugees and migrants despite growing international criticism. [...] The detention of asylum-seekers in the country continued to be implemented without the necessary safeguards to ensure that it was lawful, necessary and proportional. [...] The government spent over €20 million on communication campaigns labelling refugees and migrants as criminals and threats to national security. In October, it held a national referendum on its opposition to the relocation of asylum-seekers to Hungary within an EU-wide scheme. The referendum was invalid due to insufficient turnout. (Amnesty International 2017, 181, 182, 183)

Hungary's prime minister, Viktor Orbán, spoke of migration as 'poison, we don't need it and won't swallow it' and said that 'every single migrant poses a public security and terror risk' (*Guardian* 2016). In summer 2017, Orbán's Fidesz movement ran a campaign that used posters showing a picture of philanthropist George Soros and the messages 'Don't let Soros have the last laugh' as well as '99% reject illegal immigration'. The posters created the impression that Soros fostered illegal immigration to Hungary. The campaign was widely condemned as being anti-Semitic.

In Austria, the Freedom Party (FPÖ) under Heinz Christian Strache used election campaign slogans such as 'Homeland instead of Islam: WE are for YOU',[2] 'Vienna must not turn into Istanbul'[3] or 'More courage for our "Viennese Blood": Too much foreignness is not good for anyone'.[4] In the run-off 2016 presidential election, the FPÖ's candidate, Norbert Hofer, achieved 46.2 per cent of the votes.

In France, the leader of the National Front, Marine Le Pen, calls immigration 'an organized replacement of our population. This threatens our very survival. We don't have the means to integrate those who are already here. The result is endless cultural conflict' (RT 2011). In the Netherlands, Party for Freedom (PVV) politician Geert Wilders suggested a 'head rag tax' of €1,000 that he justified by saying that he believes in the 'polluter pays' principle (Steen 2010).[5]

In the 2016 UK referendum on leaving the European Union (EU), Nigel Farage's UK Independence Party (UKIP) used posters that read: 'BREAKING POINT: The EU has failed us all. We must break free of the EU and take back control of our borders'. The posters showed an image of thousands of refugees. Some observers pointed out parallels with Nazi propaganda films that showed images of Jews accompanied by the message, 'These are the type of Eastern Jews who flooded Europe's cities after the last war – parasites, undermining their host countries, threatening thousand-year-old cultures and bringing with them crime, corruption and chaos' (Bartlett 2016).

> Several European countries [in 2016] saw an increase in hate crimes targeting asylum-seekers, Muslims and foreign nationals. In Germany there was a sharp increase in attacks on shelters for asylum-seekers, and in the UK hate crimes surged by 14% in the three months after the referendum on the UK's withdrawal from the EU (Brexit) in June compared to the same period the previous year. (Amnesty International 2017, 44)

Right-Wing Authoritarianism

These are just some examples that document the prevalence of right-wing authoritarianism. We live in times of economic crises, complex wars

2. 'Daham statt Islam. WIR für EUCH'.
3. 'Wien darf nicht Istanbul werden'.
4. 'Mehr Mut für unser "Wiener Blut": Zu viel Fremdes tut niemandem gut'.
5. See also: www.watwilwilders.nl/WildersbeledigtgroepenEN.html.

and heavy political conflicts. Far-right demagogues make use of these insecurities and resulting fears. They distract attention from the complex societal and political-economic causes of crises, construct scapegoats and preach nationalism and law-and-order politics. The proliferation of new nationalisms and authoritarian politics reminds us of past times. The danger is that history might repeat itself. While there is a danger of regression to the past, at the same time we are experiencing the emergence of new technologies such as social media, big data analytics, the Internet of things, cloud computing, smart technologies that promise a new age. The old and the new are always linked in complex ways in the present. Right-wing authoritarianism celebrates new successes and is communicated through new formats, such as social media. Donald Trump as a president who uses the two communication tools of reality TV (*The Apprentice*) and social media (Twitter) is prototypical for how old ideologies are communicated through new media and how these ideologies take on new forms in the age of Internet spectacles.

This book asks: what is authoritarian capitalism? How is authoritarian capitalism communicated through social media? It formulates the foundations of a contemporary critical theory of right-wing authoritarianism and authoritarian capitalism. In doing so, it updates the Frankfurt School's critical theory of authoritarianism. It draws on and reinvigorates the works of the Frankfurt School thinkers Franz L. Neumann, Theodor W. Adorno, Erich Fromm, Herbert Marcuse, Max Horkheimer and Leo Löwenthal. It studies how right-wing authoritarianism works and is communicated on social media platforms such as Twitter and Facebook.

THE CHAPTERS IN THIS BOOK

Chapter 2 gives an introduction to the notions of ideology, nationalism and fascism from a critical theory perspective. Chapter 3 provides a theoretical framework for understanding right-wing authoritarianism and authoritarian capitalism.

If you want to go directly to the analysis of Trump's role in US capitalism and the way he uses Twitter, you may want to skip reading the theoretical foundations in Chapters 2 and 3 and go directly to Chapter 4. I recommend these two chapters as introductions to Marxist theories of nationalism, fascism and authoritarian capitalism.

Chapters 4 and 5 analyse economic power, state power and ideological power in the age of Donald Trump with the help of critical theory. They apply the critical theory approaches of thinkers such as Franz L. Neumann, Theodor W. Adorno and Erich Fromm. Chapter 4 focuses on aspects of political economy (Trumpism: Trump and authoritarian statism), while Chapter 5 concentrates on Trump's ideology (Trumpology).

Chapter 4 analyses changes of US capitalism that have, together with political anxiety and demagoguery, brought about the rise of Donald Trump. The chapter draws attention to the importance of state theory for understanding Trump and the changes to politics that his rule may bring about. In this context it is important to understand the complexity of the state, including the dynamic relationship between the state and the economy, the state and citizens, intra-state relations, inter-state relations, semiotic representations of and by the state, and ideology. Trumpism and its potential impacts are theorised along these dimensions.

Chapter 5 focuses on the ideology of Trump (Trumpology). Trumpology has played an important role not just in Donald Trump's business and brand strategies, but also in his political rise. The (pseudo-) critical mainstream media have helped create Trump and Trumpology by providing platforms for populist spectacles that sell as news and attract audiences. Through Trump making news in the media, the media make Trump. An empirical analysis of Trump's rhetoric and the elimination discourses in his NBC show *The Apprentice* underpins the analysis of Trumpology. The combination of Trump's actual power and Trump as spectacle, showman and brand makes his government's concrete policies fairly unpredictable. An important question that arises is what the role of social scientists should be in the conjuncture that the world is experiencing.

Chapter 6 analyses how Donald Trump uses Twitter for communicating authoritarian ideology. It uses the critical theory of the authoritarian personality for theoretically framing right-wing authoritarianism and engages with the works of Wilhelm Reich, Erich Fromm and Theodor W. Adorno. The chapter identifies hierarchical leadership, nationalism, the friend/enemy scheme and militaristic patriarchy as four key elements of right-wing authoritarianism. Using this theory framework, it presents a critical discourse analysis of 1,815 tweets posted by Donald Trump between July 2016 and January 2017. The chapter gives insights into how right-wing authoritarianism works on social media platforms such as Twitter.

This book contributes to the study and critical theory of nationalism in the age of social media (nationalism 2.0). Some conclusions are drawn in Chapter 7. This work stands in the tradition of theoretical and empirical ideology critique. Ideology, nationalism and right-wing authoritarianism are general key concepts used throughout the book. It therefore makes sense to briefly outline the understanding of these concepts, which will be the task of Chapter 2.

2
Ideology, Nationalism and Fascism

This chapter engages with the book's foundational theoretical categories, namely ideology,[1] nationalism and fascism.

IDEOLOGY

There are different traditions regarding how to define and study ideology. Approaches include Marx's theory of commodity fetishism, Lukács' theory of reification, Gramsci's theory of hegemony, the Frankfurt School, Hallian cultural studies, various forms and schools of critical discourse analysis, Foucauldian discourse analysis and Althusserian ideology theory (Eagleton 1991, Rehmann 2013, Žižek 1994). These theories do not form a consensus on what ideology is and how it should be defined. Two major schools in the critical study of ideology go back to Antonio Gramsci and Georg Lukács.

Six Understandings of Ideology

Terry Eagleton (1991, chapter 1) discerns various understandings of ideology by identifying six theoretical approaches:

1. Ideology as the 'production of ideas, beliefs and values in social life' (28) (= ideology as culture) (28);
2. Ideas and beliefs of 'a specific, socially significant group or class' (29) (= ideology as worldview);
3. The '*promotion* and *legitimation* of the interests' of a group 'in the face of opposing interests' (29);
4. The 'promotion and legitimation of sectoral interests' in the 'activities of a dominant social power' (29) (= ideology as dominant worldviews);

1. Acknowledgement: the ideology section of this chapter has been reproduced from Fuchs (2016d), which was published based on a Creative Commons CC-BY license.

5. '[I]deas and beliefs which help to legitimate the interests of a ruling group or class specifically by distortion and dissimulation' (30);
6. '[F]alse or deceptive beliefs [...] arising not from the interests of a dominant class but from the material structure of society as a whole' (30).

Gramsci and Lukács

Whereas Gramsci's approach can be characterised as ideology theory, Lukács' can be seen as ideology critique (Fuchs 2015, chapter 3). Gramsci understands ideology as worldviews, the 'superstructure of a particular structure' (Gramsci 1988, 199) and a 'conception of the world' (Gramsci 1988, 343). Lukács, based on Marx's theory of commodity fetishism, sees ideology as reified thought emerging in reified societies. He therefore argues that the 'emergence and diffusion of ideologies appears as the general characteristic of class societies' (Lukács 1986, 405).

Ideology Critique

Marx, Lukács and the Frankfurt School in particular have influenced the theoretical concept of ideology used in this book and the Marxian theory approach that underlies it (Fuchs 2015). The notion of ideology employed relates to Eagleton's fifth and sixth meanings of ideology. By ideology, I understand thoughts, practices, ideas, words, concepts, phrases, sentences, texts, belief systems, meanings, representations, artefacts, institutions, systems or combinations thereof that represent and justify one group's or individual's power, domination or exploitation of other groups or individuals by misrepresenting, one-dimensionally presenting or distorting reality in symbolic representations (Fuchs 2015). Ideology is not simply an abstract structure, but has a concrete, lived reality: ideological workers produce and reproduce ideologies (Fuchs 2015, chapter 3). Marx characterises the producers of ideology as 'the thinkers of the [ruling] class', its 'active, conceptive ideologists', who, based on a division of labour within the ruling class, 'make the formation of the illusions of the class about itself their chief source of livelihood' (Marx and Engels 1845, 68).

The definition taken in the theory approach underlying this work implies moral realism and socialist praxis: humans can analyse and understand the world's reality and the real causes of complex problems. Ideology critique is the deconstruction of falsehood, of knowledge that is presented as truth but is deceptive. Socialist moral realism implies that dominative and exploitative societies negate humans' general interests. They therefore should from a political point of view be abolished and replaced by a societal formation that benefits everyone economically, socially, politically and culturally. Such a society of the commons is a socialist society. Eagleton's fifth and sixth meanings of ideology are based on a dialectical contradiction of class societies and socialism. These are critical political understandings that imply political praxis and the transcendence of class, capitalism and domination.

General Theories of Ideology

Not everyone agrees with such a definition of ideology. General theories of ideology generally disagree. For Louis Althusser (2005), ideology is an 'organic part of every social totality' (232). 'Ideology is a system (with its own logic and rigour) of representations (images, myths, ideas or concepts, depending on the case) endowed with a historical existence and role within a given society' (231). Althusserian ideology theory has been influential.

Stuart Hall (1986/1996, 26) defines ideology as 'the mental frameworks – the languages, the concepts, categories, imagery of thought, and the systems of representations – which different classes and social groups deploy in order to make sense of, define, figure out and render intelligible the way society works'. Hall (1982) identifies the critical paradigm in media studies with the study of ideology. The origin would have been the Frankfurt School's challenge of behaviourist media effects research. Hall's notion of ideology is grounded in structural linguistics and the works of Gramsci, Althusser and Laclau.

Criticisms of General Ideology Theories

The problems in Hall's understanding are twofold. First, humans are denied subject positions. Discourse and ideological structures are turned into subjects. Such structuralism becomes evident when structures are presented as actively doing something and humans are seen as structure's objects. Hall (1982) for example writes that humans are positioned and languaged (80), ideological discourses win their way (80) and discourse speaks itself through him/her (88). It is then not humans who communicate ideology and discourse through language, but ideology that languages, speaks, communicates, etc. Ideology is in this approach an articulation of linguistic elements, of rules, codes, linguistic systems, classificatory systems, matrixes and sets of elements. Missing is the insight that ideology is an active communicative process and a social relation, in which humans, groups and classes produce and reproduce power relations. Production and reproduction of power entails the possibilities to undo, perturb, challenge and oppose existing power relations just like it entails the possibilities of taking over, justifying, sustaining, and legitimating such relations.

The second problem is associated with the first: in a structuralist approach social struggle becomes a struggle between ideologies. It is not seen as a power relation between humans, in which they actively produce and reproduce discourses and ideologies. It is not ideologies that struggle with each other, but humans, human groups and classes that struggle against each other with various means, including the means of communication, and with specific capacities to mobilise power. Such resources in ideological and other struggles have specific distributions that enable various degrees of power. Hall's (1982) approach is a relativistic determinism, in which ideological struggles and alternative interpretations emerge with necessity. He therefore speaks of ideology as a 'site of struggle' (between competing definitions) (70) and of significations as 'controversial and conflicting' (70). There is certainly always the possibility of contestation, but no necessity for it. Asymmetric power relations can equip humans, groups and classes to different degrees with the capacities to speak and communicate, to be heard, be visible and be listened to, and to get information across to others.

Horkheimer and Adorno's Criticisms of General Ideology Theory

General understandings of ideology represent the first and second meanings identified by Eagleton. The problem is that such a generalist understanding is morally and politically relativist. If the views that 'Jews are inferior beings, that women are less rational than men, that fornicators will be condemned to perpetual torment' are 'not instances of false consciousness, then it is difficult to know what is; and those who dismiss

12

the whole notion of false consciousness must be careful not to appear cavalier about the offensiveness of these opinions' (Eagleton 1991, 15). If democratic socialism and anti-fascism are the dominant paradigms in a society, then in such a societal context, fascism, racism and capitalism are understood in a general way to be forms of ideological critique. Such a generality is a disservice to a critical theory of society. Max Horkheimer (1972, 28) makes such a remark about Karl Mannheim's general theory of ideology, saying that these general approaches 'thoroughly purge from the ideology concept the remains of its accusatory meaning'. According to Adorno (1981, 38), generalising theories of ideology employ 'the terminology of social criticism while removing its sting'. Whereas the critique of ideology is 'determinate negation in the Hegelian sense, the confrontation of the ideational with its realization' (Adorno 1972, 466), general theories of ideology replace the determinate negation by the analysis of 'general worldviews' (Adorno 1972, 472).

Eagleton's fifth and sixth definitions do not imply, as claimed by Stuart Hall (1986/1996, 30), 'economic and class reductionism'. In the theory of false consciousness and false society, class background and position do not determine, but condition, consciousness. A dominant class is often organised in competing class factions that also have competing ideologies. The example of Marx and Engels, who came from quite bourgeois families, shows that individuals are not trapped in certain ideologies because of their background. Consciousness is dynamic and reflects in complex non-linear ways the total of an individual's experiences, social positions and social relations in society.

Critical Discourse Analysis

In the tradition of critical discourse analysis (CDA), there are different understandings of ideology. Norman Fairclough (2010, 73) distinguishes between critical and descriptive concepts of ideology. Teun van Dijk (1998, 8) has a more descriptive approach and defines ideology as a mental framework that is 'the *basis of the social representations shared by members of a group*' that allows the organisation of the group members' social beliefs and practices. In contrast to van Dijk, Fairclough defines ideology as 'representations which contribute to the constitution, reproduction, and transformation of social relations of power and domination' (Fairclough 2010, 73). His understanding is close to the fourth, fifth and sixth meanings of ideology identified by Eagleton. Reisigl and Wodak (2009, 88) understand ideology as a 'one-sided perspective or world view' of a particular social group that is a means for 'establishing and maintaining unequal power relations through discourse'. Wodak explicitly acknowledges the influence of Frankfurt School critical theory on the discourse-historical approach of CDA (Wodak 2009, 34–5; Reisigl and Wodak 2001, 32).

Adorno: Ideology Critique in Action

Theodor W. Adorno's works show ideology critique in action. The dominant tendency is to reduce Adorno to the critique of the culture industry (Horkheimer and Adorno 2002, 94–136; for a discussion and critique of this tendency, see: Fuchs 2016b, chapter 3). Such readings overlook the wealth of Adorno's ideology critique, which also includes studies of the ideology of anti-Semitism (Horkheimer and Adorno 2002, 137–72), fascist and authoritarian ideology (Adorno 1955, 1956, 1973), ideologies in everyday life (Adorno 1951b), astrology, superstition and occultism (Adorno 1955, 1962), ideology and its critique in education (Adorno 1971), etc. Adorno understands ideology in a Lukácsian sense as 'a consciousness which is objectively necessary and yet at the same time false, as the intertwining of truth and falsehood' (Adorno 1954, 189). For Adorno (1954, 190), the need for ideology critique follows from the existence of ideology. The understanding of ideology underlying this book stands in the tradition of Marx, Lukács and the Frankfurt School. Jürgen Ritsert (1972), based on the Frankfurt School tradition, has defined empirical ideology critique as a method of critical social research. In this book, ideology critique combines critical theory and empirical social research. It is both a theory and a theory-based empirical research method.

The methodological approach taken combines immanent ideology critique, critical theory of society and praxeological reflections. It critically analyses and theorises mediated *texts* in their *contexts* in order to advance the *prospects* for progressive changes of society. It uses immanent critique for analysing the inherent contradictions of texts by comparing their claims to reality and pointing out divergences. Single comments and tweets stand in the broader context of power relations in society. Right-wing authoritarianism aims at a particular model of society that wants to organise power relations by hierarchic leadership, nationalism, polarisation into friends and enemies, patriarchy and militarism. Using critical theory for the analysis means to theorise the broader context of right-wing authoritarianism, i.e. to embed the analysis into the critical theory of authoritarianism. It also requires us to think about the potential consequences of the presented results for praxis. The approach taken is not explicitly based on, but not unrelated to Fairclough's understanding of CDA as the unity of normative critique, explanatory critique and praxis: 'CDA is normative critique of discourse, leading to explanatory critique of relations between discourse and other social elements of the existing social reality, as a basis for action to change reality for the better' (Fairclough 2015, 48). CDA combines text-immanent critique, socio-diagnostic critique and prospective critique (Reisigl and Wodak 2001, 31–5).

NATIONALISM

The nation is a complex term. It can on the one hand be understood as a territorial state and on the other hand as national identity (Jessop 2016, 149–50). Nationalism is a particular national ideology that primarily takes place at the level of national identity, but tends towards defining who should be included in and excluded from the citizenship of a territorial state.

'Immigrants take away "our" jobs and dump our wages': this claim is one of the most frequently used xenophobic, new racist and nationalist statements. It is an ideological claim that exemplifies the connection between nationalism and capitalism. Nationalism, racism and xenophobia displace class struggle by focusing the attention on foreigners who allegedly attack the nationalist collective.

Otto Bauer's Concept of Nationalism

The Austrian socialist politician and Marxist theorist Otto Bauer created an influential analysis of nationalism. Bauer (1924/2012, 52) argues that the nation grows out of a 'community of destiny rather than from a mere similarity of destiny'. The decisive characteristic of a nation would not be class, but the commonality of language, communication, upbringing, moral values, traditions, customs and law. Bauer didn't just reify the nation, but also misjudged the resistance of the working class to nationalism:

> [The] working class welds the knife of criticism against everything that is historically transmitted. [...] Since the national cultural values are not in the possession of the proletariat, national valuation is not the proletarian valuation. [...] There is no class that is inwardly more completely free from national valuation than the proletariat that has been freed from all tradition by the destructive power of capitalism. (Bauer 1924/2012, 65–6)

Bauer's assumption has been falsified by the fact that European far-right movements today find massive support among blue-collar workers. A Bauerian approach to nationalism cannot explain that the '"disappearance" of the working class [...] fatally unleashes its reappearance in the guise of aggressive nativism' (Žižek 2000/2006, 40), and that the 'populist Right moves to occupy the terrain evacuated by the Left, as the only "serious" political force that still employs an anti-capitalist rhetoric – even if thickly coated with a nationalist/racist/religious veneer' (Žižek 2000/2006, 33–4).

Rosa Luxemburg's Critique of Nationalism

Rosa Luxemburg was one of the first Marxist theorists to formulate an ideology critique of the nation and nationalism. For Luxemburg (1976), the modern nation state organises its national territory as a market for commodities and labour that it protects through internal defence (law, police) and external defence (military) (162). It also organises infrastructures (162) and population policies as conditions of capital accumulation. Capitalist imperialism is an inherent feature of the modern nation state (130, 172). The capitalist state is the social form of nationalism (165–6). The state is, however, also dialectical because certain modern social forms, especially the democratic system and culture (education system, science, media, arts, intellectual life), can also advance the emancipation of the working class (175, 257). Knowledge is power 'in the sense of knowledge as a lever of class struggle, as the revolutionary consciousness of the working masses' (257).

Luxemburg questions the political demand 'that all nationalities forming the state have the right to self-determination' (Luxemburg 1976, 102). She argues that the nation is a bourgeois principle and the right to national self-determination a 'metaphysical cliché' (110). Socialism only knows 'a general socialist principle: sympathy for the proletariat of all suppressed nationalities and the recognition of their *right* to self-determination' (Luxemburg 1976, 108).

Luxemburg applies Marx's notion of fetishism to the nation and nationalism, arguing that nationalist ideology 'ignores completely the fundamental theory of modern socialism – the theory of social classes' (135). Nationalism is a 'misty veil' that 'conceals in every case a definite historical content' (135). 'In a class society, "the nation" as a homogeneous socio-political entity does not exist. Rather, there exist within each nation, classes with antagonistic interests and "rights"' (135). Nationalism is an ideology that veils and distracts attention from society's class division. In a comparable manner, Étienne Balibar (2007, 71) argues that there is not just economic fetishism, but also a 'juridical fetishism'. The fetishism of the nation and the nation state is an example of this political form of fetishism. For Luxemburg, socialist internationalism is incompatible with any form of nationalism. She expresses this political attitude in the following words in a letter: 'I feel at home in the entire world, wherever there are clouds and birds and human tears' (Luxemburg 2013, 376).

On 4 August 1914, 78 parliamentarians of the German Social Democratic Party (SPD) voted in favour of the Reichstag's support of war loans, while 14 opposed them. The SPD thereby gave up its opposition to the First World War. Rosa Luxemburg, Karl Liebknecht and others who opposed the war founded the Spartacus League that in 1918 became the Communist Party of Germany (KPD). Luxemburg argued in the *Junius Pamphlet* that the nationalist ideology of national self-determination had corrupted the SPD and had turned it into a party that supported imperialism. '*This world war* means a reversion to barbarism' (Luxemburg 1970, 388). Nationalism resulted in the fact that 'working men kill and destroy each other' and in 'an abyss between the commandments of international solidarity of the proletariat of the world and the interests of freedom and nationalist existence of the people' (391). Luxemburg's critique of nationalism as a fetishistic ideology that denies class conflict attained a very practical political relevance in the First World War: the

SPD was 'refuting the existence of class struggle' (428). For Luxemburg, the critique of nationalism is also the critique of imperialist warfare. Such 'bloody nightmare of hell will not cease until the workers […] clasp each others' hands in brotherhood and will drown the bestial chorus of war agitators and the hoarse cry of capitalist hyenas with the might cry of labor, "Proletarians of all countries, unite!"' (472). 'The workers' fatherland, to the defense of which all else must be subordinated, is the socialist International' (477).

Critical Theories of Nationalism

There are some important general insights one can learn from critical theories of nationalism (Özkirimli 2010): nationalism is both an ideology and a political movement. It originated in the West during the eighteenth and nineteenth centuries in the context of Romanticism and Enlightenment thought. In the English language, the term *nationalist* emerged in the eighteenth century and the word *nationalism* in the nineteenth century (Williams 1983a, 213). Fetishistic concepts of the nation naturalise the nation and argue that it develops naturally and inevitably in any society. Ethnosymbolist and primordialist concepts of the nation and nationalism, in particular, face the risk of fetishism. Anthony D. Smith (1991, 14), for example, defines a nation as a common population with a common territory, culture, economy, common legal rights and duties, common myths, common memories and a common history. The problem with such general definitions is that they make the nation almost synonymous with society and risk not just fetishising the nation, but also reifying nationalism as a behaviour common to humans in all societies. Conceiving nationalism as an ideology that constructs nations and national pride is the best way to avoid fetishising nationalism. '[N]ationalism comes before nations. Nations do not make states and nationalisms but the other way round' (Hobsbawm 1992, 10).

Eric Hobsbawm: The Nation as Invented Tradition

Authors such as Eric Hobsbawm have challenged fetishism by arguing that nations and nationalism are invented traditions (Hobsbawm and Ranger 1983). To argue that the nation and nationalism are invented differs from Benedict Anderson's (1991) claim that the nation is an imagined political community that is so large that its citizens cannot all know each other personally and therefore have to imagine shared characteristics. Imagination has to do with creativity, which implies a positive concept of the nation, whereas critical theories of nationalism stress its ideological character. Invention resonates with fabrication, falsity and ideology (Özkirimli 2010, 107).

Nationalistic fetishism tends to take on two forms. Biologistic nationalism argues that there is a natural bond between humans of the same biological 'race'. It is inherently racist because it assumes that there is a bond based on blood and that different human races exist. Cultural nationalism assumes that nations develop in any society because of shared language, experiences, values and morals, customs and traditions, religion, means of communication, emotions, affects and identity. Bob Jessop (2016, 152–5) distinguishes in this context between the ethnic and the cultural understanding of the nation. He adds that there is also a civic understanding, in which identity is defined by 'loyalty to and identification with the constitution and political arrangements of the state' (Jessop 2016, 154).

Banal Nationalism

Nationalism reproduces itself through banal everyday symbols, phenomena and practices such as flags, national anthems, politicians' rhetoric, sports, news media, television and radio, national currencies, coins, bank notes, national days, stamps and celebrities (Billig 1995). Nationalism makes identity claims, temporal claims and spatial claims:

> The nationalist discourse divides the world into 'us' and 'them', 'friends' and 'foes', positing a homogeneous and fixed identity on either side and stressing the characteristics that differentiate 'us' from 'them'. [...] The nationalist discourse always looks back in time, seeking to demonstrate the 'linear time of the nation', its undisputed diachronic presence. [...] The nationalist discourse is also haunted by a fixation on territory, the quest for a 'home', actual or imagined. This involves the reconstruction of social space as national territory. (Özkirimli 2010, 208–9)

Étienne Balibar: Nationalism as Fictive Ethnicity

Étienne Balibar terms the nationalist Us/Them distinction the construction of *fictive ethnicity* (Balibar and Wallerstein 1991, 49, 96–100): it involves the construction of a fictive collective. Individuals are 'represented in the past or in the future *as if* they formed a natural community' (96). There are two dominant forms of fictive ethnicity (98–105). A first version of fictive ethnicity is the ideological construction of a linguistic community through general communication and in schools. A second version is the construction of a racial community through the family and based on the principles of genealogy and kinship.

Balibar argues that there is a necessary dialectic of racism and nationalism (50). 'Racism is constantly emerging out of nationalism [...] and nationalism emerges out of racism' (53). Racism is a super-nationalism and integral nationalism that calls for preserving the nation's cultural and/or biological origin and purity (59). Racism 'constantly induces an excess of "purism" as far as the nation is concerned: for the nation to be itself, it has to be racially or culturally pure' (59–60). Stuart Hall (1993, 356) argues in this context that nation states are never pure; they 'are without exception ethnically hybrid – the product of conquests, absorptions of one peoples by another'. 'The building of states, at whatever level, is intrinsically a ruling-class operation' (Williams 1983b, 181).

Balibar (Balibar and Wallerstein 1991, 38–9) distinguishes between internal (within the nation) and external racism (directed to groups outside the nation), auto-referential and hetero-referential racism, institutional and sociological racism, exclusive and inclusive racism. The 'racism of *extermination* or elimination (an "exclusive" racism)' wants to 'purify the social body of the stain or danger the inferior races may represent', whereas the 'racism of *oppression* or exploitation (an "inclusive" racism)' seeks 'to hierarchise and partition society' (39). Nazism is the typical example of exterminatory racism, colonialism the typical example of exploitative racism.

Balibar bases his analysis on an anti-humanist and institutional Althusserian theory of ideology and society that is based on Engels' late works (Balibar 1994, chapter 4). He assumes that ideologies are tied to state apparatuses (Balibar 1994, 113–15) and that the state is the 'first ideological power' (Balibar 2007, 78). In the case of the analysis of nationalism, he therefore stresses the role of institutions such as the family and schools (Balibar and Wallerstein 1991, 100–5). The anti-humanist concept of ideology becomes evident when Balibar (Balibar and Wallerstein 1991, 58–9, 63–4) argues that racism and socialist humanism share the stress on theoretical humanism, essence, the human species and universalisation. Balibar misses the point that racism is necessarily particularistic because it proclaims certain negative biological and/or cultural essences for specific groups (lazy, parasitic, criminal, unintelligent, subhuman, etc.). Socialist humanism in contrast is truly universalistic in that it stresses positive characteristics and the social and cooperative character of *all humans*. Balibar (2007, 27–33) is, however, not opposed to humanism and argues for a practical humanism that uses a transindividual ontology of social relations, in which human essence is the ensemble of social relations. Practical humanism is for Balibar the foundation for anti-racism and allows that arguing for '[a]bsolute civic equality' takes 'precedence over the question of "belonging" to a particular state' (Balibar and Wallerstein 1991, 63–4).

Balibar's anti-humanist notion of ideology results in a dualistic model of society that separates the economy from the state and ideology. There are mere interactions between the economic and non-economic for Balibar. He leaves society's realms separate and does not see how the economy operates inside of the state and ideology. For him, ideologies are relatively abstract. But an ideology needs to be produced and reproduced by human labour. Culture, ideology and politics are both economic and non-economic (Fuchs 2015, chapters 2 and 3). So, for example, a specific representation of British national identity is one of the tasks of the British Broadcasting Corporation ('the accurate and effective representation of British life, institutions and achievements', BBC Agreement). This ideological strategy is not simply a text, but has a context in which the BBC management and the secretary of state produce such a legal statement and BBC employees produce programmes that enact it. Cultural and ideological labour is an economic dimension operating inside of cultural and ideological organisations such as media organisations, schools, universities, research institutes, consultancies and think tanks.

Immanuel Wallerstein: Capitalism, Racism, Sexism

Immanuel Wallerstein argues that capitalism requires inclusive racism because it seeks ways to minimise the costs of production by keeping wages low (Balibar and Wallerstein 1991, 33). This assumption, however, implies that exclusive racism plays no necessary role in capitalism. The argument overlooks capitalism's necessary economic and political fetishistic structure. In order to justify, reify, veil and legitimatize class inequality, capitalism needs to ideologically construct scapegoats and steer hatred and the population's aggressions against the out-group, which comes along with desires for exclusion, the deprivation of rights, deportation, incarceration, internment or extermination. Racism and nationalism form one of capitalism's key political fetishisms. Racist exploitation has a more direct economic form in capitalism, whereas racist ideology takes on a more intermediate role that mediates between culture and the economy.

Wallerstein argues that racism and sexism are necessary elements of capitalism. Racism and xenophobia are in capitalist strategies to 'minimize the costs of production' and to 'minimize the costs of political disruption (hence minimize – not eliminate, because one cannot eliminate – the protests of the labour force)' (Balibar and Wallerstein 1991, 33). Sexism invents houseworkers and asserts they are 'not "working", merely "keeping house"' (35). Housework is not just reproduced labour power, but is also an 'indirect subsidy to the employers of the wage labourers in these households' (34). The connection of sexism and (new) racism in capitalism is that they are both anti-universalist ideologies that legitimate low- and no-wage labour and discrimination.

New Racism

Classical nationalism often constructed the outsider in biological terms as a 'race', whereas today it has become more common to define the outsider in cultural and political terms. Whereas some observers therefore like to distinguish between racism and xenophobia, Étienne Balibar has coined the notion of the new racism to describe ideological continuities and parallels:

The new racism is a racism of the era of 'decolonization' [...] [It] fits into the framework of 'racism without races' [...] It is a racism whose dominant theme is not biological heredity but the insurmountability of cultural differences, a racism which, at first sight, does not postulate the superiority of certain groups or peoples in relation to others but 'only' the harmfulness of abolishing frontiers, the incompatibility of life-styles and traditions; in short, it is what P. A. Taguieff has rightly called a *differentialist racism.* (Balibar and Wallerstein 1991, 21)

Pierre-André Taguieff, to whom Balibar refers, argues that racism ideologically naturalises differences, 'either by scientistic biologization or by ethnicization or "culturalist" fixing' (Taguieff 2001, 200). He distinguishes between two basic types of racism. Racism type 1 biologises differences and argues that one postulated 'race' is superior to another and that such differences are natural and eternal. Racism type 2 culturalises and celebrates differences. It concludes that specific cultures should therefore not mix. 'Naturalization is therefore either *biologizing* or *culturalist*' (207). Both versions draw comparable political conclusions that include the erection and defensive closure of borders, ending migration, and the opposition to multiculturalism:

> Irreducible, incomparable, and unassimilable, the human types that differ (the reasons for difference are infinite), moreover, may not communicate with each other, neither de facto nor de jure. The impossibility of a human community beyond the enclosures is the ultimate conclusion of the thesis of *incommunicability.* Hence the violent denunciations of 'cosmopolitanism' or 'globalism', processes and ideals that are supposed to destroy singular and closed communities, and, more profoundly and less distinctly, their 'identity.' (204)

Taguieff's key insight, on which Balibar builds, is that there are biologistic and culturalist versions of racism.

Five Dimensions of Nationalism

We can summarise the key points made by critical theories of nationalism. They will inform the empirical analysis presented in this book:

- *Ideology.* Nationalism is an ideology that constructs an Us/Them difference, in which the in-group is conceived as a unitary, homogeneous collective defined either by common claims to biology, genealogy, kinship and family ('race') or by claims to a common culture (commonality of language, communication, upbringing, moral values, traditions, customs, law, religion, emotions, experiences, identity, means of communication), a common state/political system/constitution or a common economy. Nationalism as ideology makes claims to territorial power for organising a national economic and a national political system. Nationalism constructs/invents/fabricates the nation and fictive national identity. Nationalist identity stresses fixity and homogeneity, whereas in reality all societies are complex, hybrid and diverse.

- *Dialectic of racism/xenophobia and nationalism.* Racism/xenophobia and nationalism are inherently linked. Xenophobia is an ideological construction of the out-group that is not part of the illusionary national collective.
- *Political fetishism.* Nationalism, xenophobia and racism are a form of political fetishism that ideologically distracts from how society's class antagonisms bring about social problems. The distraction from and veiling of class are often achieved by the construction of scapegoats and by steering hatred against them.
- *Forms of nationalism.* Nationalism, xenophobia and racism can be directed against an inner enemy (migrants, minorities) or an outer enemy (other nations, foreign groups). One can draw a distinction between sociological and institutional racism/nationalism and between inclusive (exploitative) and exclusive (exterminatory) racism/nationalism. Furthermore, there are biological and cultural forms of racism/nationalism.
- *Militarism.* Nationalism is associated with internal militarism (repression and law-and-order politics directed against immigrants and minorities) and external militarism (imperialist warfare).

FASCISM AND CAPITALISM

What is Fascism?

If one argues in a historiographical manner that fascism includes only the societies associated with Hitler in Germany and Mussolini in Italy, then one risks not being able to argue for the potential historical return of fascism. Such a theoretical understanding is devoid of the dynamic historical adaptability of the concept of fascism. It underestimates the possibility that certain political systems can emerge under different historical contexts with particular features. At the same time one must bear in mind that the industrial extermination of six million Jews by the Nazis is incomparable to other forms of violence and that comparisons downplay the singularity of this horror. It is therefore feasible to not speak of Nazi Germany as 'fascism', but always as 'Nazi-fascism'.

Daniel Woodley (2010) discusses features of a critical theory of fascism. He bases his theoretical understanding on Marx and Moishe Postone (1980, 1993, 2003) in order to connect fascism to the fetishism concept. Woodley sees fascism as 'a populist ideology which seeks, through a mythology of unity and identity, to project a 'common instinctual fate' (uniform social status) between bourgeois and proletarianized groups, eliding the reality of social distinction in differentiated class societies' (Woodley 2010, 17).

Fascism aims at creating a particular model of society.

[F]ascism must *itself* be understood as a political commodity: Fascism is not simply a subjectively generated, reactive strategy – a desperate attempt by atomized individuals to overcome the disenchantment and inauthenticity of modernity – but an aesthetic innovation which transcends existing patterns of differentiation and political subjectification to disrupt established narratives of history and progress. [...] the fetishization of communal identities which conceal the true nature of the commodity as a structured social practice, bridging the gap between the specificity of the nation-state (as the nexus linking culture and power) and the rationalization of circuits of capital. (Woodley 2010, 17–18)

Nazi-Fascism

Nazi-fascism was the historically most violent form of fascism. It aimed at the extermination of Jews, minorities and all political opponents and establishing the world dominance of Germany. Understanding Nazi Germany is therefore a key aspect of general analyses of fascism. Authoritarianism is also an element of economic fascism in respect to the economy, where it means the leadership of monopoly capitalist corporations. Reinhard Kühnl (1990) argues that Nazi-fascism represented large industry's capital interests (216) and destroyed the labour movement, and that the Nazi Party repressed all other political forces with terrorist means (218). For Kühnl (1998, 31–2, 107–22), the main features of fascism in general are that it is anti-Marxist, anti-democratic, racist, patriarchal, populist, terroristic, capitalist, imperialistic and social Darwinist. The specificities of Nazi-fascism would be the level of terror, its extremely activist and fanatic form and its exterminatory anti-Semitism (122–5).

Tim Mason (1995, 68) argues that under the Nazis, monopoly capitalism was developed further as rearmament advanced the monopoly power of, for example, Siemens in the electrical industry, IG-Farben in the chemical industry or Reichswerke Hermann Göring in the metal and iron industry. There was a coalition of the fascist party, the state and big business. 'The economic rulers were to a much higher degree "dependent" on this fascist leadership than in the Weimar Republic or the Federal Republic of Germany' (Kühnl 1990, 219). Mason (1995, 53–76) therefore speaks of the primacy of politics over the economy in Nazi Germany. Corporations can only survive in a fascist society if capitalists closely align themselves with the fascist regime. Big state and big capital tend to form a symbiotic unity.

Franz L. Neumann: Nazi-Fascism as the *Behemoth*

Franz L. Neumann (1900–54) was a German, Jewish political scientist. After Hitler came to power, he first fled to England and then went on to the USA in 1936. At the time of the Second World War, in the years 1943–8, he worked for the Office of Strategic Services. He also worked as an analyst for the prosecutors in the Nuremberg Trials. In 1948, he became a professor of political science at Columbia University. Neumann's (1944/2009) book *Behemoth: The Structure and Practice of National Socialism 1933–1944* has become a classic work in the analysis of authoritarianism. One of the book's basic hypotheses is that Nazism was not a state, but a lawless and irrational political monster that he based on Thomas Hobbes' *Behemoth*. Neumann argues that Nazism repealed the rule of law and substituted it by irrationality: 'Behemoth, which depicted England during the Long Parliament, was intended as the representation of a non-state, a situation characterized by complete lawlessness' (Neumann 1944/2009, 459).

Neumann (1943, 27–8) stresses that anti-Semitism was 'the most constant single ideology of the Nazi Party. [...] We may, indeed, say that anti-Semitism is the sole ideology that can possibly cement the Nazi Party [...] Anti-Semitism is thus the spearhead of terror'. Nazi-fascist capitalism was labour-fetishistic: for its war-orientation, it introduced a compulsory labour service and used terror, control, propaganda and wage increases in order to raise productivity (Neumann 1944/2009, 340–9). Neumann argues that the Nazis claimed to have substituted class society by one based on 'occupation and training', whereas in reality they deepened class antagonisms (Neumann 1944/2009, 367).

The book brings together economic, political and ideological analysis. Neumann starts with an introduction that focuses on Nazism's pre-history and context in the Weimar Republic. The book's first part ('The Political Pattern of National Socialism)' starts with remarks on Nazi ideology. Neumann (1944/2009, 38) argues that it is opposed to 'all traditional doctrines and values', including liberalism, democracy and socialism. The second part focuses on the 'Totalitarian Monopoly Economy'. The third part is about 'The New Society' and analyses Nazism's class structure. So part one analyses Nazism's political system, while parts two and three focus on its economic system.

In his analysis of Nazism's political system, he shows how leadership ideology, anti-Semitism and racist imperialism shaped politics under Hitler. 'The justification of this [leadership] principle is charismatic: it rests on the assertion that the Leader is endowed with qualities lacking in ordinary mortals. Superhuman qualities emanate from him and pervade the state, party, and people' (Neumann 1944/2009, 99). Nazism is ideologically an 'Anti-Semitic movement' that advocates 'the complete destruction of the Jews' (111). The compulsory acquisition of Jewish property and Jews' deprivation of rights strengthened big business (117) and satisfied 'the anti-capitalistic longings of the German people' (121). So terroristic state power had both economic and ideological dimensions and was driven by the political-ideological motive to annihilate the Jews. Nazism ideologically justified the Second World War as a war against 'plutocratic-capitalistic-Jewish democracies' (187). Imperialist warfare was justified as the 'Aryan race's' 'proletarian' warfare against an imagined unity of capitalism, democracy, liberalism, socialism and Marxism. Neumann speaks of the ideology of racial proletarianism (188). Nazism's military strategy as a form of politics both has an ideological aspect (the destruction of perceived enemies) and an economic dimension (the creation of a *Lebensraum* for the biological expansion of 'Aryans' and the biological and economic expansion of Germany).

In part two, Neumann shows that Nazism's economy featured compulsory cartelisation; the organisation of the entire economy based on the leader; the growth of monopolies via 'Aryanisation', Germanisation, technological progress in the heavy industries and the elimination of small and medium businesses; as well as state intervention into the economy via the control of prices, investments, trade and the labour market (abolishment of workers' rights, ban of trade unions and collective bargaining, compulsory labour). Neumann shows how ideology (leadership ideology, anti-Semitism), militarism, the command economy and totalitarian politics were fused into a total system of control, annihilation, accumulation, expansion and imperialist warfare.

In section three, Neumann shows how Nazism's ideology and class system interacted. Ideologically, Nazi-fascism 'claims to have [...] created a society differentiated not by classes but according to occupation and training' (367). But in reality, under the ideological guise of racism and nationalism, it 'deepened and solidified' class antagonisms (367). Nazism organised society in 'a monistic, total, authoritarian' (400) manner that was ideologically presented as an 'abstract "people's community,"' which hides the complete depersonalization of human relations and the isolation of man from man' (402).

> The essence of National Socialist social policy consists in the acceptance and strengthening of the prevailing class character of German society, in the attempted consolidation of its ruling class, in the atomization of the subordinate strata through the destruction of every autonomous group mediating between them and the state, in the creation of a system of autocratic bureaucracies interfering in all human relations. (367)

Nazism's totalitarian monopoly capitalism deepened capitalist class structures via a terroristic state driven by anti-Semitic and racist ideology, abolished the rule of law and exercised the utmost violence.

Nazi Germany's Economy: Totalitarian State Capitalism or Totalitarian Monopoly Capitalism?

Franz L. Neumann (1944/2009, 116–20, 275) argues that the 'Aryanisation' of Jewish property served the expansion of German monopoly capitalist interests such as those of Otto Wolff AG (steel), Friedrich Flick's conglomerate (steel, iron, coal), or Mannesmann (steel, iron) (Neumann 1944/2009, 275, 288–92). Also, the Germanisation of conquered economies would have been part of German Nazi imperialism (275–7). Corporations in Nazi Germany were large cartels and combines that were based on the leadership principle (233). Cartels were brought about by compulsory cartelisation (Neumann, Marcuse and Kirchheimer 2013, 270, 273–4).

Neumann argues that Nazism consists of four groups all functioning based on the leadership principle: monopoly capital, the party, the military and bureaucracy:

Under National Socialism, however, the whole of the society is organized in four solid, centralized groups, each operating under the leadership principle, each with a legislative, administrative, and judicial power of its own. Neither universal law nor a rationally operating bureaucracy is necessary for integration. Compromises among the four authoritarian bodies need not be expressed in a legal document nor must they be institutionalized (like the 'gentlemen's agreements' between monopolistic industries). It is quite sufficient that the leadership of the four wings agree informally on a certain policy. The four totalitarian bodies will then enforce it with the machinery at their disposal. There is no need for a state standing above all groups; the state may even be a hindrance to the compromises and to domination over the ruled classes. The decisions of the Leader are merely the result of the compromises among the four leaderships. (Neumann 1944/2009, 468–9)

Friedrich Pollock (1941a, 1941b) argues that Nazism was a totalitarian state capitalism, where 'the profit motive is superseded by the power motive' (1941b, 207) and there is 'masochistic submission to all kinds of commands, to suffering, sacrifice, or death' (1941a, 449). Totalitarian state capitalism was to be a new order that succeeded private capitalism (450).

The recognition of an economic sphere into which the state shall not and cannot intrude, so essential for the era of private capitalism, is being radically repudiated. In consequence, execution of the program is enforced by state power and nothing essential is left to the functioning of laws of the market or other economic 'laws.' The primacy of politics over economics, so much disputed under democracy, is clearly established. (Pollock 1941a, 453)

Max Horkheimer (1940, 1941) followed Pollock's state capitalism approach, although he foregrounded aspects of ideology and instrumental reason. 'State capitalism is the authoritarian state of the present. [...] The self-movement of the concept of the commodity leads to the concept of state capitalism' (Horkheimer 1940, 96, 108).

Neumann disagreed with Friedrich Pollock's assessment that Nazism was a new order of state capitalism that had replaced monopoly capitalism. In state capitalism, there would be a primacy of politics over the economy. Horkheimer largely followed Pollock's approach. Neumann did not share the assumption that state power strongly limited capital's power in Germany. He rejected the term state capitalism and characterised Nazism as totalitarian monopoly capitalism. Neumann argues that Nazism combined monopoly capitalism and a command economy and did thereby not bring about a new order and did not replace monopoly capitalism. 'The German economy of today has two broad and striking characteristics. It is a monopolistic economy – *and* a command economy. It is a private capitalistic economy, regimented by the totalitarian state. We suggest as a name best to describe it, "Totalitarian Monopoly Capitalism"' (Neumann 1944/2009, 261). There were both capitalist and state interests (the latter involving the Nazi Party, bureaucracy and the military) in Nazism that converged in the war economy: the Nazi regime wanted to arm Germany for an imperialist world war in order to accumulate power. Germany's large industry welcomed such efforts because armament meant its expansion and possibilities for capital accumulation. Whereas Pollock stresses the discontinuities between capitalism and Nazism, Neumann tends to foreground the continuities.

Underlying Neumann's critique of the term totalitarian state capitalism is the assumption that 'a state is characterized by the rule of law' (Neumann 1944/2009, 467) and that Nazi Germany was therefore not a state. Certainly not everyone will agree with such a concept of the state. Neumann (1936b) argues that the state in Nazi Germany was a racist state (559) and leadership state (562), in which the 'law is the will of the Leader in the form of law' (562). The rule of law did not exist (571). Instead Hitler and his cabinet passed laws per decree. The independence of the judiciary did not exist, the judge was 'the absolute servant of the law, i.e., of the will of the Leader. [...] The judge was to serve the Leader' (573–4). There was no separation of legislative, executive and judiciary power. Hitler had 'supreme legislative and executive power' and also took on 'judicial functions' (577). Neumann therefore concludes that the Nazi state was 'in no way a Rechtsstaat' (570). He here differentiates between the state and a state under the rule of law, and makes clear that Nazi Germany was a state without the rule of law. This does not imply that it was not a state. It was not an *Unstaat* (non-state), but rather an *Unrechtsstaat* (state of injustice, an unjust/tyrannical state).

Eric Hobsbawm (1994, 129) stresses that monopoly capitalism is not an exclusive economic feature of fascism, but can also exist in parliamentary democracies and other political systems. In Nazi Germany fascism would, however, have benefited big business because of the repression of the workforce, the destruction of the labour movement, the expropriation of Jews, the introduction of slave labour, etc. (Hobsbawm 1994, 129).

The Problems of Theories of Totalitarianism and Theories of Social Fascism

In theories of totalitarianism, comparisons of Nazi-fascism to the Soviet Union have often been made. For example, the German historian Ernst Nolte argued in the Historians' Dispute (*Historikerstreit*): 'Auschwitz is not primarily a result of traditional anti-Semitism and was not just one more case of "genocide". It was the fear-borne reaction to the acts of annihilation that took place during the Russian Revolution' (Nolte 1980/1993, 13–14). In the introduction to *The Black Book of Communism*, Stéphane Courtois wrote that '[c]ommunist regimes have victimized approximately 100 million people in contrast to the approximately 25 million victims of the Nazis' (Courtois et al. 1999, 15). Jürgen Habermas criticised such positions by saying that in them, the 'Nazi crimes lose their singularity by being made comprehensible as the answer to a Bolshevist threat of annihilation' and by stressing that thereby 'Auschwitz is reduced to the format of a technical innovation' (Habermas 1989, 224).

In the 1920s, many communists saw social democracy as a form of social fascism. The Communist International's president, Grigory Zinoviev, at the International's fifth congress in 1924, formulated this hypothesis: he argued that 'the Social-Democratic Party has been converted into a wing of fascism' (Bay Area Study Group 1979, 195). Stalin (1924, 295) shared the view that social democracy is 'objectively the moderate wing of fascism. […] Fascism is the bourgeoisie's fighting organisation that relies on the active support of Social-Democracy'. The social fascism hypothesis misunderstood the character of fascism, which resulted in the fact that communists did not work together with social democrats and others against the fascist threat, but rather tended to assume that only a working-class revolution organised by the Communist Party could stop fascism, that capitalism would collapse before or during fascism, or that fascism would not be able to survive politically. These assumptions were proven wrong. Mussolini and Hitler outlawed, imprisoned and killed communists just like social democrats, trade unionists, anarchists and liberals. Also, many social democrats viewed communists as equally dangerous as fascists. Karl Kautsky (1932), for example, said that 'any cooperation between Communists and Socialists […] against Hitlerism' was 'impossible' because the idea of a united front would have been 'a convenient Communist maneuver to destroy the Socialists'. The rise of Hitler and the Nazis was certainly helped by both the communists and social democrats' rejection to cooperate and to consider the Nazis and fascism as the highest threat.

The United Front Strategy

In the mid-1930s, the Soviet Union changed its position and called for 'a united proletarian front against fascism on an international scale' (Dimitrov 1935). Fascism was defined as 'the open terrorist dictatorship of the most reactionary, most chauvinistic and most imperialist elements of finance capital' (Dimitrov 1935). Non-Stalinist communists had called much earlier for a united front against fascism. Trotsky, for example, spoke in 1930 of the 'tremendous possibilities' of the 'policy of a united front of the workers against fascism' (Trotsky 1968). August Thalheimer was a founding member of the Communist Party of Germany, who, because of his anti-Stalinism, was expelled from the party and, together with Heinrich Brandler, formed the Communist Party Opposition in 1928. In 1921, Thalheimer had already called for a united front strategy of the Communist Party (Thalheimer 1932).

Thalheimer (1930) argued based on Marx's (1871) 'The Civil War in France' that fascism was a particular form of Bonapartism. For Thalheimer, Bonapartism means 'the independence of the executive power' in the form of 'the open dictatorship of capital' and the 'subordination of all the rest of the social classes to the executive' that takes on the form of an independent power. The Bonapartist element of fascism is 'the political subjugation of all the masses [...] beneath the fascist state power. [...] Fascism, like Bonapartism, wants to be the joint benefactor of all classes' (Thalheimer 1930).

Is Fascism a Petty Bourgeois Movement?

Notwithstanding the differences between the many shades of the political and theoretical left in the 1920s and 1930s, the position of many of its representatives converged regarding the question of what fascism's class base was. Classical Marxist theories of fascism argued that such movements' supporters could predominantly be found among the 'middle class' (especially the self-employed and white-collar workers), peasants and the army (Hobsbawm 1994, 121–2; Kitchen 1976; Kühnl 1998, 33–4; Mason 1995, 56; Poulantzas 1974).

Antonio Gramsci (1971, 219–23) characterised Mussolini's fascism as a form of Caesarism, another term for Marx's notion of Bonapartism. Caesarism according to Gramsci has its foundation in the *morti di fame*, the degraded and impoverished middle class (203, 273–4). Georgi Dimitrov (1935) said that 'fascism has managed to gain the following of the mass of the petty bourgeoisie that has been dislocated by the crisis, and even of certain sections of the most backward strata of the proletariat'. Otto Bauer (1938, 175) stressed that the Nazis had 'the support of the petty bourgeois and peasant masses impoverished by the crisis'. For August Thalheimer (1930), fascism's class basis, followers and 'social composition' are made up of 'the declassed of all classes, the nobility, bourgeoisie, urban petty bourgeoisie, peasantry and workers'. He also spoke with respect to Bonapartism's social composition about the 'declassed elements of all classes', the '[e]conomically and socially rootless elements', those 'who are excluded from direct production'. When detailing who the workers are that support fascism, he spoke of 'the lumpenproletariat' and 'the labour aristocracy and bureaucracy'. Leon Trotsky (1968) argued that the 'genuine basis (for fascism) is the petty bourgeoisie. In Italy, it has a very large base – the petty bourgeoisie of the towns and cities, and the peasantry. In Germany likewise, there is a large base for fascism.' Through fascism, capitalism would set 'in motion the masses of the crazed petty bourgeoisie and the bands of declassed and demoralized lumpenproletariat'. 'The main army of fascism still consists of the petty bourgeoisie and the new middle class: the small artisans and shopkeepers of the cities, the petty officials, the employees, the technical personnel, the intelligentsia, the impoverished peasantry' (Trotsky 1931). 'Fascism is a specific means of mobilizing and organizing the petty bourgeoisie in the social interests of finance capital. [...] The passage to fascism, on the contrary, is inconceivable without the preceding permeation of the petty bourgeoisie with hatred of the proletariat' (Trotsky 1934).

Martin Kitchen (1976, 84–5) summarises these widespread assumptions about the class foundation of fascism in the following words:

> [fascism] recruits its mass following from a politicised, threatened, and frightened petite bourgeoisie. Artisans, small independent businessmen who are threatened by monopolisation and severely hurt by the economic crisis flock to the fascists, attracted by their political rhetoric, in the hope of finding economic and social salvation, where they join forces with white-collar workers and lower civil servants who are determined to ward off the immanent threat of being cast down into the ranks of the proletariat. In some instances they are joined by members of the 'aristocracy of labour' who no longer identify with the working class and see in fascism a means of enhancing their social status.

Turning petite-bourgeois support into a definitional criterion makes fascism an inflexible concept and idealises blue-collar workers, who are categorically excluded from supporting fascism. Past and present empirical evidence also negates the claim that fascism and right-wing authoritarianism are movements of the petty bourgeois class.

The Nazi Party's Membership Structure

One of the reasons why there has been the widespread assumption that the Nazi Party (NSDAP) was a 'middle class' party is that Hitler came from a 'middle class' family. His father worked as a civil servant in the customs service, his mother was a housewife. Both came from families with a farming background. For a long time the party's published membership statistics, which are methodologically limited and disputed, was the only data source for the social background of members (Mühlberger 1996, 48–9).

Jürgen W. Falter (2013) analysed the NSDAP's membership based on sample membership cards archived in the Berlin Document Center. His analysis shows that during the years 1925–33, blue-collar workers accounted on average for 40 per cent of all new party members, white-collar workers and civil servants for 21 per cent, the self-employed for 31 per cent and those without job for 8 per cent (Falter 2013, table 1). In 1933, these group's shares were 33 per cent, 30 per cent, 31 per cent and 5 per cent.

Mühlberger (1996) compared four newer studies of NSDAP membership that were based on samples of membership data for the period between 1925 and January 1933, mostly obtained from the Berlin Document Center. He concludes that blue-collar workers 'provided a *minimum* of around 40 percent of members in the period between 1925 and the end of January 1933' (Mühlberger 1996, 53). Mühlberger's analysis indicates that workers who were members of the NSDAP were predominantly semi-skilled and skilled and working in the secondary sector. According to the data, there was a clear overrepresentation of toolmakers, joiners, bakers, mechanics, drivers, bricklayers, butchers, painters, fitters, gardeners, tailors and shoemakers in the NSDAP membership (Mühlberger 1996, 64). 'Metalworkers, building workers, woodworkers, and transport workers [...] formed the majority of blue-collar workers in the NSDAP' (Mühlberger 1996, 68). Mühlberger (1996, 54–5) argues that such data show that the NSDAP was not a petty bourgeois party, but a mass integration party focused on appealing to all German citizens with the concept of the German *Volksgemeinschaft* (national ethnic community). The NSDAP was 'a catch-all party attracting followers from across the social spectrum' (Brustein 1996, 137).

A volume edited by Jürgen W. Falter (2016) presents the results of studies of the NSDAP's membership. According to calculations, 9.8 million individuals became party members between 1925 and 1945 (Falter 2016, 175, 187). The highest issued membership number was 10,174,581 (Falter 2016, 175, 178). The study analysed membership data of 15,364 'young fighters', who were ideologically highly committed to Nazi ideology and who joined the party either in its early phase (1925–33) or in the late phase between 1942 and 1945 when there was a general admission stop and one could only become a new member under special circumstances. Of the 'young fighter-Nazis', 98.4 per cent were aged between 17 and 29 when they joined the party, which explains their characterisation (Falter 2016, 211); 49.9 per cent of them were blue-collar workers, 21.0 per cent white-collar employees and public servants, 5.8 per cent family workers, 1.6 per cent self-employed and 9.1 per cent without occupation[2] (Falter 2016, 213). Skilled workers in trade and industry made up the largest share of workers and accounted for a total of 30.4 per cent of the 'young fighter-Nazis' (Falter 2016, 213).

An analysis of a sample of 1,264 Austrian NSDAP members (period of analysis, 1926–44) shows that blue-collar workers (including crafts-people) accounted for 40.2 per cent, public servants for 20 per cent, white-collar employees for 15.3 per cent, farmers for 12 per cent, the self-employed for 7.1 per cent, freelancers for 3.4 per cent and students for 2 per cent (Falter 2016, 448). These analyses confirm that blue-collar workers constituted a very significant part of the NSDAP's membership and especially of the ideologically highly committed members.

Germany was hit hard by unemployment in the course of the world economic crisis that started in 1929. It rose from 1.3 million (4.5 per cent) in 1929 to six million (24 per cent) in 1932 (Dimsdale, Horsewood and Van Riel 2004, 3). The governments led by Brüning and Papen implemented austerity measures, including wage cuts and the reduction of welfare support, unemployment benefits and disability benefits, while giving tax breaks to employers (Brustein 1996, 141–3). In the Weimar Republic, the export industries (machinery, metal-finishing, chemical industries, electro-technical industry) flourished, whereas the domestic industries (mining, coal, metal) stagnated and suffered from

---

2. For 12.7 per cent of the sample, there was no indication of the occupation on the membership cards or the information was unreadable.

rationalisation, low wages and profits, dequalification and growing unemployment (Brustein 1996, 143–7). Brustein (1996, 156–7) analysed data indicating that on average, between 1925 and 1932, 55 per cent of the new blue-collar workers who joined the NSDAP as new members worked in stagnating industries.

Who Voted for Hitler?

Falter conducted studies of who voted for and supported Hitler. The share of workers in the electorate who voted for the NSDAP increased from 2 per cent in 1928 to 33 per cent in 1933 (Falter 1996, 35; Falter and Hänisch 1986, table 13). The NSDAP's share of voters in the quartile of districts with the highest share of workers in employment increased from 1.8 per cent in 1928 to 16 per cent in 1930, 34.6 per cent in July 1932 and 42.2 per cent in March 1933 (Falter 1996, 12). The 'higher the proportion of employed workers, the better the NSDAP's performance tends to be after 1928' (Falter 1996, 13).

Falter found that the degree of urbanisation and religion were two important factors influencing the share of NSDAP voters between 1930 and 1933. There was a strong growth in rural Protestant areas (Falter 1996, 22–6). In rural districts at large, the NSDAP in March 1933 reached 44 per cent of the registered electorate. In predominantly Protestant rural areas, the share was 50 per cent. In Protestant rural areas with a predominantly working-class population, the share was 47 per cent, whereas in other Protestant rural areas the share was 54 per cent (Falter 1996, 28). 'Workers who were economically active, unemployed, or retired along with heir dependents', according to Falter's calculations, accounted for 'under 40 percent of National Socialist voters (as against 45 percent of all registered voters), members of the old middle classes around 45 percent and members of the new middle classes some 17 percent' (Falter 1996, 40). Falter does not dispute that the 'middle class' played an important role in supporting the Nazis, but he doubts that one can speak of a 'middle-class party' (Falter 1996, 40). The NSDAP was rather an integrative Nazi protest movement (Falter 1996, 40), 'a mass integration party which aimed to win support in all social milieux' (35) by trying ideologically to construct an 'Aryan' national unity that veiled class conflict. The Nazis' *Volksgemeinschaft* (national ethnic community) was an ideology that tried to mobilise a cross-class mass movement in the name of the nation by trying to unite hatred against those who were constructed and presented as being enemies of the German nation (Jews, communists, socialists, liberals, people of colour, etc.). There was also Nazi election propaganda specifically directed at workers (36–8).

According to data, in the German federal election 1933, in which 39 per cent of the eligible voters cast their ballot for the Nazis, 33 per cent of all blue-collar workers voted for them, 28 per cent of the white-collar workers and public servants, 47 per cent of the self-employed, 53 per cent of those without occupation and 37 per cent of the houseworkers (Falter and Hänisch 1986, table 13; Falter 1987, 229). According to data, the NSDAP became the largest working-class party in July 1932, when only 23 per cent of all blue-collar workers voted for the Social Democrats (SPD), who had held 31 per cent of the blue-collar workers' votes in 1928, and 27 per cent voted for the Nazis (Falter and Hänisch 1986, table 14; Falter 1996, 34, 44). In the November 1932 and March 1933 elections, the Nazis also held the largest share of blue-collar workers' votes. In the 1933 election, they obtained 33 per cent of blue-collar workers' votes, the SPD 21 per cent and the Communists (KPD) 17 per cent (Falter and Hänisch 1986, table 14; Falter 1996, 34, 44).

Nazi-Fascism's *Volksgemeinschaft* Ideology

Empirical research seems to indicate that the NSDAP's members and voters were not simply 'petty bourgeois', but that it was rather a party that used the ideology and politics of the *Volksgemeinschaft* for trying to achieve support throughout the population and distract attention from class conflicts. Hitler continuously stressed the *Volksgemeinschaft* ideology and made pleas for how it should unite Germans with nationalist sentiments across class boundaries. For example, he argued in a speech given on 18 May 1930, in Regensburg: 'First of all we are Germans, and then workers, entrepreneurs and public servants'[3] (Hitler 1992, Volume 3, 197). In another speech, Hitler said on 24 September 1931, in Hamburg: 'We are members of a people, and a common fate unites us. It must stop that one divides oneself into bourgeois, public servants, proletarians, etc. We first have to be Germans. [Thundering

---

3. Translation from German, original: 'Zuerst sind wir Deutsche, dann Arbeiter, Unternehmer und Beamte'.

applause]. If fate blesses us, we want to create German unity, for which we will sacrifice us. Then we will arrive at a kingdom of power, greatness and glory'[4] (Hitler 1992, Volume 4, 115). The quote shows that Hitler presented the superiority of the German *Volksgemeinschaft* as determined by nature ('common fate', 'fate'). He uses religious language for romanticising German unity and glorifying German nationalism. He calls for Germans to 'sacrifice' themselves in the name of the nation, which is a military connotation calling for a German war of aggression in order to create a great 'kingdom'.

Especially after the economic crisis had started, the Nazis tried to win working-class support using targeted policies. The NSDAP's economic programme propagated Germany's economic autarky, state intervention into the economy that creates jobs by state investments into infrastructure projects (highways, housing, etc.), the introduction of a compulsory labour service, opposition to free trade, strengthening the domestic economy, the introduction of protective tariffs and the demand that Germany cancels and demands back all First World War reparation payments (Brustein 1996, 146–56).

The Nazis argued that reparations and foreign workers caused unemployment. They opposed the Young Plan that reduced Germany's reparation debts because they demanded full cancellation of Germany's payments. The Nazis opposed the SPD and presented it as betraying the German working class by not opposing First World War reparation payments effectively. And the NSDAP portrayed the KPD as wanting to turn Germany into a Soviet colony.

The Nazis' Economic Programme

As part of its campaign for the July 1932 Reichstag election, the Nazis issued an Emergency Economic Programme. It formulated the foundations of the Nazis' economic policies (NSDAP 1932):

---

4. Translation from German, original: 'wir sind Glieder eines Volkes und uns alle bindet ein Schicksal. Aufhören muß es, daß man sich trennt in Bürger, Beamte, Arbeiter, Proleten [sie!] usw. Wir müssen zuerst Deutsche sein. [Beifallssturm.] [...] Wir wollen, wenn das Schicksal uns segnet, die deutsche Einheit schaffen, für die wir uns opfern werden. Dann kommen wir zu einem Reich der Kraft, der Größe und der Herrlichkeit' (Hitler 1992, Volume 4, 115).

Previous economic policy has aimed above all at increasing German exports, which has disrupted the domestic market in the interests of our ability to complete on the world market. [...] Creating jobs requires refocusing the German economy on the domestic market. [...] Focusing on the domestic market requires an increase in agricultural production. [...] [We demand] [b]uilding roads, canals, etc., to support the domestic exchange of goods, settling people in the East, and loosening the hold of big cities. [...] Only the state can accomplish these tasks. [...] The reparations policies of post-war governments have made Germany one of the poorest civilized nations. [...] National Socialism demands that the needs of German workers no longer be supplied by Soviet slaves, Chinese coolies, and Negroes. National Socialism is determined to eliminate the barriers between the cultural level of German workers and German farmers. Therefore, import restrictions must be implemented when the result will be work for the German worker or the German farmer. National Socialism opposes the liberal world economy, as well as the Marxist world economy. Instead, it demands that each people's comrade be protected from foreign competition. [...] Before the war, Germany was one of the great powers. Today, it is a second class country. Its raw materials come primarily from abroad, the transportation routes to which can be instantly severed, for Germany is not in a position to maintain and protect the routes to these sources of raw materials. Therefore, a guideline of National Socialist policy is to cover the German people's needs by its own production as far as possible, securing the amount in excess of domestic production from friendly European states, particularly if they are willing to accept industrial products from Germany as payment. [...] The bourgeois-liberal and Marxist governments of the post-war period have burdened the German people with foreign debts that are currently about 22 billion marks. These private debts were loaded on to the German people to cover a part (10.3 billion) of the outrageous reparations payments, in part also (6.3 billion) to pay for imports of colonial goods and delicacies, not life necessities for the German people, and also to pay for foodstuffs that could have been produced domestically'.

There are certainly parallels between the NSDAP's and Donald Trump's economic policies, especially with respect to the foregrounding of the joint national interest of capital and labour; the scapegoating of immigrants, foreign capital and labour; the opposition to free trade; the view that foreign influences have weakened the national interest and that nationalist politics will make the nation 'great again' (compare Hitler's promise that he will turn Germany into a 'kingdom of power, greatness and glory' and Trump's promise to 'make America great again'); the focus on infrastructure projects, etc. The Nazis did not advocate internationalist working-class politics, but nationalist politics promising social advantages for both the German working class and the German bourgeoisie. Trump advocates nationalist politics that promise to benefit both US workers and US capital.

Although there are certain similarities, one cannot simply argue that Trump is the new Hitler. The project of Hitler and the Nazis was inherently anti-Semitic and built on the idea of exterminating the Jews, to 'Aryanise' Jewish property, to destroy all political opposition and to kill critics. Trump focuses on scapegoating immigrants and other nations, overreacts to any criticism and constantly criticises the media that criticise him, but one cannot say that he practices a project of extermination, industrial mass murder and outlawing and killing the political opposition. Trump has an authoritarian personality, but thus far the institutions of American liberal democracy have exerted limits on his politics. The future will show if they will be undermined by him, initiate an impeachment, or if there will be another development.

The argument advanced in this book is that Trump stands for an authoritarian form of capitalism (see Chapters 4 and 5). As the discussion will show, Trump's authoritarian capitalism includes to a certain degree an apologetic attitude towards right-wing extremist movements that relate positively to him. Authoritarian capitalism features a far-right political strategy and political economy, but is qualitatively different from Nazi-fascism. There are commonalities between authoritarian capitalism and fascist capitalism, but in the first the rule of law and democracy remain intact, whereas in the second they are abolished. This book shows that Trump's vision of a society that corresponds to his own personality structure is highly problematic.

Who Votes for Marine Le Pen?

In the first round of the 2012 French presidential election, Marine Le Pen achieved 17.9 per cent of the vote, including 33 per cent of votes among manual workers, 23 per cent among routine non-manual workers, 20 per cent among the self-employed (shopkeepers, artisans), 12 per cent among lower service employees and 8 per cent among upper service employees (Mayer 2013). The share was also higher among those living in villages and those who only completed primary or secondary education. The typical Le Pen voter is a male manual worker who has a low level of education and lives in a rural area.

Who Votes for the Austrian Freedom Party?

The Austrian Freedom Party (FPÖ) has, under the leadership first of Jörg Haider (1986–2000) and then Heinz Christian Strache (since 2005), been one of the world's most successful far-right parties in elections. In 1999, it achieved 26.9 per cent of the votes cast in the Austrian federal election. In 2016, its candidate Norbert Hofer was, with 35.1 per cent of the vote, the winner of the presidential election's first round. Data show that in the 2013 federal elections, the FPÖ was the strongest party among men, the age group 16–29, blue-collar workers, and those with low educational achievements.[5] In the 2016 Austrian presidential election's first round, FPÖ candidate Hofer was strongest among men in all age groups (especially those aged 16–29), blue- and white-collar workers (72 per cent of the blue-collar workers, 37 per cent of the white-collar workers) and those who had not taken school leaving examinations.[6]

Who Voted for Donald Trump?

The American presidential election shows that Trump's voting base is comparable to one of the European far-right parties. Trump won the 2016 presidential election because he flipped the vote from Democratic to Republican in deindustrialised Rust Belt states. A post-election study conducted by Emsi in the Rust Belt states of Michigan, Ohio, Minnesota, Wisconsin, Indiana and Pennsylvania showed that:

> 437 of the 489 counties in the six states analyzed [...] voted for Trump. [...] almost without exception [...] the counties with the highest con-

---

5. FPÖ bei Arbeitern, SPÖ bei Pensionisten vorne. *Der Standard Online*, 29 September 2013.
6. Österreichs neue Politlandkarte. *ORF Online*, 24 April 2016.

centration of manufacturing, agriculture, and mining and oil and gas extraction employment voted for Trump. [...] The same counties who overwhelmingly voted for Trump have seen an increased dependence the last 15 years on factory jobs and ag and mining employment. [...] Many of the 52 counties in these states where Clinton won are more urban and have a more diverse mix of large-employing industries. Manufacturing employment in the U.S. has declined 25 per cent since 2001. That's more than four million lost jobs in a sector that typically brings new income into regions through the products it exports. (Wright 2017; see also Paquette 2017)

Brexit

According to a poll, 71 per cent of routine manual workers and 59 per cent of those who were not in paid work voted in favour of Brexit (Goodwin and Heath 2016), while 64 per cent of those belonging to the C2 (skilled manual workers) and DE (semi-skilled and unskilled manual workers, casual workers, pensioners, the unemployed) social groups voted for Brexit (Ashcroft 2016). Of the 'Remainers', 79 per cent thought immigration was good, while 80 per cent of the 'Leavers' thought that it was bad. Of the 'Leave' voters participating in the poll, 39 per cent described themselves as English and not British or as more English than British, whereas the share among 'Remainers' was just 18 per cent. The data indicate that English nationalism seems to be more prevalent among those who voted for Brexit.

Clarke, Goodwin and Whiteley (2016) constructed a regression model that was based on data from one pre- and one post-Brexit survey (N_1 = 2,218, N_2 = 1,993). The study showed that age, education, social class and attitudes towards immigration had a significant impact on voting behaviour:

[V]oters with highly negative attitudes about immigration were more likely than other people to extol the benefits of Brexit and to minimize the costs of doing so. [...] older voters and voters from university educated people and those in higher social grades were significantly less likely to see the benefits of leaving the EU than were other people. In contrast, older voters were more likely to judge that Brexit would have benefits by helping to control immigration and reducing the threat of terrorism. (Clarke, Goodwin and Whiteley 2016, 20)

'[E]ffects associated with socio-demographic characteristics including age, education and social class were observed' (Clarke, Goodwin and Whiteley 2016, 24). Older people with lower education coming from the working class and opposing immigration were very likely to vote for 'Brexit'.

Blue-Collar Right-Wing Authoritarianism

The example data from France, Austria, the USA and the UK indicate that blue-collar workers have in recent times voted to a significant degree in favour of right-wing authoritarian parties, leaders and causes. It is therefore not feasible to assume, as many classical Marxist theories did, that the petty bourgeoisie is the class base of right-wing authoritarianism. It is much more feasible to assume that right-wing authoritarianism in specific political contexts, and with the help of stereotypes and scapegoating, appeals to classes and groups that have been declassed or have fears of social downfall. Especially when there is a weak and disjointed left-wing opposition and there are classes and groups that are particularly affected by, threatened by or afraid of social decline, such appeals can be fruitful and result in victories for the far right.

Far-right parties and movements are not simply 'middle-class' groups, but have historically and today often tried to appeal to blue-collar workers and other social groups. Woodley (2010, 76) says in this context that 'the social function of fascism is to create a unity of social forces incorporating propertied interests, lower-middle-class voters and plebeian elements'. The ideological construction of national and/or racial unity deflects attention from class conflicts. It uses nationalist, xenophobic and racist demagogy to appeal to a large part of the population across classes and social strata. Right-wing authoritarianism in its various forms tries to construct a national unity that is held together by hatred of imagined enemies and outsiders, which results in the ideological deflection of political attention away from class structures and class struggles. The political-economic role of right-wing authoritarianism is that it tries to subvert class struggles by advancing nationalist struggles.

Ideological Bonapartism

Marx (1852) introduced the term Bonapartism for analysing the rule of Napoleon III, who came to power in France through a coup d'état in

1851. A feature of Bonapartism is that 'the state seem[s] to have made itself completely independent' (Marx 1852, 186):

> Marx described Bonapartism as the dictatorship of the most counter-revolutionary elements of the bourgeoisie. Its distinguishing features were: a policy of manoeuvring between classes to create a state power seen to be ruling over all alike; crude demagogy camouflaging the defence of the interests of the exploiters, combined with political terrorism; the omnipotence of the military machine; venality and corruption; the employment of criminals, and the widespread use of blackmail and bribery. (Marx and Engels 1975–2005, Preface to Volume 11, xviii)

Absolutist state rule is not just a feature of fascism, but of all absolute forms of political reign, including absolutist monarchies. Fascism is always capitalist in character, it presupposes capitalist rule. Absolute state power in the form of the military, the police and terror is used for enforcing capitalist rule. Marx mentioned another feature of Bonapartism: it 'professed to save the working class by breaking down Parliamentarism, and, with it, the undisguised subserviency of Government to the propertied classes. It professed to save the propertied classes by upholding their economic supremacy over the working class; and, finally, it professed to unite all classes by reviving for all the chimera of national glory' (Marx 1871, 330). Here Marx foregrounds the role of nationalism as an ideology that constructs a fictive ethnicity in order to distract attention from class antagonism. Bonapartism is not just a dictatorial form of politics, but also a particular form of nationalist ideology that tries to deflect attention from class structures. Marx leaves open how the working class positions itself towards the ruling class within Bonapartism. This certainly includes the possibility that it actively supports the regime because it believes in the 'chimera of national glory'. That Marx in these passages speaks of 'chimera' and 'professing' shows that he considers ideology to be an integral part of any form of Bonapartism.

These introductory theoretical remarks on key concepts such as ideology, nationalism and fascism should equip the reader for the chapters that follow. In Chapter 3 we will turn to the question of how to understand right-wing authoritarianism and authoritarian capitalism.

3

Right-Wing Authoritarianism
and Authoritarian Capitalism

INTRODUCTION

This chapter introduces the notions of right-wing authoritarianism and authoritarian capitalism. This book's understanding of these terms is grounded in the Frankfurt School's critical theory of authoritarianism. Based on the Frankfurt School, and especially some of its authors such as Theodor W. Adorno, Franz L. Neumann and Erich Fromm, we can develop an understanding of right-wing authoritarianism and authoritarian capitalism. Doing so also requires us to reflect on what the role of the state is in capitalist society.

THE FRANKFURT SCHOOL'S CRITICAL THEORY OF AUTHORITARIANISM

Wilhelm Reich: *The Mass Psychology of Fascism*

Classical Frankfurt School critical theory combined the approaches of Karl Marx and Sigmund Freud in order to understand how authoritarian thought works. Wilhelm Reich was a psychoanalyst and theorist who influenced the Frankfurt School's study of the authoritarian personality. Reich (1972) argues in his book *The Mass Psychology of Fascism* that fascism and authoritarianism don't just have political-economic, but also ideological and psychological, foundations. In his writings Reich is especially interested in the question of how fascism operates with emotional, unconscious and irrational elements, and why certain humans actively reproduce fascist propaganda in their consciousness. As a consequence, it does not suffice that anti-fascism operates by criticising poverty, hunger and inequality. It has to take the psychology of fascism into account too. Economy, ideology and psychology interact in society. According to Reich, the fact that everyday people follow fascism shows the materiality and material effectiveness of fascist ideology and its political psychology. Ideology would embed the 'economic process in the *psychic structures of the people who make up the society*' (Reich 1972, 18).

Reich shows how Hitler operated upon 'the *emotions* of the individuals in the masses' and avoided '*relevant arguments* as much as possible' (Reich 1972, 34). 'Hitler repeatedly stressed that one could not get at the masses with arguments, proofs, and knowledge, but only with feelings and beliefs' (Reich 1972, 83). 'Every form of totalitarian-authoritarian rulership is based on the irrationalism inculcated in masses of people' (Reich 1972, 312). Reich argues that one needs to explain *why* individuals are accessible to ideology. Authoritarian fathers, bosses and political leaders would play an important role in the formation of individuals' authoritarian character structure. Authoritarianism culminates in the identification with a political Führer (Reich 1972, 62–3).

Wilhelm Reich and the Frankfurt School

Frankfurt School thinkers such as Erich Fromm, Herbert Marcuse, Theodor W. Adorno, Franz L. Neumann, Leo Löwenthal and Max Horkheimer took an approach comparable to and influenced by Reich. They stress that fascism cannot be explained by capitalism alone, but that its analysis needs to take ideology, political psychology and the role of the state into account. The Frankfurt School argued for an interdisciplinary approach to understanding fascism and authoritarianism.

Reich complained that Erich Fromm 'managed to disregard completely the sexual problem of masses of people and its relationship to the fear of freedom and craving for authority' (Reich 1972, 219). Fromm (1933) reviewed Reich's 1932 book *Der Einbruch der Sexualmoral* (*The Imposition of Sexual Morality*). He remarked that Reich was 'one of the few authors, who based on the results of Freud's psychoanalysis and Marx's sociology, came to new and fruitful sociological results' (Fromm 1933, 119). In the Frankfurt School's *Studie über Autorität und Familie* (*Study on Authority and Family*), Max Horkheimer (1936a, 69) referenced Reich in a footnote and Erich Fromm (1936, 113) wrote that Reich's analysis of masochism was fruitful, but that Reich's works were characterised by the 'physiologistic overestimation of the sexual factor'.

The first German edition of Reich's *The Mass Psychology of Fascism* was published in 1933. The Frankfurt School's *Zeitschrift für Sozialforschung* published a short review, in which Max Horkheimer's friend Karl Landauer (1934) mentioned that Reich overestimated genital sexuality. This remark may be characteristic for the Frankfurt School's general assessment of Reich's approach. The Frankfurt School authors respected Reich's general approach of combining Marx and Freud in the analysis of the interaction of capitalism and the human psyche. Reich laid some of the foundations for this analysis, but on the other hand Fromm, Adorno and their colleagues also felt that Reich overstressed the sexual factor.

In his book *Eros and Civilization: An Inquiry into Freud*, Herbert Marcuse (1955, 239) writes that Reich made a 'serious attempt to develop the critical social theory implicit in Freud', but also formulated the criticism that 'Reich rejects Freud's hypothesis of the death instinct' and the sex instinct's 'fusion with the destructive impulses'.

> Consequently, sexual liberation *per se* becomes for Reich a panacea for individual and social ills. The problem of sublimation is minimized; no essential distinction is made between repressive and non-repressive sublimation, and progress in freedom appears as a mere release of sexuality. The critical sociological insights contained in Reich's earlier writings are thus arrested; a sweeping primitivism becomes prevalent, foreshadowing the wild and fantastic hobbies of Reich's later years. (Marcuse 1955, 239)

The Frankfurt School's first generation seemed to sympathise with Reich's general approach of combining psychoanalysis and Marxism, and with his assumption that the analysis of authoritarianism needed to take ideology and psychology into account. At the same time they were highly sceptical of Reich's analysis of sexuality, and considered his approach as a form of sexual reductionism that reduced authoritarianism to the suppression of sexual instincts and saw sexual uninhibitedness as a panacea against fascism and authoritarianism. The Frankfurt School's theorists did not share sexual reductionist assumptions such as the claim that 'suppression of the natural sexuality of children and adolescents serves to mold the human structure in such a way that masses of people become willing upholders and reproducers of mechanistic authoritarian civilization' (Reich 1972, 322).

Max Horkheimer on Authority

Max Horkheimer (1936b, 70) defines authority as 'internal and external behaviors in which men submit to an external source of command'. The Enlightenment challenged the authority of the church and the monarch, but set up capital as the new authority:

> Bourgeois thought begins as a struggle against the authority of tradition and replaces it with reason as the legitimate source of right and truth. It ends with the deification of naked authority as such (a conception no less empty of determinate content than the concept of reason), since justice, happiness, and freedom for mankind have been eliminated as historically possible solutions. [...] That the struggle against dependence on authority should in modern times change directly into a deification of authority as such is a development rooted in the origins of the struggle. (72, 76)

Capitalist authority is shaped by the irrationality of the 'blind power of chance' and crisis in capitalism (82), and 'the reified authority of the economy' (83) that expresses itself as the class relationship between capital and labour. Horkheimer also stresses the role of the family, and writes that the patriarchal family is 'the creator of the authority-oriented cast of mind' (112). In capitalist patriarchy, authority in the family has to do with the social position of the father and the mother in earning the family's living (122). The need to sell one's labour power always carries with it the threat of poverty and of not being able to feed one's children. Marcuse (1936, 210) argues in this context that discipline at work is an inherent feature of the organisation of the labour process. The need to conform to the market and to the boss is built into capitalism, which influences the family's structure.

Erich Fromm on the Authoritarian Personality

Erich Fromm (1984) conducted a survey among German workers. The data collection took place from 1929 until 1931 and resulted in a total of 584 responses. For analysing personality types (radical, authoritarian, compromise-oriented) he used a total of ten questions, grouped into three domains: political opinions, attitudes to authority and attitudes towards fellow human beings. The analysis showed, for example, that workers in larger companies and urban centres were more radical and less prone to authoritarianism than those in smaller companies and rural areas. Workers who identified as communists, left socialists or social democrats were less authoritarian than those identifying as Nazis or as supporting bourgeois parties. A limit of the study was that only 17 Nazis participated; 29 per cent of social democrats, 7 per cent of left socialists, 8 per cent of communists showed some authoritarian leaning. In this study, Fromm defined the authoritarian attitude as the personality of someone who 'affirms, seeks out and enjoys the subjugation of men under a higher external power, whether this power is the state or a leader, natural law, the past or God' (209–10), and opposed this outlook to the radical attitude that shows 'a demand for freedom, for oneself and for all human beings [...] on the basis of solidarity with others' (209).

Fromm (1936) argues that the patriarchal family that has a dominant father is one of the authoritarian personality structure's sources. The same mode of projection and identification with authority takes place in other parts of society too, where individuals positively affirm leaders such as politicians, managers, bosses or teachers. Fromm argues (unlike Reich) that childhood experiences do not determine political positions taken in adulthood, but constitute predispositions (86). A decisive aspect would be the human desire to be loved and the fear of being deprived of love and being rejected (78, 96). Fromm argues that Freud disregards the 'relationship of family structure with the structure of the totality of society' (88). The level of authority of the father in the family would be mediated with 'the societal totality's authority structures' (88). The operation of the Oedipus complex would depend on societal structures, which means that the son does not always and does not necessarily perceive his father as a sexual rival. The implication is that a lower level of authority in education can result in less psychosocial rivalry and less search for identification with authority.

For Fromm (1936), not all authority and suppression of instincts are authoritarian: he distinguishes between supportive authority that helps individuals to develop, and repressive authority that aims at exploitation and domination (111, 135). Fromm characterises the authoritarian personality as a sadomasochistic character type that feels pleasure in both submission to authority and the subjection of underdogs. Authoritarian societies foster sadomasochistic personalities (117–18). Authoritarian personalities therefore show 'aggression against the defenceless and sympathy for the powerful' (115). Authoritarianism has an extremely polarised relationship with the powerful and the weak: 'To the one group all good characteristics are ascribed and they are loved, and to the other group all negative characteristics are ascribed and they are hated' (116). Authorities would often support and promote this dual structure in order to reach the double goal of on the one hand keeping the relationship with one group 'free from hatred and directing on the other hand hatred against forces that it wants to combat with the help of the subaltern' (116). 'Finally overcoming sadomasochism is only thinkable in a society, in which humans govern their lives planfully, reasonable and actively and where not the bravery of suffering and obedience, but the courage for happiness and the overcoming of fate form the highest virtue' (122).

Adorno's Study of the Authoritarian Personality

Adorno et al. (1950), in their study *The Authoritarian Personality*, empirically studied the question: 'If a potentially fascistic individual exists, what, precisely, is he like? What goes to make up anti-democratic thought? What are the organizing forces within the person?' (2). The study focused on American citizens. Methodologically it used questionnaires with factual, opinion and projective questions as well as in-depth interviews. There were four versions of the questionnaire in which the research team developed four versions of the F scale (fascism scale) that measured the extent to which a person had a fascist leaning: form 78, form 60, form 45, and form 40. The forms were named according to the number of questions they consisted of. All versions of the questionnaire had nine dimensions in common, and included a series of questions for each of these dimensions. A Likert scale ranging from −3 ('I strongly disagree') to +3 ('I strongly agree') was used. The scores were recoded ranging from 1 (strong disagreement) to 7 (strong agreement). The dimensions used were as follows (see Adorno et al. 1950, 228):

1. Conventionalism: adherence to middle-class values;
2. Authoritarian submission: submission to authorities and leaders;

3. Authoritarian aggression: opposition to people who violate conventional values;
4. Anti-intraception: opposition to the subjective, the imaginative and the tender-minded;
5. Superstition and stereotypy: belief in rigid categories, mysticism and predetermined fate;
6. Power and 'toughness': identification with leaders, power figures, strength and toughness;
7. Destructiveness and cynicism: general hostility towards humans;
8. Projectivity: belief that the world is wild and dangerous;
9. Exaggerated concerns with sex.

The study showed that these nine dimensions tended to appear together in authoritarian consciousness (Adorno et al. 1950, 751). Dimensions two and six both refer to the belief in leadership figures and top-down power politics. The stereotype aspect of dimension five as well as dimensions three and seven refer to a negative view of the world, which is seen as hostile and as being polarised into friends and enemies. It is not clear why, in dimension five, superstition and stereotyping have been combined. These seem to be two different aspects of authoritarianism. Dimensions one, eight and nine have to do with a patriarchal and militaristic view of the world, in which conservative moral values dominate, women are reduced to housework, traditional gender roles prevail, men are seen as dominant, the ideal man is a warrior and soldier who confronts a wild and dangerous world, and there is a constant threat of war for which one has to be prepared. The belief in superstition is a form of naturalism that focuses on the disbelief in the human capacity to change society for the better, the fetishistic belief in mechanic determination and society's rule by mystical forces that humans cannot influence. It is surprising that collective identity, i.e. nationalism and ethnocentrism, does not form a separate dimension of the F scale. Whereas fascist worldviews may have some variety in terms of the enemies they perceive, oppose, hate and want to destroy, all of them seem to have the closed and rigid we-identity of a national or ethnic community. Daniel Woodley (2010) argues, in his comprehensive review of critical theories of fascism, that although nationalism comes in a variety of forms that change historically, 'nation and nationhood are central components of fascist political discourse' (Woodley 2010, 185). Adorno et al.'s study used a separate ethnocentrism scale (E scale) that focused on attitudes towards people of colour, minorities, patriotism and anti-Semitism (Adorno et al. 1950, chapter 4). It is somewhat surprising that parts of the E scale have not been included in the F scale, because such a separation implies that there can be fascism without nationalism and ethnocentrism.

Right-Wing Authoritarianism's Four Dimensions

One problem with the F scale is that its dimensions are overlapping and incomplete. A more comprehensive understanding of right-wing authoritarianism focuses on four dimensions:

1. Authoritarianism and leadership: belief in the importance of strong authorities and leaders.
2. Nationalism, ethnocentrism: belief in the superiority of a particular community that is conceived as forming a nation or ethnicity. Nationalism and the friend/enemy scheme (see dimension 3) serve the purpose of distracting attention from the class conflict that shapes capitalism. Fascism is a particular form of capitalist ideology and political practice.
3. Friend/enemy scheme: the national community is defined in relation to one or more constructed out-groups that are portrayed as dangerous enemies that should be opposed, fought and eliminated. There is a rigid distinction between groups that are conceived as being strictly different, separate and opposed. Adorno et al. (1950, 113) found that 'ethnocentric hostility toward outgroups is highly correlated with ethnocentric idealization of ingroups' and that there is a general opposition to all kinds of out-groups among ethnocentrists.
4. Patriarchy and militarism: there is a belief in conservative values, including traditional gender roles, sexism and the heroism of warriors and soldiers, whose task it is to defend the nation and fight against the perceived enemies. Society is seen as being shaped by a dichotomy between strength and weakness. The world is conceived as a wild and dangerous place with a constant threat of war and the need to defend the nation against enemies. This conservative picture of the world often comes with a stress on the importance of nature, the human body and physical strength.

Levels of Right-Wing Authoritarianism

Right-wing authoritarianism, right-wing extremism and fascism are not just ideologies and psychological dispositions, but can also be political movements that can turn into societal systems. When discussing questions such as 'Is X right-wing authoritarian/right-wing extremist/fascist?', one must always be clear about which level of being one is talking about: one must clarify whether one is talking about the level of consciousness, psychology/character structure, ideology, political movements/groups/parties, institutions or society. There can, for example, be fascist ideology and character structures within a democratic society that either has organised fascist movements or does not. The basic distinction that needs to be drawn is the one between the levels of the individual, social groups, institutions and society. There is a micro (individuals), a meso (groups and institutions) and a macro (society) level of the far right. Right-wing authoritarianism involves all of the four elements mentioned above. There can be right-wing authoritarian individuals, groups and institutions and a right-wing authoritarian society. Right-wing extremism and fascism are an intensification of right-wing authoritarianism so that an increase of quantity turns into a new quality: fascists favour terror and violence for attaining their goals (hierarchic leadership, nationalism, opposing perceived enemies, patriarchy, militarisation). Fascism's final factor 'is the reliance upon terror, i.e., the use of non-calculable violence as a permanent threat against the individual' (Neumann 1957, 245). A right-wing authoritarian individual, group, institution or society does not necessarily favour terror and a police state that represses all opposition, but right-wing authoritarianism can turn into fascism. A fascist society presupposes fascist individuals, groups and institutions.

Adorno's F Scale and Related Studies

A number of studies have built on Adorno et al.'s F scale. Altemeyer (1996, 6) defines right-wing authoritarianism as a combination of authoritarian submission, authoritarian aggression and conventionalism. His right-wing authoritarianism (RWA) scale uses 30 items that are scored on a Likert scale ranging from -4 (strong disagreement) to $+4$ (strong agreement). The answers are recoded so that -4 corresponds to 1 and $+4$ to 9. The RWA scale for a particular individual therefore ranges from a minimum of 30 to a maximum of 270. Altemeyer (1996, 47) argues that his approach is different to the one used by Adorno et al. (1950). But at the same time he admits that Adorno et al.'s model was the starting point and got him interested in studying right-wing authoritarianism (45).

Duckitt et al. (2010) developed the authoritarianism-conservatism-traditionalism scale (ACT) that consists of 36 items. Each of the three dimensions consists of twelve items. Altemeyer's three dimensions were renamed: authoritarian aggression was called authoritarianism (A), authoritarian submission was called conservatism (C) and conventionalism was called traditionalism (T). Based on Altemeyer's scale, Dunwoody and Funke (2016) developed the aggression-submission-conventionalism scale (ASC). The difference is that Altemeyer's scale uses single-, double- and triple-barrelled questions, whereas Dunwoody and Funke's 18 items avoid multi-barrelled questions. The items in the scales used by Altemeyer, Duckitt et al., and Dunwoody and Funke are organised along the first three of Adorno et al.'s (1950) dimensions. Aspects of nationalism, patriarchy and warfare are not present in the RWA, ACT and ASC scales. The important aspect, however, is that such research confirms the continued relevance of Adorno's empirical method.

In the next section, we will take a closer look at right-wing authoritarianism's four levels.

RIGHT-WING AUTHORITARIANISM AND AUTHORITARIAN CAPITALISM

Nationalism is a particular ideology that constructs fictive ethnicity and the nation as communities in order to distract attention from class conflicts and other forms of social antagonism. Right-wing authoritarianism is a concept that is based on the critical theory of the authoritarian personality that was developed by Frankfurt School authors such as Erich Fromm and Theodor W. Adorno. Hierarchical leadership, nationalism, the friend/enemy scheme, patriarchy and militarism are the key elements of right-wing authoritarian personality, ideology, movements, institutions and systems.

A Model of Right-Wing Authoritarianism

It is common linguistic use to speak of right-wing extremist individuals or movements, but the term right-wing extremist society is hardly used.

Right-wing extremism is an ideology, political goal and movement, but not a type of society (Holzer 1993, 31–2). Right-wing extremism is a militant and violent form of right-wing authoritarian consciousness, ideology, social movements and organisations, whereas fascism can potentially be found at the level of the individuals, groups, organisations and society. One can speak of fascist individuals, fascist consciousness, fascist ideology, fascist social movements, fascist organisations, fascist institutions and a fascist society. Each of these levels presupposes the previous ones, but the lower organisational levels do not necessarily imply and require the upper ones. A difference between right-wing extremism and fascism is that right-wing extremists exhibit a latency towards accepting and favouring violence against political opponents, and attacks are mostly limited to political style as well as communicative, ideological and symbolic violence (Bailer-Galanda and Neugebauer 1997, 55; Schiedel 2007, 29). Fascists and fascist societies, in contrast, use violence and terroristic means in order to try to harm, imprison, ban, kill or exterminate their opponents and scapegoats. The boundary is blurry because psychological intimidation and threats (for example online and on social media) are also a form of violence aimed at harming individuals.

Figure 3.1 shows a model that visualises right-wing authoritarianism. Right-wing authoritarianism's four elements (authoritarian leadership, nationalism, the friend/enemy scheme, patriarchy and militarism) often interact with each other. It uses political fetishism: it fetishises the nation in order to deflect attention from class contradictions and power inequalities. Nationalism constitutes a we-identity by constructive fictive ethnicity. Authoritarian leadership is the way in which the power of this national collective is organised, namely in a top-down manner, in which a leader rules and the followers submit to their authority. Authoritarian leadership and leader fetishism is used as a political organisation principle that often also extends to the organisation of the capitalist economy, culture and everyday life. Right-wing authoritarianism sees hierarchic, authoritarian leadership as the basic organisational principle for economic, political and cultural systems and relations in society. The friend/enemy scheme constructs enemies and scapegoats in order to distract from class and capitalist relations. It is about 'Them', the 'Other', the 'Enemies'. Militant patriarchy has to do with the relationship between 'Us' and 'Them'. It glorifies the soldier and warrior and sees law-and-order,

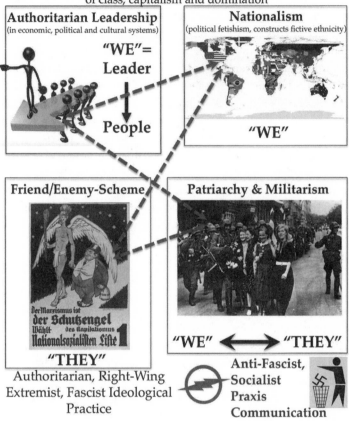

Figure 3.1 Model of right-wing authoritarianism

repression, exploitation, domination, politics, violence, imperialism and war as the appropriate ways for organising social relations. The more militant, terroristic and violent right-wing authoritarianism and authoritarian capitalism become, the more they become right-wing extremism and fascism.

Right-wing authoritarianism is an ideological practice, which means that it is not just a worldview and thought system, but also a form of human action and organisation in the economy, the political system and culture. It can just be organised on the level of ideas, which is a cognitive and communicative social practice in itself. But it can also be the guiding principle of how to organise social relations. Such ideological practices can take place at the level of the individual, group, institution or society as a whole. Right-wing authoritarianism at such a level always presupposes that it exists at the previous level as a necessary condition.

Anti-fascism is an anti-ideological praxis that challenges and questions right-wing authoritarianism, right-wing extremism and fascism. It is not just practice, but praxis, a particular form of practice – socialist practice. Because right-wing authoritarianism tries to deflect attention from the true causes of society's problems through nationalism and the friend/enemy scheme, socialism is the appropriate praxis response that sheds light on social problems' rootedness in power, exploitation and domination and offers perspectives that transcend capitalism, domination and class. Praxis communication is communication that acts within democratic-socialist structures or aims at establishing such structures and a society built on them.

Authoritarian Capitalism

The capitalist economy is a class economy, in which labour produces commodities that are privately owned and sold to the benefit of capitalists trying to accumulate ever more capital. Capitalism is a particular form of society that combines the exploitation of labour and the accumulation of monetary capital, the accumulation of political decision-making power, and the accumulation of cultural definitional and reputational power. Authoritarian capitalism is a specific type of capitalism. Authoritarian capitalism is a capitalism that uses repressive state power in order to advance capitalist interests, which features a blurring of the boundaries between the state and big capital, state intervention into the economy in favour of big capital, law-and-order politics, armament and militarism, and a certain degree of repressive politics against immigrants, the political opposition and other constructed enemies. Fascism is a particular form of authoritarian capitalism. Any authoritarian capitalism is not necessarily fascist, but can turn into fascism. Authoritarian capitalism has tendencies towards limiting the opposition's and perceived enemies' freedom, whereas fascism eliminates them. The basic difference between authoritarian capitalism and fascism is one between repressive limitation and elimination.

Franz L. Neumann's Definition of Fascism

Franz L. Neumann defines fascism as 'the dictatorship of the Fascist [...] party, the bureaucracy, the army, and big business, the dictatorship over the whole of the people, for complete organization of the nation for imperialist war' (Neumann 1936a, 35; see also Neumann 1944/2009, 360). Fascism refuses 'groups with an independent existence of their own, groups which come between the state and the individual' (Neumann 1936a, 35), such as independent trade unions, meeting points, movements and parties. There is an assimilation (*Gleichschaltung*) of groups and organisations. In fascism, 'the state is everything, the individual nothing' (Neumann 1936a, 36). Fascism robs workers of their rights (42). Workers have no influence in the economy and the state (43). Neumann stresses both the political-economic and ideological character of fascism. He points out the role of the authoritarian state that represents the interests of capital and the fascist party/leader in order to destroy any influence of the working class and other potential oppositional movements. An aspect that is missing here is the role of nationalism as an ideology that constructs a fictive unity of capital and labour as nation.

Neumann stresses that state apparatuses (bureaucracy, army, party) become fused under the control of the state. As a consequence, no independent groups are allowed to exist within the state, economy or society. Fascism is for Neumann an inherently imperialist and war-waging type of society. This aspect relates to the characteristic of militarism. Two elements that he does not discuss are the connection between militarism and patriarchy as well as the friend/enemy scheme and exterminatory and repressive politics that are based on it. In his later book, *Behemoth*, Neumann (1944/2009) discusses all aspects of fascism in detail, including nationalism, the friend/enemy scheme and patriarchy.

Charismatic Leadership

NEUMANN AND WEBER ON CHARISMATIC POWER

Charismatic power and the leadership principle form an important element of right-wing authoritarianism. Neumann characterised charismatic leadership in the following way: 'The justification of this [leadership] principle is charismatic: it rests on the assertion that the Leader is endowed with qualities lacking in ordinary mortals. Superhuman qualities emanate from him and pervade the state, party, and people' (Neumann 1944/2009, 99). In authoritarian ideologies and systems, the 'principle of leadership [...] dominates all social and political organizations' (Neumann 1944/2009, 83). The concept of charismatic leadership does not mean an individualistic analysis that just focuses on the role of single persons as leaders. It rather stresses that citizens follow, legitimate, enable and support authoritarian rule and in specific societal and organisational contexts enact the leadership principle and act as small leaders. Max Weber (1978, 243) therefore speaks of the connection of a charismatic leader to a charismatic community that is 'based on an emotional form of communal relationship'.

ADORNO ON AUTHORITARIAN LEADERS

Adorno (1951a) points out the importance of the leadership principle in right-wing authoritarianism. The leader presents himself as a 'threatening authority' (137). Psychology is an important element for making individuals follow authoritarian rule and collectively projecting themselves into the leader. 'It is precisely this idealization of himself which the fascist leader tries to promote in his followers, and which is helped by the *Führer* ideology' (140). Collective narcissism is a psychological dimension of authoritarianism. The image of the strong leader creates the psychological 'enlargement of the subject: by making the leader his ideal he loves himself, as it were, but gets rid of the stains of frustration and discontent which mar his picture of his own empirical self' (140). 'The narcissistic *gain* provided by fascist propaganda is obvious' (145). An authoritarian leader presents himself as superman and ordinary, as a 'great little man' (142). This 'unity trick' (146) tries to construct a feeling of union within the national community in order to advance hatred against out-groups.

IAN KERSHAW AND NEUMANN ON HITLER'S CHARISMATIC LEADERSHIP

Hierarchic leadership is a necessary, but not sufficient element of right-wing authoritarianism. Historically speaking it formed an important feature of all fascist systems. Ian Kershaw (2008) wrote a widely acclaimed biography of Hitler. He does not consider Hitler's personality to be the key feature of Nazi-fascism, but a specific form of charismatic rule. Kershaw (2004) argues that Nazi-fascism combined 'Hitler's "charismatic authority"', the cult and myth of the Führer, 'and its promise of national salvation' (Kershaw 2004, 246). Nazi-fascism aimed at 'racial cleansing and imperialism' (249), the Shoah and a world war, and used a modern military and state for putting its ideology into political practice. Nazi-fascism's ideology featured the '"removal of the Jews" [...]; attaining "living space" to secure Germany's future (a notion vague enough to encompass different strands of expansionism); race as the explanation of world history, and eternal struggle as the basic law of human existence' (Kershaw 2004, 252). Neumann (1944/2009, 83–97) agrees with the analysis that Hitler was a charismatic leader, whom the Germans saw as possessing '[s]uperhuman qualities' (85). But he stresses that hierarchic leadership was not confined to the Nazi state and its political groups, but extended to all realms of Nazi society. The 'principle of leadership [...] dominates all social and political organizations' (83). Hitler was 'the leader of the party, the army, and the people' (84).

Nationalism

Nationalism is a key feature of right-wing authoritarianism, and we discussed it in more detail in Chapter 2. It forms the part of right-wing ideology that constructs the inner logic of society, whereas the friend/enemy scheme constructs the other logic of society (see 'The Friend/Enemy Scheme' section below).

MYTHIC COLLECTIVES

Right-wing authoritarianism appeals to a mythic collective such as the nation, ethnicity and race. It thereby diverts attention from class conflicts. '[R]acism and Anti-Semitism are substitutes for the class struggle' (Neumann 1994/2009, 125). '[B]lood, community, folk, are devices for hiding the real constellation of power' (Neumann 1994/2009, 464). Right-wing authoritarianism uses reactionary collectivism as an ideology for claiming that it can overcome the social problems of capitalism, modernity and globalisation.

Right-wing authoritarian language centres on "'irrational" ideas such as folk, race, blood and soil, Reich' (Marcuse 1998, 150). It often employs the 'verbalization of nouns, a shrinking of the synthetical structure of the sentence, and a transformation of personal relations into impersonal things and events' (150). Right-wing authoritarianism is irrational because concepts such as race, ethnicity and nation do not have reasonable foundations (Marcuse 1934). But this political irrationality is rationalised and put into political practice by rational means, especially state power.

The Friend/Enemy Scheme

CARL SCHMITT

The friend/enemy scheme is an important element of right-wing authoritarianism. It is an ideology that constructs scapegoats who are presented as enemies of the nation in order to deflect attention from the real conflicts and contradictions in society. Carl Schmitt was a German legal scholar who sympathised with the Nazis. He became a member of the Nazi Party in 1933 and was editor of the judicial journal *Deutsche Juristen-Zeitung.*

Schmitt formulated the logic of the friend/enemy scheme in the following way:

The specific political distinction to which political actions and motives can be reduced is that between friend and enemy [...]. Insofar as it is not derived from other criteria, the antithesis of friend and enemy corresponds to the relatively independent criteria of other antitheses: good and evil in the moral sphere, beautiful and ugly in the aesthetic sphere, and so on. [...] The distinction of friend and enemy denotes the utmost degree of intensity of a union or separation, of an association or dissociation. [...] Emotionally the enemy is easily treated as being evil and ugly, because every distinction, most of all the political, as the strongest and most intense of the distinctions and categorizations, draws upon other distinctions for support. [...] The enemy is solely the public enemy, because everything that has a relationship to such a collectivity of men, particularly to a whole nation, becomes public by virtue of such a relationship. [...] War follows from enmity. War is the existential negation of the enemy. It is the most extreme consequence of enmity. It does not have to be common, normal, something ideal, or desirable. But it must nevertheless remain a real possibility for as long as the concept of the enemy remains valid (Schmitt 1932/1996, 26, 27, 28, 33).

REFUGEES AND IMMIGRANTS AS NEW ENEMIES IN FAR-RIGHT IDEOLOGY

In far-right and white supremacist ideologies, Muslims and Eastern and Southern immigrants are often defined as the enemy. On the one hand, biologistic forms of racism are still prevalent. But on the other hand a culturalised form of racism and xenophobia has emerged, in which foreigners are said to have a culture different from and incompatible with the majority culture. The political conclusion is that cultures should never mix and borders be shut to immigrants and refugees. The notion of the enemy also plays a geopolitical role today: Western military interventions in Iraq, Afghanistan, Libya and Syria have not helped to stabilise the political situation in the Middle East, but have further destabilised the region.

Wars and destabilisation are the causes of refugees in the Middle East leaving their home countries. Europe and other parts of the world have not responded in a coordinated manner, but have in many respects violated the human right to asylum. Refugees and immigrants have been constructed as new enemies flooding Europe and bringing terror and non-European values and lifestyles to the continent. Even those who at first seemed to be welcoming, like Germany, finally used the friend/enemy scheme because of the fear of losing elections when being perceived as too refugee-friendly. European countries have blamed each other. The results are the erection of borders and quotas, and the spread of nationalism, racism and xenophobia. The EU has made a dodgy political deal with Turkey about the return of refugees to a country whose political climate means high insecurity and risks for refugees. The economic crisis of capitalism has turned into a highly dangerous political crisis in Europe and the world system, in which nationalism and the friend/enemy logic are rapidly spreading and expanding.

ANTI-SEMITISM

Nazi-fascism is anti-Semitic, but the question arises as to whether all fascism and right-wing authoritarianism has to be anti-Semitic.

Mussolini took on anti-Semitism from Hitler in 1938 (Hobsbawm 1994, 116), but Italian fascism largely dispensed with anti-Semitism before Italy entered into an alliance with Nazi Germany. It is clear that the construction of a national collective needs to define itself against an enemy which is considered to threaten the unity of the imagined national community. It is, however, relatively open which group far-right ideology chooses as its main scapegoat. Fascism is an annihilationist and exterminatory ideology, but the choice of its enemies is not strictly determined. The imagined Other is presented as being powerful and depriving the national community of opportunities.

Nazi-fascism uses racism and anti-Semitism for justifying 'unequal citizen rights' (Neumann 1944/2009, 99). According to Neumann (1944/2009, 110–11), Nazi anti-Semitism blamed the Jews for economic problems, identified capitalism with Judaism, claimed that the Jews were 'the leaders of Marxist socialism' (111) and was based on the conspiracy that they have set out to destroy 'Aryanism'. Neumann argues that anti-Semitism was 'the sole ideology that can possibly cement the Nazi Party. [...] Anti-Semitism is [...] the spearhead of terror' (Neumann, Marcuse and Kirchheimer 2013, 27).

Fascism is a form of repressive, exterminatory dualism. Fascist anti-Semitism builds on the ideology and politics of exterminatory dualism. The Nazis opposed a productive industrial Aryan capitalism with a parasitic, unproductive financial Jewish capitalism. They did not criticise capitalism, but biologised and racialised the sphere of circulation and finance.

MOISHE POSTONE: ANTI-SEMITISM AND CAPITALISM

According to Moishe Postone, Auschwitz was the result of capitalism's logic. The Nazis created Auschwitz as a negative factory for the destruction of Jewishness that they considered to be the abstract cause of modernity's evils:

Auschwitz was a factory to 'destroy value', that is, to destroy the personifications of the abstract. Its organization was that of a fiendishly inverted industrial process, the aim of which was to 'liberate' the concrete from the abstract. The first step was to dehumanize and reveal the Jews for what they 'really are' – ciphers, numbered abstractions. The second step was to then eradicate that abstractness, trying in the process to wrest away the last remnants of the concrete material 'use-value': clothes, gold, hair [...] Modern anti-Semitism emerged from the fetishistic structure of capitalism. It is 'a particularly pernicious fetish form' [...] The Jews were held responsible for economic crises and identified with the range of social restructuring and dislocation resulting from rapid capitalist industrialization. [...] [The] specific characteristics of the power attributed to the Jews by modern anti-Semitism – abstractness, intangibility, universality, mobility – are all characteristics of the value dimension of the social forms fundamentally characterizing capitalism. (Postone 2003, 95, 89, 91).

Hitler constantly voiced anti-Semitic stereotypes. He for example spoke of the 'despotism of international world finance, Jewry!' (Hitler 1941, 674) and of 'international world finance Judaism's goal of enslaving the world' (875). Anti-Semitic stereotypes are not a necessary element of right-wing authoritarianism because the friend/enemy scheme poses a certain ideological flexibility, but it nonetheless can often be found in far-right thought. Socialism, finance capitalism and Jewry were identical for Hitler: he for example wrote that the 'Marxist shock troops of international Jewish stock exchange capital' want to 'definitely break the spine of the German national state' (905).

Speaking of Jewish finance is a short-circuited, biologistic assessment of capitalism typical of fascist thought. It discerns between an unproductive, parasitic sphere of circulation and finance on the one side, and a productive sphere of industrial capital on the other. Anti-Semitic fascism biologises this dualism by characterising the first as Jewish and the second as Aryan. Postone argues that modern anti-Semitism is a biologisation and naturalisation of the commodity fetish. It is based on the 'notion that the concrete is "natural"' and that the 'natural' is 'more "essential" and closer to origins' (Postone 1980, 111). 'Industrial capital then appears as the linear descendent of "natural" artisanal labor', 'industrial production' appears as 'a purely material, creative process' (110). Anti-Semitic fascism separates industrial capital and industrial labour from the sphere of circulation, exchange and money that is seen as 'parasitic' (110). In Nazi ideology, the 'manifest abstract dimension is also biologized – as the Jews. The opposition of the concrete material and the abstract becomes the racial opposition of the Arians and the Jews' (112). Modern anti-Semitism is a one-sided 'critique' of capitalism that sees the sphere of circulation as the totality of capitalism, biologistically inscribing Jewishness into circulation and capitalism. It sees technology and industry that are perceived as productive and Aryan as standing outside of capitalism. In this ideology, capitalism 'appeared to be only its manifest abstract dimension, which was in turn held responsible for the economic social, and cultural changes associated with the rapid development of modern industrial capitalism' (Postone 2003, 93).

THE NAZIS' RACIAL IMPERIALISM

The reason why Jews have historically been somewhat overrepresented in the realms of trade and banking has to do with an anti-Semitic division of labour that banned them from taking on certain occupations. William Brustein (2003) argues in his book *Roots of Hate: Anti-Semitism in Europe before the Holocaust* that in 1925, the year when Hitler published the first volume of *Mein Kampf*, 17.6 per cent of the German banks had Jewish owners. This means that 82.4 per cent of the banks in Germany had non-Jewish owners. Claims about 'Jewish finance' are a pure myth that serves ideological purposes.

Neumann (1944/2009), in his study of Nazi Germany's political economy and ideology, stresses that the Nazis' racial imperialism was a peculiar political form that merged imperialism, anti-Semitism and racism. The ideology of the friend/enemy scheme is connected to violence because it can motivate imperialism and extermination. 'The essence of the theory is extremely simple. Germany and Italy are proletarian races, surrounded by a world of hostile plutocratic capitalistic-Jewish democracies. [The war is thus a war for] [...] the attainment of a better life for the master race through reducing the vanquished states and their satellites to the level of colonial peoples' (Neumann 1944/2009, 187, 193). An important element of Nazi imperialism was the ideology of producing 'Aryan' living space (*Lebensraum*) through military conquest (130). Nazi imperialism postulated that the 'Aryans' are proletarian have-nots who are under threat by Jews, democracy and socialism and therefore must defend themselves (221).

Militarism and Patriarchy

MARCUSE ON INSTRUMENTAL REASON AND CYNICAL MATTER-OF-FACTNESS

In respect to nature, biology and gender, right-wing authoritarianism tends to idealise the body, nature, male supremacy, the population's fitness and health, physical labour and toil, the soldier, the army and the importance of procreation. It tends to define ideologically the sphere of production as a masculine realm and reproduction as a feminine sphere.

Marcuse (1998, 142–3) argues that right-wing authoritarian ideology is highly instrumental. Everything is considered to be an instrument for the rule of the national collective and the leader. Marcuse speaks of cynical matter-of-factness (142), a technological rationality that 'measures all issues in terms of efficiency, success and expediency' (143). The fascist would think 'in quantities: in terms of speed, skill, energy, organization, mass' (143).

Militaristic ideology and practices are the consequence of this high level of instrumental reason. For achieving its goals, right-wing authoritarianism requires, to a certain degree, a militarised and repressive state that uses the law, the police, the military, education, science, etc. – state apparatuses and ideological apparatuses – as instruments of governmental power in order to militarise and control all aspects of everyday life. Right-wing authoritarianism believes in the necessity of the 'statisation' of society. Marcuse (1998, 142) speaks in this context of 'integral politicalization': 'Social as well as private existence, work as well as leisure, are political activities. The traditional barrier between the individual and society, and between society and the state has disappeared' (142). Put into political practice, right-wing authoritarianism 'tends to abolish any separation between state and society' (70). In fascist forms of right-wing authoritarianism, the militarisation of society is directed against inner enemies that are intimidated, controlled, repressed and killed. Violence is also directed against outer enemies that are attacked with the machinery of imperialist warfare.

HORKHEIMER AND ADORNO ON MILITARISM

Militarism is a form of violence that not just postulates law and order and the use of arms and guns as responses to social problems and conflicts, but also operates on the psychological level. Horkheimer and Adorno describe the pleasure and joy of hatred and violence associated with militarism in the following way:

> A creature which has fallen attracts predators: humiliation of those already visited by misfortune brings the keenest pleasure. The less the danger to the one on top, the more unhampered the joy in the torments he can now inflict: only through the hopeless despair of the victim can power become pleasure and triumphantly revoke its own principle, discipline. Fear averted from the self bursts out in hearty laughter, the expression of a hardening within the individual which can only be lived out through the collective. (Horkheimer and Adorno 2002, 88)

PATRIARCHY IN RIGHT-WING AUTHORITARIANISM AND FASCISM

In the realm of the family and personal relations, right-wing authoritarianism is radically dualist. This gendered dualism is one of fundamental inequality. It ideologically defines the realms of production and the public as male and those of reproduction and the private as female. Right-wing authoritarianism is based on ideological dualisms between men/women, society/nature, body/mind, rationality/irrationality, production/reproduction, war/peace, public/private, intellectuality/emotionality, aggression/love, activity/passivity, etc. Right-wing authoritarianism's model of society is an extremely hierarchical and militarised form of patriarchy, in which there is a strict gender division of labour and the male soldier is seen as the ideal citizen.

In fascist societies, the private realm becomes militarised, statised and subordinated to nationalism and racism. Procreation is defined as a national duty. The model of the soldier defines images and practices of health, sports, fitness and the body. Also the motive of the competitive, physically strong male soldier can be found in fascist culture. An example is Leni Riefenstahl's movie *Olympia*. Not just the body, but also nature is part of fascist ideology that often presents blood, soil and love of nature as part of the homeland.

Fascism tends to view homosexuality 'as a threat to the integrity of the race-nation' (Woodley 2010, 228). Klaus Theweleit argues that fascism is sexually schizophrenic because it is based on the double bind 'thou shall love men' (Theweleit 1989, 339) that includes the contradictory principles of 'love for the leader' (Theweleit 1987, 60) and 'thou shall not be homosexual' (Theweleit 1989, 339). Theweleit sees a connection between fascism's 'male bonding and the white terror – a connection that provides the pleasure of power' (325).

In Nazi-fascism, sexism took on a particular form of population politics that fused patriarchy and militarism. There was a double goal: (a) the commandment of women to 'produce children'; (b) the SS's 'commandment to kill those who are not fit to live' (Neumann 1944/2009, 112). The Nazis' militaristic-patriarchal principle was: 'Produce as many children as possible so that the earth can be ruled by the master race; kill the unhealthy so that the masters need not be burdened by the care of the weak' (112).

Jill Stephenson (2001, 18) argues in her book *Women in Nazi Germany*:

> The ideal remained the married woman who bore several children and worked contentedly at maintaining a clean and orderly home, shopping thriftily and making limited demands as a consumer, educating her children to be both conscious of their racial identity and eager to engage in a life of service to the 'Aryan' community. The woman who devoted herself unstintingly to these tasks yet still found time to serve her community, through participation in a Nazi women's organization, could be satisfied that she was both 'conscious of her responsibility' (verantwortungsbewusst) to her nation and 'ready to make sacrifices' (opferbereit) to further its interest.

Authoritarian capitalism as a social system combines big capital and the big state. State power is used for enforcing capitalist interests in a repressive and authoritarian manner. For understanding authoritarian capitalism, we therefore need to understand what the state is all about.

THE STATE AND AUTHORITARIAN CAPITALISM

Bob Jessop: What is the State?

State theorist Bob Jessop (2016, 49) argues that there are four elements of the state: the state system/apparatus, the state territory, the state population and state ideas.[1] He defines the state in the following way:

---

1. Acknowledgement: the fourth section of this chapter, 'The State and Authoritarian

The core of the state apparatus comprises a relatively united ensemble of socially embedded, socially regularized, and strategically selective institutions and organizations [*Staatsgewalt*] whose socially accepted function is to define and enforce collectively binding decisions on the members of a society [*Staatsvolk*] in a given territorial area [*Staatsgebiet*] in the name of the common interest or general will of an imagined political community identified with that territory [*Staatsidee*]. (Jessop 2016, 49)

In comparison to Jessop's (1990, 341) earlier definition of the state, his newer understanding adds a cultural dimension (the nation as imagined political community). This reflects Jessop's insight that French regulation theory, an approach that he used earlier (see Jessop 1990) and completely dropped in his 2016 book, does not adequately take into account culture and ideology, and that a cultural political economy approach is needed (Sum and Jessop 2013; for a critique of this approach see Fuchs 2017a; Fuchs 2015, chapter 2). By using the concept of the imagined political community, Jessop refers to Benedict Anderson's (1991) understanding of the nation. Eric Hobsbawm, in contrast to Anderson, argues that nations and nationalism are *invented* traditions (Hobsbawm and Ranger 1983). To say that the nation and nationalism are invented differs from the claim that the nation is an *imagined* political community that is so large that its citizens cannot all know each other personally and therefore have to imagine shared characteristics.

Imagination has to do with creativity, which implies a positive concept of the nation, whereas critical theories of nationalism stress the nation and nationalism's ideological character. Invention resonates with fabrication, falsity and ideology (Özkirimli 2010, 107). One must certainly take into account that Jessop here provides a general definition of the state, but the question is whether in a democratic-socialist society a form of 'civic nationalism' can exist, and if not whether any form of nationalism always has within itself the threat of genocide so that a free society must strive to overcome all national borders and all forms of national identity.

Capitalism', was first published as part of the following article in the open access journal *tripleC: Communication, Capitalism & Critique*: Christian Fuchs. 2017. Donald Trump: A Critical Theory-Perspective on Authoritarian Capitalism. *tripleC: Communication, Capitalism & Critique* 15 (1): 1–72. www.triple-c.at/index.php/tripleC/article/view/835. Reprinted and updated with permission by *tripleC*.

Doubts arise as to whether the ideological concept of the imagined community should be included in the definition of the state.

Jessop's general definition of the state leaves out the relationship of the state to the economy. Any state relies for its existence on material inputs from the economy. Any state's collective decisions regulate the economy and society at large. In a capitalist state, these collective decisions reflect capitalist interests to a significant degree. But given that a state is not necessarily a capitalist and class state, the relationship of the state to capitalism and class should not be part of the definition of the state in general, but only of the capitalist state and the class state. Jessop's definition, however, lacks a focus on the relationship between economic and political systems.

Defining the State

If we assume that society is made up of dialectical relations between the economic, the political and the cultural realms (Fuchs 2008b, 2015, 2016b), where each realm is a realm of production and has relative autonomy, then the implication is that we need a definition of the state that focuses on the relationships of the state to the economy, politics (including self-referential relations within the state system as well as relationships to other states) and culture.

In modern society, the state regulates working conditions (labour time, wage levels, holiday entitlements, safety, etc.); ownership (monopolies, intellectual property rights, competition policies, legal defence of property against theft, etc.); monetary policies (interest rates, monetary supply); trade (protectionist vs free market); the level and rights of the immigrant workforce, fiscal policy (taxation, government spending) in respect to (a) taxation (capital, labour) and (b) state spending, borrowing and investments in infrastructure; the private, public or hybrid ownership character of infrastructures (science and technology, schools, universities, roads, railways, bridges, hospitals, communications, housing, waste disposal, energy supply, water supply, pension system, etc.); inheritance policies; population policies (financial support for families, etc.); and external and internal defence (military, police, secret services, prison system).

The officials, members and supporters of political parties to specific degrees represent the capitalist class, the working class and different class fractions. The state is a political site, where these interests meet and contradict each other in the collective decision-making process. Collective decision making in parliaments or other political institutions is a site where different political interests relate to each other. In capitalism, the state regulates class conflict. For example, it has positive or negative effects on profits and wages through taxation, minimum wage policies and decisions on the public or private provision of basic services. The state's economic policies influence the rate of profit and the rate of surplus value. Its innovation and infrastructure policies also shape the organic composition of capital. This also means that the capitalist class, the working class, ideological struggles and the state influence class struggles. Crises of capitalism are often triggers for the restructuring of the state and its policies that regulate capitalism. Politicians are also producers of collective decisions who earn a wage paid for by taxation.

Taking these reflections into account, we can define the state as an ensemble of institutions and organisations that produce and practice collective decisions that are binding for all members of society and that thereby regulate economic, political and cultural life within the territorial boundaries of society. State power involves certain relations between the economy and the state, intra-state relations between the state's institutions, inter-state relations that define the relationship between states, semiotic representations by the state (discourses by the state) and semiotic representations of the state (discourses on the state). Table 3.1 present a systematic model of the state.

Table 3.1 Dimensions of the state

Dimension
(1) Relationship of the state to the economy
(2) Relationship of the state to the citizens
(3) Intra-state relations
(4) Inter-state relations
(5) Semiotic representations by the state (discourses by the state)
(6) Semiotic representation of the state (discourses on the state)

The Capitalist State

The capitalist economy is a regime of monetary capital accumulation that is based on class relations that define and enable the private ownership of the means of production, the exploitation of labour and the dominant class's dispossession of the products and value that labour produces. The logic of accumulation can extend beyond the economy. As a consequence, modern politics and the state are systems for the accumulation of influence and decision-power. Further, modern culture is an ideological system for the accumulation of reputation, meaning-making-power and definition-power (Fuchs 2017d, chapter 3).

Modern society therefore not just entails a capitalist economy, but is a capitalist society. A state is capitalist to the extent that its role is to support, enable, defend and legitimise the accumulation of economic capital, the accumulation of political power (at the internal level of the state via mechanisms that allow elite control of politics, and at the international level of the state via imperialist mechanisms that allow control of the international economy, international politics and international ideological hegemony) and the accumulation of cultural power.

Culture, worldviews and ideologies matter for the state in several respects:

- The state is a site for the formulation of political positions, government programmes and opposition programmes that express particular worldviews.
- In political institutions, different worldviews collide, contradict each other and may also temporarily align with each other.
- Policies and political values influence and are influenced by everyday worldviews and ideologies, and by intellectuals and lobbies that try to shape political programmes and positions.

Economic reductionism sees the state as the instrument for the rule of the capitalist class. It overlooks the fact that the working class can have influence on state power. Political reductionism sees the state as an autonomous and neutral institution that, depending on who controls it, determines the economy in particular ways. A dialectical view sees the modern state and the modern economy as identical and non-identical. They are both based on the logic of accumulation (of political power and capital). The state is always a system of political domination; class society is always a system of exploitation. The state as the site of political accumulation and domination stands in a contradictory relation to the capitalist economy as the site of economic accumulation and exploitation.

State and Economy

The state regulates and depends on the capitalist economy, and at the same time has relative autonomy from it. The tightness or looseness of the coupling between the capitalist economy and the state depends on specific political, cultural and ideological conditions and the temporary results of social conflicts and struggles. '[S]tate power is capitalist to the extent that it creates, maintains or restores the conditions required for capital accumulation in given circumstances and is non-capitalist to the extent that these conditions are not realized' (Jessop 1990, 117). The political elite can at certain times operate relatively autonomously from the capitalist class's influence and shape the development of the capitalist economy, especially if there is a socialist government.

Jessop (1990, 150) assumes that there is an 'institutional separation of the economic and political' so that one 'cannot reduce state power to questions of the class background, affiliation or sympathies of the state elite'. 'The separation of the economic and the political orders excludes an immediate isomorphism between economic class relations and relations among political categories. Indeed the legitimacy of the modern state would disappear if the state unequivocally served the immediate economic interests of the dominant class(es)' (102). The question is whether this relation is changing under Trump.

The Theory of State Monopoly Capitalism

The tradition of state theory that Jessop represents assumes that the economy and politics are relatively separate and autonomous. The theory of state monopoly capitalism (Stamocap) in contrast takes a more traditional approach, in which the economy largely determines the political system. It defines the state as a foundational structure and the mode of functioning of modern capitalist society. Key characteristics of state monopoly capitalism are:

- a high degree of concentration, centralisation and monopolisation of private capital;
- the bourgeois state's steady and extensive presence and intervention into the economic reproduction process;

- significant influence of the leading monopolies on state policies regulating the economy and other realms of society. (Huffschmid 1990, 758)

'By the interlocking of and relations between the state and corporations and influences by the latter on the first, the leading corporations' interests influence and shape state politics to a great degree' (Huffschmid 2010, 148). This influence can take the form of corporate lobbying; the strategic role of corporations in cities, regions and countries; and the exchange of personnel between the state and corporations, i.e. between political and economic elites. Stamocap theories assume that the state acts on behalf of capitalist monopolies' interests and that the class affiliations of the state's officials are key. State officials would be the political representatives of monopoly capital's interests. In state monopoly capitalism, there would be heavy state intervention (including nationalisation) to support monopolies because the profit rate would tend to fall.

Stamocap Theories' Problems

One problem of many Stamocap theories is that they assume that state monopoly capitalism results in the breakdown of capitalism and the transition to socialism. Paul Boccara (1982) stresses in this context the role of state intervention, the nationalisation of industries, new transport and communication technologies, intellectual labour, cybernetics and automation. He argues that in the state monopoly stage, capitalism reaches the 'uttermost limit' of its decay. 'Collective ownership and the socialist plan become immediately necessary for economic practice' (103, translation from German). We of course know today that state capitalism and the information economy have not given rise to a post-capitalist society. Rather, state monopoly capitalism was followed by yet another stage of capitalist development, namely neoliberal capitalism.

Jörg Huffschmid (2010, 149–1), who in the 1960s and 1970s was one of West Germany's leading Stamocap theorists, argues that Stamocap theories overlook the fact that small and medium-sized companies can also play an important role in capitalism's development, that capital's interests and the state are contradictory, that the internationalisation of capital poses challenges for Stamocap theories and that the environmental crisis and patriarchy cannot be reduced to the role of monopolies in capitalism.

Stamocap theories have been criticised for reducing the state to an instrument of the monopoly bourgeoisie and for thereby advancing an economic-reductionist and monolithic approach that overlooks the fact that the state is itself a realm, in which conflicts between classes and class factions are politically fought out and condensed into temporary, fragile unity and alliances (Hirsch, Kannankulam and Wissel 2015).

The approaches of Antonio Gramsci, Nicos Poulantzas and other materialist theories of the state assume, in contrast, a relative autonomy of the state and capitalism. The question, however, arises in this context as to how the phenomenon of Donald Trump can be explained based on the assumption of relative autonomy, as his victory in the US presidential election seems to be indicative for a temporary close coupling and overlap of the US's economic and the political system. Whereas state monopoly capitalism cannot explain the state's relative autonomy from capital in other situations, relative autonomy theories have trouble explaining Donald Trump.

Stamocap theories tend to assume that the capitalist economy and the capitalist state interlock and interact functionally, institutionally and in respect to personnel. However, it tends to stress that both realms remain separate because otherwise the orthodox assumption that the economic base determines the political and ideological superstructure cannot be upheld (see IMSF 1981, 226–44). Interlocking and interaction would take place in the form of committees, boards, lobbying organisations, industry associations, consultancies, bourgeois academia and science, bourgeois media, research groups, working groups, etc. (IMSF 1981, 257–76). The state's leading group of career politicians would have specific career paths separate from the ones of the capitalist class. The contact between the two would take on the form of 'working groups, contact groups, research groups' and institutions (IMSF 1981, 274).

The Dynamic Relationship of Political and Economic Systems

Relative autonomy theories and Stamocap theories cannot adequately explain the fact that Donald Trump is both a capitalist (among the richest Americans) and US president. There is a direct overlap between monopoly capital and the state in the form of one person, who is among the most powerful capitalists and has become the world's most powerful politician. Trump is not a career politician, but a capitalist-turned-politician, who fuses economic and political interests into one person. Trump says in this context: 'I am the richest presidential candidate in history. I'm the only billionaire ever to run' (Trump 2015a, 148).

There is always a dialectic of the state and the economy in capitalism, but this relationship involves a specific power distribution that is dynamic and can shift historically. Neumann (1957, 12) argues in this context that politics and the economy are always dialectically interconnected: 'Economics is as much an instrument of politics as politics is a tool of economics'. The specific relation between the two realms depends on society's historical context (14). So for example in Nazi Germany, there was the primacy of the state over the economy. In the Keynesian state, there is an interaction of two poles of power. In the neoliberal state, there is a primacy of the economy over the state via structural mechanisms. In the Trump state, there may be a primacy of the economy over the state via a capitalist-turned-politician.

Transformations of Capitalism

Keynesian capitalism as a democratic form of state monopoly capitalism ruled in Western capitalist societies until the 1970s, and was then gradually supplanted by neoliberal capitalism that privatised state-owned industries and reduced the level of state intervention in specific parts of the economy. The rise of neoliberal capitalism stood in the context of the crisis of Fordism and the crisis of the Keynesian state. Two important changes that the emergence of neoliberal capitalism brought about were the privatisation of state-owned industries and the internationalisation of capitalism that brought about competition states. The role of finance capital and new technological capital increased. The role of classical industry in capitalism was reduced. The role of the capitalist state shifted in light of these transformations. States compete for deregulating the welfare state and social protection in order to attract capital. This does, however, not mean that state power has been weakened. It has merely been transformed and changed its role. Capital's structural and indirect influence as a collective political actor on the state has been strengthened. In neoliberal capitalism, state politics primarily focus on (a) the politics of privatisation, deregulation, market liberalisation, low tax and free trade policies in order to enable commodification; and (b) the politics of militarisation and securitisation in order to exert international and national control that protects the overall political-economic system.

Yet another shift of the role of the state was indicated by the bailout of banks and corporations in the course of the capitalist crisis that started in 2008. Nation states strongly intervened in the economy by saving crisis-struck finance capital and capital in the car industry with taxpayers' money. Results of this interventionist move were hyper-neoliberal austerity politics that hit the poorest and weakest in society and further advanced inequalities.

There is certainly always an institutional separation of the capitalist state and the capitalist economy, which means that both systems have different organisations, logics, rules and structures. However, at times there can be a direct overlap of personnel so that capitalists become part of the ruling political elite, and Donald Trump as US president consti-tutes an important transition in this regard. With the rise of Donald Trump to becoming the USA's head of state, there is now a much more direct influence of the capitalist class on political power because there is an overlap of personnel in the form of the president, who is also a billionaire capitalist.

Monopoly-Finance Capitalism

John Bellamy Foster and Robert W. McChesney (2012) explain the rise of multinational corporations as part of capital's attempt to overcome long-term economic stagnation and to attain global monopoly profits. Multinationals aim to drive down the wage share globally and increase their profits by installing a system of global competition among workers. The consequence is a worldwide increase in the rate of exploitation that Foster and McChesney, drawing on Stephen Hymer's work, call a 'strategy of divide and rule' (Foster and McChesney 2012, 114–15, 119). Foster (2006, 11) argues that monopoly-finance capitalism is a 'new phase' of capitalist development. He explains its genesis:

At the brink of the twentieth century, capitalism underwent a major transformation, marked by the rise of the giant corporation. The early decades that followed were dominated by world wars and a depression associated with this great transformation. Following the Second

World War the new stage of capitalism was fully consolidated, particularly within the United States, the most advanced capitalist economy. The result was a situation in which a handful of giant corporations controlled most industries. (Foster 2006, 2)

Financialization can be defined as the shift in the center of gravity of the capitalist economy, from production to finance. [...] Growth of finance relative to the real economy also meant the appearance of financial bubbles that threatened to burst. [...] Economic power was shifting from corporate boardrooms to financial institutions and markets, affecting the entire capitalist world economy in complex ways, through a process of financial globalization. [...] The growing role of finance was evident not just in the expansion of financial corporations but also in the growth of the financial subsidiaries and activities of non-financial corporations, so that the distinction between the financial and non-financial corporations, while still significant, became increasingly blurred. Financialization in the 1980s and '90s was the main new force in the much longer-term globalization process, and was the defining element in the whole era of neoliberal economic policy. (Foster 2010, 5–6).

This ballooning of finance produced new outlets for surplus in the finance, insurance and real estate sector of gross domestic product (GDP) in the form of new investment in buildings, office equipment, etc. Nevertheless, the great bulk of the money capital devoted to finance was used for speculation in securities, real estate and commodities markets rather than for investment in capital goods, and thus did not feed into the growth of GDP, which continued to stagnate (Foster 2006, 4–5).

CONCLUSION

The Critical Theory of Authoritarianism

Frankfurt School scholars such as Erich Fromm, Theodor W. Adorno, Franz L. Neumann, Leo Löwenthal and Otto Kirchheimer stress that capitalism has inherently authoritarian tendencies that in situations of crisis can be activated when authoritarian populists gain voice, visibility and large support. They show that the authoritarian personality could take on both the form of authoritarian leaders and authoritarian followers. If both coincide, then democracy can come under attack and the danger of authoritarian capitalism becomes very real. Authoritarianism has economic, political, ideological and psychological dimensions. It is a way of organising society and the economy and therefore can take on the form of authoritarian capitalism, a specific type of capitalism and social formation.

Authoritarianism can also take on the form of authoritarian political movements, leaders, groups or parties in the political system. Authoritarianism is also an ideology that propagates itself in order to manage societal contradictions through leadership, nationalism, law and order, militarism and violence. Often it takes on the ideological role of deflecting attention from the real causes of social problems and from class conflicts, by constructing and blaming scapegoats and presenting workers and capital as unified in a national community whose existence is under threat by dark forces. Finally, for authoritarianism to work, there must also be a psychological basis, a structure of feeling, experience and thought that makes individuals believe in authoritarianism. This psychological structure is also termed the authoritarian personality.

Authoritarian Capitalism

The state involves relationships between the political and the economic systems, relations to citizens, intra-state relations, inter-state relations, discourses by the state and discourses on the state. In the capitalist state, all levels are organised in ways that advance capitalist interests. The relationship between the state and capitalism is shaped by a specific distribution of power. In authoritarian capitalism, state power and the power of the political leader play a powerful role in society and the economy, and authoritarian state power is used for enforcing capitalist interests. Authoritarian capitalism is a type of capitalist society that embodies the four principles of right-wing authoritarianism: authoritarian leadership, nationalism, the friend/enemy scheme and patriarchy/militarism.

Given these theoretical foundations, in Chapters 4 and 5 we will analyse how US capitalism is changing under Donald Trump's rule.

4

Trumpism: Donald Trump and Authoritarian-Capitalist Statism

INTRODUCTION

The task of this chapter is to outline how the US state is changing under Donald Trump's presidency.[1] Based on the concepts of the state and authoritarian capitalism outlined in Chapter 3, this chapter explores the transformations of state power and capitalism under Trump's rule.

The next section gives an overview of the data that deal with who voted for Trump. Section three deals with the question of why Trump won the 2016 US presidential election and the conditions that led to his victory. The fourth section focuses on the relationship between the state and the economy under Trump. Section five analyses civil liberties and state institutions under Trump. The fifth section discusses international relations under Trump.

WHO VOTED FOR TRUMP?

On 8 November 2016, the Republican Party nominee Donald Trump won the US presidential election against the Democratic Party candidate Hillary Clinton. According to statistics, Trump is the 156th richest American.[2] Clinton achieved two million votes more than Trump in the popular vote, but given the USA's majority voting system – and that Trump achieved the majority in 30 out of 50 states – he won the election. Table 4.1 shows exit poll data. Some observers argue that, based on

1. Acknowledgement: this chapter was first published as part of an article in the open access journal *tripleC: Communication, Capitalism & Critique*: Christian Fuchs. 2017. Donald Trump: A Critical Theory-Perspective on Authoritarian Capitalism. *tripleC: Communication, Capitalism & Critique* 15 (1): 1–72. www.triple-c.at/index.php/tripleC/article/view/835. Reprinted and updated with permission from *tripleC*.
2. www.forbes.com/forbes-400/list, accessed on 27 November 2016.

income data, Trump supporters are not working class (Silver 2016). The problem with such an analysis is that class is not defined by income, but by the position in the relations of production. A highly skilled blue-collar worker can have the same income as a low-level manager. So for example in the USA, the average annual salary of a food service manager was in 2016 US$56,010, of a structural iron and steel worker US$56,030, and of a vocational education teacher US$55,730 (data source: Bureau of Labor Statistics[3]). In this example, the salaries of managers, blue-collar workers and white-collar workers are comparable. Discerning class by income is not a meaningful distinction.

According to the data in Table 4.1, the income group earning between US$0 and US$49,999 was more likely to vote for Clinton than for Trump. This is a very wide income range (although in the analysis itself it was subdivided into two income groups). Both groups also contain a wide range of occupations. As an example, a precarious freelancer, a self-employed shopkeeper, a waitress, a call centre agent and a cleaner can earn comparable incomes. A more fine-grained analysis is therefore needed.

Rothwell (2016) analysed data from a Gallup poll that focused on attitudes towards Trump and that had 87,428 respondents. The data were aggregated at county level and presented together with other county-level data entered into a multi-variable regression analysis:

Trump's supporters are older, with higher household incomes, are more likely to be male, white non-Hispanic, less likely to identify as LGBTQ, less likely to hold a bachelor's degree or higher education, more likely to be a veteran or family member of a veteran, more likely to work in a blue-collar occupation, and are more likely to be Christian and report that religion is important to them. Those who view Trump favorably are slightly less likely to be unemployed and more likely to be self-employed. Labor force participation is lower among Trump supporters, but not after adjusting for age. Trump supporters are much more likely to be retired. Trump supporters live in smaller commuting zones with lower college attainment rates, a somewhat higher share of jobs in manufacturing, higher mortality rates for middle-aged whites,

---

3. www.umass.edu/preferen/You%20Must%20Read%20This/Rothwell-Gallup.pdf, accessed on 13 April 2017.

Table 4.1 Exit poll showing the share of voters who fall into a specific category

Group	Trump (%)	Clinton (%)
Men	53	41
Women	42	54
White	58	37
Black	8	88
Age 18–29	37	55
Age 30–44	42	50
Age 45–65	53	44
Age 65+	53	45
High-school education or less	51	45
Postgraduate study degree	37	58
Income under $30,000	41	53
$30,000–$49,999	42	51
$50,000–$99,999	50	46
$100,000–$199,999	48	47
$200,000–$249,999	49	48
$250,000+	48	46
City over 50,000 population	35	59
Suburbs	50	45
Small city, rural	62	34
Those who think that immigration is the most important political issue	64	32
Those who think that the US economy is in a poor condition	79	15
Those whose financial situation has become worse since 2012	78	19
Those who are angry about the federal government	90	6

Data source: *New York Times*, www.nytimes.com/interactive/2016/11/08/us/politics/election-exit-polls.html?_r=0

and a higher segregation. [...] workers in blue collar occupations (defined as production, construction, installation, maintenance, and repair, or transportation) are far more likely to support Trump, as are those with less education. People with graduate degrees are particularly unlikely to view Trump favorably. Since blue collar and less educated workers have faced greater economic distress in recent years, this provides some evidence that economic hardship and lower-socio-economic status boost Trump's popularity. [...] People living in commuting zones with higher white middle-aged mortality rates are much more likely to view Trump favorably. [...] Racial isolation and lack of exposure to Hispanic immigrants raise the likelihood of Trump support. Meanwhile, Trump support falls as exposure to trade and immigration increases. [...] He is the only candidate who receives significantly more favorable ratings in racially isolated neighborhoods and in areas with high middle-aged white mortality rates, conditional on individual factors. [...] social well-being, measured by longevity and intergenerational mobility, is significantly lower among the communities of Trump supporters. (Rothwell 2016, 7–12)

One of the factors in Trump's win was that he flipped the vote from Democratic to Republican in deindustrialised Rust Belt states (Michigan, Ohio, Wisconsin and Pennsylvania). A post-election study conducted by Emsi in the Rust Belt states Michigan, Ohio, Minnesota, Wisconsin, Indiana and Pennsylvania showed that '437 of the 489 counties in the six states analyzed [...] voted for Trump. [...] [A]lmost without exception [...] the counties with the highest concentration of manufacturing, agriculture, and mining and oil and gas extraction employment voted for Trump' (Wright 2017).

Overall, such data indicate that the experience and/or fear of social downfall affecting the self-employed and blue-collar workers seem to have played a role in Trump's success. Also the deprivation of social services, lower education level, higher age and a low level of contact with immigrants and minorities seem to have been factors. Franz L. Neumann (1957, 250–1) argues that disenfranchised groups and groups that are threatened with decline or doom tend to be more likely to support right-wing authoritarianism. Experience and fear of declassification seems to play a role in the support of right-wing authoritarianism. Declassification is understood in this context as the loss of one's class status, where class in a Bourdieuian sense means the combination of economic class, social status and cultural status as defined by the level of control of economic power, political power and cultural power of a particular individual or group.

Voter Turnout

Changes in the turnout also influenced the result. According to the data, the turnout increased by 0.7 per cent for white, non-college voters, who tended to cast their ballot for Trump, whereas it decreased by 7.1 per cent among African Americans and 0.4 per cent among Hispanics, two groups who tended not to vote for Trump (Griffin, Halpin and Teixeira 2017).

Who Voted for Brexit?

The data indicate that the typical Donald Trump voter is an older white man, who lives in rural America, is self-employed or a blue-collar worker, has a low level of education, has fears about immigration and economic decline, and is angry with the government. This voting pattern is not a unique case. The typical pro-Brexit voter lived in rural Britain, had a low income, low education and was older and white (Table 4.2).

Table 4.2 British Election Study of voters in the EU Referendum 2016

Group	% of votes in favour of Brexit
Household income > £60,000	35
Household income < £20,000	58
Routine manual worker	71
Higher professional	41
Not in paid work	59
Postgraduate degree	27
No qualifications	75
Age 66+	59
Age 18–25	28
Women	50
Men	52
Black, Asian and minority ethnic	36
White British	52

Data source: Goodwin and Heath (2016).

Trump promised radical change and opposed the political elite. He managed to become the projection mechanism of the discontented and those who are afraid of social decline. Here's his typical characterisation of this elite: 'Typical politician. All talk, no action. Sounds good, doesn't work. Never going to happen. Our country is suffering because people like Secretary Clinton have made such bad decisions in terms of our jobs and in terms of what's going on' (Clinton and Trump 2016a). 'Finally, I realized that America doesn't need more "all-talk, no-action" politicians running things. It needs smart businesspeople who understand how to manage. We don't need more political rhetoric – we need more common sense. "If it ain't broke, don't fix it" – but if it is broke, let's stop talking about it and fix it. I know how to fix it' (Trump 2015a, 4).

What Trump suggests is to substitute the political elite with the economic elite so that the latter has direct influence on policymaking: '[I]t's about time that this country had somebody running it that has an idea about money' (Clinton and Trump 2016a). 'And if we could run our country the way I've run my company, we would have a country that you would be so proud of [...]. We have the greatest businesspeople in the world. We have to use them to negotiate our trade deals' (Clinton and Trump 2016c). The rise of Trump is the story of how a billionaire came to political power. He did not bring about a non-elitist people's politics, but the rise of the capitalist class as directly ruling and dominating politics.

WHY DID TRUMP WIN THE US PRESIDENTIAL ELECTION?

Anxiety and Politics Today

Neumann (1957/2017) argues in his essay 'Anxiety and Politics' that the rise of authoritarian politics is a combination of economic, political and psychological processes. Situations of anxiety in society can in such cases result in a vast number of people identifying with a leader. Leadership ideology would come along with the hatred of identified enemies:

> Just as the masses hope for their deliverance from distress through absolute oneness with a person, so they ascribe their distress to certain persons, who have brought this distress into the world through a conspiracy. The historical process is personified in this manner. Hatred, resentment, dread, created by great upheavals, are concentrated on certain persons who are denounced as devilish conspirators. (618)

In such situations, the 'fear of social degradation [...] creates for itself "a target for the discharge of the resentments arsing from damaged self-esteem"' (624). Alienation for Neumann has psychological, socioeconomic and political dimensions.

Collective anxiety can emerge when one or several of the following factors are present (Neumann 1957/2017, 624–8): (a) the alienation of labour; (b) destructive competition; (c) social alienation – a group fears or is threatened by the decline of 'its prestige, income, or even its existence' and 'does not understand the historical process or is prevented from understanding it' (626); (d) political alienation in respect to the political system; (e) the institutionalisation of anxiety (for example in the form of a totalitarian movement, propaganda or terror); and (f) destructive psychological alienation and persecutory anxiety.

Neumann summarises these aspects the following way:

> Neurotic, persecutory anxiety can lead to ego-surrender in the mass through affective identification with a leader. This caesaristic identification is always regressive, historically and psychologically. An important clue for the regressive character is the notion of false concreteness, the conspiracy theory of history. [...] The intensification of anxiety into persecutory anxiety is successful when a group (class, religion, race) is threatened by loss of status, without understanding the process which leads to its degradation. Generally, this leads to political alienation, i.e., the conscious rejection of the rules of the game of a political system. The regressive mass movement, once it has come to power must, in order to maintain the leader-identification, institutionalize anxiety. The three methods are: terror, propaganda, and, for the followers of the leader, the crime committed in common. (Neumann 1957/2017, 628)

Capitalist Development in the USA: The Alienation of Labour

Neumann's notions of crisis and authoritarianism can help us to understand the political situation in the USA and Europe that has developed since the start of the capitalist crisis in 2008. A *first element* is the alienation of labour. *Neoliberal capitalism* is the struggle of the ruling class against everyday people that is fought via the commodification of everything, state support for capitalist interests and ideology. Figures 4.1 and 4.2 show the development of the wage share and the capital share in the USA and the EU. The wage share is the share of total wages in GDP, the capital share the share of total capital in GDP. The two variables are inversely proportional: the higher the capital share, the lower the wage share. Since the mid-1970s, the wage share has dropped by around 5 per cent in both the USA and the EU.

Figure 4.1 The wage share's development in the USA and the EU15 countries (data source: AMECO)

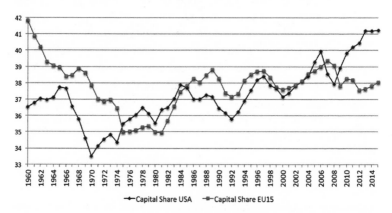

Figure 4.2 The capital share's development in the USA and the EU15 countries (data source: AMECO)

The Contradiction of the Rate of Surplus Value and the Organic Composition of Capital

The rate of profit measures an economy's relationship of annual profits to investments. The rate of surplus value is the relationship of profits to wages. The organic composition of capital is the relationship of capital investments to wages. The rate of surplus value indicates how high the exploitation of labour is in an economy, the organic composition measures the importance of technology and other fixed assets.

The rate of profit is directly proportional to the rate of surplus value and indirectly proportional to the organic composition of capital. Figures 4.3 and 4.4 show the development of these three macroeconomic variables in the USA and the EU15 countries.

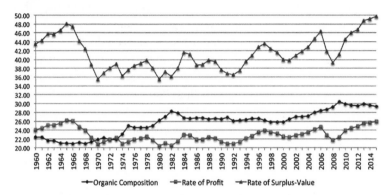

Figure 4.3   Macroeconomic development in the USA (data source: AMECO)

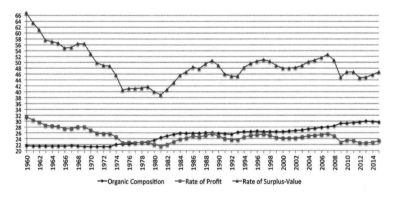

Figure 4.4   Macroeconomic development of the EU15 countries (data source: AMECO)

In the EU and the USA, the rate of surplus value and the organic composition of capital have both increased since the mid-1970s. Given that the two variables contradict each other and exert contradictory pressures on the profit rate, the result was that the profit rate fluctuated and could not reach the same levels as it had in the 1950s and 1960s. Pressures on wages were combined with a low-tax regime. In the USA, the level of capital taxation decreased from 0.4 per cent of GDP to 0.1 per cent in 2016 (data source: AMECO).

Although capital and the capitalist state exerted downward pressure on wages, the rising costs for capital investments acted as a counter-tendency. This can be observed as the increasing organic composition of capital. Technology investments advancing computerisation and other innovations are capital-intensive. Capital therefore tried to find other ways to increase profits. The result was an increase in the economy's financialisation, which included the growth of high-risk financial derivatives. According to estimations, the value of over-the-counter derivatives in 2008 was US$600 trillion (Sundaram 2012). World GDP was around US$63 trillion in 2008 (data source: World Bank Statistics), which means that over-the-counter derivatives amounted to 9.5 times the value of global GDP. In many countries, the squeeze on wages resulted in large increases in personal debt: in the USA, the share of loans to GDP increased from 63 per cent in 1995 to 93.5 per cent in 2008 (data source: Fuchs 2017d, table 10.1). In the UK, there was an increase from 64 per cent to 93.3 per cent during the same time period (data source: Fuchs 2017d, table 10.1). Inequality also rose massively. In 1979, the richest 0.1 per cent owned 7 per cent of the total US wealth, whereas in 2016 this share had increased to 22 per cent (Sanders 2016b, 207). In 2008, the US housing market's financial bubble burst, which triggered a major economic crisis and a long depression. Given that financial markets are global and networked, the crisis spread and took on an international dimension.

Capital Export and Deindustrialisation

A *second factor* was that the international competition of transnational corporations brought about *capital export* and *deindustrialisation* in the West. In 2008, capital export (measured as foreign direct investment, FDI, outward flows) accounted for 2.74 per cent of world GDP.[4] The Organisation for Economic Co-operation and Development (OECD)

---

4. Source for all FDI data: OECD statistics; source for world GDP data: World Bank Statistics.

countries accounted for 81.9 per cent of these exports. The EU (43.6 per cent) and the USA (19.0 per cent) were the largest exporters of capital; 53.9 per cent of all FDI flows went to OECD countries, including 19.7 per cent to the USA and 20.1 per cent to the EU. Other important destinations for capital exports were China (10.9 per cent), Russia (4.8 per cent), Canada (3.9 per cent), Australia (2.97 per cent), Brazil (2.87 per cent), India (2.76 per cent) and Saudi Arabia (2.51 per cent).

In 2015, the share of capital export in world GDP had decreased to 2.2 per cent (−0.5 per cent since 2008). Whereas the US's share increased from 19.0 per cent in 2008 to 20.1 per cent in 2015, the EU's share decreased from 43.6 per cent to 33.3 per cent. China's share increased from 3.3 per cent to 11.7 per cent. What is also significant is that the total volume of capital export decreased from US$1.4 trillion in 2008 to US$1.2 trillion in 2015. The US's total volume of FDI outflows during this period shrank from US$329.1 billion to US$322.5 billion. The EU's total volume went from US$752.4 billion down to US$532.5 billion. These data provide indications that *capitalism* has to a significant degree *deglobalised* since the start of the capitalist crisis in 2008. Capitalism is still to a significant degree global capitalism, but there is a tendency towards the annual increase of capital export shrinking absolutely and slowing down relatively.

Social Alienation

Social alienation has constituted a *third factor*. Given a more unequal world, many people fear a decline of their social status. The share of those US citizens who indicated in the World Values Survey that they are rather or completely dissatisfied with the financial situation of their household increased from 29.7 per cent in 2000 to 36.9 per cent in 2010.[5] Politics in Europe and North America reacted to the world economic crisis not by questioning, but by intensifying neoliberal governmentality: states bailed out banks and corporations with taxpayers' money and implemented hyper-neoliberal austerity measures that focused on cutting expenditures for the welfare state. The bailout as such is a

---

5. Data source: World Values Survey, www.worldvaluessurvey.org. This item was measured with a Likert-scale ranging from 1 (completely dissatisfied) to 10 (completely satisfied). Here the relative share of the total of answers lying between 1 and 5 is reported.

state-interventionist and therefore state-capitalist measure, in which the state mobilises public money in order to pay for the debt of private corporations. So this form of state-capitalist intervention turns public into private money. In 2015, the EU under German leadership answered the election of the left-wing Syriza government in Greece with brutal financial repression. In summer 2015, it put a gun to the Greek government's head, saying, 'Implement more neoliberal austerity measures or we will shoot and kill your banking system and your economy'. Even now, the EU, driven by German financial interests, refuses a haircut of Greece's debt. Greece's debt is the result of the combination of Europe's core–periphery structure and Greek neoliberalism (Laskos and Tsakalotos 2013). Furthermore, the decline of blue-collar labour in total occupation and value added is a factor that has contributed to feelings of social alienation (Fuchs 2014, chapter 5).

Political Alienation

Given the decades-long persistence of politics that advance capitalist interests and squeeze everyday citizens, it is no wonder that normal people as a *fourth factor* feel *politically alienated* from the political system, political parties and politicians. Whereas in 1960, the voter turnout in the US presidential election was 62.8 per cent of the voting-age population, it was less than 54 per cent in 2016.[6] The average turnout in EU parliamentary elections decreased from 62 per cent in 1979 to 42.6 per cent in 2014.[7] These are indications that citizens feel that the political system does not represent their interests. Confidence in political systems seems to be generally low: in the World Values Survey (2010–14 wave), 85.3 per cent of US participants indicated that they have low or no confidence in political parties;[8] 65.3 per cent indicated they had low or no confidence in the government. In an earlier wave of this survey (2005–9), 63.6 per cent of UK participants expressed low or no trust in the government and 76.9 per cent in political parties. Low trust in the political system, political parties and politicians also has to do with the fact that social

6. Data sources: www.presidency.ucsb.edu/data/turnout.php, www.electproject.org/2016g, accessed on 17 February 2017.
7. www.ukpolitical.info/european-parliament-election-turnout.htm, accessed on 17 February 2017.
8. Source for all data from the World Values Survey: www.worldvaluessurvey.org.

democracy has shifted towards the political right in many countries, and has become indistinguishable from conservative and liberal forces.

The Institutionalisation of Anxiety and Persecutory Anxiety

The *fifth factor* is the *institutionalisation of anxiety*. Particularly since the capitalist crisis started, far-right populists like Donald Trump in the USA, Nigel Farage in the UK, Geert Wilders in the Netherlands, Marine Le Pen in France, or Heinz Christian Strache in Austria have gained in prominence and poularity. The practices of such forces constitute the *sixth factor, persecutory anxiety*: they blame immigrants and refugees for social problems and advance nationalist sentiments. In the 1980s the Austrian politician Jörg Haider was already a prototype for this kind of new right populist politics that plays with nationalism and xenophobia (Fuchs 2016a, 2016d).

In countries such as the UK and the USA, the combination of these six factors has resulted in an increase in nationalist and xenophobic sentiments and in the election of Donald Trump and the UK's decision to leave the EU.

Of those who voted for 'Leave' in the Brexit referendum, 79 per cent thought that immigration was bad for society, and 71 per cent argued that multiculturalism is bad. The levels among those who voted for Britain to remain in the EU were, in contrast, 19 per cent and 20 per cent (Ashcroft 2016). The share of 'Leave' voters among those who described themselves as English and not British was 79 per cent (21 per cent 'Remain' voters), whereas the share of 'Remain' voters among those who saw their identity as British and not as English was 60 per cent (40 per cent 'Leave' voters). Furthermore, 84 per cent of those who said in an exit poll that illegal immigrants working in the USA should be deported were Trump voters (Huang et al. 2016).

The fourth section in Chapter 3, 'The State and Authoritarian Capitalism', outlined a model of the state. The following subsections in this chapter and the following section will focus on this model's dimensions and apply them to Trump:

- 'The Relationship of the State to the Economy under Trump' (section five)
- 'The Relationship of the State to its Citizens: Civil Liberties and State Institutions under Trump' (section six)

- 'International Relations under Trump' (section seven)
- 'Trumpology: Donald Trump's Ideology' (Chapter 5)

Note that dimensions two and three of the state model (relationship of the state to citizens, intra-state relations) have been combined. Both relate to the political system's internal organisation, focusing on (a) the relationship of the state to civil society and (b) the relationship among state institutions. The first dimension covers the relationship of the state to the economy. The model's fifth and sixth dimensions focus on the relationship of the state to culture and have also been combined. The cultural-ideological dimension analyses ideological representations by the state and of the state in the age of Trump.

THE RELATIONSHIP OF THE STATE AND THE ECONOMY UNDER TRUMP

Trump's Economic Empire

For reflecting on how US capitalism may change under Trump, we need a better understanding of Trump's economic empire. According to the Forbes list of the world's billionaires, in 2016 Trump was the 324th richest billionaire, with an estimated wealth of US$4.5 billion.[9] However, measuring the exact extent of Trump's wealth has been a matter of controversy (O'Brien 2016).

The Trump Organization builds, owns and operates real estate, towers and skyscrapers, hotels, golf courses, casinos, residential towers, luxury entertainment and leisure resorts. Trump also owns Trump Productions LLC that produces the reality TV show *The Apprentice*, hosted by Donald Trump from 2004 until 2015. Table 4.3 shows, according to a financial disclosure statement, Trump's ownership involvement in companies with a value larger than US$50 million around the time he ran for US president.

Trump and Corporate Interlocking

Table 4.4 shows, according to a 2016 financial disclosure, examples of industries with which Donald Trump's economic activities are inter-

---

9. www.forbes.com/billionaires/list/, accessed on 28 November 2016.

Table 4.3 Donald Trump's companies that have a value of at least US$50 million

Company name	Minimum value	Company and revenue type
40 Wall Street LLC	$50,000,000	Commercial real estate, rent
401 North Wabash Venture LLC	$50,000,000	Residential and commercial real estate, rent, condo sales
DJT Operations	$50,000,000	Aircraft, rent
Fifty-Seventh Street Associates LLC	$50,000,000	Real estate, rent
Trump National Golf Club – Jupiter	$50,000,000	Golf club
Trump National Golf Club – Bedminster	$50,000,000	Golf club
Mar-a-Lago Club, LLC	$50,000,000	Resort
Trump Turnberry	$50,000,000	Golf courses and resort
The Trump Corporation	$50,000,000	Management company
Trump National Doral	$50,000,000	Golf courses and resort
Trump International Golf Links – Scotland	$50,000,000	Golf course
Trump International Hotels Management LLC	$50,000,000	Management company
Trump National Golf Club – Colts Neck	$50,000,000	Golf club
Trump National Golf Club – Westchester	$50,000,000	Golf club
Trump National Golf Club – Washington, DC	$50,000,000	Golf club
Trump Old Post Office LLC	$50,000,000	Hotel
Trump Park Avenue LLC	$50,000,000	Residential and commercial real estate: rent, condo sales
Trump Ruffin Tower I LLC	$50,000,000	Commercial real estate, condo sales, hotel-related revenue
Trump Tower Commercial LLC	$50,000,000	Commercial real estate, rent
Trump National Golf Club – Los Angeles	$50,000,000	Golf course and unsold lots, golf related revenue and land sales
HWA 555 Owners, LLC	$50,000,000	Commercial real estate, rent
1290 Avenue of the Americas	$50,000,000	Commercial real estate, rent
Trump Tower Triplex	$50,000,000	Residential real estate
Total:	>$1,150,000,000	

Data source: Donald Trump Executive Branch Personnel Public Financial Disclosure Report, OGE Form 278e, 16 May 2016; unchanged on an updated form released on 14 June 2017

Table 4.4 Donald Trump's connections to other industries and companies via shareholding

Industry	Example companies
Agricultural products and services	Agrium
Clothing	Nike, VF Corporation
Computer hardware and software	Apple, Cisco, General Electric, Intuit, Microsoft
Defence	Raytheon
Electronic instruments	Ametek, Parker Hannifin, Roper Technologies
Finance	Advantage Advisers Xanthus Fund, AG Eleven Partners LP, Ameriprise Financial, Baron Growth Fund, Baron Partners Fund, Baron Real Estate Fund, BlackRock, Caterpillar, Citigroup, Deutsche Money Market Series, Deutsche X-trackers MSCI Hedged Equity, Discover Financial Services, General Electric, Invesco European Grow, JPMorgan Chase, MidOcean, Paulson & Co, Prudential Financial, Swiss Re, Vanguard, Visa, Wells Fargo
Food and consumer products	Ecolab, Kraft Heinz, Mead Johnson, PepsiCo, Procter & Gamble, Sealed Air, WhiteWave Foods
Health and biotechnology	Ecolab, General Electric, Gilead Sciences, Hospital Corporation of America, Johnson & Johnson, McKesson Corporation, Merck & Co, Pfizer, Thermo Fisher Scientific
Media content	Comcast, 21st Century Fox
Natural resource extraction and sale, utilities	American Water Works, BHP Billiton, Chevron, ConocoPhillips, EOG Resources, ExxonMobil, Freeport-McMoRan, General Electric, Halliburton, NextEra Energy, Phillips 66, Royal Dutch Shell, Schlumberger, Total S.A., Valero Energy
Pulp and paper	International Paper
Retail and wholesale	Costco Wholesale, Home Depot, L Brands Inc, TJX, Walmart
Storage	Extra Space Storage
Telecommunications and Internet infrastructure	AT&T, CenturyLink, Comcast, Crown Castle, General Electric, Telenor, Verizon Communications
Transport	Boeing, Borg Warner, Caterpillar, Norfolk Southern Railway

Data source: Donald Trump Executive Branch Personnel Public Financial Disclosure Report, OGE Form 278e, 16 May 2016 locked via investments and share ownership. Industries outside his core economic area of real estate and entertainment into which he has invested include finance, natural resource extraction, utilities, transport, health, biotechnology, food, retail, telecommunications and Internet.

Given the Trump empire's interlocking with core sectors of US capitalism, it is interesting to have a look at how Trump stands on policies that affect these industries.

Infrastructure

Trump's campaign said that he wants to start a massive project for the construction of infrastructure. 'Our airports, bridges, water tunnels, power grids, rail system – our nation's entire infrastructure – is crumbling, and we aren't doing anything about it' (Trump 2015a, 120). The programme aims to:

- Create thousands of new jobs in construction, steel manufacturing, and other sectors to build the transportation, water, telecommunications and energy infrastructure needed to enable new economic development in the U.S., all of which will generate new tax revenues.
- Put American steel made by American workers into the backbone of America's infrastructure.
- Leverage new revenues and work with financing authorities, public–private partnerships, and other prudent funding opportunities.[10]

So the idea is that the state invests into the construction of infrastructure. But given that taxpayers' money will be used, it is not made obvious in this plan that this will be publicly owned infrastructure. It rather seems that fostering public–private partnerships could mean that the state pays for infrastructure projects that are carried out by private companies that then also own this infrastructure. So it could very well turn out that the state is neither the employer of infrastructure workers nor the owner of newly built infrastructure, but only the financer, which basically

10. www.donaldjtrump.com/policies/an-americas-infrastructure-first-plan/, accessed on 17 February 12017.

means the tax-funded creation of profits and private property. The very question that arises is whether, in the case where taxpayers' money is used for investments, the created resources should be owned publicly or privately. Such projects clearly benefit the real estate industry that Trump comes from.

The Trump administration announced a US$1 trillion infrastructure programme that consists of US$200 million of investments and US$800 million of tax breaks for developers. One of the key slogans in this context is that to 'rebuild America's infrastructure' the government wants to 'unleash private sector capital and expertise'.[11] Private developers receive taxpayers' money and tax credits for building infrastructure such as roads, bridges, tunnels, airports, dams, schools, hospitals and water systems that they own and for the use of which they can charge the public.

Labour

ANDREW F. PUZDER: THE NOMINATION OF A FAST FOOD CEO AS SECRETARY OF LABOUR

Trump appointed Andrew F. Puzder as secretary of labour. Puzder was, from 2000 until 2017, the CEO of CKE Restaurants which owns the fast food chains Carl's Jr., Hardee's, Green Burrito and Red Burrito. Fast food jobs tend not to be very well paid, which is why the demand for a living wage of US$15 per hour has arisen in this industry particularly. California has passed a law to increase the minimum wage to US$15 until 2022. Puzder opposes such an increase (Hiltzik 2016).

In 2014, Puzder spoke out against minimum wage increases from US$7.25 to US$10.10:

Unfortunately, this 40 per cent minimum-wage hike would also reduce employment opportunities for those who need them most. [...] Let's examine how it would affect a restaurant franchisee, a typical small business owner attempting to run a profitable enterprise. My company, CKE Restaurants, has more than 200 franchisees running about 2,000 restaurants nationwide. Our typical franchised restaurant employs 25 people and earns about $100,000 a year in pretax profit –

11. www.whitehouse.gov/blog/2017/06/08/president-trumps-plan-rebuild-americas-infrastructure, accessed on 7 August 2017.

about 8% of the restaurant's $1.2 million annual sales. […] But here's what middle-class business owners, who live in the real world, will do when faced with a 40% increase in labor costs. They will cut jobs and rely more on technology. Such changes are already happening in banks, gas stations, grocery stores, airports and, more recently, restaurants. Almost every restaurant chain in the country from Applebee's to McDonald's is testing or already implementing automated ordering with tablets or kiosks. The only other option is to raise prices. Yet it would be near-impossible to increase prices enough to offset the wage hike, particularly given today's economic conditions. (Puzder 2014)

When wages increase, Puzder only sees two possible responses by companies, namely that they either increase prices or try to enforce automation in order to lay off workers. The point is that he leaves out the option that companies accept lower profit rates. This does not seem to be an option for Puzder because he represents the interests of capital and not of labour. It is quite likely that a businessman as secretary of labour will do anything to keep minimum wages low, to limit their increase and to limit the power of workers. A law taxing machinery that comes along with minimum wage increases could easily secure avoiding wage increase-based incentives for automation. In the light of Puzder's appointment, it seems likely that Trump's goal of keeping capital in and attracting capital to the USA is not a project that is concerned about good earnings for workers, but is all about growing corporations' profits.

Given that fast food jobs represent highly alienated labour, automating these activities should not automatically be dismissed. The point is that well-paid skilled jobs are needed. But the USA's elitist higher education system plunges young people and their parents into debt. Neoliberal capitalism enforces low-paid, precarious labour. Progressive forms of automation must therefore stand in the context of discussions about how to secure a good life for all, for example in the form of a basic income guarantee that is funded out of capital taxation (Fuchs 2008a).

In February 2017, Puzder withdrew his nomination for secretary of labour. He had come under severe criticism in the Senate hearings that have to confirm nominations. The former attorney for the Southern District of Florida, Alexander Acosta, became Trump's secretary of labour. But the fact that Puzder was the first choice shows that Trump favours labour policies that represent capitalist interests.

Healthcare

Trump opposes Obama's health reform and wants to advance what he terms consumer-driven healthcare. 'Bad health care at the most expensive price. We have to repeal and replace Obamacare' (Clinton and Trump 2016c). 'We want competition. You will have the finest health care plan there is' (Clinton and Trump 2016b). Trump's plan aims to:

- Repeal and replace Obamacare with Health Savings Accounts (HSAs). [...]
- Allow people to purchase insurance across state lines, in all 50 states, creating a dynamic market. [...]
- President Obama said his health plan would cut the cost of family premiums by up to $2,500 a year. Instead, premiums have gone up by almost $5,000 since Obamacare passed. [...]
- Premiums have skyrocketed across the nation, with a national average of almost 25 per cent, with some states experiencing rate increases up to 70 per cent. [...]
- People are going without needed medical care because they can't afford these amounts.[12]

The argument that capitalist competition makes things cheaper is not automatically true, as the privatisation of railways in the United Kingdom and of telecommunications in the EU shows. Capitalism has an inherent monopoly tendency so that for-profit orientation and competitive markets tend to result in oligopolies and monopolies. If there is a private health insurance market, then the goal of the companies involved is to maximise profits. The way to do this is to aim at keeping the number and level of insurance claims low. Michael Moore's (2007) film *Sicko* illustrates the fact that privatised health care can result in denials from health insurance companies to cover costs. In contrast, if health insurance is a public service funded out of contributions paid in by employees and employers, then the logic of insurance denial can more easily be avoided. Only a public health system can guarantee universal coverage and access. A private for-profit system makes patients vulnerable to the whims of private insurance companies that want to increase their profits.

---

12. www.donaldjtrump.com/policies/health-care/, accessed on 17 February 2017.

Trump's interest in fostering private health care may not just result from the fact that he, as shareholder, has business interests in this industry, but it may very well come from a general ideological conviction that health and other social services should be organised as capitalist businesses that accumulate capital.

Climate and the Environment

US CAPITALISM

Table 4.5 shows how the share of total US GDP of the 500 largest US companies has developed. Given that the share has increased from 57.9 per cent in 1996 to 65.4 per cent in 2016, we can say that US capitalism has become more monopolistic. The data show that the information, finance, health/pharmaceuticals/biotech, transport, food and energy industries form US capitalism's key sectors. It may therefore not be an accident, but a business strategy, that Donald Trump has invested in exactly these sectors.

According to the data used in Table 4.5, the US energy industry made massive losses in 2016. The combined loss of the largest energy companies was US\$44.4 billon. These included companies such as Apache (−\$23.1 billion), Chesapeake Energy (−\$14.7 billion), Devon Energy (−\$14.5 billion), Freeport-McMoRan (−\$12.2 billion), Occidental Petroleum (−\$7.8 billion), Anadarko Petroleum (−\$6.7 billion), NRG Energy (−\$6.4 billion), Energy Future Holdings (−\$5.3 billion), EOG Resources (−\$4.5 billion), ConocoPhillips (−\$4.4 billion), Hess (−\$3.1 billion), Marathon Oil (−\$2.2 billion), Baker Hughes (−\$2.0 billion) and Peabody Energy (−\$2.0 billion).

The *Wall Street Journal* observed:

Low fuel prices and new climate policies are rapidly transforming the American energy sector, while escalating wars in the Middle East and a nuclear deal with Iran are clouding the global oil picture. [...] What's harder to develop is the political consensus to transition to pricing carbon emissions. Right now, climate policy is being implemented piecemeal around the world. That, combined with current low oil and gas prices, has increased the investment risk associated with future energy production. (Cook 2015)

Table 4.5   Share of the 500 largest companies' revenues in the USA's GDP, share of specific industries' profits in the total profits of the USA's 500 largest companies

	1996	2007	2016
Share of the top 500 companies' revenues of US GDP (%)	57.9	68.4	65.4
Largest industry's share in the Fortune 500 companies' total profits (%)	Finance, 25.2	Finance, 29.4	Information, communication and computing, 27.3
Second largest industry's share (%)	Energy, 13.7	Energy, 18.8	Finance, 26.8
Third largest industry's share (%)	Transport, 11.1	Information, communication and computing, 13.7	Health, pharmaceuticals and biotech, 14.2
Fourth largest industry's share (%)	Information, communication and computing, 10.3	Health, pharmaceuticals and biotech, 9.5	Transport, 11.9
Fifth largest industry's share (%)	Health, pharmaceuticals and biotech, 8.7	Food, 5.7	Food, 8.6
Share of hotel, restaurant and leisure industry (%)	0.6	1.3	1.8
Share of engineering and construction industry (%)	−0.2	0.9	0.6
Share of real estate industry (%)	0	0.2	0.5

Data sources: Fortune US 500 (revenues, profits), various years; OECD Stat & BEA (GDP)

Trump's says he favours oil and coal in energy politics over alternative forms of energy:

We invested in a solar company, our country. That was a disaster. They lost plenty of money on that one. Now, look, I'm a great believer in all forms of energy, but we're putting a lot of people out of work. Our energy policies are a disaster. Our country is losing so much in terms of energy, in terms of paying off our debt. You can't do what you're looking to do with $20 trillion in debt. [...] There has been a big push to develop alternative forms of energy – so-called green energy – from renewable sources. That's a big mistake. To begin with, the whole push for renewable energy is being driven by the wrong motivation, the mistaken belief that global climate change is being caused by carbon emissions. If you don't buy that – and I don't – then what we have is really just an expensive way of making the tree-huggers feel good about themselves. [...] Until we get this country's lifeblood – oil – back down to reasonable rates, America's economy will continue to slump, jobs won't get created, and American consumers will face ever-increasing prices.[13]

'Our first priorities need to be approving the Keystone XL Pipeline and starting to drill everywhere oil is accessible' (Trump 2015a, 65).

CLIMATE CHANGE SCEPTICISM

On 6 November 2012, Trump voiced climate change scepticism on Twitter: 'The concept of global warming was created by and for the Chinese in order to make U.S. manufacturing non-competitive.' His election campaign announced that it wants to '[u]nleash America's $50 trillion in untapped shale, oil, and natural gas reserves, plus hundreds of years in clean coal reserves.'[14] He made it clear that he favours not just oil, but also coal:

[E]nergy is under siege by the Obama administration. [...] we need much more than wind and solar. [...] Hillary Clinton wants to put all the miners out of business. There is a thing called clean coal. Coal will last for 1,000 years in this country. Now we have natural gas and so many other things because of technology. [...] I will bring our energy companies back. They'll be able to compete. They'll make money. They'll pay off our national debt. They'll pay off our tremendous budget deficits, which are tremendous. (Clinton and Trump 2016b)

After the election, Tump said in a *New York Times* interview about climate change:

---

13. www.ontheissues.org/2016/Donald_Trump_Energy_+_Oil.htm, accessed on 17 February 2017.
14. www.donaldjtrump.com/policies/energy/, accessed on 17 February 2017.

I have an open mind to it. We're going to look very carefully. It's one issue that's interesting because there are few things where there's more division than climate change. [...] I think there is some connectivity [between human activity and climate change]. There is some, something. It depends on how much. It also depends on how much it's going to cost our companies. You have to understand, our companies are noncompetitive right now. (Trump 2016e)

Trump in general favours deregulation. 'The misguided passion of environmentalists today makes building anything much more difficult. Now we have crazy overregulation. You can barely buy a paper clip without being in violation of some governmental policy' (Trump 2015a, 82). Trump appointed Scott Pruitt as head of the Environmental Protection Agency. The *New York Times* argues that Pruitt, as the Oklahoma attorney general, worked 'with some of the largest oil and gas companies, and the state's coal-burning electric utility, to try to overturn a large part of the Obama administration's regulations on air emissions, water pollution and endangered animals' (Davenport and Lipton 2016). Pruitt and Strange (2016) say about climate change: 'Scientists continue to disagree about the degree and extent of global warming and its connection to the actions of mankind. That debate should be encouraged.'

Trump's focus on the oil industry may not just result from the fact that he as shareholder had business interests in this industry, but it may very well come from a general ideological belief that the oil industry is needed as US capitalism's driver. Given his opposition to green energy, it could very well be that Trump's environmental policies will foster an increase in carbon dioxide emissions and environmental pollution.

On 1 June 2017, Donald Trump announced: 'In order to fulfil my solemn duty to protect America and its citizens, the United States will withdraw from the Paris Climate Accord' (*CNN*, 21.38 Central European Time). Countries that signed this agreement committed themselves to reduce their greenhouse gas emissions. Trump argued that the accord 'disadvantages the United States to the exclusive benefit of other countries'. It would mean 'lost jobs, lower wages, shuttered factories, and vastly diminished economic production'. There would be a loss of GDP and jobs in industries such as car production, paper, cement, iron, steel, coal and natural gas. Trump thinks that withdrawing from the Climate Accord is in America's economic interest and won't matter much to the climate. He puts capitalist interests over environmental interests. At the same time he seems to assume that climate change is not a massive environmental problem and that there are technological fixes.

Taxation

LOW CORPORATION TAX

Trump promises low taxes for corporations: 'The Trump Plan will lower the business tax rate from 35 percent to 15 percent, and eliminate the corporate alternative minimum tax. This rate is available to all businesses, both small and large, that want to retain the profits within the business.'[15] He speaks of creating 'the lowest tax rates since before World War II' (Trump 2015a, 153). No 'business of any size will pay [...] more than 15 percent of their business income in taxes' (Trump 2015a, 153). There will 'be only four [tax] brackets: 0%, 10%, 20%, and 25%' (153). What one must note in this context is that when Trump came to power in 2016, the highest tax bracket was 39.6 per cent for single filers' incomes over US$415,050.

Trump expects that a low level of corporation tax will keep US companies from outsourcing jobs:

Our jobs are fleeing the country. They're going to Mexico. They're going to many other countries. You look at what China is doing to our country in terms of making our product. [...] So Ford is leaving. You see that, their small car division leaving. Thousands of jobs leaving Michigan, leaving Ohio. [...] But we have to stop our jobs from being stolen from us. We have to stop our companies from leaving the United States and, with it, firing all of their people. All you have to do is take a look at Carrier air conditioning in Indianapolis. They left – fired 1,400 people. They're going to Mexico. So many hundreds and hundreds of companies are doing this. We cannot let it happen. Under my plan, I'll be reducing taxes tremendously, from 35 percent to 15 percent for companies, small and big businesses. That's going to be a job creator like we haven't seen since Ronald Reagan. It's going to be a beautiful thing to watch. Companies will come. [...] I'm going to cut regula-

---

15.   www.donaldjtrump.com/policies/tax-plan/, accessed on 17 February 2017.

tions. I'm going to cut taxes big league, and you're going to raise taxes big league, end of story. (Clinton and Trump 2016a)

CHINA AND MEXICO

Trump furthermore announced that American companies that outsource production to Mexico and other countries, but bring their products back to the USA in order to sell them, will face tariffs of 35 per cent:

> Companies, like Carrier are firing their workers and moving to Mexico. Ford is moving all of its small car production to Mexico. When I'm President, if companies want to fire their workers and leave for Mexico, then we will charge them a 35% tax when they want to ship their products back into the United States. That means the companies won't leave in the first place and, if they do, we'll at least make money when they ship their products across the border.[16]

Such a measure is a clear state intervention into the free market. The purpose of this idea is, as we shall see, not to guarantee decent wages but profitability within the USA. Trump believes in a *national capitalism*, in which US companies produce commodities in the USA by exploiting US workers and exporting to other countries. Trump's version of national capitalism is not predominantly based on capital export and finance, but on construction, manufacturing, real estate and oil.

The logic that jobs are being stolen blames countries such as Mexico and China for capitalism's structural problems. Companies are driven by the imperative of profit maximisation and the logic of competition. They will therefore tend to seek out every opportunity to maximise profits. If outsourcing to another country is possible and poses the opportunity to increase profits, then there will be a tendency for companies to seek this opportunity. The problem arises from the combination of capitalism's structural logic of accumulation and the competition state. Competition with low-wage economies can easily result in vicious downward spirals of wage dumping and precarious working conditions. The quotes above show that Trump also advocates massive tax cuts for corporations. But

16. www.donaldjtrump.com/press-releases/donald-j.-trump-proposes-american-desk-protect-economic-and-national-intere, accessed on 17 February 2017.

such tax cuts tend to reduce the federal budget. Such reductions tend to hit the poorest if they are offset by cuts of public services.

THE NEED FOR NEW ECONOMIC MODELS

The logic of capitalism's international division of labour has advanced deindustrialisation and low-wage economies. One factor of Trump's success is the discontent associated with these changes. In the quote above, he refers to these discontents. But are there alternatives to the low-wage economy? One alternative that can be implemented in any location is the transformation of companies into worker-owned cooperatives. In such companies, the workers are the collective owner and take all decisions together. This structure advances a company interest that makes workers' interests the core of the company interest. Bernie Sanders argues for 'new economic models' that provide support for the creation of worker-owned businesses:

> Unlike large corporations that have been shipping jobs overseas, employee-owned businesses, by and large, are not shutting down and moving their businesses [...] employee-owned businesses boost morale, because workers share in profits and have more control over their work lives. The employees are not simply cogs in a machine owned by somebody else. They have a say in how the company is run. (Sanders 2016b, 260–1)

POTENTIAL IMPACTS OF TRUMP'S TAX PLANS

The Tax Policy Institute analysed Trump's revised tax plans and concluded:

> The top quintile – or fifth of the distribution – would receive an average tax cut of $16,660 (a 6.6 percent increase in after-tax income), the top 1 percent an average tax cut nearly 13 times larger ($214,690, or 13.5 percent of after-tax income), and the top 0.1 percent an average tax cut approaching $1.1 million (14.2 percent of after-tax income). In contrast, the average tax cut for the lowest-income households would be $110, 0.8 percent of after-tax income. Middle-income households would receive an average tax cut of $1,010, or 1.8 percent of after-tax income. (Nunns et al. 2016, 9)

According to these calculations, the wealthy will be better off with these tax cuts and inequality will increase. The Tax Policy Institute also argues that as a result of Trump's plans for lowering income and business taxes, 'the federal debt would increase by at least $7.0 trillion over ten years' (Nunns et al. 2016, 1). The plans would 'substantially increase budget deficits unless offset by spending cuts' (9). And if there were spending cuts and privatisations in realms such as education, social security and health care, then lower-income groups would be hit hardest because they cannot easily afford private services.

CARRIER

Carrier is a US company that produces air conditioning, ventilation and heating systems. It planned to outsource up to 2,000 manufacturing jobs from Indianapolis to Mexico. Trump had conversations with the company's management and as a result announced that it would only outsource parts of the jobs to Mexico:

> We have negotiated an agreement with the incoming administration that we believe benefits our workers, the state of Indiana and our company. We are announcing today that Carrier will continue to manufacture gas furnaces in Indianapolis, in addition to retaining engineering and headquarters staff, preserving more than 1,000 jobs. [...] Today's announcement is possible because the incoming Trump-Pence administration has emphasized to us its commitment to support the business community and create an improved, more competitive U.S. business climate. The incentives offered by the state were an important consideration.[17]

Bernie Sanders (2016a) commented:

> It is not good enough to save *some* of these jobs. Trump made a promise that he would save all of these jobs, and we cannot rest until an ironclad contract is signed to ensure that all of these workers are able to continue working in Indiana without having their pay or benefits slashed. In exchange for allowing United Technologies to

---

17. www.carrier.com/carrier/en/us/news/news-article/carrier_statement_regarding_indianapolis_operations.aspx, accessed on 17 February 2017.

continue to offshore more than 1,000 jobs, Trump will reportedly give the company tax and regulatory favors that the corporation has sought. Just a short few months ago, Trump was pledging to force United Technologies to 'pay a damn tax.' He was insisting on very steep tariffs for companies like Carrier that left the United States and wanted to sell their foreign-made products back in the United States. Instead of a damn tax, the company will be rewarded with a damn tax *cut*. Wow! How's that for standing up to corporate greed? How's that for punishing corporations that shut down in the United States and move abroad? In essence, United Technologies took Trump hostage and won. And that should send a shock wave of fear through all workers across the country.

STEVEN MNUCHIN AND WILBUR ROSS: CAPITALIST INTERESTS IN GOVERNMENT

On 30 November 2016, Trump announced the appointment of Goldman Sachs banker Steven Mnuchin as treasury secretary. Mnuchin was active in the motion picture industry (RatPac Entertainment), hedge funds and banking. He was involved in purchasing the mortgage corporation IndyMac that went bankrupt during the 2008 economic crisis and offered high-risk mortgages. It was turned into the OneWest bank. Mnuchin announced the 'largest tax change since Reagan' and said that 'we are going to cut corporate taxes. [...] We are gonna get to 15 percent' (Jopson, Murphy and Sevastopolu 2016).

Trump also announced picking Wilbur Ross as secretary of commerce. In 2016, Ross was the 232nd richest American. He had an estimated wealth of around US$2.9 billion.[18] Ross is an investor who restructured companies in industries such as steel, coal and textiles and invested into oil, gas, shipping and transportation (Levine 2016). The underlying rationale may be that Ross is an expert in industries that Trump sees as forming key economic sectors. At the same time it is clear that Ross is close to the financial interests of these industries. Commenting on Trumponomics, Ross argues: 'America in general would be good because it isn't just trade that Trump is gonna fix, it's the corporate tax. Reducing the corporate tax rate from 35 percent to 15, means that given

---

18. www.forbes.com/forbes-400/list/#version:static_search:wilbur%20ro, accessed on 17 February 2017.

the amount of pre-tax earnings will throw off 30 percent more after tax'
(Levine 2016).

The examples of Mnuchin and Ross show how Trump brings representatives of the corporate class, who support hyper-capitalist politics, into
key political positions. They support policies that favour corporations
and the rich, and will further advance the tendency that corporations
pay little in taxes.

Education

BETSY DEVOS: SECRETARY OF EDUCATION

Donald Trump appointed Betsy DeVos as education secretary. She
comes from a billionaire family that owns Amway, a company that sells
beauty and health products. In 2016 her husband, Richard DeVos, had
an estimated wealth of US$5.4 billion, making him the eighty-eighth
richest American[19] and the world's 308th richest person.[20] According
to news sources, Betsy DeVos 'has long supported using taxpayer funds
for voucher programmes, parochial schools and charters, all of which
undermine and replace public schools and locally-elected school boards'
(Lazare 2016).

DeVos describes her involvement in educational reform the following
way: 'Today there are about 250,000 students in 33 publicly funded,
private-choice programs in 17 states and the District of Columbia. The
movement's growth is accelerating. [...] We think of the educational
choice movement as involving many parts: vouchers and tax credits,
certainly, but also virtual schools, magnet schools, homeschooling, and
charter schools.'[21]

DeVos is the chairperson of the American Federation for Children,
whose task involves advancing private schools:

> The American Federation for Children envisions an education
> system where parents are empowered to choose the best educational

---

19. www.forbes.com/forbes-400/list/#version:static, accessed on 28 November 2016.
20. www.forbes.com/billionaires/list/#version:static_search:devos, accessed on 28
November 2016.
21. www.philanthropyroundtable.org/topic/excellence_in_philanthropy/interview_
with_betsy_devos, accessed on 17 February 2017.

environment for their child, where innovation and entrepreneurism revolutionizes our education system, ensuring all children, especially low-income children, are provided with the opportunity to receive the finest education possible, whether it be in a traditional public school, public charter school, virtual learning, private school, home school or blended learning.[22]

Trump's campaign supported these kinds of policies and promised to 'add an additional federal investment of $20 billion towards school choice. This will be done by reprioritizing existing federal dollars.'[23]

What could be the consequences of such policies? The National Education Association's president, Lily Eskelsen García, commented on DeVos's appointment:

[Her] efforts over the years have done more to undermine public education than support students. She has lobbied for failed schemes, like vouchers – which take away funding and local control from our public schools – to fund private schools at taxpayers' expense. These schemes do nothing to help our most-vulnerable students while they ignore or exacerbate glaring opportunity gaps. She has consistently pushed a corporate agenda to privatize, de-professionalize and impose cookie-cutter solutions to public education. By nominating Betsy DeVos, the Trump administration has demonstrated just how out of touch it is with what works best for students, parents, educators and communities.[24]

From Millionaire Politics to Billionaire Politics

THE WEALTH OF US PRESIDENTS

Most US presidents have certainly been wealthy. Barack Obama's wealth was estimated at US$12.2 million in 2016.[25] The estimation of Bill Clinton's wealth was US$80 million in 2016.[26] George W. Bush's wealth

---

22. www.federationforchildren.org/about-us/mission/, accessed on 17 February 2017.

23. www.donaldjtrump.com/policies/education/, accessed on 17 February 2017.

24. www.nea.org/home/69329.htm, accessed on 17 February 2017.

25. www.therichest.com/celebnetworth/politician/president/barack-obama-net-worth/, accessed on 17 February 2017.

26. www.therichest.com/celebnetworth/politician/president/bill-clinton-net-worth/, accessed on 17 February 2017.

was, according to estimations, US$35 million in 2016.[27] Barack Obama's 2014 and 2015 public financial disclosure reports[28] show that he owned no significant shares in companies, but had income from pension investments and book royalties. Hillary Clinton's 2015 financial disclosure report[29] shows, just like the ones from her husband Bill, that they both earn significant incomes from speaking fees. According to estimates, Bill Clinton earned more than US$100 million from talks he gave in the years from 2001 until 2013.[30] Bernie Sanders criticised the fact that Hillary Clinton received US$225,000 for a talk she gave in 2013 at a Goldman Sachs conference. He said that finance capitalism

> brought this country into the worst economic downturn since the Great Recession, the Great Depression of the '30s, when millions of people lost their jobs, their homes and their life savings. The obvious response to that is that you have got a bunch of fraudulent operators and that they have got to be broken up. [...] Now Secretary Clinton was busy giving speeches to Goldman Sachs for 225,000 dollars a speech. (Griffin, Fitzpatrick and Devine 2016)

Whereas Hillary and Bill Clinton interlock with corporate elites via giving talks, which means that they provide a service for relatively high fees, Donald Trump's interlocking is of a different nature and involves the ownership of shares.

GEORGE W. BUSH

George W. Bush was US president from 2001 to 2009. In the 1970s and 1980s, he was involved in the oil business as part of the companies Arbusto Energy, Bush Exploration, Spectrum 7 and HKN Inc. His

---

27. www.therichest.com/celebnetworth/politician/president/george-w-bush-net-worth/, accessed on 17 February 2017.

28. www.whitehouse.gov/sites/default/files/docs/oge_278_cy_2014_obama.pdf, www.whitehouse.gov/sites/whitehouse.gov/files/documents/oge_278_cy_2015_obama_051616.pdf, accessed on 17 February 2017.

29. assets.documentcloud.org/documents/2082788/hillary-clinton-financial-disclosure-form.pdf, pfds.opensecrets.org/N00000019_2015_Pres_A.pdf, pfds.opensecrets.org/N00000019_2015_Pres.pdf, accessed on 17 February 2017.

30. www.therichest.com/celebnetworth/politician/president/bill-clinton-net-worth/, accessed on 17 February 2017.

1999/2000 financial disclosure report[31] shows that Bush earned income from savings and real estate investments, and capital gains from the ownership of the Texas Rangers baseball team. A group around Bush owned the Texas Rangers from 1989 until 1998. His real estate and financial income included the George W. Bush Qualified Diversified Trust and ownership of 1,583 acres in McLennan County in Texas. Both assets had a value of over US$1 million. In 1978, Bush was an unsuccessful candidate for the House of Representatives. He was involved in his father's presidential campaigns in the late 1980s and early 1990s. So, although having had connections to politics, Bush did not enter politics fully before 1995 when he became the governor of Texas.

Bush was just like Trump – a capitalist-turned-politician. The difference is that Bush came from a Republican family involved in both the oil business and politics. Donald Trump has been a businessman all his life and turned very late towards politics. He became US president at the age of 70 and is thus the oldest president in US history. Another important difference between Bush and Trump is that Bush is certainly rich, but Trump is super-rich and part of the elite of the world's richest people. According to his 2016 financial disclosure statement, Trump was before the election involved in at least 500 companies.[32] According to estimations,[33] Trump's wealth was more than 128 times as large as Bush's in 2016. High quantity can turn into a different quality, which means that the number of Trump's connections and amount of economic power may trigger a qualitative transformation of the US state.

TRUMP: THE BILLIONAIRE PRESIDENT

Donald Trump is a billionaire whose status as president and as a well-connected billionaire impinges on the structure of the US state where capitalist and state interests directly interlock and overlap. Traditionally this interlocking was more indirect. Trump is a billionaire turned president who has lots of connections to many different capitalist industries. The interlocking of the state and capital, and Trump's representation of the interests of big capital, can be observed in suggestions

---

31. news.findlaw.com/hdocs/docs/gwbush/gwbush-sf278.pdf.
32. pfds.opensecrets.org/N00023864_2016_Pres.pdf, accessed on 17 February 2017.
33. www.therichest.com/celebnetworth/politician/president/george-w-bush-net-worth/, www.forbes.com/forbes-400/list, accessed on 27 November 2016.

that aim at advancing a low-tax economy that benefits big capital, and state intervention that favours capital interests in industries such as private education, private health care, the pharmaceutical industry, the oil, gas and coal industries, the construction industry and the transport industry.

On 30 November 2016, Donald Trump announced on Twitter that he 'will be leaving' his 'business in total in order to fully focus on running the country' and that 'legal documents are being crafted which take me completely out of business operations'.[34] On 11 January 2017, Trump gave a news conference in which he announced that his business would be conveyed to a trust and that his sons Donald Jr. and Eric would take over the Trump Organization's management. He said that he would not have any influence on business operations during his presidency. An ethics adviser would vet national deals made by the Trump Organization for potential conflicts of interest. No international deals would be made. It is important to stress that Trump did not sell the Trump Organization and did not divest, which would have been a way towards eliminating possible conflicts of interest. 'Trump's commitment falls short of the recommendations from the Office of Government Ethics and former chief White House ethics advisors for both parties, who say the only way for Trump to fully inoculate himself from conflicts is to fully divest his business holdings and clearly break from financial interests' (Harwell 2017).

Observers commented that these changes

fell short of the recommendations of ethics experts in both parties who have said the only way for Mr. Trump to genuinely eliminate potential conflicts is to place all his real estate holdings and other business ventures in a blind trust over which neither he nor his family has any control, severing him entirely from the enterprise. [...] Mr. Trump's influence over foreign and domestic policy as president has raised questions about whether American policy could affect his bottom line. For instance, he will oversee the regulation of banks, some of which lend money to his company, and he will have frequent contact

---

34. twitter.com/realDonaldTrump/status/803926488579973120, twitter.com/realdonald trump/status/803927774784344064, twitter.com/realDonaldTrump/status/80393149051 4075648.

with foreign heads of state, including some who run countries where he does business. (Haberman, Hirschfeld Davis and Lipton 2017)

Although there is not a direct and simultaneous double role of Trump as businessman and president, his decades-long business practices certainly involve capitalist interests that he cannot easily leave behind. 'The emphasis on "business operations", not on ownership, hinted that Mr. Trump is not ruling out retaining a financial stake in the Trump Organization or putting his children in control of the company. Ethics experts said such moves would leave Mr. Trump vulnerable to accusations that his official actions are motivated by personal financial interests' (Shear and Lipton 2016).

The State and Capitalism in Other Parts of the World

The changing relationship between the state and capitalism is an important dimension in the analysis of Trump. State capitalism in the case of Trump means that to a certain degree the state and capitalism intersect in the form of capitalists turned politicians such as Donald Trump, Rex Tillerson, Steven Mnuchin, Wilbur Ross and Betsy DeVos.

STATE CAPITALISM

When talking about state capitalism, one should not forget that although Europe and North America dominate world trade and capital exports, their companies and states are not the only economic and political actors in the world system. Kurlantzick (2016) argues in his book, *State Capitalism: How the Return of Statism is Transforming the World*, that over the past two decades state-capitalist economies have grown. He defines state capitalism as a political economy, in which the state exerts significant influence over at least one-third of the 500 biggest companies, and the state directly intervenes to a significant degree in the management of the economy (Kurlantzick 2016, 9). He argues that state capitalism exists, for example, in China, Brazil, India, Russia, Indonesia, Saudi Arabia, Argentina, Norway, Iran, Thailand, the United Arab Emirates, Malaysia, Singapore, Egypt, Kazakhstan, Algeria, Qatar, Venezuela, Vietnam and Kuwait. Kurlantzick argues that state capitalism can be accompanied by different political systems, ranging from liberal democracy to authoritarianism.

China would be the most striking example of state capitalism. Only three of the 42 largest Chinese companies are privately owned (Kurlantzick 2016, 4). The role of the Chinese state doesn't just involve tight political control of the country, but also an important role for state-owned enterprises, and the state intervening in and putting limits on financial markets during the 2015/16 stock market crisis. Public investments in city infrastructure form another element of Chinese state capitalism. China also subsidised some of its exports, and established export-processing zones through state regulation, in which foreign capital has access to cheap labour. However, one needs to take into account the fact that, according to statistics, capitalist ownership dominates the Chinese economy (see Fuchs 2015, chapter 7). According to official statistics, in 2015 state-owned and collective enterprises accounted for 12.3 per cent of industrial profits, shareholding companies for 46 per cent, private enterprises for 24.9 per cent and foreign investors' companies for 16.8 per cent (National Bureau of Statistics of China 2016). One of the problems with Kurlantzick's book is that he sets the United States up in opposition to state capitalism. He argues that the USA could save the world from state capitalism's negative impacts. With the rise of Donald Trump, however, one cannot rule out the possibility that US society will take on certain elements of state capitalism.

THE RELATIONSHIP OF THE STATE TO ITS CITIZENS: CIVIL LIBERTIES AND STATE INSTITUTIONS UNDER TRUMP

Authoritarian Statism

In contemporary politics, authoritarian politicians such as Rodrigo Duterte (Philippines), Recep Tayyip Erdoğan *(Turkey)*, Nigel Farage (UK), Jarosław Kaczyński and Beata Szydlo (Poland), Marine Le Pen (France), Narendra Modi (India), Viktor Orbán (Hungary), Vladimir Putin (Russia), Heinz Christian Strache (Austria) or Geert Wilders (Netherlands) play a role in many countries. Donald Trump's presidency is the most powerful expression of the rise of right-wing authoritarianism. The key question with respect to state institutions and civil liberties is whether Trump's presidency could result in an authoritarian form of US capitalism. In the age of Trump, we should think about how to understand authoritarian capitalism.

Lenin (1917, 398) argues that a 'democratic republic is the best possible political shell for capitalism'. The problem with this assumption is that Nazi Germany shows that capitalism and democracy do not form a necessary unity. In contrast to fascist capitalism, the ground for opposition is much larger in liberal democracies. Bob Jessop (2016, 212) argues that under specific circumstances, authoritarian statism can become the best possible shell for capitalism.

State theorist Nicos Poulantzas argues that authoritarian statism transfers powers of legislation and the judiciary to the executive power of the president/prime minister. Authoritarian statism is a state form that features 'intensified state control over every sphere of political democracy' and the 'draconian and multiform curtailment of so-called "formal" liberties' (Poulantzas 1980/2000, 203–4). There is a decline in the rule of law, also evident in 'the increasing concern for the pre-emptive policing of the potentially disloyal and deviant'. There is an encouragement of 'the fusion of the three branches of the state – legislature, executive and judiciary' (Jessop 1990, 67).

Nazi-fascism was a particular form of authoritarian state capitalism that ruled Germany at the time of the Second World War. In a similar way to Kurlantzick (2016), critical theorist Friedrich Pollock (1975) argues that state capitalism has two characteristic forms: democratic and totalitarian state capitalism. His analysis refers to Fordist capitalism. By totalitarian state capitalism, he primarily means Nazi Germany. Fascist societies have powerful states. The historian Tim Mason (1995, 53–76) therefore characterises Nazi Germany as a society in which there was a primacy of politics over the economy. This means that companies had to support Hitler's regime if they wanted to survive. The state and capital formed a unity. Capitalism in Nazi Germany was based on combines and cartels that all used the leadership principle as organisational means (Neumann 1944/2009, 233). The leadership principle was taken over from the Nazi state and applied to the economy. 'The underlying [Nazi] ideology is racism, the sovereignty of the racial people incarnated in the Leader. The whole structure is at the service of two ideas, the New Order and proletarian racism' (Neumann 1944/2009, 221). Cartels were formed by state power in the form of compulsory cartelisation (Neumann, Marcuse and Kirchheimer 2013, 270, 273–4).

Neumann (see 1944/2009, 221–34) disagrees with Pollock's view that during the Nazi era there was totalitarian state capitalism in Germany. Pollock (1941a, 445) writes that Hitler 'transformed monopoly capitalism into state capitalism'. Neumann, in contrast, suggests that Nazi Germany's economy was 'a monopolistic economy – *and* a command economy. It is a private capitalistic economy, regimented by the totalitarian state. We suggest as a name best to describe it, "Totalitarian Monopoly Capitalism"' (Neumann 1944/2009, 261). Neumann (1944/2009, 116–20, 275) says that the 'Aryanisation' of Jewish property played an important role in Nazi Germany's monopoly capitalism. It helped to advance monopoly capital's interests. Examples were Otto Wolff AG (steel), Friedrich Flick's conglomerate (steel, iron, coal) or Mannesmann (steel, iron) (275, 288–92). Nazi imperialism also involved the 'Germanisation' of militarily conquered economies (275–7).

Neumann described proletarian racism as an aspect of fascist capitalism:

> Racial proletarianism is the genuine theory of National Socialism and its most dangerous expression. [...] The essence of the theory is extremely simple. Germany and Italy are proletarian races, surrounded by a world of hostile plutocratic-capitalistic-Jewish democracies. [...] It exploits hatred of the Jews, aversion to capitalism, and, finally, utilizes Marxist phraseology and symbolism to an ever increasing extent. It is clear that the very purpose of the doctrine of racial proletarianism is to entice the working classes. (Neumann 1944/2009, 188, 187, 188)

Nazism had a short-circuited critique of capitalism that pitted industrial capital against finance capital. It biologised and racialised this difference.

Is Trump a Fascist?

NEUMANN: FIVE ELEMENTS OF THE AUTHORITARIAN STATE

Neumann (1957, 244–5) argues that modern dictatorship, or what he also terms the authoritarian state, consists of five elements:

1. A police state substitutes the rule of law: 'The rule of law is a presumption in favour of the right of the citizen and against the coercive power of the state' (244);

2. The centralisation of political power;
3. The existence of a monopolistic state party;
4. Totalitarian social controls extending to all realms of society in the form of the leadership principle, the synchronisation of social organisation, the substitution of bureaucracies by private leadership groups, the destruction of social organisations that are substituted by undifferentiated mass organisations and atomise the individual, and the transformation of culture into propaganda; and
5. The reliance on terror.

These elements relate to the relationship of the state to itself, the economy and citizens/civil society.

Since the start of the crisis in 2008, it has become evident that the contradiction between global capitalism and politics at the level of the nation state has implications at the level of subjectivity. There has been a backlash so that the contradiction has been sublated into the strengthening of authoritarian statism and authoritarian populist ideology. Bob Jessop argues in this context:

> We should particularly note the continued decline of parliament and rule of law, the growing autonomy of the executive, the increased importance of presidential or prime ministerial powers, the consolidation of authoritarian, plebiscitary parties that largely represent the state to the popular masses, and – something neglected by Poulantzas – the mediatization of politics as the mass media play an increasing role in shaping political imaginaries, programmes, and debates. A stronger emphasis on issues of national security and pre-emptive policing associated with the so-called war on terror at home and abroad has reinforced the attack on human rights and civil liberties. (Jessop 2016, 245–6)

In the times we live in, states of emergency have become very realistic and real aspects of politics. 'States of emergency are declared, commissarial dictatorships are appointed, or (quasi-)sovereign dictatorships seize power in response to threats to the state' (Jessop 2016, 218). This can involve the suspension of elections, the centralisation and monopolisation of power (bans of and limitations on political opposition), the concentration of state powers (legislative power, executive power, judiciary power), the suspension of the rule of law, the use of repressive state apparatuses against political opponents (control, surveillance, policing, law-and-order politics, police killings, covert secret service operations, militarisation, war, etc.) and an ideological offensive that includes real and ideological violence against foreigners, immigrants, migrants, people of colour and other minorities.

ROBERT O. PAXTON: IS TRUMP A FASCIST?

Influenced by Franz Neumann's works, Robert O. Paxton (2004, 218) defines fascism as 'a form of political behaviour marked by obsessive pre-occupation with community decline, humiliation, or victimhood and by compensatory cults of unity, energy, and purity, in which a mass-based party of committed nationalist militants, working in uneasy but effective collaboration with traditional elites, abandons democratic liberties and pursues with redemptive violence and without ethical or legal restraints goals of internal cleansing and external expansion'. Elements of fascism are a sense of crisis, nationalism, ideological discourse of the national community as a victim and being in decline, victimisation discourse, exclusionary violence, authoritarianism and leadership ideology, Darwinian struggle and the suspension of the rule of law (219–20). This is certainly a comprehensive definition. However, it lacks any focus on the economy. For Neumann, fascism was the combination of a repressive, racist and terrorist political system, racist monopoly capitalism, and the ideologies of leadership, nationalism and proletarian racism.

Paxton (2016) argues that Donald Trump personifies 'self-indulgent demagoguery on behalf of oligarchy':

> Superficially, he seems to have borrowed a number of fascist themes for his presidential campaign: xenophobia, racial prejudice, fear of national weakness and decline, aggressiveness in foreign policy, a readiness to suspend the rule of law to deal with supposed emergencies. His hectoring tone, mastery of crowds, and the skill with which he uses the latest communications technologies also are reminiscent of Mussolini and Hitler. And yet these qualities are at most derivative of fascist themes and styles; the underlying ideological substance is very different, with the entitlements of wealth playing a greater role than fascist regimes generally tolerated. Trump's embrace of these themes

and styles is most likely a matter of tactical expediency – a decision taken with little or no thought about their ugly history. Trump is evidently altogether insensitive to the echoes his words and oratorical style evoke, which should not be surprising, given his apparent insensitivity to the impact of every other insult that he hurls.

Given that Paxton leaves out the economic dimension in his definition of fascism, it is no wonder that his stress on oligarchy is quite vague and does not play a role in the conclusions he draws. One cannot rule out the possibility that elements of extreme authoritarianism will emerge under Donald Trump's presidency. It may or may not be the case. Trump is quite unpredictable, and it is not certain to what extent he will put into action and radicalise what he said during his election campaign. The decisive question is whether his policies advance the interests of US monopoly capital, limit civil liberties, limit or repress democratic opposition, advance racism, nationalist division and violence against minorities, militarise the country and engage in imperialist war.

ROGER GRIFFIN: IS TRUMP A FASCIST?

Roger Griffin takes an approach on Trump that is comparable to Paxton's. Griffin (1993, 44) defines fascism as:

> a genus of political ideology whose mythic core in its various permutations is a palingenetic form of populist ultra-nationalism. The fascist mentality is characterized by the sense of living through an imminent turning-point in contemporary history, when the dominance of the allegedly bankrupt or degenerate forces of conservatism, individualistic liberalism and materialist socialism is finally to give way to a new era in which vitalistic nationalism will triumph. To combat these rival political ideologies and the decadence they allegedly host (for example the parasitism of traditional elites, materialism, class conflict, military weakness, loss of racial vitality, moral anarchy, cosmopolitanism), fascist activists see the recourse to organized violence as both necessary and healthy. Though they may well make some concessions to parliamentary democracy in order to gain power, the pluralism of opinion and party politics upon which it rests is anathema to their concept of national unity, which implies in practice the maximum

totalitarian control over all areas of social, economic, political and cultural life.

Based on this understanding, Griffin argues that Trump is not a fascist: 'You can be a total xenophobic racist male chauvinist bastard and still not be a fascist. [...] As long as Trump does not advocate the abolition of America's democratic institutions, and their replacement by some sort of post-liberal new order, he's not technically a fascist' (cited in Matthews 2016).

SLAVOJ ŽIŽEK: 'EVERYTHING UNDER HEAVEN IS IN UTTER CHAOS; THE SITUATION IS EXCELLENT'

Slavoj Žižek (2017) argues that the 'fear that a Trump victory could turn the US into a fascist state is a ridiculous exaggeration'. He says that the 'US has such a rich texture of divergent civic and political institutions' that such a focus distracts attention from the 'true political divisions' that are based on the liberal capitalism that Hillary Clinton stands for, and that 'popular rage is by definition free-floating and can be redirected'. Žižek embraces Trump's victory as the opportunity that 'the Left will be mobilized only through such a threat of catastrophe'. 'Trump's victory provides a unique chance for the renewal of the Left'.

Fascism is certainly a potential situation lying dormant in capitalism. But this does not mean that the dangers of liberal capitalism are larger than those of authoritarian capitalism and neofascism and that one should therefore embrace the latter as an opportunity to fight the former. The years 1933 and 1968 show why Žižek is wrong: historically, the Western Left was defeated in 1933 precisely when Hitler came to power and a world war was looming, and became empowered in 1968 under the conditions of liberal democratic, imperialist welfare capitalism. There is great political danger in repeating the logic of the social fascism hypothesis today. Trump is certainly an impetus for Left alternatives and struggles, but such struggles do not necessarily emerge or succeed in situations where civil liberties are limited or under threat. Trump is not a secondary problem reducible to the 'real problem' of Clinton and liberalism. Rather, he is the intensification of the capitalist problem because he epitomises the convergence of capitalism and the state.

NOAM CHOMSKY: IS TRUMP A FASCIST?

Noam Chomsky takes an approach that differs from Paxton and Griffin. Chomsky argues that Trump is unpredictable and that one therefore cannot tell whether he will advance authoritarian statism and/or a me-ideology that aims at increasing his popularity:

> For many years, I have been writing and speaking about the danger of the rise of an honest and charismatic ideologue in the United States, someone who could exploit the fear and anger that has long been boiling in much of the society, and who could direct it away from the actual agents of malaise to vulnerable targets. That could indeed lead to what sociologist Bertram Gross called 'friendly fascism' in a perceptive study 35 years ago. But that requires an honest ideologue, a Hitler type, not someone whose only detectable ideology is Me. The dangers, however, have been real for many years, perhaps even more so in the light of the forces that Trump has unleashed. (Chomsky 2016b)

CORNEL WEST AND JOHN BELLAMY FOSTER: TRUMP AND NEOFASCISM

Cornel West (2017) argues that Trump's presidency means 'a neofascist era: a neoliberal economy on steroids, a reactionary repressive attitude toward domestic "aliens", a militaristic cabinet eager for war and in denial of global warming'.

John Bellamy Foster (2017) argues that there are obvious differences between Trump and classical fascism, such as the lack of black or brown shirts, paramilitary violence or storm troopers. But Trump for Foster means 'that liberal or capitalist democracy in the United States is now endangered'. He argues that Trump aims at the Gleichschaltung of US society, including the state administration, the economy, the intelligence apparatus, the media and the education system.

> Neofascist discourse and political practice are now evident every day in virulent attacks on the racially oppressed, immigrants, women, LBGTQ people, environmentalists, and workers. [...] neofascism today also has as its aim a shift in the management of the advanced capitalist system, requiring the effective dissolution of the liberal-democratic order and its replacement by the rule of represen-

tatives of what is now called the 'alt-right', openly espousing racism, nationalism, anti-environmentalism, misogyny, homophobia, police violence, and extreme militarism. The deeper motive of all these forms of reaction, however, is the repression of the work force. […] Islamophobia merges with China-phobia – and with Latino-phobia, as represented by the so-called 'defense of the U.S. southern border.' In the Trump vision of the restoration of U.S. geopolitical and economic power, enemies are primarily designated in racial and religious terms. A renewed emphasis is put on placing U.S. boots on the ground in the Middle East and on naval confrontation with China in the South China Sea, where much of the world's new oil reserves are to be found. (Foster 2017)

ROBERT KAGAN: IS TRUMP A FASCIST?

Historian Robert Kagan (2016) argues that Trump has commonalities with fascist leaders:

His incoherent and contradictory utterances have one thing in common: They provoke and play on feelings of resentment and disdain, intermingled with bits of fear, hatred and anger. His public discourse consists of attacking or ridiculing a wide range of 'others' – Muslims, Hispanics, women, Chinese, Mexicans, Europeans, Arabs, immigrants, refugees – whom he depicts either as threats or as objects of derision. His program, such as it is, consists chiefly of promises to get tough with foreigners and people of nonwhite complexion. He will deport them, bar them, get them to knuckle under, make them pay up or make them shut up. […] [Fascist movements] play on all the fears, vanities, ambitions and insecurities that make up the human psyche. In democracies, at least for politicians, the only thing that matters is what the voters say they want – *vox populi vox Dei*. A mass political movement is thus a powerful and, to those who would oppose it, frightening weapon. When controlled and directed by a single leader, it can be aimed at whomever the leader chooses. […] He might be the highest-ranking elected guardian of the party's most cherished principles. But if he hesitates to support the leader, he faces political death.

NEIL FAULKNER: CREEPING FASCISM

Neil Faulkner (2017) understands fascism as 'the active mobilisation of atomised "human dust" around the right-wing nexus of nationalism, racism, sexism, and authoritarianism' (64). Neoliberal capitalism would have created a 'human dust' of 'individuals acting not on a class basis but as formless social detritus cast adrift by the capitalist crisis' (188). Faulkner argues that Trump, Brexit, Marine Le Pen, Geert Wilders, Norbert Hofer, etc. constitute the 'danger of "creeping fascism"; that the film of the 1930s is running in slow motion; that we have begun a journey, and that if we continue on the same road, our destination could be something akin to Auschwitz' (22). Fascism would today avoid the style of paramilitarism, Blackshirts, storm troopers, and combat boots and rather practice 'cyber-fascism' (122) that uses Facebook, Twitter, fake news, the mainstream media, etc. 'Trump represents a qualitative shift towards far more militant expressions of nationalism, racism, sexism, authoritarianism, and militarism; towards, that is, an explicitly fascist form of politics' (150).

IS THIS FASCISM OR NOT?

Those who say that Trump is not a fascist tend to argue that to speak of fascism there needs to be a terroristic regime that destroys all opposition and constructed enemies and implements a totalitarian form of capitalism. In contrast, those who disagree with this position tend to stress that fascism changes historically. Gáspár Miklós Tamás (2000) speaks in this context of post-fascism. Post-fascism would be a 'cluster of policies, practices, routines, and ideologies' that takes on non-classical forms, but shares with all fascisms the 'hostility to universal citizenship' so that a differentiation is made between nation/enemies and citizens/ non-citizens. 'Post-fascism does not need stormtroopers and dictators. [...] Cutting the civic and human community in two: this is fascism'. Post-fascism argues for installing the constructed enemies' 'suspension of [...] civic and human rights'. Tamás uses Ernst Fraenkel's (1941) concept of the dual state that consist of the normative state that guarantees rights for regular citizens and the prerogative state that neglects, marginalises, discriminates and represses the constructed non-citizens and enemies.

The discussion shows that there are differing opinions on the questions of what fascism means today, whether it exists and whether we are on the way towards it or not. The two positions outlined above may appear to be mutually exclusive. However, classical concepts of fascism and concepts such as post-fascism (Tamás 2000), creeping fascism (Faulkner 2017, Gross 1980) and friendly fascism (Gross 1980) share the stress of certain core elements that Neumann (1936a, 1944/2009, 1957, 1957/2017) saw as characteristic for any form of right-wing authoritarianism: nationalism, the friend/enemy scheme, a leadership ideology and repression of constructed enemies. The disagreement is on whether one should speak of fascism only if terroristic methods are used or not. The concept of right-wing authoritarianism is the common core of both positions. The fact that there are individual, group, institutional and societal dimensions to right-wing authoritarianism and fascism makes the matter even more complex. So if we agree with the position that a fully developed fascist system is, as Neumann also argues, one that uses terrorist methods for installing capitalism and racist imperialism, then this does not exclude the assumption that elements of fascism can and do also exist without a fully developed fascist system. We therefore need to discern between elements of right-wing authoritarianism whose existence can be observed or not, as well as different levels of organisation. The analysis must therefore proceed by critically studying both elements and levels of right-wing authoritarianism. The decisive criteria for judging the extent to which capitalism turns into authoritarian or fascist capitalism are whether one can observe the decline of the rule of law, the concentration of power and the limitation of political opposition in order to enforce policies that support the capitalist class, the leadership principle and leadership ideology, and nationalism combined with the friend/enemy scheme.

Naomi Klein (2017) argues that crises such as '[e]conomic shocks', 'security shocks', 'weather shocks', 'industrial shocks' and – we can add – truth shocks often result in exceptional situations that are seized in order to push through extraordinary political measures and to 'declare some sort of state of exception or emergency, where the usual rules no longer apply' (6). In a society that is in turmoil and crisis, such measures can easily advance authoritarian capitalism. Klein argues that Trump's politics counts on the generation of 'wave after wave of crises and shocks' (Klein 2017, 6). She says that the political shock caused by 9/11 put progressive social movements and NGOs on the defensive, which 'left a vacuum for Trump and far-right parties' to step into (111–12).

CHARLOTTESVILLE: TRUMP AND AMERICAN FASCISM

In August 2017, right-wing extremists gathered in Charlottesville, Virginia, for the Unite the Right rally. There were anti-fascist counter-demonstrations. James Alex Fields Jr., in a terrorist attack on counter-demonstrators, drove a car into a crowd of anti-fascists and killed one activist, the thirty-two-year-old anti-fascist Heather Heyer, and injured 19 more people.

In a press conference, Donald Trump said that 'we condemn in the strongest possible terms this egregious display of hatred, bigotry, and violence on many sides. [...] No child should ever be afraid to go outside and play or be with their parents and have a good time'. He tweeted: 'We ALL must be united & condemn all that hate stands for. There is no place for this kind of violence in America. Lets come together as one! We must remember this truth: No matter our color, creed, religion or political party, we are ALL AMERICANS FIRST. Condolences to the family of the young woman killed today, and best regards to all of those injured, in Charlottesville, Virginia. So sad!' (Twitter, @RealDonaldTrump, 12 August 2017).

Trump uses two generalisations here: he argues that violence was committed on 'all sides', and that there are no grounds for it because those involved are 'all Americans'. Many observers criticised him for not condemning the attacks as fascist terrorism and for not directly addressing and condemning the white supremacists. Trump uses a generalising synecdoche (Reisigl and Wodak 2001, 57): fascists exerted political terror against citizens, but he says that there was violence on 'all sides'. Trump is indeed one of the first to condemn Islamist terrorism around the world whenever it happens and to call it by this name. For example: 'The threat from radical Islamic terrorism is very real, just look at what is happening in Europe and the Middle-East. Courts must act fast!' (Twitter, @RealDonaldTrump, 6 February 2017).

In contrast to Trump, Bernie Sanders tweeted on the day of the attack: 'The white nationalist demonstration in #Charlottesville is a reprehensible display of racism and hatred. This has no place in our society' (Twitter, @BernieSanders, 12 August 2017). In respect to Trump, Sanders criticised: 'No, Mr. President. This is a provocative effort by Neo-Nazis to foment racism and hatred and create violence. Call it out for what it is' (Twitter, @SenSanders, 12 August 2017).

Two days after the terrorist attack, and following lots of criticism, on 14 August Trump made a further statement on the attack, in which he said: 'Racism is evil – and those who cause violence in its name are criminals and thugs, including KKK, Neo-Nazis, White Supremacists, and other hate groups are repugnant to everything we hold dear as Americans.' Trump started the statement by talking about trade deals, jobs and the economy, which resulted in criticism that he should have put the issue of fascist terrorism first. That this public statement was influenced by media and public pressure became evident from the fact that Trump tweeted a couple of hours later: 'Made additional remarks on Charlottesville and realize once again that the #Fake News Media will never be satisfied ... truly bad people!' (Twitter, @RealDonaldTrump, 14 August 2017). Breitbart commented approvingly on Trump's tweet by saying: 'President Donald Trump defied the media for continuing to hammer him for failing to immediately condemn alt-right protesters in Charlottesville, asserting that both sides were to blame for the violence' (Spiering 2017).

In a press conference on 16 August, Trump answered questions by reporters and said: 'Excuse me, what about the alt-left that came charging at, as you say the alt-right? Do they have any semblance of guilt?' 'You had a group on one side that was bad and you had a group on the other side that was also very violent [...] You had a group on the other side that came charging in, without a permit, and they were very, very violent'. 'Not all of those people were neo-Nazis. Not all of those people were white supremacists. [...] Those people were also there to protest the taking down of the statue of Robert E. Lee. [...] So this week it's Robert E. Lee. I noticed that Stonewall Jackson is coming down. I wonder, is it George Washington next week? And is it Thomas Jefferson the week after? You know, you really do have to ask yourself, where does it stop?' 'You had a group on one side and you had a group on the other and they came at each other with clubs. And it was vicious and it was horrible. [...] But there is another side. There was a group on this side, you can call them the Left, you've just called them the Left, that came violently attacking the other group. [...] There is blame on both sides.'[35]

---

35.   www.washingtonpost.com/news/the-fix/wp/2017/08/15/trumps-off-the-rails-news-conference-on-charlottesville-the-alt-left-and-infrastructure-annotated/?utm_term=.ob1d73fd1d3a, www.whitehouse.gov/featured-videos/video/2017/08/15/president-trump-gives-statement-infrastructure-discussion, accessed on 16 August 2017.

Many observers argued that Trump characterised counter-demonstrators, who protested against racism and fascism, as similarly violent as those among whom there was a fascist terrorist who killed an anti-fascist. The former Ku Klux Klan leader David Duke commented on Trump's remarks: 'Thank you President Trump for your honesty & courage to tell the truth about #Charlottesville & condemn the leftist terrorists in BLM/Antifa' (Twitter, @DrDavidDuke, 16 August 2017).

When, eight days after the Charlottesville attack, Islamist terrorists conducted a car attack in Barcelona that killed 13 people, Donald Trump rapidly took to Twitter, where he said: 'The United States condemns the terror attack in Barcelona, Spain, and will do whatever is necessary to help. Be tough & strong, we love you! Study what General Pershing of the United States did to terrorists when caught. There was no more Radical Islamic Terror for 35 years!' (Twitter, @RealDonaldTrump, 17 August 2017).

Observers remarked that in the case of Nazi-terrorism it took Trump days to issue a half-hearted and relativistic condemnation, while in the case of Islamic terrorism he responded much quicker and more directly. Users for example commented on Twitter: 'When did you get the FACTS on events in Barcelona? How come it took 48 hours to get FACTS in the USA & you got them in 2 minutes from Spain?', 'You have YET to call the attack in Charlottesville that killed #HeatherHeyer a terror attack though it clearly was. Why is that? (We know.) Which was immediately contradicted when you RT'd a notorious Nazi and then completely undermined when you said there were "peaceful" Nazis. This attack happened two hours ago. It took you two days to read a speech supposedly condemning the violence in Charlottesville.'

Later in August, Stephen Bannon left his position as White House chief strategist and rejoined Breitbart as executive chairman. Trump thanked Bannon publicly on Twitter and wrote: 'Steve Bannon will be a tough and smart new voice at @BreitbartNews ... maybe even better than ever before. Fake News needs the competition!' The tweet is an indication that Bannon left because of the bad political aesthetic he gives to Trump after the Charlottesville terror, but that they will remain right-wing comrades in arms and that Breitbart under Bannon will continue to give huge support to Trump.

Law-and-Order Politics

Trump stands for law-and-order politics:

> And we need law and order. If we don't have it, we're not going to have a country. [...] We have to bring back law and order. Now, whether or not in a place like Chicago you do stop and frisk, which worked very well [...] We have gangs roaming the street. And in many cases, they're illegally here, illegal immigrants. And they have guns. And they shoot people. And we have to be very strong. And we have to be very vigilant. (Clinton and Trump 2016a)

Opponents

ROSIE O'DONNELL

In 2006, Donald Trump said about comedian Rosie O'Donnell, who had criticised him: 'If you take a look at her, she's a slob. How does she even get on television? If I were running *The View*, I'd fire Rosie. I'd look her right in that fat, ugly face of hers and say, "Rosie, you're fired"' (Oppenheim 2016). Other comments he made about her include the following: 'She came to my wedding. She ate like a pig. And – I mean, seriously, the wedding cake was – was – it was like missing in action. I couldn't stand there' (Zaru 2016). 'She is an unattractive person both inside and out' (Trump and Zanker 2007, 187–8). 'I think I can cure her depression. If she'd stop looking in the mirror I think she'd stop being so depressed' (189). 'I hit that horrible woman right smack in the middle of the eyes' (190). In the 2016 presidential election, Trump defended these comments: '[S]omebody who's been very vicious to me, Rosie O'Donnell, I said very tough things to her, and I think everybody would agree that she deserves it and nobody feels sorry for her' (Clinton and Trump 2016a).

In his book *Think Big: Make It Happen in Business and Life*, Trump writes: 'When somebody screws you, screw them back in spades. [...] When someone attacks you publicly, always strike back. [...] Go for the jugular so that people watching will not want to mess with you' (Trump and Zanker 2007, 199).

Democratic politics involves opposition. Opposition not just means disagreement, but also public disagreement, in which nice words are not the only ones used. If, however, the logic of retaliation is used in politics by someone coming to power, and if somebody in this position hits back in spades and goes for the opponents' jugulars, then actual dangers for democracy can arise.

Donald Trump repeatedly made highly problematic comments about women and others. In a leaked videotape recorded in 2005, he says: 'You know I'm automatically attracted to beautiful – I just start kissing them. It's like a magnet. Just kiss. I don't even wait. And when you're a star they let you do it. You can do anything. Grab them by the pussy. You can do anything.'[36] Information about other alleged problematic comments and behaviour has also been published (see e.g. Kranish and Fisher 2016, 55–7, 63–9, 88–91, 109, 150, 163–5, 167, 217, 257–8, 278–9).

It seems that Trump cannot deal with or take any criticism, he takes any critique and opposition personally, is easily provoked, has to go on the offensive whenever challenged, and in numerous instances shows reactions that are hot-headed, sexist or a form of symbolic violence. The most fundamental question in this context is what might happen in world politics if a powerful person with such an authoritarian personality feels provoked by other international politicians in emergency situations, and what reactions might follow?

HILLARY CLINTON

Donald Trump has at different times expressed various opinions on the question of whether he wants to have a special prosecutor who looks into Hillary Clinton's email affair. The danger is that the appointment of such a special prosecutor could very well be interpreted as a form of political revanchism directed against a political opponent.

In the second television debate with Clinton, Trump said:

> If I win, I am going to instruct my attorney general to get a special prosecutor to look into your situation, because there has never been so many lies, so much deception. There has never been anything like it, and we're going to have a special prosecutor. [...] The people of this country are furious. [...] There has never been anything like this where e-mails ... And you get a subpoena. You get a subpoena, and

---

36. www.youtube.com/watch?v=C-Rr7CO59HY, accessed on 17 February 2017.

after getting the subpoena, you delete 33,000 e-mails. And then you acid wash them or bleach them, as you would say. [...]

Clinton: It is just awfully good that someone with the temperament of Donald Trump is not in charge of the law in our country.

Trump: Because you'd be in jail! (Clinton and Trump 2016b)

After the election, Trump came back to this issue in an interview with the *New York Times*:

Trump: I want to move forward, I don't want to move back. And I don't want to hurt the Clintons. I really don't. She went through a lot. And suffered greatly in many different ways. And I am not looking to hurt them at all. The campaign was vicious. They say it was the most vicious primary and the most vicious campaign. [...]

Deputy Managing Editor: So you're definitely taking that off the table? The investigation? [...]

Trump: No, no, but it's just not something that I feel very strongly about. (Trump 2016e)

TRUMP'S SCOTTISH GOLF COURSE IN BALMEDIE

In 2006, Donald Trump bought land in Balmedie, a village near Aberdeen in Scotland, in order to build a golf course and a hotel. This Trump estate is described in the following words on its website:

This opulent five-star property provides exquisite superior and deluxe guestrooms, intimate bar and dining facilities [...] MacLeod House & Lodge offers luxury and comfort in a secluded and dramatic location. [...] MacLeod House & Lodge is ideally situated for visitors, business travellers and golfers. [...] The golf course follows a classic pattern of two out-and-back loops of nine holes. All 18 holes thread their way engagingly through the dunes, rising here to find views of the sea and the coastline, plunging there into secluded valleys, offering a sequence of superlative topographies, landscapes, alternating between spaciousness and enclosure, then panoramic view, and the whole time a rich texture of vegetation and wildlife habitats surrounding the golf holes.[37]

37. www.trumpgolfscotland.com/Default.aspx?p=dynamicmodule&pageid=100012&ssid=100034&vnf=1, accessed on 30 November 2016.

Anthony Baxter's (2011) documentary *You've Been Trumped* paints a less idyllic picture and shows the conflicts between Trump and Balmedie's residents. Some locals, including the farmer Michael Forbes, refused to sell their land to Trump. Donald Trump, in an interview shown in the movie, said about Forbes: 'His property is terribly maintained. It's slum-like. It's disgusting. [...] He lives like a pig' (Baxter 2011). The documentary shows how the residents, who stayed, faced problems with their new neighbour. A public statement by Trump says that Forbes

> has always been dirty, sloppy and unkempt in his personal appearance and demeanor. He is a loser who is seriously damaging the image of both Aberdeenshire and his great country. [...] His property is a disgusting blight on the community and an environmental hazard, with leaking oil containers, rusted shacks and abandoned vehicles dumped everywhere. It is a very poor image and representation for the world to see of Scotland. (Carrell 2009)

> Trump claimed in 2008 that his planned resort would employ 1,200 people; it currently employs 95, many of whom will be seasonal. [...] Despite the bitter opposition of all Scotland's environment agencies and charities, Scottish government ministers, who were backed by local business and council leaders, decided the scheme was of national importance. In November 2008 they ruled that this allowed Trump to bulldoze through a third of the Foveran dunes complex, a legally protected site of special scientific interest, and breach the council's structural plans, which defined Menie as green belt land. (Carrell 2016)

The example shows how Trump in this case resorted to personal abuse of an economic opponent, who had different interests than the billionaire businessman.

Breitbart

STEPHEN BANNON

Trump appointed Stephen Bannon as chief White House strategist. In the late stage of the presidential election, Bannon was the Trump campaign's chief executive officer. Bannon had worked in the navy, for Goldman Sachs and as producer of right-wing documentaries. In Hong Kong, Bannon was part of Internet Gaming Entertainment, a company that hired so-called 'goldfarmers', low-paid computer gamers who create in-game goods in video games such as World of Warcraft (Green 2017, 81–2). Bannon's advancement of the alt-right and Breitbart was inspired by the culture surrounding online boards such as 4chan, 8chan, Thottbot, reddit, Wowhead, or Allakhazam (83, 145–6). Bannon supplied Trump's campaign with a coherent nationalist worldview, and helped Trump by having worked on damaging Hillary Clinton's reputation over many years (46–7). Bannon's ideology has been strongly influenced by René Guénon. Guénon's writings are anti-modern and believe in the existence of a long dark age that could only be overcome by restoring old traditions (204–8).

Bannon was a founding member and executive chair of Breitbart, a far-right news blog. In late 2016, Breitbart was the 671st most accessed website in the world and the 127th most accessed platform in the USA.[38] Breitbart has received funding from Robert Mercer, the owner of Renaissance Technologies, who also supported Trump's campaign financially and invested in the data company Cambridge Analytica that worked for Trump. It attracts more online readers than, for example, Bloomberg, the *New York Post*, ABC News, Slate, CNBC, *Time Magazine*, Mashable, NYDailyNews, BBC, Reuters, CBS, TheDailyBeast, the *Atlantic*, CBS Local, and the *New Yorker*. Breitbart's US readership increased from 7.4 million in September 2014 to 15.8 million in September 2016 (Booth et al. 2016). In August 2017, Breitbart was the world's 309th most read web platform and the USA's sixty-ninth most read.[39]

Bannon called Occupy activists shown in a movie he made the 'greasiest, dirtiest people you will ever see' (cited in Friedersdorf 2016). Commenting on Black Lives Matter and police shootings of black Americans, Bannon said: 'What if the people getting shot by the cops did things to deserve it? There are, after all, in this world, some people who are naturally aggressive and violent.'[40]

BREITBART ARTICLES

One gets an impression of the world according to Breitbart by having a look at the types of articles it publishes and how it portrays society in

---

38. www.alexa.com/siteinfo/breitbart.com, accessed on 28 November 2016.
39. www.alex.acom/siteinfo/breitbart.com, accessed on 4 August 2017.
40. www.breitbart.com/big-journalism/2016/07/10/sympathy-devils-plot-roger-ailes-america/, accessed on 17 February 2017.

them. An article by David Horowitz called the conservative commentator William Kristol a 'renegade Jew'[41] for being critical of Donald Trump. One article had the title 'Birth Control Makes Women Unattractive and Crazy'.[42] Abortion was compared to the Holocaust:

> Planned Parenthood can attribute a good portion of their boffo baby-killing business to their president since 2006, Cecile Richards. Richards is well on her way to personally matching Hitler's body count. Breitbart has done the grim maths so you don't have to. Using a conservative estimate of 300,000 abortions a year – or 300 kiloscrapes, using the technical metric measure – Cecile Richards has presided over three million abortions, or three megascrapes in her ten years as president of the organisation. This has earned her 'half Holocaust' status. Full Holocaust seems eminently reachable given Planned Parenthood's growing hegemony in the abortion industry.[43]

On black Americans: 'After 50 years of celebrating MLK's [Martin Luther King's] civil rights legacy, black people now commit a catastrophically high amount of crime. [...] So how is it then that there are five times fewer black people than white people in America and, yet, we consistently carry out a larger share of the crimes?'[44]

On white Americans:

> Anti-White Racism: The Hate That Dares Not Speak Its Name [...] A principal source of the war on white people generally and law enforcement in particular is our leftwing university and literary culture, which for forty years has taught college students that it is politically correct to hate white people; which fosters a hatred of America so virulent, that it has inspired millennials to flock to a lifelong supporter of communist causes like Bernie Sanders and to avert its own gaze from this impertinent fact: the largest, most oppressive and most

---

41.   www.breitbart.com/2016-presidential-race/2016/05/15/bill-kristol-republican-spoiler-renegade-jew/, accessed on 17 February 2017.

42.   www.breitbart.com/tech/2015/12/08/birth-control-makes-women-unattractive-and-crazy/, accessed on 17 February 2017.

43.   www.breitbart.com/big-government/2015/08/22/godwins-law-planned-parenthoods-body-count-is-up-to-half-a-holocaust/, accessed on 17 February 2017.

44.   www.breitbart.com/big-hollywood/2016/01/21/10-things-black-people-should-worry-about-that-arent-oscar-so-white/, accessed on 17 February 2017.

violent inner cities in America are 100% controlled by the Democratic Party – the party of slavery and segregation – and have been for fifty to a hundred years.[45]

On illegal immigrants:

If you think data about illegal alien crime is hidden from public, just try to find information on the contagious diseases brought across our borders by illegal aliens from nearly 100 countries. If we survey the anecdotal and sporadic official data of the past fifteen years, there is no doubt we are being invaded daily by dangerous diseases. There is good reason to believe the government is minimizing this risk as part of its disinformation campaign to sanitize illegal immigration and to portray all critics as 'anti-immigrant.' Although the U.S. Border Patrol publishes frequent reports on the number of individuals apprehended crossing the border, no agency publishes reports on the diseases they bring with them and then carry into our communities. […] What should scare us most is not what we know about the health of 700,000 illegal aliens arriving each year *but what we do not know*. When the Obama administration goes to great lengths to hide the truth about so many of its activities, there is no reason to trust what they are telling us about the health profiles of hundreds of thousands of illegal aliens released into the American heartland. […] If an illegal alien from Brazil or Vietnam can carry an infectious disease across the border by accident, what kind of diseases can be carried and spread by Islamic jihadis who are on a suicide mission? […] The public health ramifications of our scandalous open borders are possibly even more dangerous and far-reaching than the economic and political consequences.[46]

Such articles give an impression of the ideology and conspiracies that Breitbart advances, in which white America is under attack by illegal immigrants, Muslims, liberals, leftists, feminists, etc. Breitbart supports Donald Trump, who promised in his election campaign to 'make

45. www.breitbart.com/big-journalism/2016/04/26/anti-white-racism-hate-dares-not-speak-name-2/, accessed on 17 February 2017.
46. www.breitbart.com/big-government/2015/12/25/why-are-many-diseases-back-decades-after-being-wiped-out-in-the-u-s/, accessed on 17 February 2017.

America great again'. Trump responded to the criticisms of Bannon and Breitbart by stating that:

> I've known Steve Bannon a long time. If I thought he was a racist, or alt-right, or any of the things that we can, you know, the terms we can use, I wouldn't even think about hiring him. [...] Breitbart cover things, I mean like The New York Times covers things. [...] Breitbart, first of all, is just a publication. [...] Now, they are certainly a much more conservative paper, to put it mildly, than The New York Times. But Breitbart really is a news organization that's become quite successful. (Trump 2016e)

HAMILTON

Mike Pence, Trump's vice president, visited the Broadway musical *Hamilton* on 18 November 2016, ten days after Trump had been elected. Brandon Victor Dixon, one of the actors, addressed Pence on behalf of the crew, saying:

> Vice President-elect Pence, we welcome you and we truly thank you for joining us here at Hamilton. We, sir, we are the diverse America who are alarmed and anxious that your new administration will not protect us, our planet, our children, our parents, or defend us and uphold our inalienable rights, sir. What we truly hope is that this show has inspired you to uphold our American values and to work on behalf of all of us.[47]

Obviously, this message was an expression of concerns that Donald Trump's administration could limit diversity and impose discriminatory policies. Donald Trump reacted to it in a tweet: 'The Theater must always be a safe and special place. The case of Hamilton was very rude last night to a very good man, Mike Pence. Apologize!' (Twitter, @ RealDonaldTrump, 19 November 2016, 5.56 am)

Trump does not seem to see any problems with Breitbart, a publication that expresses highly intolerant views, but denunciates the Hamilton crew's call for tolerance in a message posted to his (at the time) 16

---

47. www.thestar.com/entertainment/2016/11/19/mike-pence-sees-hamilton-gets-sharp-personalized-speech-from-cast.html, accessed on 29 November 2016.

million followers on Twitter. Trump shows tolerance towards intolerant, right-wing extremist supporters and intolerance towards critics who call for a tolerant society.

Immigration

TRUMP TOWER

In 1979, Donald Trump bought the department store Bonwit Teller located at 6th Avenue and 56th Street in New York. He demolished the building in order to build Trump Tower. Libby Handros (1991) argues in her documentary film *Trump: What's the Deal?* that for the demolition William Kaszycki's company hired more than 200 Polish immigrants 'with no working papers, who were paid one third the union rate and worked under difficult conditions' (Handros 1991, 31.41–31.47). One worker says in the documentary, 'all the wires, lots of construction, it was covered with asbestos' (32.29–32.39). Kranish and Fisher (2006, 88), in their book *Trump Revealed*, argue about the working conditions at the demolition site: 'The men toiled through spring and summer of 1980 with sledgehammers and blowtorches, but without hard hats, working twelve- to eighteen-hour days, seven days a week, often sleeping on Bonwit Teller's floors. They were paid less than $5 an hour, sometimes in vodka. Many went unpaid and were threatened with deportation if they complained.' In 1983, Harry Diduck filed a lawsuit against Donald Trump, arguing that workers were cheated in pension and welfare fund contributions not paid for the wages of the Polish workers (Justia 1991). There was a collective bargaining agreement between Kaszycki & Sons and the House Wreckers Union Local 95. The case carried on until 1999 when a sealed settlement was reached (Robbins 1999).

TRUMP ON IMMIGRATION

This case provides indications that seem to suggest that illegal immigrants worked under horrible conditions at the Trump Tower construction site. Trump's campaign made immigration a key issue and blamed immigrants for destroying American jobs and lowering wages: 'Donald J. Trump's Vision: – Prioritize the jobs, wages and security of the American people. – Establish new immigration controls to boost wages and to ensure that open jobs are offered to American workers first. [...] Donald J. Trump's

10 Point Plan to Put America First: 1. Begin working on an impenetrable physical wall on the southern border, on day one. Mexico will pay for the wall'.[48] 'The first thing we need to do is secure our southern border – and we need to do it now. We have to stop that flood, and the best way to do that is to build a wall. [...] Nobody can build a wall like me. I will build a great wall on our southern border' (Trump 2015a, 23–4).

In a speech on immigration, Trump said:

When politicians talk about immigration reform, they usually mean the following: amnesty, open borders, and lower wages. [...] [w]e have to listen to the concerns that working people have over the record pace of immigration and its impact on their jobs, wages, housing, schools, tax bills, and living conditions. These are valid concerns, expressed by decent and patriotic citizens from all backgrounds. [...] [t]here is the case of 90-year-old Earl Olander, who was brutally beaten and left to bleed to death in his home. The perpetrators were illegal immigrants with criminal records who did not meet the Obama Administration's priorities for removal. [...] [t]here is only one core issue in the immigration debate and it is this: the well-being of the American people. [...] [t]here are at least 2 million criminal aliens now inside the country. We will begin moving them out day one, in joint operations with local, state and federal law enforcement. Beyond the 2 million, there are a vast number of additional criminal illegal immigrants who have fled or evaded justice. But their days on the run will soon be over. They go out, and they go out fast. [...] Let's secure our border. [...] Together, we can save American lives, American jobs, and American futures. Together, we can save America itself. Join me in this mission to Make America Great Again. (Trump 2016a)

In this speech, Trump doesn't once mention and criticise how American capitalists exploit foreign workers, whom they pay extremely low wages in order to maximise profits. Instead he argues that illegal immigrants are criminal and have negative impacts on jobs, wages, housing, schools, etc. Observers of both illegal workers on Trump's construction site and his election campaign could argue that his position is hypocritical. Trump, in his speech, does not condemn companies' illegal exploitation of immigrants, a strategy they use for wage dumping in general, but

---

48.   www.donaldjtrump.com/policies/immigration, accessed on 17 February 2017.

rather blames immigrants themselves for social dumping, which deflects attention from the real structural causes of social problems.

MEXICANS AS TRUMP'S SCAPEGOATS

Trump announced in his election campaign that he wants to 'begin working on an impenetrable physical wall on the southern border [between the USA and Mexico], on day one. Mexico will pay for the wall'.[49] Repeatedly he argued that such a wall is needed to stop crime: 'Now, I want to build the wall. We need the wall. And the Border Patrol, ICE, they all want the wall. We stop the drugs. We shore up the border' (Clinton and Trump 2016c). '[W]e are letting people into this country that are going to cause problems and crime like you've never seen. We're also letting drugs pour through our southern border at a record clip. At a record clip. And it shouldn't be allowed to happen. [...] She wants amnesty for everybody. Come right in. Come right over. It's a horrible thing she's doing' (Clinton and Trump 2016b). 'When Mexico sends its people, they are not sending their best. [...] They are bringing drugs, they are bringing crime, they are rapists. And some, I assume, are good people.' 'It's not only Mexico [...]. They're coming from all over. [...] So we have this open border [...] And it's not just Mexicans. [...] And certainly we do have killers and plenty of other problems coming over. We take them because other countries don't want them. We are like a dumping ground.'[50]

Such statements associate migration with crimes, drugs, rape and killings. The point is that in such speeches and discussions there is hardly any mention of immigrants from Mexico and Latin America in general, who as everyday people live in the United States and work hard, pay taxes and contribute to community life and civil society. By focusing on the exception from the rule, the impression is created that the exception is the norm. A study on immigrants and crime conducted by the American Immigration Council (2015) concluded:

According to an original analysis of data from the 2010 American Community Survey (ACS) conducted by the authors of this report, roughly 1.6 percent of immigrant males age 18–39 are incarcerated, compared to 3.3 percent of the native-born. This disparity in incar-

---

49. www.donaldjtrump.com/policies/immigration/, accessed on 17 February 2017.
50. edition.cnn.com/videos/tv/2015/06/25/exp-presidential-candidate-donald-trump-immigration-intv-erin.cnn, accessed on 17 February 2017.

ceration rates has existed for decades, as evidenced by data from the 1980, 1990, and 2000 decennial censuses. [...] The 2010 Census data reveals that incarceration rates among the young, less-educated Mexican, Salvadoran, and Guatemalan men who make up the bulk of the unauthorized population are significantly lower than the incarceration rate among native-born young men without a high-school diploma. In 2010, less-educated native-born men age 18–39 had an incarceration rate of 10.7 percent – more than triple the 2.8 percent rate among foreign-born Mexican men, and five times greater than the 1.7 percent rate among foreign-born Salvadoran and Guatemalan men. (American Immigration Council 2015, 1–2)

Generalising logic could also be found in a 2015 statement of the Trump campaign that said that 'Donald J. Trump is calling for a total and complete shutdown of Muslims entering the United States until our country's representatives can figure out what is going on. According to Pew Research, among others, there is great hatred towards Americans by large segments of the Muslim population' (Trump 2015b).

Donald Trump has blamed immigrants for social problems, played with the fire of nationalism, made ambivalent announcements about investigating Hillary Clinton and foreign workers were highly exploited in at least one of his construction projects; he has resorted to personal abuse, and seems to have no problem with Breitbart's intolerance, while condemning concerned citizens expressing fears about the increase of intolerance. Such circumstances indicate an authoritarian tendency. One will have to wait and see if, and if so how and to which extent, this approach translates into authoritarian statism.

INTERNATIONAL RELATIONS UNDER TRUMP

International trade policies and foreign politics are two key aspects of international relations. We shall look at each in turn.

International Relations 1: International Trade Policies

THE NORTH AMERICAN FREE TRADE AGREEMENT

The first dimension of international relations is that Trump promised, with respect to trade policies, to renegotiate or withdraw from free trade agreements such as the North American Free Trade Agreement (NAFTA) and the Trans-Pacific Partnership (TPP).

Trump announced that 'NAFTA will be renegotiated to get a better deal for American workers'[51] and that he will '[w]ithdraw from the Trans-Pacific Partnership, which has not yet been ratified'.[52] His election programme argued that Trump will '[t]ell NAFTA partners that we intend to immediately renegotiate the terms of that agreement to get a better deal for our workers. If they don't agree to a renegotiation, we will submit notice that the U.S. intends to withdraw from the deal. [We will] Eliminate Mexico's one-side backdoor tariff through the VAT and end sweatshops in Mexico that undercut U.S. workers'.[53]

Trump is sceptical of free trade agreements because he argues that they result in the undercutting of wages and the destruction of US manufacturing jobs: 'America has lost nearly one-third of its manufacturing jobs since NAFTA and 50,000 factories since China joined the World Trade Organization'.[54] 'So my plan – we're going to renegotiate trade deals. We're going to have a lot of free trade. We're going to have free trade, more free trade than we have right now. But we have horrible deals. Our jobs are being taken out by the deal that her husband signed, NAFTA, one of the worst deals ever. Our jobs are being sucked out of our economy. [...] Our jobs have fled to Mexico and other places' (Clinton and Trump 2016c). 'Look, our country is stagnant. We've lost our jobs. We've lost our businesses. We're not making things anymore, relatively speaking. Our product is pouring in from China, pouring in from Vietnam, pouring in from all over the world. [...] I've visited so many communities' (Clinton and Trump 2016c).

> The NAFTA agreement is defective. [...] And what you do is you say, fine, you want to go to Mexico or some other country, good luck. We wish you a lot of luck. But if you think you're going to make your air conditioners or your cars or your cookies or whatever you make and bring them into our country without a tax, you're wrong. And once you say you're going to have to tax them coming in, and our politi-

---

51.   www.donaldjtrump.com/press-releases/fact-sheet-donald-j.-trumps-pro-growth-economic-policy-will-create-25-milli, accessed on 17 February 2017.

52.   www.donaldjtrump.com/policies/trade/, accessed on 17 February 2017.

53.   www.donaldjtrump.com/policies/trade/, accessed on 17 February 2017.

54.   www.donaldjtrump.com/policies/trade/, accessed on 17 February 2017.

cians never do this, because they have special interests and the special interests want those companies to leave, because in many cases, they own the companies. (Clinton and Trump 2016a)

Taken together, Trump makes two arguments in respect to free trade agreements:

1. As a result of free trade agreements, cheap commodities are flooding the US market.
2. As a result of free trade agreements, US manufacturing jobs are leaving the USA and are being conducted for lower wages in other countries. The solution would be tariffs and the renegotiation of trade agreements that does not eliminate free trade, but transforms it.

Trump (2016l) sees NAFTA as a 'one-way street', which creates the impression that other countries and people living there have only benefited and the USA has only had disadvantages from NAFTA. NAFTA came into effect on 1 January 1994, and subsequently eliminated constraints on cross-border capital investments in and trade between Canada, Mexico and the United States. On 2 January 1994, the Zapatista uprising started in Chiapas, Mexico's poorest region. It was explicitly directed against NAFTA. In 1991, Mexico's President Salinas abolished the system of land tenure to qualify for NAFTA participation. In 1992, 'he removed existing restrictions on the size of the large estates and abolished the Ejido Law in order to clear the way for privatization of the land and thus allow national and foreign agribusiness to grow cash crops for export, violating the inalienability of *ejido* lands in Article 27 of the Mexican Constitution of 1917' (Marcos 2002, 429). The Zapatista rebels assessed 'that NAFTA will not bring them benefits, but "a death sentence"' (Marcos 2002, xxv).

MEXICO AND NAFTA

Mexico's socio-economic situation has not really improved through NAFTA: in the period from 1994 to 2013, Mexico's GDP increased on average by only by 0.9 per cent per year. Mexico's poverty rate in 2012 was 52.3 per cent but 52.4 per cent in 1994, so the country stayed extremely poor during NAFTA's first 20 years, and in addition real wages stagnated (Weisbrot, Lefebvre and Sammut 2014).

NAFTA removed tariffs (but not subsidies) on agricultural goods, with a transition period in which there was a steadily increasing import quota for certain commodities. The transition period was longest for corn, the most important crop for Mexican producers, only ending in 2008. Not surprisingly, U.S. production, which is not only subsidized but had higher average productivity levels than that of Mexico, displaced millions of Mexican farmers. (Weisbrot, Lefebvre and Sammut 2014, 13)

In the years 1991–2007, Mexico lost more than two million jobs in agriculture and forestry, a drop of 19 per cent (13).

The number of Mexican Maquiladora factories has been notably expanding since NAFTA came into effect. Maquiladoras exist as part of Special Economic Zones, especially in northern Mexican border cities such as Ciudad Juárez, Heroica Nogales, Matamoros, Mexicali and Tijuana. They make use of NAFTA for importing materials tariff- and duty-free, are known for low wages and harsh working conditions, and export the end products back to the countries of the resources' origins. Important industries involved in maquiladoras are those that produce machinery, chemicals, automotive parts, furniture, electronics, textiles, packaging, plastics, metal, medical devices and call centre services (Dorocki and Brzegowy 2014, figures 3 and 4). 'The mission of the maquiladoras' is 'lowering labor costs by importing and processing raw materials to be exported as finished products back to the country of origin – normally to the United States' (94). In the period from 1994 until 2006, US companies accounted for 88.4 per cent of all capital investments in Mexican maquiladoras (table 1). In 2012, there were more than 5,000 maquiladoras with a total of more than 2 million employees (table 2). Piece wages are common in maquiladoras, and maquiladora workers tend to be paid a fraction of their US equivalents and work long hours in difficult working conditions.

The 2017 Californian minimum wage is US$10.50 per hour for companies that employ more than 25 employees and US$10 for smaller companies.[55] The 2017 Mexican daily minimum wage is 80.04 pesos[56]

---

55. www.govdocs.com/california-15-statewide-minimum-wage/, accessed on 17 February 2017.
56. zetatijuana.com/2016/12/01/la-consami-sube-7-36-pesos-al-salario-minimo-a-partir-del-2017/, accessed on 17 February 2017.

(approximately US$3.90). In September 2016, the Mexican average daily wage was 316.57 pesos (around US$15.30).[57] In November 2016, the average daily earnings of employees in the USA were around US$178.[58] This means that the average wage is twelve times higher in the USA than in Mexico. Tijuana is a town located in the Mexican state of Baja California. It is based right on the border with California. In Tijuana, one of the maquiladora industry's centres, manufacturing workers' average monthly salary was in the year 2016 US$304 for unskilled workers and US$368 for highly skilled workers.[59] In California, production workers' average monthly salary was US$2,980.[60] So the average manufacturing wage was ten times lower in Tijuana than in California. The implication is that US companies can use NAFTA for reducing labour costs by a factor of around ten in order to maximise their profits.

The point is that NAFTA helps both US corporations as well as Mexican suppliers to increase their profits, whereas Mexican workers are paid at relatively low levels and US manufacturing workers lose their jobs. The international working class is the overall loser. The problem with Trump's analysis is that he presents NAFTA in a one-sided and nationalist manner as an issue of nations, whereas it is in reality an issue of class. Trump seems only to care about US corporations' profits, whereas the reality is that through NAFTA international capital takes advantage of the working class in Mexico, the USA and Canada.

Robert Scott (2011, 2) argues in an analysis published by the Economic Policy Institute that NAFTA has been the context for the circumstance that 'U.S. trade deficits with Mexico as of 2010 displaced production that could have supported 682,900 U.S. jobs'. The basic reason would have been US capital FDI in Mexico – 22 per cent of these jobs would have been in the manufacturing of computer and electronic parts, and 15.8 per cent in the manufacturing of cars and the production of automotive parts.

When Trump argues that NAFTA destroys US jobs and therefore should be renegotiated or abolished, in a nationalist manner he only sees

57.   www.tradingeconomics.com/mexico/wages, accessed on 17 February 2017.
58.   Calculation based on: www.bls.gov/news.release/empsit.t19.htm, accessed on 17 February 2017.
59.   www.estradayasociados.com.mx/area-information/baja-california/labor-wages, accessed on 17 February 2017.
60.   Data source: Bureau of Labour Statistics, www.bls.gov/oes/current/oes_ca.htm#51-0000, accessed on 4 December 2016.

the US side of the coin, but disregards that NAFTA seems to have also destroyed over two million agricultural jobs in Mexico because of the USA's export of subsidised corn and cheap grain.

CHINA

The same issue arises with respect to China. Trump argues: 'And Apple, and our other major companies, will start making their iPhones, computers and other products inside of the United States – not in China, and all over the world' (Trump 2016l). 'There are people who wish I wouldn't refer to China as our enemy. But that's exactly what they are. They have destroyed entire industries by utilizing low-wage workers, cost us tens of thousands of jobs, spied on our businesses, stolen our technology, and have manipulated and devalued their currency, which makes importing our goods more expensive – and sometimes, impossible' (Trump 2015a, 43). The basic problem is that the international division of labour does not benefit Chinese and American workers, but both Apple that exports capital and Foxconn, in whose Chinese factories Apple tools are assembled under precarious conditions (Fuchs 2017d; Qiu 2016).

For Trump the issue is one of nation and nationalism, not one of capitalism's structural contradictions. He uses the friend/enemy scheme when opposing the Chinese nation to the American nation.

TRUMP'S BUSINESS PRACTICES

Donald Trump criticises China's export of subsidised steel at cheap prices: 'You take a look at what's happening to steel and the cost of steel and China dumping vast amounts of steel all over the United States, which essentially is killing our steelworkers and our steel companies' (Clinton and Trump 2016b). *Newsweek* reports that an investigation it conducted

> has found that in at least two of Trump's last three construction projects, Trump opted to purchase his steel and aluminium from Chinese manufacturers rather than United States corporations based in states like Pennsylvania, Ohio, Michigan and Wisconsin. [...] Of Trump's last three construction projects, the first to use Chinese steel was Trump International Hotel Las Vegas, which opened in 2008. [...] According to government documents, the Chinese entity chosen

by Trump to provide steel for the Las Vegas property is a holding company called Ossen Innovation Co. Ltd. – formerly known as Ultra Glory International Ltd. [...] Another recent Trump building that has used metal from China is Trump International Hotel and Tower in Chicago, which opened in 2009. [...] Because American businesses have been turning to cheaper aluminium from overseas, the industry is collapsing. For example, in just the last two years, more than half of the country's aluminium smelters in states like Ohio, West Virginia and Texas have closed as a result of being undercut on price by competition from overseas. (Eichenwald 2016)

So it looks like although Trump criticises capitalists making use of structural advantages for increasing their profits at the expense of US workers, according to these reports his own company made use of such mechanisms, which questions how credible and authentic his political commitments are.

How does Trump respond to this type of criticism?

The same thing is true with having my products made in China or Mexico or other countries. Some have attacked me for urging that we complain about these countries at the same time I'm having goods manufactured there. My response: I'm a realist. I'm a competitor. When I am working on a business deal, I make the best deal. But we should be changing the business climate so that manufacturers can get the best deal right here in the US. Right now it doesn't work that way. We need legislation that gives American companies the tax priorities and financial support to create more of their technology and to redirect more of their manufacturing here at home. (Trump 2015a, 86)

Trump's answer is to create investment conditions for capital in the USA that keep capital there and attract new capital. Given the contradictory nature of capitalism, a good business climate also tends to mean, as the example of China shows, low wages in order to increase profits. When Trump talks about his vision of making the American economy great again, increasing minimum wages, guaranteeing everyone earns a living wage, and the importance of trade unions are missing (see Trump 2015a).

International Relations 2: Foreign Politics

Foreign politics constitutes the second element of international relations. Donald Trump announced that other NATO members would have to contribute more to the alliance's budget if they wanted to count on the USA's support. He planned a trade war with China, cooperation with Russia and Syria, a military offensive against ISIS and a tough stance on the Iran nuclear deal. He aims to:

- End the current strategy of nation-building and regime change. [...]
- Pursue aggressive joint and coalition military operations to crush and destroy ISIS, international cooperation to cutoff their funding, expand intelligence sharing, and cyberwarfare to disrupt and disable their propaganda and recruiting. [...]
- Suspend, on a temporary basis, immigration from some of the most dangerous and volatile regions of the world that have a history of exporting terrorism.[61]

In respect to NATO, Trump said:

Number one, the 28 countries of NATO, many of them aren't paying their fair share. Number two – and that bothers me, because we should be asking – we're defending them, and they should at least be paying us what they're supposed to be paying by treaty and contract. And, number two, I said, and very strongly, NATO could be obsolete, because [...] they do not focus on terror. [...] we pay approximately 73 percent of the cost of NATO. It's a lot of money to protect other people. But I'm all for NATO. But I said they have to focus on terror, also. (Clinton and Trump 2016a)

We defend Germany. We defend Japan. We defend South Korea. These are powerful and wealthy countries. We get nothing from them. (Trump 2015a, 34)

On ISIS: 'I think we have to get NATO to go into the Middle East with us, in addition to surrounding nations, and we have to knock the hell out of

---

61. www.donaldjtrump.com/policies/foreign-policy-and-defeating-isis/, accessed on 17 February 2017.

ISIS, and we have to do it fast, when ISIS formed in this vacuum created by Barack Obama and Secretary Clinton' (Clinton and Trump 2016a).

On Putin and Russia:

Now we can talk about Putin. I don't know Putin. He said nice things about me. If we got along well, that would be good. If Russia and the United States got along well and went after ISIS, that would be good. He has no respect for her [Hillary Clinton]. He has no respect for our president. And I'll tell you what: We're in very serious trouble, because we have a country with tremendous numbers of nuclear warheads – 1,800, by the way – where they expanded and we didn't, 1,800 nuclear warheads. And she's playing chicken' (Clinton and Trump 2016c).

On Cuba:

Today, the world marks the passing of a brutal dictator who oppressed his own people for nearly six decades. [...] Fidel Castro's legacy is one of firing squads, theft, unimaginable suffering, poverty and the denial of fundamental human rights. While Cuba remains a totalitarian island, it is my hope that today marks a move away from the horrors endured for too long, and toward a future in which the wonderful Cuban people finally live in the freedom they so richly deserve. [...] Though the tragedies, deaths and pain caused by Fidel Castro cannot be erased, our administration will do all it can to ensure the Cuban people can finally begin their journey toward prosperity and liberty. I join the many Cuban-Americans who supported me so greatly in the presidential campaign, including the Brigade 2,506 Veterans Association that endorsed me, with the hope of one day soon seeing a free Cuba. (Scott 2016)

'If Cuba is unwilling to make a better deal for the Cuban people, the Cuban/American people and the U.S. as a whole, I will terminate deal'.[62] In June 2017, Trump signed an order that revoked part of the Obama administration's policies on Cuba. Travel by US citizens to and US trade with Cuba thereby became more restricted again.

---

62. twitter.com/realDonaldTrump/status/803237535178772481, accessed on 17 February 2017.

THE FRIEND/ENEMY SCHEME

Trump seems to operate with a clear friend/enemy scheme, in which the enemies must be crushed and one keeps out of alliances that do not tackle these enemies. It might very well be that Trump's foreign politics will not be isolationist, but unilateralist and highly unpredictable so that the future of the world may be at risk. In any case, he argues for massive armament:

> 'Iron Mike' Tyson, the famous fighter, once explained his philosophy, saying, 'Everybody has a plan until they get punched in the mouth.' The first thing we need to do is build up our ability to throw that punch. We need to spend whatever it takes to completely fund our military properly. [...] Everything begins with a strong military. Everything. We will have the strongest military in our history, and our people will be equipped with the best weaponry and protection available. Period. That means the best missile systems, the best cyber-warfare training and equipment, and the best-trained soldiers. (Trump 2015a, 32–3, 47)

Trump describes himself as 'aggressive in military and foreign policy' (Trump 2015a, 98). 'No enemy, and no enemy leader, should misinterpret our resolve to fight to the death – their death' (Trump 2015a, 138). The problem of the complexity of international political relations involves the possibility of nuclear warfare. So fighting a nation to its death may at the same time mean the end of life on Earth.

Trump appointed US Marine General James Mattis as defence secretary. According to news reports, Mattis said: 'Actually, it's a lot of fun to fight. You know, it's a hell of a hoot. [...] It's fun to shoot some people. I'll be right up front with you, I like brawling'; 'You go into Afghanistan, you got guys who slap women around for five years because they didn't wear a veil. [...] You know, guys like that ain't got no manhood left anyway. So it's a hell of a lot of fun to shoot them' (Associated Press 2016).

NUCLEAR ARMS

Trump argues: 'When somebody screws you, screw them back in spades. [...] When someone attacks you publicly, always strike back. [...] Go for the jugular so that people watching will not want to mess with you'

(Trump and Zanker 2007, 199). Given that Trump believes in a world that is full of enemies, what he does in a situation of a highly polarised political conflict could be quite unpredictable. In international politics, it is not always clear what the frontlines are and who the political aggressor is. The Soviet Union felt threatened by the deployment of US nuclear weapons in Italy and Turkey. The USA felt threatened by the deployment of Soviet nuclear weapons in Cuba. Each blamed the other. The problem is that warfare, competition and conflict often result in vicious cycles of aggression, violence and armament. In such situations it is difficult to make out who started the conflict and each side blames the other for it. If a highly polarised international political situation occurred under Donald Trump's presidency and he applied the logic 'When somebody screws you, screw them back in spades. When someone attacks you publicly, always strike back. Go for the jugular so that people watching will not want to mess with you', then a nuclear war might be the result.

On 22 December 2016, Trump tweeted about expanding the USA's nuclear armament: 'The United States must greatly strengthen and expand its nuclear capability until such time as the world comes to its senses regarding nukes' (Twitter, @RealDonaldTrump, 22 December 2016, 8.50 am).

On the same day, Vladimir Putin said Russia needs 'to strengthen the military potential of strategic nuclear forces'.[63] Given Putin and Trump's announcements, a new nuclear arms race seems to be in the making that certainly increases the chances of a nuclear war and planetary destruction. Trump commented: 'Let it be an arms race. We will outmatch them at every pass and outlast them all.'[64] The point is that not armament, but only disarmament will end the threat of such a catastrophe that could easily wipe out humankind.

DONALD TRUMP AND VLADIMIR PUTIN

Trump's relationship with Russia shows how variable and unpredictable his foreign policies are. During his electoral campaign and the first months of his presidency, Trump stressed the necessity of building

---

63. www.itv.com/news/2016-12-22/donald-trump-vladimir-putin-us-russia-nuclear-weapons/, accessed on 17 February 2017.
64. www.cnbc.com/2016/12/23/trump-to-putin-lets-have-a-nuclear-arms-race.html, accessed on 17 February 2017.

friendly relations with Russia and his admiration for Putin. For example, on 7 January 2017, he tweeted:

> Having a good relationship with Russia is a good thing, not a bad thing. Only 'stupid' people, or fools, would think that it is bad! We have enough problems around the world without yet another one. When I am President, Russia will respect us far more than they do now and both countries will, perhaps, work together to solve some of the many great and pressing problems and issues of the WORLD! (Twitter, @RealDonaldTrump, 7 January 2017)

US intelligence reports say that Russian intelligence hacked the Democratic National Committee's server, leaked the obtained information to WikiLeaks and tried to influence the US presidential election in Trump's favour (ODNI 2017). Michael Flynn resigned as Trump's security advisor in February 2017 for having provided incomplete information regarding contacts with Russian officials. In March 2017, FBI Director James Comey, in a House Intelligence Committee hearing on Russian interference in the 2016 Presidential election, confirmed that 'the FBI, as part of our counterintelligence mission, is investigating the Russian government's efforts to interfere in the 2016 presidential election and that includes investigating the nature of any links between individuals associated with the Trump campaign and the Russian government and whether there was any coordination between the campaign and Russia's efforts' (*Washington Post* 2017). In May 2017, Trump dismissed Comey as FBI Director. Comey released his introductory statement to a testimony in the Senate Select Committee on Intelligence in advance. In it he wrote:

> I had understood the President to be requesting that we drop any investigation of Flynn in connection with false statements about his conversations with the Russian ambassador in December. [...] I could be wrong, but I took him to be focusing on what had just happened with Flynn's departure and the controversy around his account of his phone calls. Regardless, it was very concerning, given the FBI's role as an independent investigative agency. (Comey 2017)

Asked if Trump tried to obstruct justice by trying to stop an FBI investigation of Mike Flynn, Comey said a conversation he had with Trump about Flynn, in which Trump allegedly said 'I hope you can see your way clear to letting this go, to letting Flynn go', was a 'very disturbing thing, very concerning'. Comey said that special counsel Robert Mueller would have to look into this issue in order 'to try and understand what the intention was there, and whether that's an offense'. In May 2017, Robert Mueller was appointed as the special counsel investigating possible links between the Trump campaign and the Russian government. Comey also mentioned: 'I believe [...] that I was fired because of the Russia investigation' (Senate Intelligence Committee 2017).

In July 2017, an email exchanged between Donald Trump Jr. and the publicist Rob Goldstone was published, in which the latter offered to arrange a meeting with Russian lawyer Natalia Veselnitskaya, who was said to offer 'some official documents and information that would incriminate Hillary and her dealings with Russia and would be very useful to your father'. Trump Jr. answered: 'Seems we have some time and if it's what you say I love it especially later in the summer.' He agreed to meet the Russian lawyer.

US IMPERIALISM, RUSSIAN IMPERIALISM

The USA and Russia are imperialist powers aiming to secure political-economic influence in the world. That the USA and Russia compete for global power explains why in the USA there is a certain unease about Trump's attitudes towards Russia and Putin. In respect to ISIS, Russia and the USA's interests partly converge because this death cult threatens both countries' geopolitical interests. One can only speculate why Trump has certain sympathies for Putin. Trump may also have an interest in creating a climate that fosters more investments of US capital in Russia. Trump and Putin are two of the most powerful world leaders. They are both white, Christian men, whose attitudes towards power and authority show similarities. Trump may very well see himself in Putin. But such psychological ties and projections are unstable, contradictory and prone to disruption.

After a chemical weapons attack in Syria had killed 80 people, Trump in April 2017 spoke of an 'egregious crime' by Bashar al-Assad and ordered the firing of 59 cruise missiles on a military base of the

Syrian government. Vladimir Putin stressed his support for the Syrian government and argued that the attack might have been staged by Assad's opponents in order to provoke US military intervention. Russia vetoed a UN Security Council resolution put forward by the USA that called for a UN investigation into the attack. After a meeting between Putin and US Foreign Secretary Tillerson, Trump stressed: 'We're not getting along with Russia at all. […] We may be at an all time low' (Borger and Luhn 2017). A statement issued by the Kremlin stressed: 'The President of Russia regards the US airstrikes on Syria as an act of aggression against a sovereign state delivered in violation of international law under a far-fetched pretext. […] This move by Washington [the US airstrike on an air base in Syria] has dealt a serious blow to Russian-US relations, which are already in a poor state.'[65] In June 2017, the US navy shot down a Syrian government warplane after Assad's forces had bombed the Syrian Democratic Forces that include Kurdish and other fighters who are allied with the USA. Russian Deputy Foreign Minister Sergei Ryabkov spoke of an 'act of aggression'.

The example of how Putin turned from Trump's friend into his enemy shows that Trump's policies and political positions can change fairly quickly and are rather unpredictable. The USA and Russia both oppose Daesh in Syria, but have differing geopolitical interests: whereas Russia just like Iran is a military and political ally of Assad, the USA would like to see him removed and replaced. The problem is that the political situation in Syria is highly complex and that military intervention by the USA could backfire and provoke a conflict between the USA and Russia. Given that both countries are nuclear powers, such a conflict could have devastating consequences, as would a conflict between the USA and China or North Korea. We live in a world of competing imperialisms, in which the threat of nuclear Armageddon is looming when the world's military superpowers enter into direct conflict.

In July 2017, the US Congress passed a bill that aimed at introducing new economic sanctions against Russia. Congress argued that this was necessary because of Russia's interference in the US presidential election, its role in Crimea and Ukraine, and the violation of human rights. Trump did not veto the bill. Vladimir Putin reacted by ordering that more than 700 US diplomats had to leave Russia.

---

65. en.kremlin.ru/events/president/news/54241, accessed on 13 April 2017.

In the global oil and gas industry, there are both strong US and Russian corporations. In 2017, US oil and gas company ExxonMobil was the world's thirteenth largest company and the largest company in the oil and gas industry.[66] The corporation's 2016 profits amounted to US$7.8 billion. Other large transnational US oil and gas corporations include Phillips 66 (in 2017 the world's 210th largest company), Valero Energy (#211), Marathon Petroleum (#287), Chevron (#359), ConocoPhillips (#519), Anadarko Petroleum (#770), EOG Resources (#831), Devon Energy (#888), Apache (#1,133), Hess (#1,187), Marathon Oil (#1,277), Pioneer Natural Resources (#1,306), Noble Energy (#1,389), Targa Resources (#1,407), Cheniere Energy (#1,466), Continental Resources (#1,541), Concho Resources (#1,586), EQT (#1,692), PBF Energy (#1,737), Penn Virginia (#1,771), Chesapeake Energy (#1,822) and HollyFrontier (#1,972). Sixteen of these 23 transnational US corporations made absolute losses in 2016, which indicates that the US oil and gas industry is in crisis.

With profits of US$12.1 billion, in 2016 the Russian company Gazprom was the world's most profitable oil and gas corporation and the fortieth largest global company. Other large Russian oil and gas corporations include Rosneft (the world's eighty-second largest transnational corporation in 2017), LukOil (#129), Surgutneftegas (#305), Novatek (#542) and Tatneft (#673). All six of these companies made large profits in 2016. Ranked by profits, five of these six Russian companies and only one US company (ExxonMobil) were among the world's most profitable oil and gas corporations in 2016. The capitalist oil and gas industry is a realm of heavy imperialist rivalry between US corporations and Russian corporations. In 2016, the USA was the world's largest exporter of petroleum oils and bituminous minerals containing more than 70 per cent oil, whereas Russia was the second largest exporter of this type of oil. So Russia and the USA are the world's heaviest competitors in the sale of this type of oil.

Table 4.6 shows that Russia's share of world oil and gas exports has consistently been around 10 per cent over the past 20 years, whereas the United States' share increased from 1.4 per cent in 1995 to 5.8 per cent

---

66.   Source of all data in this and the following paragraphs: Forbes 2000, 2017 list, www. forbes.com/global2000/, accessed on 27 July 2017. Note that the Forbes ranking of the world's 2,000 largest publicly traded corporations is based on a composite indicator taking sales, profits, capital assets and stock market value into account. A ranking of the Forbes 2000 based on profits is therefore different from the general ranking.

Table 4.6   The development of Russian and US exports of oil and gas

	1995	2000	2005	2010	2016
Russia (thousands of US$)	32,230,220	50,513,704	143,841,732	248,756,458	138,648,277
USA (thousands of US$)	4,696,637	8,222,809	18,665,649	61,178,365	76,917,944
World total (thousands of US$)	327,232,725	608,266,463	1,324,167,741	2,128,096,913	1,330,005,464
Russian share in world total (%)	9.8	8.3	10.9	11.7	10.4
US share in world total (%)	1.4	1.4	1.4	2.9	5.8

Data source: UNCTAD Stat; the data are a combination of the following product categories: 333 petroleum oils, oils from bitumen; materials, crude; 334 petroleum oils or bituminous minerals > 70 per cent oil; 343 natural gas; 344 petroleum gases, other gaseous hydrocarbons, n.e.s.

in 2016. In 1995, oil and gas made up 6.4 per cent of world exports. In 2016, this share had increased to 8.3 per cent. Fossil fuels are one of the capitalist world system's most important export commodities. Oil and gas accounted for 0.8 per cent of the USA's monetary export value in 1995 and 5.3 per cent in 2016. Oil and gas made up 41.2 per cent of Russian export value in 1995 and 48.8 per cent in 2016 (data source: UNCTAD Stat).

Table 4.7   Destination region's shares of the value of US and Russian exports of oil and gas in 2016

	Europe	Developing American economies	Developed American economies	Developing Asian economies	Developed Asian economies	African economies
Russia	61.8%	1.2%	2.1%	23.1%	4.9%	1.2%
USA	15.1%	58.3%	18.3%	5.8%	0.7%	1.5%

Data source: UNCTAD Stat

Table 4.7 shows the destinations of the USA's and Russia's oil and gas exports. Almost two-thirds of the value of Russian oil and gas exports in 2016 came from Europe, while 58.3 per cent of the USA's oil and gas exports came from developing American economies, 18.3 per cent from developed American economies and 15.1 per cent from Europe.

Given the importance of oil and gas for the Russian economy, US economic sanctions against Russia, including export sanctions, can harm not just the profits of Russian oil and gas corporations, but the Russian economy at large. The US oil and gas industry has been struggling, and sanctions that reduce Russian competition can help open up Russian oil and gas markets, especially in Europe, for US companies. Given the imperialist rivalry between the US and Russian oil and gas corporations, it is no surprise that Russia's deputy foreign minister, Sergey Ryabkov, commented that US sanctions were 'a very serious step towards destroying any potential for normalizing relations with Russia' (RT 2017b). Given Europe's dependence on Russian gas exports and Germany's cooperation with Russia in building the Nord Stream-2 natural gas pipeline from Russia to Germany, the EU also reacted with criticism: the president of the European Commission, Jean-Claude Juncker, argued that 'America first cannot mean that Europe's interests come last' (RT 2017a).

In 2016, the USA accounted for 8.4 per cent of Iraq's export value of petroleum oils from bitumen minerals and crude oil. In 2010, the year before the Syrian civil war started, the USA's share of Syria's export value of petroleum oils or bituminous minerals containing more than 70 per cent oil was 38.9 per cent. These data indicate that the USA has economic interests in Iraq and Syria. Russia in contrast has much less economic involvement in either country, but Syria is an old Russian military ally. The alliance goes back to the time of the Cold War. The Syrian port in Tartus is Russia's only naval base in the Middle East. This naval base is of strategic military importance for Russia because it allows Russian warships access to the Mediterranean Sea and thereby to North Africa and the Middle East without having to cross the Black Sea that borders NATO member Turkey. So whereas the USA has a strong economic interest in Syria and Iraq, Russia has a strategic military interest in Syria. Russia and the USA both see ISIS as a force that threatens their interests in the Middle East. Specific political and economic interests explain the involvement of the USA and Russia in the Syrian civil war: Russia supports the Assad government, the USA the Syrian Democratic Forces that are made up of left-wing Kurdish and other oppositional groups.

DONALD TRUMP AND KIM JONG-UN

The political polarisation between the USA and North Korea widened in March and April 2017 when the USA together with Japan and South Korea conducted joint military exercises, North Korea test-fired four banned ballistic missiles, the USA dropped a MOAB thermobaric bomb (at 10,000 kg the largest conventional bomb thus far developed and used) on an ISIS cave in Afghanistan, which Pyongyang perceived as the threat that a similar bomb might be dropped on North Korea, Trump ordered the USS *Carl Vinson* aircraft carrier to be stationed in the western Pacific Ocean close to the Korean peninsula, and the North Korean military, in a parade that took place on the 105th birthday of the country's founder and first president Kim Il Sung, displayed new missiles, including inter-continental ballistic missiles that may be capable of reaching the US West Coast.

Trump said about the aircraft carrier heading towards North Korea: 'We are sending an armada, very powerful. We have submarines, very powerful. Far more powerful than the aircraft carrier, that I can tell you. And we have the best military people on the Earth' (cited in Osborne 2017). Trump also repeatedly communicated military threats against North Korea via Twitter: 'North Korea is looking for trouble. If China decides to help, that would be great. If not, we will solve the problem without them! U.S.A.' (Twitter, @RealDonaldTrump, 11 April 2017). 'North Korea just stated that it is in the final stages of developing a nuclear weapon capable of reaching parts of the U.S. It won't happen!' (Twitter, @RealDonaldTrump, 2 January 2017). Choe Ryong-hae, a member of North Korea's Politburo and a high-ranking political and military official, said that North Korea was prepared to use nuclear bombs: 'We're prepared to respond to an all-out war with an all-out war. […] We are ready to hit back with nuclear attacks of our own style against any nuclear attacks' (BBC 2017a). North Korea's vice foreign minister, Han Song-ryol, argued that Trump was inflaming tensions with North Korea via Twitter: 'Trump is always making provocations with his aggressive words' (Sullivan 2017). He said: 'If the US is planning a military attack against us, we will react with a nuclear pre-emptive strike by our own style and method' (BBC 2017b).

North Korea's leader, Kim Jong-un, is determined to increase the country's nuclear armament. He said in his New Year Address 2017:

We will continue to build up our self-defence capability, the pivot of which is the nuclear forces, and the capability for pre-emptive strike as long as the United States and its vassal forces keep on nuclear threat and blackmail and as long as they do not stop their war games they stage at our doorstep disguising them as annual events. We will defend peace and security of our state at all costs and by our own efforts. (Kim 2017)

On 4 July 2017 (US Independence Day), North Korea tested the intercontinental ballistic missile Hwasong-14. It stayed in the air for 37 minutes, which means that it could reach Alaska and Hawaii. The USA saw this test as military escalation and responded by conducting a joint missile exercise with South Korea. China and Russia called for de-escalation and negotiations. They said that North Korea should commit to stop further nuclear testing and the USA should not engage in joint military exercises with South Korea. On 29 July North Korea tested another Hwasong-14. According to estimations, the test showed that this type of missile could, if directed at the USA, reach cities such as Los Angeles or New York City. The USA and South Korea reacted with joint military exercises close to North Korean territory. Trump threatened in August 2017: 'North Korea best not make any more threats to the United States. [...] They will be met with fire, fury and frankly power the likes of which this world has never seen before.' (Sciutto 2017)

On 9 August, North Korea said that US planes stationed on the US Anderson Air Base on Guam frequented South Korean air space to provoke the North. It threatened to strike US airbases on Guam, an island located in the western Pacific Ocean. A spokesman of the Korean People's Army (KPA) said:

The KPA Strategic Force is now carefully examining the operational plan for making an enveloping fire at the areas around Guam with medium-to-long-range strategic ballistic rocket Hwasong-12 in order to contain the U.S. major military bases on Guam including the Anderson Air Force Base in which the U.S. strategic bombers, which get on the nerves of the DPRK and threaten and blackmail it through their frequent visits to the sky above south Korea, are stationed and to send a serious warning signal to the U.S. (KCNA, 9 August 2017)

Donald Trump tweeted in reaction: 'My first order as President was to renovate and modernize our nuclear arsenal. It is now far stronger and more powerful than ever before. [...] Hopefully we will never have to use this power, but there will never be a time that we are not the most powerful nation in the world!' (Twitter, @RealDonaldTrump, 9 August 2017). On 11 August, Trump tweeted further war threats: 'Military solutions are now fully in place, locked and loaded, should North Korea act unwisely. Hopefully Kim Jong-un will find another path!' (Twitter, @RealDonaldTrump, 11 August 2017).

On 3 September 2017, North Korea tested a thermonuclear hydrogen bomb (H-bomb). Trump commented on Twitter: 'South Korea is finding, as I have told them, that their talk of appeasement with North Korea will not work, they only understand one thing! [...] The United States is considering, in addition to other options, stopping all trade with any country doing business with North Korea' (Twitter, @RealDonaldTrump, 3 September 2017).

In this conflict both the USA and North Korea use the power of words and display of military force to threaten each other. China's Foreign Minister Wang Yi urged both sides that a nuclear war couldn't be won by anyone: 'We urge all parties to refrain from inflammatory or threatening statements and deeds to prevent the situation on the Korean Peninsula from becoming irreversible. [...] Once a war really happens, the result will be nothing but loss all around. No one can become a winner' (Li 2017).

The problem is that both Donald Trump and North Korean President Kim Jong-un are fairly unpredictable. They both believe in military force as a way of resolving conflicts. A pre-emptive strike by the USA could result in North Korea launching nuclear missiles on Japan and South Korea, setting off a vicious cycle of nuclear bombings that could eradicate life on Earth. Incautious comments by Trump on Twitter or elsewhere could be interpreted by Pyongyang as an imminent threat and result in a pre-emptive attack on South Korea. Trump's Twitter account could in this case become a communication tool that triggers a nuclear war. The other way round, North Korea's nuclear tests could provoke Trump to undertake a pre-emptive strike on North Korea. In any case, the result is likely to be an uncontainable spiral of military violence.

When the world's last Stalinist dictatorship and an authoritarian-capitalist democracy threaten to engage in warfare with each other, it becomes evident that the Cold War and the threat of nuclear annihilation of human life persist. The election of Donald Trump has certainly intensified this threat.

GÜNTHER ANDERS: APOCALYPTIC BLINDNESS IN THE AGE OF AUTHORITARIAN CAPITALISM

The Austrian critical theorist of technology Günther Anders (1956, 243) argued that the nuclear war age could be characterised by the sentence that 'Humanity as a whole is exterminable'[67] (for a detailed discussion of the relevance of Anders' philosophy in the digital age, see Fuchs 2017c). The possibility for human extinction has, according to Anders, become automated and computerised so that responsibility can be blamed on 'electronic consciousness automata'[68] (Anders 1956, 245). The computerisation of warfare is connected to what Anders terms the 'Promethean gap' – gaps between what humans can technologically produce and what they can imagine, between action and imagination, production and ideology, doing and feeling, technology and the human body (Anders 1956, 16): 'The volume of what we can produce, do or think is larger than the volume of what our imagination or even our feelings can achieve'[69] (Anders 1956, 270). The Promethean shame is associated with the Promethean gap: if it just takes pressing some buttons to wipe out humanity, then the difference between human actions as well as its products on the one side, and the imagination of their potential consequences on the other side, is so large that the inhibition to kill is undermined.

If there are political leaders, as we find them today, who have an almost religious ideological belief in war, the military and authoritarianism, then the Promethean shame takes on a new dimension. Authoritarian personalities lack the moral phantasy and scruple (Anders 1956, 273) to imagine that the products and technologies they control could wipe out humanity. They suffer from what Anders terms apocalyptic blindness. The atomic bomb constitutes an absolute gap between technological possibilities and moral desirability: what is technologically possible is morally reprehensible. Authoritarian personalities' nihilistic glorification

---

67. Translation from German: 'Die Menschheit als ganze ist tötbar'.
68. Translation from German: 'elektronische Gewissens-Automaten'.
69. Translation from German: 'Volumen dessen, was wir herstellen, tun oder denken können, größer ist als das Volumen dessen, was unsere Vorstellung oder gar unser Fühlen leisten kann'.

of war, or what Walter Benjamin (1930, 240) called 'the apotheosis of war', has turned into apocalyptic blindness and annihilism – annihilatory nihilism.

SOCIAL DARWINISM'S LOGIC OF EXTINCTION AND ANNIHILISM (ANNIHILATORY NIHILISM)

What lots of people fear is that Trump's personality is too uncontrolled and too revengeful, which could be dangerous in a tricky political situation. The fear is that he may press the nuclear button. Whereas toughness, retaliation and brutality are core features of capitalism, with which capitalist corporations are confronted day by day in the competition to survive, the rest of society does not automatically follow the same logic. Although the logic of survival of the fittest also tends to be imitated in politics, there are boundaries to this logic that when crossed result in situations of no return, in which political violence escalates. In politics the logic of social Darwinism can easily lead to annihilism and the extinction of mankind.

The point is that such dangerous situations can only be overcome if both sides talk to each other, overcome their individual standpoints, and make compromises. For example, the Cuban missile crisis could only be overcome because John F. Kennedy and Nikita Khrushchev communicated with each other and Robert Kennedy and the Soviet Ambassador Anatoly Dobrynin met secretly and agreed that the USA would remove its missiles from Turkey and Italy and the Soviet Union its missiles from Cuba. Diplomacy and communication seem to be the important features of mastering such dangerous situations in international politics. So the question is whether Donald Trump has what it takes for international diplomacy. If it turns out that the answer is 'No', the world may come to an end.

EXXONMOBIL'S CEO REX TILLERSON: SECRETARY OF STATE

In 2016, ExxonMobil was the world's ninth largest transnational company and the largest oil and gas corporation.[70] In 2015, it made profits of US$16.2 billion. Donald Trump appointed ExxonMobil's CEO Rex Tillerson as US secretary of state. As secretary of state, Tillerson

---

70. Data source: Forbes 2000, 2016 list.

does of course not keep up his role as CEO. But having spent more than 40 years working for ExxonMobil, it is unlikely he can easily leave behind his past and the interests of the industry that he represented for decades.

The US secretary of state is in charge of foreign policy and diplomacy and is one of the US cabinet's most influential politicians. Wars have been fought over oil because oil is such a crucial resource for keeping fossil fuel capitalism going. If the oil and gas industry's interests determine foreign policy, then there is a danger that not only prospects for democracy and human rights, but business interests, determine international relations. Eric Ferrero, director of communications for Amnesty International USA, asked: 'We know that Tillerson has been successful in safeguarding the interests of a massive oil company – will he be as invested in safeguarding human rights abroad?'[71] John Sauven, who is Greenpeace UK's executive director, commented: 'So a real-life JR Ewing becomes America's chief diplomat as Donald Trump does away with the usual intermediaries and directly outsources foreign policy to the fossil fuel industry. We spent years warning that Exxon was too close to the US government. Now they are the government' (Gambino and Yuhas 2016).

ExxonMobil has been subject to a lawsuit concerning allegations of human rights violations:

In 2001, eleven Indonesian villagers filed suit against ExxonMobil in US federal court alleging that the company was complicit in human rights abuses committed by Indonesian security forces in the province of Aceh. The plaintiffs maintain that ExxonMobil hired the security forces, who were members of the Indonesian military, to protect the natural gas extraction facility and pipeline which ExxonMobil was operating. The plaintiffs further claim that ExxonMobil knew or should have known about the Indonesian military's human rights violations against the people of Aceh. The plaintiffs allege that they suffered human rights violations, such as murder, torture and rape, at the hands of these security forces. [...] In a decision issued in July 2015, a US federal court ruled that the plaintiffs' claims sufficiently 'touch and concern' the United States and may proceed in US court.[72]

---

71.   www.amnestyusa.org/news/press-releases/trump-s-proposed-state-department-leadership-deeply-concerning, accessed on 17 February 2017.
72.   business-humanrights.org/en/exxonmobil-lawsuit-re-aceh, accessed on 17 February 2017.

CONCLUSION

This chapter has outlined how US capitalism is changing under Trump. Key aspects include the following:

- State and the economy – big capital and state power. Trump is not a career politician, but a capitalist-turned-politician, who fuses economic and political interests in one person. Donald Trump's presidency means that the billionaire class and specific factions of capital (such as construction, real estate, health and biotechnology, utilities, transport, entertainment, natural resource extraction or finance) have direct influence on state power. There is a direct personnel overlap between the capitalist and billionaire class and the political elite.
- State and the economy – economic policies. Trump's economic policies feature low taxes for US corporations and protectionism that limits US capital's export. It uses state intervention in the form of protectionist trade policies. At the same time he advances neoliberal privatisation policies (for example in health care and education). It also uses a form of 'Keynesian neoliberalism' that invests taxes into infrastructure projects carried out by private corporations that own the resulting infrastructures.
- State and citizens. Trump stands for law-and-order politics and friend/enemy politics that feature constant attacks on opponents and scapegoating.
- International relations – foreign trade. Trump scapegoats other nations (such as Mexico and China) for capitalism's problems. He distracts from the class conflict between labour and capital by presenting capitalist power as a conflict between nations. Trump argues for US capital and US labour to be united against other nations. For Trump, international political economy is an issue of nations and nationalism, not one of capitalism's structural contradictions. For Trump, capitalism is the competition between nations.
- International relations – foreign policy. Trump's foreign politics is on the one hand unilateral and on the other hand highly polarising, which has raised concerns about armament and the threat of a nuclear war in particular.

In Chapter 5 we will turn to aspects of Trump and ideology (Trumpology).

5

Trumpology: Donald Trump's Ideology

INTRODUCTION

Donald Trump is a capitalist and a politician.[1] But at the same time he is a celebrity who advances a particular form of ideology (Trumpology), makes use of reality TV and Twitter, and organises politics like a media spectacle. This chapter analyses Trump's ideology.

The second section analyses Trumpology's four elements. Sections three and four discuss Trump's use of the media, especially social media (Twitter) and reality TV (*The Apprentice*). The fifth section draws conclusions from Chapters 4 and 5.

There is a complex relationship between politics and culture in general, and between the state and ideology in capitalist society. The state's collective and individual actors produce meanings about society, and individuals and groups in society make meaning of the state. We can therefore distinguish between discourses by the state and discourses on the state.

Discourses by the State and Discourses on the State

In discourses by the state, politicians, parties, governments, political institutions or communication workers employed by such state institutions produce and communicate specific interpretations of society to the public. A government or party programme is an example. In discourses

1. Acknowledgement: this chapter was first published as part of an article in the open access journal *tripleC: Communication, Capitalism & Critique*: Christian Fuchs. 2017. Donald Trump: A Critical Theory-Perspective on Authoritarian Capitalism. *tripleC: Communication, Capitalism & Critique* 15 (1): 1–72. www.triple-c.at/index.php/tripleC/article/view/835. Reprinted and updated with permission by *tripleC*.

on the state, individuals and groups in society interpret what state actors and institutions are doing and express and communicate these interpretations in semiotic forms. Examples are a conversation about the government between friends, media reports about a political event or a consultancy agency's development of a communication strategy for a political party. Discourses are semiotic representations of reality through which humans communicate and make meanings of certain aspects of the world. Discourses by the state can therefore also be called semiotic representations by the state. Discourses on the state can also be termed semiotic representations of the state.

Discourses by and on the state are to specific degrees ideological in character, i.e. ideologies by the state and ideologies on the state. In ideologies by the state, state actors justify domination and/or exploitation. In ideologies on the state, individuals or groups justify state actions that enact, practice or justify domination and/or exploitation. The distinction between discourses and ideologies points towards the potentially contradictory character of discourses by the state and discourses on the state so that they may have a contested character.

TRUMPOLOGY'S FOUR ELEMENTS

Given that Trump is the US president, his general view of the world is relevant for understanding the state's ideology (ideology by the state) during his rule. Having a look at his ideological views may also reveal what role he assigns to the state in society (ideology on the state). Trumpology is Trump-style ideology. It is not the ideology of a single person, but rather a whole way of thought and life that consists of elements such as hyper-individualism, hard labour, leadership, the friend/enemy scheme and social Darwinism.

Possessive Hyper-Individualism

'I', 'I', 'I'

Hyper-individualism is Trumpology's first element. Trump is a brand. Trump is a strategy. Trump is entertainment. Trump is a spectacle. Trump is politics. Trump is the instrumentalisation of everything surrounding him. Trump is the absolute commodification of the self.

Donald Trump has made a career by branding and selling himself. His presidential campaign was also focused on Trump as brand, celebrity, billionaire and political leader. As a consequence, Trump likes talking in the first-person singular. 'I', 'me', 'my' and 'mine' are among his most frequently used words. Trumpology is about possessive individualism, the individual as owner.

Consider the following example:

> Whenever I start something new, I know I have tons to learn. I see each new project as a blank page that I can't wait to fill. I get excited because I love to investigate, dig in new areas, acquire information, put it together, and gain an in-depth understanding of something completely new. I've had this feeling at every stage of my career; it's how I begin every successful project. I consider it a sign; if I don't feel excited, I usually pass on the opportunity, even if it could produce huge profits. My enthusiasm drives me to learn, and what I learn gives me more control. My knowledge also helps me avoid mistakes and eliminate problems that could arise. I studied up on travel before starting GoTrump.com, my travel agency. I studied the men's fashion industry for my Donald J. Trump Signature Collection of menswear. I researched and read carefully before starting Trump University; and that's just to name a few examples. (Trump 2007, 94–5)

This short passage from Trump's book *Trump 101: The Way to Success* consists of nine sentences, in which the term 'I' occurs 16 times, 'my' five times and 'me' three times. This means that in this passage, Trump on average uses the first-person singular 2.3 times per sentence.

POSSESSIVE INDIVIDUALISM

The philosopher Erich Fromm (1997, 91–2) characterises possessive individualism as a having-centred ideology of accumulation:

> Speaking more generally, the fundamental elements in the relation between individuals in the having mode of existence are competition, antagonism, and fear. The antagonistic element in the having relationship stems from its nature. If having is the basis of my sense of identity because 'I am what I have,' the wish to have must lead to the desire to

have much, to have more, to have most. In other words, *greed* is the natural outcome of the having orientation. It can be the greed of the miser or the greed of the profit hunter or the greed of the womanizer or the man chaser. Whatever constitutes their greed, the greedy can never have enough, can never be 'satisfied'. In contrast to physiological needs, such as hunger, that have definite satiation points due to the physiology of the body, mental greed – and all greed is mental, even if it is satisfied via the body – has no satiation point, since its consummation does not fill the inner emptiness, boredom, loneliness and depression it is meant to overcome. In addition, since what one has can be taken away in one form or another, one must have more, in order to fortify one's existence against such danger. If everyone wants to have more, everyone must fear one's neighbor's aggressive intention to take away what one has. To prevent such attack one must become more powerful and preventively aggressive oneself.

Trump summarises his philosophy: 'A big ego is a positive thing' (Trump and Zanker 2007, 280). His individualism is his capital accumulation strategy. His self is the commodity he sells.

Performance and the Ideology of Hard Labour

Trumpology's second element is the ideology of hard labour. 'My father didn't give me much money, but what he did give me was a good education and the simple formula for getting wealthy: work hard doing what you love' (Trump and Zanker 2007, 44). 'Hard work is my personal method for financial success' (32). 'You can help create your own luck, you can make things happen through hard work and intelligence. You can become luckier' (114). 'The harder you work, the luckier you get' (135). Celebrities, billionaires, successful businesspeople and superstars' 'attitudes, actions, persistence, and passion […] separate the winners from the losers' (1).

The implication is that the poor do not work or do not work hard enough. News sources say that Trump's father Fred, a rich real estate developer, supported his son financially in a significant manner at the start of his career, on other occasions and when Donald faced financial problems (Kranish and Fisher 2016, 75, 95, 124–5, 201, 294). Of course, good parents want to see their children thrive and be happy and therefore try to support them. But some parents can do so more than others, and rich parents can do so in a very powerful way. As a result, in capitalism some tend to be economically luckier than others because they had the luck to be born into wealthy families.

The Leadership Ideology

Leadership thinking is Trumpology's third element. 'I'm not bragging when I say that I'm a winner. I have experience in winning. That's what we call leadership. That means that people will follow me and be inspired by what I do. How do I know? I've been a leader my whole life' (Trump 2015a, 9).

> Leadership is not a group effort. If you're in charge, then be in charge. [...] I'm the conductor who leads the Trump Organization; I set the tempo. In my organization, I set a rapid pace, which is called allegro in symphonic circles. I pay close attention to tempo because I know that it's vital to keep the momentum going at all times. I provide strong leadership, and, at times, this can be hard and not what I want to do. (Trump 2007, 101, 125–6)

Trump also thinks of politics in terms of leadership. The very ideology of making America great again is based on the assumption that the USA needs to be the leader of the world in every respect: 'The idea of American Greatness, of our country as the leader of the free and unfree world, has vanished' (Trump 2015a, xi). In addition, Trump argues that enabling the USA to lead the world requires a strong leader who manages the country and the world like a company:

> Despite all of these challenges – and actually because of the challenges – I decided to do something about it. I couldn't stand to see what was happening to our great country. This mess calls for leadership in the worst way. It needs someone with common sense and business acumen, someone who can truly lead America back to what has made us great in the past. We need someone with a proven track record in business who understands greatness, someone who can rally us to the standard of excellence we once epitomized and explain what needs to be done. (Trump 2015a, xi)

Another, associated argument that Trump frequently employs is that career politicians are weak leaders:

> In politics, once someone gets elected, it's tough to get them out. There's no motivation to try to get anything done. [...] Career politicians like it this way; being a politician is their career. I know many of them; believe me, they couldn't get a job in private industry. They don't want anyone taking away their great pension plan and health benefits – that you are paying for. (Trump 2015a, 94)

Social Darwinism and the Friend/Enemy Scheme

Social Darwinism and the friend/enemy scheme form Trumpology's fourth dimension. Social Darwinism is a highly competitive and militaristic view of society, in which there is constant egoism, battle, conflict and war. It is based on the assumption that only the strong can and should survive and that survival requires crushing enemies.

> The world is a vicious and brutal place. We think we're civilized. In truth, it's a cruel world and people are ruthless. [...] People will be mean and nasty and try to hurt you just for sport. Lions in the jungle only kill for food, but humans kill for fun. [...]
>
> Everyone wants to kill the fastest gun. [...]
>
> The same burning greed that makes people loot, kill, and steal in emergencies like fires and floods, operates daily in normal everyday people. It lurks right behind the surface, and when you least expect it, it rears its nasty head and bites you. Accept it. The world is a brutal place. I love to crush the other side and take the benefits. Why? Because there is nothing greater. For me it is even better than sex, and I love sex. [...]
>
> When somebody screws you, screw them back in spades. [...] Go for the jugular so that people watching will not want to mess with you. (Trump and Zunker 2008, 29, 176, 48, 199)

Using such descriptions, Trump certainly gives a realist picture of capitalism. Capitalism is by definition a machine of capital accumulation that operates with economic life and death as its inputs and outputs. But if all aspects of society were driven by war-like competition then society could not exist, and expanding and intensifying this logic brings about existential threats for society. Basing politics on the logic of the 'survival of the fittest' poses the danger of military action instead of diplomatic responses to political disagreements. In such situations, where the logic of the survival of the fittest prevails among powerful nations (such as the USA on the one side and North Korea, China, Russia or Iran on the other side), spirals of violence can occur and escalate. Taking this logic to its logical conclusion means that social Darwinism in society not just poses the threat of a world war, but of nuclear destruction.

TRUMP AND THE MEDIA: SOCIAL MEDIA AND TWITTER

The Media's Making of Trump

Trumpology does not simply exist because of a single individual. Like any ideology, it requires hegemony. It requires those who admire Trump as brand and leader, and it also requires public visibility. Trumpology needs Trump as media spectacle. The Trump spectacle has two dimensions. On the one side Trump understands well how to stage himself as a scandalous spectacle in order to attract media attention. On the other side the media also needs someone like Trump for staging spectacles that attract a large audience. There is a profit motive on both sides of mediated Trumpology spectacles. The one side is looking for advertising, marketing and public relations opportunities in order to be able to better sell a range of branded commodities. The other side is looking for content that attracts a large audience and thereby allows it to sell advertising space more expensively.

The reporting and content can be quite contentious, with reporters trying to unveil ever more scandals and nastiness. The response is criticisms of the media and the claim of unfair treatment in the media. It is this contentiousness that keeps the spectacle machinery going, and creates the need for more scandals, more controversy, more spectacles and possibly more audience attention, and thereby more profits and attention for both the mainstream media and their subject. Contention and symbiosis are two poles of the Trump spectacle's dialectic that drives profitability. By Trump making news in the media, the media makes Trump.

Bernie Sanders and the Media

Bernie Sanders (2016b, 421) argues that he learned from having media exposure during the Democratic Party's primaries that 'the more important the issue is to large numbers of working people, the less interesting it is to corporate media':

> [T]he nature of media coverage today, especially on television, mostly calls for short sound bites on what the media establishment determines is the issue of the day. [...] For the corporate media, the real issues facing the American people – poverty, the decline of the middle class, income and wealth inequality, trade, health care, climate change, etc. – are fairly irrelevant. For them, politics is largely presented as entertainment. [...] Turn on CNN or other networks covering politics and what you will find is that the overwhelming amount of coverage is dedicated to personality, gossip, campaign strategy, scandals, conflicts, polls and who appears to be winning or losing, fund-raising, the ups and downs of the campaign trail, and the dumb things a candidate may say or do. Political coverage is the drama of what happens on the campaign trail. It has very little to do with the needs of the American people and the ideas or programs a candidate offers to address the problems facing the country. [...] The 'politics as entertainment' approach works very well for someone like Donald Trump, an experienced entertainer. [...] For the corporate media, name-calling and personal attacks are easy to cover, and what it prefers to cover. (Sanders 2016b, 424–5)

Trump: Mainstream Media as Gratis Advertising

Trump is quite aware of this peculiar relationship between himself and the mainstream media:

> The personal exchanges between me and others become the big story of the debate and the focus of news coverage for weeks. [...] I use the media the way the media uses me – to attract attention. [...] So sometimes I make outrageous comments and give them what they want – viewers and readers – in order to make a point. I'm a businessman with a brand to sell. [...] The cost of a full-page ad in the *New York Times* can be more than $100,000. But when they write a

story about one of my deals, it doesn't cost me a cent, and I get more important publicity. I have a mutually profitable two-way relationship with the media – we give each other what we need. And now I am using that relationship to talk about the future of America. [...] These media types sell more magazines when my face is on the cover, or when I bring a bigger audience to their television show than they normally attract, and by far. And what's funny is that it turns out the best way for them to get that attention is to criticize me. (Trump 2015a, 10, 11, 14)

Big Data in Clinton's and Trump's Campaigns

In the 2016 US presidential election, the tech pundits pronounced that big data was the factor determining election results. For example, *Wired* magazine wrote that the 'marriage of big data, social data will determine the next President' and summarised this claim in a simple formula: 'Big Data + Social Data = Your Next President'.[2] There are indications that the Clinton campaign's data spending was much higher. Data show that in October 2016, the Clinton campaign had raised US$1.3 billion, the Trump campaign just US$795 million.[3] Table 5.1 shows spending on tech and data in June 2016 for both campaigns. According to this source, the Clinton campaign not just invested a higher share of its budget on data and tech than the Trump campaign, but it spent 3.7 times what the Trump campaign invested.

Big data does not win and cannot predict elections. It is a techno-fetishistic myth to believe that the more money a campaign invests in data analytics, the larger the likelihood of electoral success. It is the complex combination of structural conditions, economic and political contradictions, crises, political subjectivities, political structures of feeling, ideological factors, organising, campaigning and communication that determines election results. Data, algorithms and tech form just a few of the many relevant factors. In the 2016 US presidential election, right-wing ideology trumped big data politics.

---

2.   www.wired.com/insights/2013/05/election-2016-marriage-of-big-data-social-data-will-determine-the-next-president, accessed on 14 October 2017.
3.   www.washingtonpost.com/graphics/politics/2016-election/campaign-finance/, accessed on 14 October 2017.

Table 5.1 Campaign spending on tech and data in June 2016

	Trump, total spending (million US$)	Trump, % of spending	Clinton, total spending (million US$)	Clinton, % of spending
Web development and digital consulting	2.5	3.3		
Telemarketing and data	1.5	1.9	0.2	0.1
Software	0.3	0.3		
Data management	0.2	0.2		
Online advertising	0.1	0.2	11.6	5.1
Digital consulting	0.1	0.1	0.7	0.3
Technology services			1.6	0.7
Computers			1.5	0.7
Database services			0.5	0.2
Technology consulting			0.4	0.2
Design and web development			0.3	0.1
Voter file			0.4	0.2
Email services			0.2	0.1
List rental			0.2	0.3
Total	4.7	6	17.6	8

Data source: Bloomberg Politics, www.bloomberg.com/politics/graphics/2016-presidential-campaign-fundraising/july/public/index.html

The Twitter Demagogue

Trump is like India's Narendra Modi a demagogical Twitter president. Trump uses Twitter as political spectacle. A study estimates that in the third US presidential election debate, political bots posted 36.1 per cent of the pro-Trump tweets and 23.5 per cent of the pro-Clinton tweets (Kollanyi, Howard and Woolley 2016). Automated politics therefore played some role in the election campaign. News articles in the mainstream media regularly focus on what Trump tweets. Some argue that we live in an age of post-truth, where ideology, personalities and emotions, rather than facts, themes and debate, shape politics. Increasingly, whatever is highly visible and emotionally attractive is considered to be the truth.

Post-Truth

The post-truth regime means distrust in experts and established politicians and the replacement of arguments and evidence by pure ideology. Trump presents himself as a post-truth politician:

> I, for one, am not interested in defending a system that for decades has served the interest of political parties at the expense of the people. Members of the club – the consultants, the pollsters, the politicians, the pundits and the special interests – grow rich and powerful while the American people grow poorer and more isolated. [...] The only antidote to decades of ruinous rule by a small handful of elites is a bold infusion of popular will. On every major issue affecting this country, the people are right and the governing elite are wrong. The elites are wrong on taxes, on the size of government, on trade, on immigration, on foreign policy. (Trump 2016g)

In the Brexit campaign, Conservative politician and then Secretary of State for Justice Michael Gove said: 'I think the people in this country have had enough of experts with organisations with acronyms saying that they know what is best and get it consistently wrong.'[4] In the 2016 Austrian presidential election, right-wing candidate Norbert Hofer said about Green Party candidate Alexander Van der Bellen: 'There is a big difference between the two of us: You have the high society behind you, and I have the people behind me. And that's the big difference'[5] (see Fuchs 2016a and 2016c for a more detailed discussion of the 2016 Austrian presidential election's political context and the use of social media in it). What all three statements have in common is that they construct a conspiratorial rule by established politicians and intellectuals and call for an anti-intellectual politics that is driven by emotions and right-wing ideology. We know today that, in the case of Trump, the call for an anti-elitist revolution resulted in the installation of members of the billionaire class into the political elite.

---

4.   www.youtube.com/watch?v=GGgiGtJk7MA, accessed on 7 August 2017.
5.   Translation from German (CF), Original: 'Es gibt einen großen Unterschied zwischen uns beiden: Sie haben die Hautvolee und ich hab die Menschen. Und das ist der große Unterschied', www.youtube.com/watch?v=YA-OHUDAXrI, accessed on 7 August 2017.

Social Media Echo Chambers

A study by Pablo Barberá (2015) analysed 15 million tweets mentioning Obama and Romney during the 2012 US presidential election: '85% of retweet interactions take place among Twitter users with similar ideological positions. [...] Political polarization is particularly intense among right-leaning Twitter users [...]. Although liberal users also present this pattern, they tend to engage more often in conversations all along the ideological spectrum' (Barberá 2015, 87).

Barberá's study seems to confirm that Twitter communication takes place in echo chambers, where users listen to, follow, like and retweet like-minded political points of view. The study also found that right-wingers are especially intolerant of opposing positions and people who do not share their opinions. The lack of debate and engagement is also expressed as online harassment, ideological violence and anonymous threats. In addition, the fast speed of Twitter also discourages debate.

Trump uses Twitter's brevity of 140 characters for a politics that does not rely on arguments, but on negative emotions that he tries to stir among his followers. Twitter is the best medium for the emotional and ideological politics of outrage, scapegoating, hatred and attack because its ephemerality, brevity and speed support spectacles and sensationalism. At the same time, the custom of liking and retweeting on Twitter appeals to Trump's narcissistic side, allowing him to indulge his status as a celebrity, brand and political leader.

Wilhelm Reich (1972) argues that authoritarianism has not just political-economic, but also ideological and psychological foundations. Reich was especially interested in the question of how authoritarianism operates with emotional, unconscious and irrational elements and why it does so successfully. 'Every form of totalitarian-authoritarian rulership is based on the irrationalism inculcated in masses of people' (Reich 1972, 312). Reich shows how authoritarianism operates upon 'the *emotions* of the individuals in the masses' and avoided '*relevant arguments* as much as possible' (Reich 1972, 34). 'Hitler repeatedly stressed that one could not get at the masses with arguments, proofs, and knowledge, but only with feelings and beliefs' (Reich 1972, 83). Twitter is a medium that supports politics that are based on feelings, beliefs and irrationality instead of arguments, proofs and knowledge. Donald Trump has made emotionally laden ideological Twitter politics a key element of his political strategy.

In the age of Trump, Twitter and reality TV, political communication is accelerated, very fast and superficial. There is no time and no space for substantial debates.

Trump's Twitter Likes

Trump makes use of Twitter for broadcasting 140-character sound bites about what he likes and dislikes.

Examples of Trump's Twitter likes include:

Vladimir Putin said today about Hillary and Dems: 'In my opinion, it is humiliating. One must be able to lose with dignity.' So true! (23 December 2016)

Yes, it is true – Carlos Slim, the great businessman from Mexico, called me about getting together for a meeting. We met, HE IS A GREAT GUY! (20 December 2016)

@BillGates and @JimBrownNFL32 in my Trump Tower office yesterday - two great guys! (14 December 2016)

The thing I like best about Rex Tillerson is that he has vast experience at dealing successfully with all types of foreign governments. (13 December 2016)

I have chosen one of the truly great business leaders of the world, Rex Tillerson, Chairman and CEO of ExxonMobil, to be Secretary of State. (13 December 2016)

Will be interviewed on @FoxNews at 10:00 P.M. Enjoy! (11 December 2016)

@TigerWoods: Can't wait to get back out there and mix it up with the boys. –TW #heroworldchallenge Great to have you back Tiger – Special! (3 December 2016)

The President of Taiwan CALLED ME today to wish me congratulations on winning the Presidency. Thank you! (2 December 2016)

I am seriously considering Dr. Ben Carson as the head of HUD. I've gotten to know him well--he's a greatly talented person who loves people! (22 November 2016)

Many people would like to see @Nigel_Farage represent Great Britain as their Ambassador to the United States. He would do a great job! (21 November 2016)

General James 'Mad Dog' Mattis, who is being considered for Secretary of Defense, was very impressive yesterday. A true General's General! (20 November 2016)

Jeb Bush, George W and George H.W. all called to express their best wishes on the win. Very nice! (13 November 2016)

Mitt Romney called to congratulate me on the win. Very nice! (13 November 2016)

Examples of Trump's Twitter Dislikes

Civil rights activist and House of Representatives member John Lewis was one of the leaders of the 1963 March on Washington. He testified in the US Senate on Donald Trump's decision to nominate Senator Jeff Sessions' for attorney general: 'It doesn't matter whether Sen. Sessions may smile or how friendly he may be, whether he may speak to you. We need someone who will stand up and speak up and speak out for the people who need help, for people who are being discriminated against.'[6] In an interview, Lewis said he did not consider Trump to be a legitimate president and that 'the Russians participated in helping this man get elected' (Todd, Bronston and Rivera 2017).

Trump commented on Twitter: 'Congressman John Lewis should spend more time on fixing and helping his district, which is in horrible shape and falling apart (not to mention crime infested) rather than falsely complaining about the election results. All talk, talk, talk – no action or results. Sad!' (14 January 2017).

After CNN had reported on an alleged Russian dossier on Trump, Trump attacked the channel in a press conference and wrote on Twitter: '@CNN is in a total meltdown with their FAKE NEWS because their ratings are tanking since election and their credibility will soon be gone!' (12 January 2016).

---

6. politics.blog.ajc.com/2017/01/11/read-john-lewis-full-testimony-against-jeff-sessions/, accessed on 14 October 2017.

Other examples include:

@NBCNews purposely left out this part of my nuclear quote: 'until such time as the world comes to its senses regarding nukes.' Dishonest! (23 December 2016)

If Russia, or some other entity, was hacking, why did the White House wait so long to act? Why did they only complain after Hillary lost? (15 December 2016)

The media tries so hard to make my move to the White House, as it pertains to my business, so complex – when actually it isn't! (15 December 2016)

Has anyone looked at the really poor numbers of @VanityFair Magazine. Way down, big trouble, dead! Graydon Carter, no talent, will be out! (15 December 2016)

Just watched @NBCNightlyNews – So biased, inaccurate and bad, point after point. Just can't get much worse, although @CNN is right up there! (11 December 2016)

Chuck Jones, who is President of United Steelworkers 1999, has done a terrible job representing workers. No wonder companies flee country! (7 December 2016)

Boeing is building a brand new 747 Air Force One for future presidents, but costs are out of control, more than $4 billion. Cancel order! (6 December 2016)

If the press would cover me accurately & honorably, I would have far less reason to 'tweet.' Sadly, I don't know if that will ever happen! (5 December 2016)

The Green Party just dropped its recount suit in Pennsylvania and is losing votes in Wisconsin recount. Just a Stein scam to raise money! (4 Decembe 2016)

Just tried watching Saturday Night Live – unwatchable! Totally biased, not funny and the Baldwin impersonation just can't get any worse. Sad. (3 December 2016)

I thought that @CNN would get better after they failed so badly in their support of Hillary Clinton however, since election, they are worse! (29 November 2016)

@CNN is so embarrassed by their total (100%) support of Hillary Clinton, and yet her loss in a landslide, that they don't know what to do. (28 November 2016)

If Cuba is unwilling to make a better deal for the Cuban people, the Cuban/American people and the U.S. as a whole, I will terminate deal. (28 November 2016)

The Green Party scam to fill up their coffers by asking for impossible recounts is now being joined by the badly defeated & demoralized Dems. (26 November 2016)

Fidel Castro is dead! (26 November 2016)

The failing @nytimes just announced that complaints about them are at a 15 year high. I can fully understand that – but why announce? (22 November 2016)

Perhaps a new meeting will be set up with the @nytimes. In the meantime they continue to cover me inaccurately and with a nasty tone! (22 November 2016)

I cancelled today's meeting with the failing @nytimes when the terms and conditions of the meeting were changed at the last moment. Not nice. (22 November 2016)

I watched parts of @nbcsnl Saturday Night Live last night. It is a totally one-sided, biased show – nothing funny at all. Equal time for us? (20 November 2016)

The cast and producers of Hamilton, which I hear is highly overrated, should immediately apologize to Mike Pence for their terrible behaviour. (20 November 2016)

The Theater must always be a safe and special place. The cast of Hamilton was very rude last night to a very good man, Mike Pence. Apologize! (19 November 2016)

Our wonderful future V.P. Mike Pence was harassed last night at the theater by the cast of Hamilton, cameras blazing. This should not happen! (19 November 2016)

The failing @nytimes story is so totally wrong on transition. It is going so smoothly. Also, I have spoken to many foreign leaders. (16 November 2016)

The @nytimes sent a letter to their subscribers apologizing for their BAD coverage of me. I wonder if it will change – doubt it? (13 November 2016)

Wow, the @nytimes is losing thousands of subscribers because of their very poor and highly inaccurate coverage of the 'Trump phenomena'. (13 November 2016)

Politics of 140-Character Sound Bites

Trump's Twitter politics is a politics of 140-character sound bites that consist of constructions of the world polarised into friends and enemies. Via Twitter, Trump broadcasts news about how his personal friend/ enemy scheme evolves. There are two sides: the side of the friends, whom he characterises as great, impressive, nice, successful and talented; and the side of the enemies, whom he characterises as bad, biased, failing, inaccurate, dishonest, nasty, not nice, one-sided, overrated, poor, rude, sad, terrible, untalented or wrong. Trump's politics is a world of polar opposites, in which representatives of the two sides have completely opposed characteristics.

Data scientists conducted a quantitative analysis of Trump's tweets. They found that Trump tends to use language that is negative and uses others as scapegoats:

But what's truly distinctive is *how* he uses adjectives: He combines an adjective followed by someone's name a stunning 10 times more than any other candidate. This is primarily because of his proclivity for using Twitter to launch personal attacks on specific individuals, like 'lightweight' Megyn Kelly, 'little' Marco Rubio, 'low-energy' Jeb Bush, 'dopey' Bill Kristol, etc. [...] Trump is also distinctive in his use of pronouns ('I', 'you', 'he', 'she', 'we', 'us', etc.). Trump uses pronouns in a very different way than the other candidates. 'I' and 'me' (as well as Trump's own name) are used much more than other candidates. While @realDonaldTrump's use of 'we' is within the range of other candidates', Trump hardly uses the pronoun 'us' – a bit surprising for a presidential candidate who is expected to lead America to a 'great' shared future. (Tsur, Ognyanova and Lazer 2016)

The Friend/Enemy Scheme on Twitter

Carl Schmitt characterised the friend/enemy scheme worldview in the following way:

> The specific political distinction to which political actions and motives can be reduced is that between friend and enemy [...] Insofar as it is not derived from other criteria, the antithesis of friend and enemy corresponds to the relatively independent criteria of other antitheses: good and evil in the moral sphere, beautiful and ugly in the aesthetic sphere, and so on. [...] The distinction of friend and enemy denotes the utmost degree of intensity of a union or separation, of an association or dissociation. [...] Emotionally the enemy is easily treated as being evil and ugly, because every distinction, most of all the political, as the strongest and most intense of the distinctions and categorizations, draws upon other distinctions for support. [...] The enemy is solely the public enemy, because everything that has a relationship to such a collectivity of men, particularly to a whole nation, becomes public by virtue of such a relationship. [...] War follows from enmity. War is the existential negation of the enemy. It is the most extreme consequence of enmity. It does not have to be common, normal, something ideal, or desirable. But it must nevertheless remain a real possibility for as long as the concept of the enemy remains valid. (Schmitt 1932/1996, 26, 27, 28, 33)

For Trump, Twitter is a symbolic and communicative battlefield. Trump calls social media his 'method of fighting back':

> It's a great form of communication. [...] I think I picked up yesterday 100,000 people. I'm not saying I love it, but it does get the word out. When you give me a bad story or when you give me an inaccurate story or when somebody other than you and another network, or whatever, 'cause of course, CBS would never do a thing like that right? I have a method of fighting back. That's very tough. [...] I really believe that the fact that I have such power in terms of numbers with Facebook, Twitter, Instagram, et cetera, I think it helped me win all of these races where they're spending much more money than I spent.[7]

---

7.   www.scribd.com/document/330970776/Trump-60-Minutes-2#download&from_
embed, accessed on 14 October 2017.

TRUMP AND THE MEDIA: TELEVISION, REALITY TV AND
THE APPRENTICE

Television

Besides Twitter, television is also a very important communication medium for Trump. The first television debate between Trump and Clinton reached a total of 84 million US viewers, including 18 million viewers on NBC, 13.5 million on ABC, 12.1 million on CBS, 11.4 million on Fox News, 9.9 million on CNN, 5.5 million on the Fox network channels, 4.9 million on MSNBC, 2.5 million on Univision and 1.8 million on Telemundo (Stelter 2016). The debate attracted the largest audience ever reached in 60 years of televised US presidential debates:

> In November, Fox averaged 3.3 million viewers in primetime, a 68% increase over November 2015. CNN averaged 1.5 million viewers, a 128% increase from last November. MSNBC attracted 1.3 million viewers, a 98% increase. [...] Strong ratings have translated into solid profits and revenues. Ad revenue for cable news may reach $2 billion this year, a 15 increase over 2015. Media analytics company SNL Kagan predicts record-breaking profits of $1.67 billion for Fox News and nearly $1 billion for CNN. (Edkins 2016)

The *New York Times* saw its paid subscriptions increasing by 132,000 during a three-week period in November 2016, a growth rate ten times higher than during the same period in 2015 (Belvedere and Newberg 2016).

In the world of the capitalist spectacle, the capitalist media need Trump just like Trump needs the media. The mainstream media helped make Trump, both economically and politically. A truly critical strategy would be to provide no free promotion to Trump by ignoring him. To say nothing, report nothing and comment on nothing that is right-wing demagogical in character has to be part of breaking the right-wing spectacle's spell. According to a report, NBC, CBS and ABC gave 23.4 times more coverage to Trump than to Sanders (Boehlert 2015). An alternative strategy also requires changing the balance of forces in media coverage.

The Apprentice: Trumpology as Reality TV Spectacle

The Apprentice is a reality TV show broadcast by NBC. It featured Donald Trump as host and juror from 2004 until 2015. The concept of the show involves a group of participants who want to become successful entrepreneurs and learn from Trump. They compete against each other by performing business tasks. Each week, Trump eliminates at least one with the words 'You're fired'. In 2008, NBC also introduced the show *The Celebrity Apprentice*, in which celebrities participate. Trump created the media company Trump Productions for producing these shows.

'Why do you think NBC gave me my own show, *The Apprentice*? They did it because I set myself apart to be a target, the big, tough employer. The result was one of the most successful shows in television history. I'm the only boss in the world who boosts a person's future status by firing them' (Trump 2015a, 12). Trump's image as a combative leader and tough businessman drove audience ratings. More than 40 million viewers watched the first season's finale in 2004 (Carter 2004).

NBC didn't just pay Trump for hosting *The Apprentice*, the show was also an opportunity for Trump to present and sell himself as a brand:

> Donald Trump built his reputation selling real estate, but the thing he had always wanted to sell was Donald Trump. His career as a reality television star would finally make Trump into a household brand – and he was determined to cash in. [...] Trump Menswear made an appearance, of course, on an episode of *The Apprentice*. So did Trump Ice, a new brand of water, and Trump Success, a new fragrance. Riding the popularity of the show, Trump licensed his name to clothes, ties, home furnishings, eyeglasses, wallets, even mattresses. (Kranish and Fisher 2016, 221, 224)

Analysis of *The Apprentice's* Elimination Scenes

I have analysed a large sample of 201 elimination scenes from *The Apprentice's* first 14 seasons (2004–15) by conducting a content analysis of the scenes in the boardroom. The analysis focused on how Trump justifies the elimination of candidates. Table 5.2 shows the results. The reasons for firing are summarised as ideal types.

Table 5.2 Frequency of Donald Trump's justifications for the elimination of participants in *The Apprentice* (2004–15), N = 201

Reason for firing	Absolute frequency	Relative frequency (%)	Example justifications
'You have no leadership capacities!'	95	47.3	'A stupid, impulsive, life-threatening decision. Frankly, if you are running a company and make that kind of decision, you destroy that company instantaneously' (S2E2)
			'You wouldn't step up as a leader' (S1E10)
			'I just don't think that you are a strong leader' (S3E11)
			'You were the team leader. The team was a mess. The project was no good. And Chris, you are fired' (S3E12).
			'Your decision making was terrible' (S4E6)
			'Lenny made a lot of mistakes. Lenny was not a good leader for this team. […] The leadership wasn't good' (S5E7)
			'You're not a proper leader. Amy, you're fired!' (S6E1)
			'You did a lousy job and you're a bad project manager' (S6E7)
			'But the concept was flawed and you were the project manager. You got killed' (S6E11)
			'You couldn't control him. You brought in no money. And you had a lousy looking store. You were not much of a team leader. […] You are fired! You were lousy last week, lousy this week. We have to do it. Go!' (S8E3)
'Your performance was poor!'	73	36.3	'You lose! I do not want to take a chance on somebody who loses all the time perhaps' (S2E13)
			'Everybody virtually said you just did not contribute, you were not a go-getter' (S2E1)
			'You are totally ineffective. You have done a terrible job' (S4E4)
			'You didn't sell. You failed' (S4E6)
			'You did not do much' (S4E7)
			'No matter which team you are on, all you do is create problems' (S4E9)
			'That suit is a loser. On this task, you did a horrible job!' (S6E2)
			'Alex sold the least. And Alex just does not seem to have the same passion as you two guys. Alex, you are fired!' (S10E2)
			'He raised no money. Gotta do it. Richard, you are fired!' (S11E5)
			'Deborah raised the least money of the people you brought back. Deborah, you are fired!' (S12E7)

Reason for firing	Absolute frequency	Relative frequency (%)	Example justifications
'You are no fighter. You are not tough. You are weak'	11	5.5	'I hated the way you took so much crap […] To me that was a form of weakness' (S1E6)
			'You did not fight for yourself and you are fired' (S1E5)
			'You are not strong enough to be here, you are just not strong enough' (S4E12)
			'It was just too much emotion […] From a pure business point of view, too much emotion can also be not so good. And therefore, Meat Loaf, you are fired!' (S11E11)
'You were disloyal to your team'	9	4.5	'You lashed out at your project leader, which was completely out of line' (S2E11)
			'What I hate is that Stacey keeps going on about responsibility, how it is never your fault. You never take responsibility. […] You can't just blame the project manager when you are unsuccessful getting your point across' (S2E7)
			'Every single woman in this room thought you were a disruptive force' (S4E1)
			'Most importantly, there was a great disloyalty to your team. Lou, you are fired!' (S12E8)
Candidate quits	6	3	
'Your behaviour is unpredictable'	4	2	'I just can't have a loose cannon on my hands' (S2E3)
'The others do not like you'	1	0.5	'Your teammates did not really like you too much' (S2E15)
'The others are more exciting than you are'	1	0.5	
Cheating	1	0.5	

The analysis shows that the justifications that Trump used most frequently for eliminated contestants were that in his opinion they showed poor leadership or performed poorly. The third most frequent elimination reason was that Trump thought candidates were weak and emotional. Taking these aspects together, it becomes clear that Trump in *The Apprentice* imagines a good business person to be a strong and hierarchic leader, who works hard, achieves high performance measured in terms of success and profits, shows no weaknesses, and is tough and ruthless.

The ideal manager and worker as portrayed in *The Apprentice* is a person who shows all the features of Trumpology: possessive individualism, performance and hard labour, top-down leadership and the belief in survival of the fittest and cut-throat competition (social Darwinism).

In the boardroom scenes, Trump often uses negative terms that can have humiliating effects on those he eliminates. Typical examples are 'stupid', 'mess', 'terrible', 'mistakes', 'not good', 'lousy', 'bad', 'flawed', 'losing', 'failing', 'ineffective', 'loser', 'horrible', 'weakness', 'not strong enough', 'too much emotion', 'unsuccessful', 'disruptive'. Such terms set up a clear binary between tough, successful, hard-working winners and weak, unsuccessful, lazy losers. *The Apprentice* conveys a picture of society as consisting only of winners and losers with nothing in-between. The winners are presented as strong and tough, like warriors in an army. The soldier is the ultimate role model, on which Trumpology and *The Apprentice* are built. There is also a patriarchal dimension that uses dualisms such as strong/weak, rational/emotional, the leaders/the led. The model of the warrior always implies the possibility for war, which is present in the dimension of cut-throat competition.

Survival of the fittest, hierarchy and performance measurement in *The Apprentice* imply that you have to make profits in order to be a winner. Those who are blamed for poor financial performance are therefore often eliminated: 'You brought in no money', 'You didn't sell. You failed', 'He sold the least', 'He raised no money', 'She raised the least money'. The unity of leadership, possessive individualism, performance measurement and social Darwinism is ideologically and socially aimed at the accumulation of money and power.

Individualism, Hard Labour, Leadership and Social Darwinism

Academic literature studying *The Apprentice* has stressed several aspects.

(1) Individualism: 'The world of *The Apprentice* is based around an extreme individualism, where everyone is a master of his (or her) own destiny, to the detriment of all others. Trump frequently describes the task themselves – from selling candy bars to constructing ad campaigns – as military operations' (Franko 2006, 255). 'The participants represent models of conduct, to be approved or disapproved according to extant

ideological criteria of "the American dream", which involves the prospect of individual ascent to the top irrespective of social background, and correct "enterprising" business practice under neoliberal conditions' (McGuigan 2008, 310–11).

(2) The ideology of hard labour: 'By presenting the "reality" of work and business in the form of highly structured entertainment, *The Apprentice* transforms the norms of the neoliberal workplace into taken-for-granted "common sense"' (Couldry and Littler 2011, 265). The 'highly distinctive *performance* norms of neoliberal business culture are themselves naturalized and objectified as part of "the real world out there" [...] neoliberal norms are reified as "rules of the game"' (Couldry and Littler 2011, 275).

(3) Leadership: 'Trump himself acts, without any irony, as the semi-autocratic ruler and the ultimate CEO' (Franko 2006, 248).

(4) Social Darwinism: 'The Apprentice is imbued with market values and seeks to validate the absolute worth of capitalist business whatever the human cost – most obviously the arduous testing of candidates in the show in order to reveal the fittest' (McGuigan 2008, 318).

The Apprentice poses questions about the relationship of play/labour, the real/the symbolic, cooperation/competition, consciousness/the unconscious, the real/the imaginary and the real/the ideological. It is a game in which real-world participants perform labour as play. It is an artificial, mediated and symbolic game that is a manifestation of neoliberal capitalism's reality. It features cooperation for the sake of competition so that feelings of solidarity are subsumed under the logic of individual survival and competition. The show allows the audience to project their desires of success and their actual experiences of stress and hardship into the candidates and Donald Trump as leader. Such projections involve both love and aggression towards particular successful and unsuccessful participants, and towards Trump's success, behaviour and aggression.

Authoritarian Spectacle

The Apprentice's competition between winners and losers is a mediated socio-psychological spectacle and drama that appeals to viewers' unconscious desires, fantasies and drives. The real and the imaginary life of both participants and viewers meet in the programme's symbolic world that is broadcast into everyday people's homes. But given the way the programme is constructed around cut-throat competition, hyper-individualism, elimination and the ruthless firing and humiliation of the least successful, *The Apprentice's* socio-psychological structure has a predominantly instrumental and ideological character. It hails the viewers as neoliberal subjects and tries to teach them neoliberal militancy and neoliberalism as a philosophy of life. *The Apprentice* portrays reality in its neoliberal version and tries to implement this image as normal reality. It is of course not certain to what extent this instrumental project is successful because audiences are complex. But we can say that the ideological dimension is the key feature of *The Apprentice*.

The Apprentice sets up an extremely polarised vision of society – a world in which there is just one winner and all others are losers, who are on their own, are eliminated, crushed and for whom there is no mercy, solidarity or support. *The Apprentice* envisions a world of untamed, pure capitalism without a welfare state and without solidarity. It wants to advance a world without elements of socialism; an unsocial world; an inhumane society; a society without society that is simply an agglomeration of egoistic individuals. *The Apprentice* is not just a TV show, but also an ideological project that tries to normalise pure capitalism.

The analysis shows that hyper-individualism, the ideology of performance and hard labour, top-down leadership, and social Darwinism, along with the friend/enemy distinction, form key elements of Trumpology. *The Apprentice* reflects the elements of this ideology in a game show that tries to normalise and justify a pure version of capitalism that lacks any elements of solidarity and social security. Imagine a society whose political system is guided by the vision advanced by Trumpology and *The Apprentice*. In such a society, large parts of the welfare state and public services are privatised. It is an autocratic society that is governed top-down with limited possibilities for opposition. Law-and-order politics impose harsh sentences even for minor crimes. It is a highly armed and militarised society threatening to use its repressive capacities against perceived enemies. Corporate taxation is low or non-existent. Workers' rights hardly exist. There is no minimum wage regulation. Trade unions have no influence on working conditions. There are close ties between big capital and the state that advances monopoly capital's interests. Culture is unitary and closed and based on a strict dichotomy of the nation and the foreign.

Ideologies always have real and fictitious dimensions. It is not prede-termined how close or distant a society governed by Donald Trump as president can come to Trumpology's dystopia. The decisive question will be to what extent Trump wants to and can realise elements of Trumpology in actual politics. This depends on the degree to which his policies are resisted by internal forces (within the Republican Party) and external forces (parliamentary opposition, civil society). In newspapers and on *The Apprentice*, Twitter and television shows, Trumpology presents itself in a rather frightening way. A key question is to what degree President Trump can put ideology into policy, words into action, and keep up and radicalise Trumpology's economic, political and ideological dimensions.

CONCLUSION: TOWARDS A CRITICAL THEORY OF CONTEMPORARY AUTHORITARIANISM, TRUMPOLOGY AND TRUMPISM

In critical theory, the leadership principle, nationalism, the friend/enemy scheme and patriarchy/militarism are seen as four important features of authoritarianism.

The Leadership Principle

The leadership principle is the first important element of authoritar-ianism. Adorno argues that an authoritarian leader 'characteristically indulges in loquacious statements about himself' (Adorno 1975, 11). We have seen in the analysis presented in this chapter that Trumpism and Trumpology are all about Trump as brand, business leader and political leader. Trump's politics and ideology are completely centred around himself. The reason why this strategy has made him President of the Unites States may be that the personality cult and the identifica-tion with one person as leader responds to the 'coldness, [...] despair, isolation, and loneliness' (11) under which individuals suffer. 'The more impersonal our order becomes, the more important personality becomes as an ideology. The more the individual is reduced to a mere cog, the more the idea of the uniqueness of the individual, his autonomy and importance, has to be stressed as a compensation for his actual weakness' (11–12). Trump's followers project their frustrations into

Trump as a symbol of their longing for love and hope. The follower, 'by making the leader his ideal [...] loves himself, as it were, but gets rid of the stains of frustration and discontent which mar his picture of his own empirical self'. There is 'identification through idealization' (Adorno 1991, 140).

The leader often presents himself as a lone wolf fighting against political elites (Adorno 1975, 14). This comes along with 'aversion to the professional politician and perhaps to any kind of expertness' (21). We have seen that Trump opposed the established political elites in the Democratic Party and the Republican Party. He cultivates the image of a lone wolf – a self-made billionaire and self-made president opposing career politicians. He presents himself as the prototypical winner of the American Dream, who by hard labour has made it to the top. The message to everyday Americans is, 'If I can make it to the top, then you can do so too!' Authoritarianism perpetuates 'actually and ideologically the necessity of hard work, this obtaining a justification for "discipline" and oppression' (Adorno 1975, 23).

Trump's demagogical, aggressive, attack-oriented, offensive, proletarian language and style make him appear as a great little man who is on top, but at the same time is an ordinary person. The great little man is 'a person who suggests both omnipotence and the idea that he is just one of the folks' (Adorno 1991, 142). 'While appearing as superman, the leader must at the same time work the miracle of appearing as an average person' (141). The great little man 'walks unrecognized in the same paths as other folks, but [...] finally is to be revealed as the saviour' (Adorno 1975, 29).

Nationalism

Nationalism is the second feature of authoritarianism. Demagogues try to create an artificial bond (Adorno 1991, 135) such as the nation. They use what Adorno calls the unity trick: they argue that everyone, except outsiders, is part of the nation and that out-groups are threatening this unity. They make use of the logic of repressive egalitarianism (146). 'They emphasize their being different from the outsider but play down such differences within their own group and tend to level out distinctive qualities among themselves with the exception of the hierarchical one' (146). They aim at 'the establishment of something utterly limited and particularistic as the totality, the whole, the community' (Adorno 1975, 58). We have seen that Trump argues that he will make 'America great again'. He promises prosperity, wealth and worldwide recognition to American citizens. But he can do so only by constructing enemy out-groups that are seen as damaging the greatness of the American nation. By playing with nationalism, Trump deflects attention from the actual class differences within the United States.

The Friend/Enemy Scheme

Authoritarianism as its third feature makes use of the friend/enemy scheme. Nationalist unity always has an outside that is portrayed as the enemy: 'the Communists, the radicals, the sceptics, and, of course, the Jews. These groups are *a priori* exempted from such a unity; they merely threaten it and must be "driven away"' (Adorno 1975, 59–60). The imagined unity is one of the 'right people' (60). The right-wing demagogue 'cannot help feeling surrounded by traitors, and so continuously threatens to exterminate them' (78). Erich Fromm (1936) characterises the authoritarian personality as a sadomasochistic character type that feels pleasure in both submission to authority and the subjection of underdogs. Authoritarian societies foster sadomasochistic personalities (117–18), and authoritarian personalities therefore show 'aggression against the defenceless and sympathy for the powerful' (115). Authoritarianism has an extremely polarised relationship with the powerful and the weak: 'To the one group all good characteristics are ascribed and they are loved, and to the other group all negative characteristics are ascribed and they are hated' (116). Authoritarian personalities would often support and promote this dual structure in order to reach the double goal of on the one hand keeping the relationship with one group 'free from hatred and directing on the other hand hatred against forces that it wants to combat with the help of the subaltern' (116).

Trump constructs out-groups such as illegal immigrants, Mexico, China, Muslims, oppositional politicians and his critics. They are presented as threatening the greatness of the American nation. According to Adorno, identification with the leader and hatred against the out-group allows emotional release (Adorno 1975, 16–20). Such a release of aggression encourages 'excess and violence' (17).

Patriarchy and Militarism

Patriarchy and militarism play a peculiar role in authoritarianism as its fourth feature. The male warrior, who fights and does not show emotions, is presented as the ideal human being that should be imitated. The 'model of the military officer' is 'transferred to the realm of politics' (Adorno 1975, 49). Love to the leader is an 'emotional compensation for the cold, self-alienated life of most people' (Adorno 1975, 37). We have seen that in Trump's world, survival, toughness, strength and the willingness to fight, lead and compete are moral norms. Any 'reference to love is almost completely excluded', and the 'traditional role of the loving father' is replaced 'by the negative one of threatening authority' (Adorno 1991, 137).

But at the same time, love for the leader is a psychological factor that allows followers to project their fears and their hope for compensation into the leader. The leader stands for 'an omnipotent and unbridled father figure', and identification is the psychological expression of an emotional tie between the leader and a community that accepts this leadership (Adorno 1991, 139). So whereas love is on the one hand excluded from politics and relegated to the realm of the family, at the same time it plays a key role in the identification with the leader that is love for the leader and at the same time the compensation for the fear of not feeling loved and accepted by society. 'The desire to be loved, no matter if it is more or less conscious, and the fear of loss even just of the possibility to be loved are the basis for admiration and obedience' (Fromm 1936, 78).

Neumann (1957/2017, 624–8) argues that political change in a specific direction can occur under the condition of the alienation of labour, destructive competition and political alienation. If such objective conditions are translated into feelings of social alienation, i.e. the collective fear by a group that 'its prestige, income, or even its existence' (626) could decline, then such change becomes more likely. Neumann adds that in such situations, institutionalised forms of anxiety such as demagogic leaders, movements and parties often bring about the transition from objective conditions and subjective anxiety into political action and change.

We have seen that the conditions of American capitalism have featured relative wage decreases, resulting in the increase of capital in total wealth, costly technological progress, fluctuating profit rates that have spurred financialisation, capital export and deindustrialisation within an international division of labour. Political alienation, i.e. the structural feeling that politicians do not represent everyday citizens, accompanies the rising power of capital. In this situation, right-wing demagogues have institutionalised anxiety by spurring nationalism and resentment against immigrants, refugees, Muslims and their opponents and critics. This means that scapegoats have become the subject of aggression and projected fears. The political trick is that ideology deflects attention from the role of class and capitalism in the creation of social problems. The paradoxical effect is that working-class voters elect a billionaire as president who represents the political interest of capital because the national interest is foregrounded against imagined enemies so that the class conflict is ideologically made invisible, although it continues to exist.

The US State under Trump

Table 5.3 summarises what the state and politics could look like under Trump's rule. The fact that a billionaire has become the president implies a significant change in the relationship between the state and the economy. Big capital has more opportunities to rule directly. The government that Trump appointed indicates the tendency towards an overlap between the political elite and the capitalist class. One has to wait and see what this means in terms of concrete economic policies. The ideological and political signs certainly point towards an even purer and untamed capitalism than before. A key question is how the realm of oppositional politics and civil liberties will develop under Trump. His political rhetoric in the election campaign and the elements of Trumpology have raised fears of what may happen. In general, threats to civil liberties create the potential for the rise of authoritarian statism.

Trumpism is not just a brand, a business strategy and a political strategy. Trumpism is also Trumpology, an ideology that stages itself as spectacle in public and in the media. Trumpology involves elements such as possessive individualism, the ideology of hard labour, performance measurements, hierarchic leadership, survival of the fittest and cut-throat competition.

For-profit mainstream media that are often (pseudo-)critical of Trump have helped to make him because they know that making Trump

Table 5.3   Dimensions of the state under Trump

Dimension	Possible changes to the state and politics under Trump
Relationship of the state to the economy	Overlap of the political elite and the capitalist class in the form of a billionaire turned politician. There is a tendency for the blurring of the boundaries between the state and big capital. Economic policies: • Low-tax economy with massive tax reductions for corporations and the rich. • Protectionism (e.g. tariffs) and deglobalisation of the US economy. • State intervention in favour of big capital (oil/gas/coal industry, healthcare and pharmaceutical industry, private education, construction, etc.) • Private–public partnerships in infrastructure projects featuring socialised financial risk and private ownership. • Logic of privatisation and for-profit in health care and education.
State institutions and the relationship of the state and citizens	Law-and-order politics. Close political ties to far-right figures, friend/enemy logic, revanchism ('screw them back in spades') and the insulting of opponents have raised fears of authoritarian statism. The scapegoating of immigrants and Muslims has raised fears of authoritarian statism.
Inter-state relations	Foreign trade: • Scepticism of international free trade agreements. • Scapegoating of other nations for socio-economic problems in the USA. Foreign policy: • Plan to build a wall between the Mexican and the US border. • Political distance and hostility towards certain countries such as China, North Korea, Mexico, Iran and Cuba. • Unilateralism. • Politics of armament. • Friend/enemy scheme.
Ideology	Trumpology: • Possessive individualism. • Ideology of hard labour and performance measurement. • Hierarchic leadership. • Social Darwinism, survival of the fittest, cut-throat competition. A key question for the future of the US state and US society is to which degree these ideological elements will be used as discourses by the state and discourses on the state that are put into political practice.

means that Trump makes them: the monetary and reputational profits of Trump and the for-profit mainstream media live in a contested but happy symbiosis within the capitalism of the spectacle. The only way of overcoming this vicious cycle that has contributed to Trump's political rise would be to slow down the speed of the media (slow media) and to stop giving so much attention to Trump. The media rather would have to give much more attention, space and time to the analysis and discussion of the big contradictions that society faces at the macro level.

Neumann: Progressive Intellectuals and Authoritarianism

The combination of Trump's actual power and Trump as spectacle, showman and brand makes his government's concrete policies fairly unpredictable. In the 1950s, Neumann wrote the essay *Anxiety and Politics*, in which he reflects on what intellectuals can do in political situations, where they face threats of the rise of authoritarianism. His words sound very topical in the world of 2017. Neumann argues that what remains is

> the dual offensive on anxiety and for liberty: that of education and that of politics. Politics, again, should be a dual thing for us: the penetration of the subject matter of our academic discipline with the problems of politics – naturally, not day-to-day politics – and the taking of positions on political questions. If we are serious about the humanization of politics; if we wish to prevent a demagogue from using anxiety and apathy, then we – as teachers and students – must not be silent. We must suppress our arrogance, inertia, and our revulsion from the alleged dirt of day-to-day politics. We must speak and write. [...] Only through our own responsible educational and political activity can the words of idealism become history. (Neumann 1957/2017, 629)

6

Trump and Twitter: Authoritarian-Capitalist Ideology on Social Media

INTRODUCTION

On 8 November 2016, Donald Trump won the US presidential election. He was inaugurated as the forty-fifth president of the USA on 20 January 2017. Trump is one of the most polarising and controversial presidents in the United States' history.

Trump stands for what can be characterised as authoritarian capitalism, based on the direct rule of the billionaire class, nationalism, scapegoating, the friend/enemy scheme, law-and-order politics and mediated spectacles (see Chapters 4 and 5). Human Rights Watch (2017, 4) wrote about Trump in its *World Report 2017*:

> Donald Trump's successful campaign for the US presidency was a vivid illustration of this politics of intolerance. Sometimes overtly, sometimes through code and indirection, he spoke to many Americans' discontent with economic stagnation and an increasingly multicultural society in a way that breached basic principles of dignity and equality. He stereotyped migrants, vilified refugees, attacked a judge for his Mexican ancestry, mocked a journalist with disabilities, dismissed multiple allegations of sexual assault, and pledged to roll back women's ability to control their own fertility.

David Renton (1999, 15) argues that '[c]apitalism, as a system, remains prone to crisis, and if crisis can return, then so can fascism'. Capitalism was hit by a major crisis in 2008 that was followed by political turmoil and transformations in many countries. New nationalisms and elements of fascism have proliferated. Bob Altemeyer (2016), an expert on the analysis of right-wing authoritarianism, argues that Trump wants to dominate everyone and he will do whatever he can get away with to become 'Number One.' Often the movement he leads becomes a personality clique, because ultimately it is really just about, only about, him. Trump appears every bit as narcissistic as he is aggressive and constantly striving for dominance. [...] The most remarkable thing about Donald Trump as an authoritarian leader, in my mind, is that he's so obvious about it.

The problem is that Trump's followers do not have a rational, but an emotional relation with him. 'I don't think you can change the minds of many Trump supporters. Winning fact-driven discussions about the man and the issues will likely make them more defensive. [...] It's based on fear that he fans and anger that he channels' (Altemeyer 2016).

By hosting *The Apprentice*, Trump became a reality TV celebrity. Twitter is his main political communication tool. Trump calls his Twitter channel 'a method of fighting back' that 'does get the word out'.[1] After the inauguration, Trump argued that he will 'keep the Twitter going' because 'it's a way of bypassing dishonest media'.[2] Such announcements show that Twitter will be a key medium of political communication and contestation during Trump's presidency. This chapter asks: how does Trump communicate ideology on Twitter? For giving an answer, it applies critical discourse analysis (CDA) to a sample of Donald Trump's tweets.

This chapter applies the Frankfurt School's critical theory of the authoritarian personality to Trump's Twitter use in an empirical case study, and the works of Wilhelm Reich, Theodor W. Adorno, Franz L. Neumann, Erich Fromm and Leo Löwenthal are of particular importance in this context. Douglas Kellner (2016) uses Fromm's approach for characterising Trump as authoritarian populist. Trump presents himself as a magic helper who will make American great again (21). Kellner expresses the view that Trump has an excessive ego (29), is a narcissistic figure (31) with deep-rooted aggression (33, 37), shows malignant aggression when he lashes out 'at anyone who dares to criticize him' (33) as well as a tendency to think in terms of things instead of living beings and their relations (37). Kellner shows on a general level how Fromm's

---

1.   www.cbsnews.com/news/60-minutes-donald-trump-family-melania-ivanka-lesley-stahl/, accessed 14 October 2017.

2.   www.mediaite.com/election-2016/should-i-keep-the-twitter-going-or-not-trump-asks-crowd-at-inaugural-ball/, accessed 14 October 2017.

analysis can be used for analysing Trump. This book undertakes a comparable approach, with the difference that (a) it uses Fromm but also the work of other critical theorists such as Adorno and Neumann; and (b) it undertakes a case study of how Trump communicates ideology and authoritarianism online.

The next section explains the methodology. Section three presents and interprets the main results. The fourth section draws conclusions.

METHODOLOGY: CRITICAL SOCIAL MEDIA DISCOURSE ANALYSIS

Big Data Analytics and Computational Social Science

Social media research is dominated by big data analytics and computational social science (Fuchs 2017b). These methods focus on the quantitative analysis of data that, due to its vast amount, cannot be analysed by humans, but only by software. Computational social science leaves out the analysis of how humans communicate and of the contexts, contradictions and power structures in which communications are embedded.

The danger of big data analytics is that the 'convergence of social-scientific methods toward those of the natural sciences is itself the child of a society that reifies people' (Pollock and Adorno 2011, 20). Critical digital and social media research, in contrast, takes a qualitative, theory-based approach that analyses the role of digital media, social media and data in the context of society's contradictions and power structures (Fuchs 2017b).

Critical Discourse Analysis

CDA is a tradition of critical analysis that studies semiotic elements (information, language, speech, images, multimedia, data, etc.) in the context of power relations (Fairclough 2009, 2015; Reisigl and Wodak 2009, 2001; Wodak and Meyer 2009). CDA analyses 'structural relationships of dominance, discrimination, power and control as manifested in language' (Wodak and Meyer 2009, 10). 'CDA combines critique of discourse and explanation of how it figures within and contributes to the existing social reality, as a basis for action to change that existing reality in particular respects' (Fairclough 2015, 6). That CDA combines discourse critique, explanation and action means that its focus is on three types of critique: CDA combines text-immanent critique, socio-diagnostic critique and prospective critique (Reisigl and Wodak 2001, 31–5). A comprehensive definition of CDA is that it critically analyses and theorises *texts* in their *contexts* in order to advance the *prospects* for progressive changes in society.

The application of CDA to social media data is still at an early stage (Khosravinik 2013; Unger, Wodak and Khosravinik 2016). Majid Khosravinik (2013, 292) argues in this context that 'critical discourse analysis appears to have shied away from new media research in the bulk of its research'. The study at hand is a contribution to the development of critical social media discourse analysis in particular, and critical digital and social media studies in general. Social media features such as user-generated content, linking, individual profiles, contact networks, hashtags, likes, retweeting, discussion groups, communities and the use of multimedia are distinct features of social media discourse (Fuchs 2017d). When conducting a critical social media discourse analysis, there are two aspects that need special planning: data collection and research ethics. Manual data collection via copy and paste is very cumbersome and can be imprecise. Therefore one should rely on automated data-collection tools.[3] Research ethics poses special challenges in respect to informed consent and the blurring boundaries between public and private communication on the Internet (Fuchs 2017d, chapter 2; Townsend et al. 2016).

Critical Social Media Discourse Analysis

In the deductive, critical theory-oriented approach taken in this chapter, critical social media discourse analysis involves the following steps (see also Fuchs 2016d, 2016e):

1. Data collection;
2. Identification of discursive macro topics;
3. Analysis of the structure of ideology and discourse for each macro topic;

---

3. For an overview of available tools, see: wiki.digitalmethods.net/Dmi/ToolDatabase, accessed 14 October 2017.

4. Analysis and theorisation of how online discourse and ideology are related to the broader societal context, i.e. the relations of the online-semiotic elements to the broader societal context;
5. Prospective critique.

The *first step* in this study collected data from Donald Trump's Twitter account @RealDonaldTrump. The collection commenced on 18 July 2016, which was the day the Republican National Convention started, where Trump was nominated as the Republican presidential candidate. Data gathering ended on 21 January 2017, one day after Trump's inauguration. This period covers two distinct phases, namely the main electoral campaign phase and the post-electoral campaign phase. After the Republican National Convention, Trump was no longer focused on internal debates, but on winning the presidency.

The tweets posted on the Twitter profile @RealDonaldTrump are targeted at the political public. Trump's tweets are forms of public political communication. In such a case, no informed consent is required for data collection, analysis and citation (Fuchs 2017d, chapter 2; Townsend et al. 2016). TAGS (Twitter Archiving Google Sheet) is a plug-in for Google Docs that supports the automated collection of specified tweets. TAGS version 6.0 was used in combination with Google Docs Sheets for collecting tweets from the Twitter handle @RealDonaldTrump. The archive created was automatically updated once an hour. Data collection resulted in a dataset consisting of 1,815 tweets.

Macro topics are the big topics that a specific discourse deals with. The conducted study takes a deductive approach: it identifies, as the *second step*, macro discourse topics of authoritarian ideology. In order to identify key features it engages with the critical theory of authoritarianism. Frankfurt School theories are of central importance in this context. The analysis then applies the theoretical foundations for investigating the ideological structure of Trump's tweets as the *third step*. This part of the chapter also relates as the *fourth step*: analysing how ideology is related to broader power structures. Steps three and four are closely related. They focus on text-immanent critique and socio-diagnostic critique. As the *fifth step*, the conclusion conducts a prospective critique that reflects on how the identified problems and contradictions could be overcome.

ANALYSIS: TRUMP ON TWITTER

There were a total of 1,815 Trump postings during the analysed period. The average number of retweets was 13,275. During the period between 18 July and 8 November 2016, there were 1,420 postings with an average of 11,099 retweets per posting. After Trump won the US presidential election on 8 November, the average retweets per posting increased to 20,959 for the period between the election win and the inauguration on 21 January 2017 (N = 395 postings). Figure 6.1 shows the development of Trump's number of followers on Twitter. Whereas the average weekly growth in the number of Trump followers was 1.8 per cent between his nomination (18 July 2016) and his victory in the presidential election (8 November 2016), it increased to an average of 5.2 per cent for the period between Trump's election win and his inauguration as US president (21 January 2017). Such data indicate that Trump's election victory further increased his social media attention and visibility.

At the end of May 2017, Trump had around 31 million Twitter followers. This number had grown by 2.3 million since the beginning of May and by seven million since early February (Dockray 2017). According to an analysis, of 'Trump's 7 million new followers, 4 million of them are egg avatars, who are disproportionately likely to be fake' (Dockray 2017). Twitter Audit[4] estimated on 31 May 2017 that 15.9 million (51.4 per cent) of Trump's followers were real and 15 million (48.6 per cent) were fake accounts. Barack Obama at the same time had 89.2 million Twitter followers, the third largest number (after Katy Perry and Justin Bieber). According to Twitter Audit, 79.3 per cent of these followers were real and 20.7 per cent fake. According to such analyses, a significant share of Trump's followers and online attention has been artificially created and sustained by an army of bots.

What Keywords Does Trump Frequently Use on Twitter?

Figure 6.2 shows a word cloud of the most frequently mentioned keywords in the analysed dataset. The terms 'https' (1,016 mentions), 'Thank' (as in 'Thank you', 275 occurrences), 'Hillary' (245), 'join' (128), 'make/making' (114, used in 'Make America Great Again'),

---

4.   www.twitteraudit.com/Realdonaldtrump, accessed 14 October 2017.

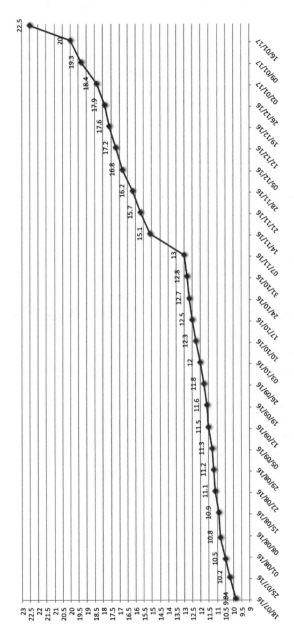

Figure 6.1 Development of the number of Donald Trump's Twitter followers (millions) (data source: Wayback Machine [twitter.com/realdonaldtrump], accessed on 2 February 2017)

'@RealDonaldTrump' (110) occur relatively frequently. This result indicates that Trump's Twitter communication is highly intertextual: he frequently links to other online material. He likes to convey and repeat simple ideological messages ('Make America Great Again'), to talk about himself, thank and appeal to his voters, allies and followers, and rant about his enemies (such as Hillary Clinton in the analysed period). It becomes evident that he uses a clear distinction between an in-group (his followers), of whom he sees himself as leader, and an out-group (all those who oppose him). Trump's online communication follows the logic of the friend/enemy scheme. According to Carl Schmitt (1932/1996, 28), the inventor of this scheme, 'nations continue to group themselves according to the friend and enemy antithesis' and an 'enemy exists only when, at least potentially, one fighting collectivity of people confronts a similar collectivity'. The use of the friend/enemy logic is often associated with nationalism.

Figure 6.2 Word cloud showing the most frequently used words in the analysed dataset of Donald Trump's tweets (generated in NVivo)

The Coding Scheme

To get a basic overview of the dataset, first a basic coding using the variables shown in Table 6.1 was conducted. Each tweet can represent several discursive macro topics. Such topics can overlap.

Table 6.1   Coding scheme

Variable	Values
Retweet	Yes/No
Macro discourse topic 'Leadership principle'	Yes/No
Macro discourse topic 'Nationalism'	Yes/No
Macro discourse topic 'Friend/enemy scheme'	Yes/No
Macro discourse topic 'Patriarchy and militarism'	Yes/No
Macro discourse topic 'Naturalism'	Yes/No
Positive in-group presentation	Yes/No
Negative other-group presentation	Yes/No
Persons mentioned	Open coding
Groups mentioned	Open coding

The Ten Most Retweeted Trump Postings

Table 6.2 shows as an example the coding of the ten most retweeted postings in the dataset.

Table 6.2 provides indications that a nationalist 'Us' versus 'Them' logic seems to attract retweets. The combination of nationalist ideology and the friend/enemy scheme seems to increase attention. Trump presents politics as a constant struggle between Americans on the one side and those whom he see as enemies such as the liberal media, protesters, Fidel Castro, etc. The table also shows that attention to what is happening on Twitter is largest at the time of special events, such as a presidential election, Christmas or an inauguration. There is a dialectic of events and social media activity and attention.

Authoritarianism and Leadership

Leadership is a first important theme in Trump's tweets: 187 out of 1,815 tweets (10.3 per cent) contained elements where Trump presented

Table 6.2 Coding of Donald Trump's postings that achieved the highest number of retweets

	Tweet	Retweets	Date	Leadership	Nationalism	Friend/ enemy	Patriarchy, militarism
1	'TODAY WE MAKE AMERICA GREAT AGAIN!'	347,979	8 November 2016	No	Yes	No	No
2	'Such a beautiful and important evening! The forgotten man and woman will never be forgotten again. We will all come together as never before'	223,083	9 November 2016	No	Yes	No	No
3	'Happy New Year to all, including to my many enemies and those who have fought me and lost so badly they just don't know what to do. Love!'	143,546	31 December 2016	No	No	Yes	No
4	'The media is spending more time doing a forensic analysis of Melania's speech than the FBI spent on Hillary's emails'	119,239	20 July 2016	No	No	Yes	No
5	'Fidel Castro is dead!'	100,739	26 November 2016	No	No	Yes	No
6	'Nobody should be allowed to burn the American flag – if they do, there must be consequences – perhaps loss of citizenship or year in jail!'	73,419	29 November 2016	No	Yes	Yes	Yes
7	'It all begins today! I will see you at 11:00 A.M. for the swearing-in. THE MOVEMENT CONTINUES – THE WORK BEGINS!'	72,556	20 January 2017	Yes	No	No	No
8	'Just had a very open and successful presidential election. Now professional protesters, incited by the media, are protesting. Very unfair!'	70,265	11 November 2016	Yes	No	Yes	No
9	'January 20th 2017, will be remembered as the day the people became the rulers of this nation again'	60,232	20 January 2017	No	Yes	Yes	No
10	'We did it! Thank you to all of my great supporters, we just officially won the election (despite all of the distorted and inaccurate media)'	59,953	19 December 2016	No	Yes	No	Yes

himself as a leader who can solve America's problems. Here are typical examples:

> Inner-city crime is reaching record levels. African-Americans will vote for Trump because they know I will stop the slaughter going on! (#470)

> http://twitter.com/realDonaldTrump/statuses/757650904896139264: 'MAKE AMERICA SAFE AND GREAT AGAIN! #TrumpPence16 https://t.co/4O4yjh7X4O https://t.co/cptBaZbV1v'. (#91)

> [Image that shows Donald Trump in a black suit and red tie in the middle, one red bar to the left of him indicating '53% TRUMP', one blue bar to the right of him indicating '42% CLINTON', text at the bottom of the image: 'WHO WOULD BETTER HANDLE TERRORISM?']

> http://twitter.com/realDonaldTrump/statuses/773584728276475905: '#AmericaFirst!' (#550)

> [Image, where Donald Trump stands in front of a portrait of Ronald Reagan; text at the bottom of the image: 'THANK YOU UNION LEAGUE OF PHILADELPHIA! Donald J. Trump 9/7/2016']

CRIME AND TERROR

Crime and terror are two typical topics that Trump uses for arguing that the USA needs strong leadership. He uses an argumentation strategy known as the topos of danger and threat (Reisigl and Wodak 2001, 77). The impression is created that crime and terror are ubiquitous and that immediate action in the form of electing a strong leader, who implements law-and-order policies, is the only solution. The second tweet shown above combines the topos of danger (the terrorist threat) with the topos of numbers that suggests that 'if the numbers prove a specific topos, a specific action should be performed' (79). The overall message communicated in visual and textual form is: 'The USA faces a constant terrorist threat. A poll says that Donald Trump as leader will handle terrorism. Hillary Clinton is weak on doing so. Elect me!' The first example tweet describes inner-city crime as 'slaughter' in order to steer emotions. It tries to appeal to those African Americans, who live in derelict inner cities and promises to improve their lives. This strategy did not work:

according to an exit poll, only 8 per cent of black voters cast their ballot for Trump and 88 per cent for Clinton (Huang 2016).

In US crime statistics, violent crime is defined as including murder, rape, robbery and aggravated assault. According to these statistics, the violent crime rate (measured as the number of violent crime per 100,000 inhabitants) in the USA decreased from 431.9 in 2009, when Obama came to power, to 372.6 in 2015 (data source: FBI 2016). The murder rate decreased from 5 to 4.9 during the same time period (FBI 2016). The claim that crime is 'reaching record levels' is an exaggeration aiming at creating the impression that urgent action is needed which can only be achieved by a strong leader.

THE ADMIRATION OF OTHER LEADERS: RONALD REAGAN

The third tweet shown above features Trump admiring a picture of former US president Ronald Reagan at the Union League of Philadelphia, where he gave a speech on 7 September 2016. The Union League of Philadelphia is a conservative private club. Trump in this tweet in a visual form makes use of an *argumentum ad verecundiam*, in which one's standpoint is backed 'by means of reference to authorities considered to be [...] competent, superior, sacrosanct, unimpeachable' (Reisigl and Wodak 2001, 72). Trump presents himself as a strong leader by reference to an authority. The image is particularly interesting because of its religious framing: Reagan's picture looks like an altar and Trump is presented as a devout worshipper. The aura of religious leadership tries to reinforce the message 'Vote for Donald Trump! He is the new Ronald Reagan'. In the speech, Trump (2016k) suggested increasing the US military's armament:

Today, I am here to talk about three crucial words that should be at the center of our foreign policy: Peace Through Strength. [...] When Ronald Reagan left office, our Navy had 592 ships. When Barack Obama took office, it had 285 ships. Today, the Navy has just 276 ships. The average Air Force aircraft is 27 years-old. We have 2nd generation B-52 bombers – their fathers flew the same plane. Our Army has been shrinking rapidly, from 553,000 soldiers in 2009 to just 479,000 today. [...] I will ask Congress to fully eliminate the defense sequester and will submit a new budget to rebuild our military. [...] We will build a Navy of 350 surface ships and submarines, as recommended by the bipartisan National Defense Panel – we have 276 ships now. And we will build an Air Force of at least 1,200 fighter aircraft, which the Heritage Foundation has shown to be needed to execute current missions – we have 1,113 now.

Peace Through Strength was a military strategy of armament used by Reagan. He described it in the following way: 'Strength is the most persuasive argument we have to convince our adversaries to negotiate seriously and to cease bullying other nations' (Reagan 1986). Like Reagan, Trump is convinced that large military spending is a primary task of the government and that heavy armament scares off enemies. Armament can, however, have the effect that all sides continuously increase the number of weapons in a self-reinforcing spiral that makes the Earth a highly militarised place which can easily be destroyed at the push of a button.

The US government's defence spending increased from US$2.86 billion in 1980 (5.86 per cent of GDP), when Jimmy Carter was president, to US$4.59 billion in 1986 (6.8 per cent of GDP) under Reagan.[5] Defence spending's share of the federal budget increased from 22 per cent in 1980 to 27 per cent in 1986 and 1988. At the same time, the share for education and training decreased from 5 per cent to 3 per cent and the share for social security from 34 per cent to 32 per cent.[6] During the Carter administration (1977–80), the average poverty rate was 11.9 per cent, whereas it was 14.1 per cent during the Reagan years (1981–8) (DeNavas-Walt and Proctor 2015, table B-1). The example provides indications that cutting social security expenditures in order to increase military spending tends to result in less human security, which makes society prone to social crisis. Not only is there no hard evidence that increased military expenditure makes the world a safer place. The neoliberal cutting of social expenditures also tends to make society more unequal, with more people living under precarious conditions. Reagan and Trump's security strategy could therefore better be called 'Inequality,

---

5. Data source: www.usgovernmentspending.com/spending_chart_1900_2020USp_XX s2li111mcn_30f_20th_Century_Defense_Spending#copypaste, accessed 14 October 2017.
6. Data source: federal-budget.insidegov.com/, accessed 14 October 2017.

Social Insecurity and Precarity through Military Armament' than 'Peace through Strength'.

TRUMP'S SELF-CENTRED TWITTER COMMUNICATION

Trump's communication is very self-centred. He likes to talk about himself and to present himself as a boss, leader and authority. Data scientists conducted a quantitative analysis of Trump's tweets (Tsur, Ognyanova and Lazer 2016) and found that Trump tends to use language that is highly self-centred, negative and scapegoating.

Irem Uz (2014) collected a large dataset of books from Google Books Ngram. It consisted of 4–6 per cent of all books ever published. She analysed how the use of pronouns is related to individualism and found that 'the relative use of first person singular pronouns over the plural pronouns is related to individualism' (Uz 2014, 1676). The relative use of first-person singular pronouns ('I', 'me') over first-person plural pronouns ('We', 'Us') in American English was 0.173, which means that on average the use of the first-person singular is 17.3 per cent higher in written American English than the use of the first-person plural.

Table 6.3 Occurrences of pronouns in the Trump Twitter dataset

First-person singular pronouns	Absolute frequency	First-person plural pronouns	Absolute frequency
'I'	363	'We'	252
'I'll'	4	'We'll'	1
'I'm'	3	'We're'	4
'I've'	4	'We've'	3
'Me'	188	'Us'	57
	$\Sigma = 562$		$\Sigma = 317$

Trump's relative use of first-person singular over first-person plural pronouns: $(562 - 317)/(562 + 317) = 0.2787$

Table 6.3 shows the absolute number of occurrences of first-person singular and first-person plural pronouns, as well as the calculation of the rate of Trump's relative use of first-person singular over first-person plural pronouns. The level of 27.9 per cent is significantly higher than the level of 17.3 per cent typical for written US American language, which is an indication of a particularly individualistic personality.

Twitter is a me-centred medium that lives through the accumulation of followers, likes and retweets. The custom of liking and retweeting on Twitter appeals to Trump's narcissism. Twitter enables him to enjoy his status as a celebrity, brand and political leader. Trump makes use of Twitter for broadcasting 140 character sound bites about what he likes and dislikes. Reality TV and Twitter are Trump's two preferred contemporary formats for public communication. In *The Apprentice*, he acted as an authoritarian business leader who ruthlessly assessed competitors and eliminated those whom he considered to be weak leaders, poor performers or disloyal (see the analysis in the section 'Trump and the Media: Television, Reality TV and *The Apprentice*' in Chapter 5). *The Apprentice* and Trump's Twitter use turn the economy and politics into spectacles that live through entertainment and the audience's observation of Trump's self-celebration as a political and business leader who claims that he is always right and knows the world better than anyone else. Trump's media use is the epitome of neoliberal subjectivity.

An authoritarian personality is, as Fromm (1936) stresses, the result of an individual's socialisation history in the family, personal relations and all experiences in social systems. The household run by Trump's parents Fred and Mary has been described by analysts as 'disciplined' and having a focus on performance (Kranish and Fisher 2016, 17). At the age of 13, Donald Trump started attending the New York Military Academy, where competition, authority and order were key aspects of education (Kranish and Fisher 2016, chapter 2). Trump describes his father as 'a very driven kind of guy. That's why I am so screwed up, because I had a father that pushed me pretty hard. My father was a tough man, but he was a good man' (Trump and Zanker 2007, 321). Family life and education, just like his role as a capitalist, certainly had an impact on the development of Trump's personality.

Nationalism

'MAKE AMERICA GREAT AGAIN'

Nationalism is a second important ideological theme in Trump's tweets: 350 out of 1,815 tweets (19.3 per cent) contained some expression of

US nationalism. The hashtag #MAGA (Make America Great Again) was present 105 times in the analysed dataset, the hashtag #AmericaFirst 52 times. The phrase 'Make America great again' could be found 37 times, 'Make America safe again' 17 times, 'Make America safe and great again' ten times. Consider the following examples:

MAKE AMERICA GREAT AGAIN! (#1,370)

The forgotten men and women of our country will be forgotten no longer. From this moment on, it's going to be #AmericaFirst. (#1,806)

The 'Rust Belt' was created by politicians like the Clintons who allowed our jobs to be stolen from us by other countries like Mexico. END! (#198)

NATIONALISM AS FICTIVE ETHNICITY

Nationalism is an ideology that constructs Us/Them differences, in which the in-group possesses a fictive ethnicity (Balibar and Wallerstein 1991, 49, 96–100), a collective identity and claimed togetherness that is said to have been created by language, family, genealogy, kinship, biology or citizenship. Nationalism always constructs an out-group of people perceived as outsiders, intruders or enemies. Nationalism is anti-universalist, anti-humanist and particularistic: it does not consider humans as equal beings. Rather it considers people as split into competing nations where one nation is considered to be superior and more important than others. The ideological construct of the nation is therefore bound up with the idea of the national interest. But nationalism also tries to construct a fictive unity of those who are said to belong to the nation. Nationalism is therefore also a 'misty veil' (Luxemburg 1976, 135) that distracts attention from class contradictions by presenting classes that have opposing interests as being part of the same nation. Nationalism makes identity claims – claims to a joint space or territory that was occupied in the past, is occupied at the moment or should be occupied in the future (Özkirimli 2010, 208–9). Nationalism therefore also has a potential for aggression that can easily result in imperialism and warfare.

US CAPITAL AND US LABOUR

Trump's tweets use a linguistic combination of collectivisation and ethnonyms (Reisigl and Wodak 2001, 48, 50): he constructs an in-group of Americans that is said to be working hard and to be economically under threat from other nations (especially Mexico and China) and by the American political elite. His main nationalist slogan – 'Make America great again!' – makes the temporal claim that once upon a time, the nation was great. It is based on the ideological assumption that foreigners and alien political groups (Mexico, China, the Washington elite, etc.) have destroyed the greatness of the American nation. A second temporal claim is that America can return to its national origin in the future if Americans vote for Trump. The demand to put 'America first' is a demand for enforcing the national interest that is said to have been subordinated to alien political and foreign economic interests that are seen as destroying the nation. In the cited tweets, Trump names such alien forces explicitly as 'the Clintons' and 'Mexico'. In the second example, he equates Americans, who lead precarious lives ('the forgotten men and women of our country') with the USA and with US interests. His rhetoric communicates that the little everyday man and the little everyday woman are being threatened by foreign nations and politicians.

http://twitter.com/realDonaldTrump/statuses/772798809508372480
'#LaborDay #AmericaFirst

Video: https://t.co/RNl7cfzkmN https://t.co/ZqRtbV4KRI'

[Text in the video:]
Donald Trump: The American worker built the foundation for the country we love and have today. But the American worker is getting crushed. Bad trade deals like NAFTA and TPP, such high and inexcusable taxes and fees on small businesses that employ so many good people. This Labor Day, let's honour our American workers, then men and women who proudly keep America working. They are the absolute best anywhere in the world. There is nobody like 'em. I'm ready to make America work again and to make America great again. That's what we are going to do on November 8. (#532)

In this video example, Trump praises American workers and presents them as having the same national interest as capital ('small businesses that employ so many good people'). In Trump's ideological world, there is no class conflict between capital and labour, but only a conflict between nations. Foreign nations and free trade agreements are for Trump enemies threatening the nation. Also the slogan 'Buy American

and hire American' (#1,651, http://twitter.com/realDonaldTrump/
statuses/814484710025994241) implies a congruency of the interest of
US workers and US capital because they both belong to the American
nation. The slogan disregards the fact that a completely nationally
contained US capitalist economy would still be facing economic crises
in which workers would lose their jobs, competition between capitals
would result in centralisation and monopolies, and capital would try
to lower wages in order to increase profits. Trump's 'America First' and
'Make America Great Again' rhetoric is an implicit communication of the
ideological topos of burdening and weighing down, in which it is argued
that 'if an institution or a "country" is burdened by specific problems,
one should act in order to diminish these burdens' (Reisigl and Wodak
2001, 78). Trump's tweets and political communication strategy suggest
that the action to be taken against un-Americanness is that Americans
vote for Trump, who promises to bring about change.

TRUMP'S IDEA OF CAPITALISM AS NATIONAL CONFLICT, NOT CLASS CONFLICT

Trump presents free trade agreements such as NAFTA as mechanisms by
which foreign nations such as Mexico exploit the USA and destroy US
jobs. He does not present the capitalist economy as being based on a class
contradiction, but on economic trade conflicts between nations. Not only
is the sphere of production disregarded and the sphere of commodity
circulation made responsible for social problems, the economy is also
presented in terms of competing nations, although it is today dominated
by transnational capital that exploits workers in many countries. Trump
never mentions the fact that, according to estimations, US subsidies for
American agricultural export products have destroyed several million
agricultural jobs in Mexico (Weisbrot, Lefebvre and Sammut 2014, 13).
Trump wants to keep US capital confined to the USA. As an incentive
to do so, he wants to radically lower corporation tax: 'The United States
also has the highest business tax rate among the major industrialized
nations of the world, at 35 percent. It's almost 40 percent when you add
in taxes at the state level. [...] Under my plan, no American company
will pay more than 15% of their business income in taxes' (Trump 2016i).
In the same speech, which defined his economic plan, Trump did not
mention increasing minimum wages and implementing a living wage.

His basic assumption seems to be that what is good for US capital is automatically good for US workers.

NATIONALIST SYMBOLS

Trump makes use of Twitter's and other social media's capacity to post images and videos that communicate nationalism. All campaign videos contain a logo that is held in the red, white and blue colours of the US flag (see http://twitter.com/realDonaldTrump/statuses/ 755972980069376000for an example, #28). The design of Trump's infographics is also typically held in the same three colours (see http:// twitter.com/realDonaldTrump/statuses/757650904896139264 for an example, #91). In some images shown in tweets, Trump also dresses in the red, white and blue colours of the US flag (for example http://twitter. com/realDonaldTrump/statuses/814484710025994241, #1,651).

The American flag is a very prominent symbol that is visible in many of the images in Trump's tweets and is prominently featured wherever he speaks (see http://twitter.com/realDonaldTrump/statuses/ 760214225830772737 for an example, #222). National flags are part of the everyday symbols through which nationalism reproduces itself culturally (Billig 1995). For Trump, the US flag is a holy national symbol, which is why he demands tough sentences against its desecration: 'Nobody should be allowed to burn the American flag – if they do, there must be consequences – perhaps loss of citizenship or year in jail!' (#1,500).

The Friend/Enemy Scheme

THE IDEOLOGICAL SQUARE MODEL

A third ideological discourse in Trump's tweets is the friend/enemy scheme. Teun van Dijk (2011) argues that ideology often operates through the positive presentation of an in-group and negative presentation of out-groups. He developed the ideological square model. It identifies four ideological strategies: (1) emphasis on positive things about the in-group; (2) emphasis on negative things about the out-groups; (3) de-emphasis on negative things about the in-group; (4) de-emphasis on positive things about the out-groups.

Table 6.4   Positive and negative references to persons and groups in Trump's tweets

	Persons	Groups	Total
Negative references	735	468	1,203
Positive references	320	279	599

Table 6.4 presents a count of positive and negative references in Trump's tweets. Overall, the number of negative references to persons and groups is twice as large as the positive ones, which shows that Trump's Twitter communication often operates by constructing scapegoats and enemies whom he attacks. Table 6.5 shows the five individuals and groups that Trump framed most frequently in a positive or negative manner in the analysed tweets.

Table 6.5   Individuals and groups whom Trump mentioned most frequently in a positive or negative manner (absolute number of mentions)

Groups negative		Groups positive		Individuals negative		Individuals positive	
Media: CNN *New York Times*	170 46 25	Fox	63	Hillary Clinton	507	Mike Pence	81
Democrats	42	American people	42	Barack Obama	93	Bernie Sanders	25
Immigrants, refugees	31	Police	30	Tim Kaine	37	Eric Trump	16
ISIS	29	Military	22	Bill Clinton	23	Ivanka Trump	16
Criminals	23	WikiLeaks	21	Bernie Sanders	11	Melania Trump	11

TRUMP AND THE MEDIA

A first important result is that Trump is obsessed with how he gets covered in the mainstream media. He frequently attacks media that cover him negatively and refers positively to those that report favourably about him. The most frequent attacks focused on CNN and the *New York Times*.

It is a common ideological strategy in the friend/enemy scheme to reference one's enemy negatively by using specific adjectives as prefixes whenever the enemy is mentioned. With respect to the media, for example, Trump speaks of 'the very dishonest and totally biased media' (#275), 'low ratings @CNN' (#5), 'failing @NYTimes' (#119), 'failing @CNN' (#323), disgusting CNN (#515), unwatchable CNN (#569), '@CNN (Clinton News Network)' (#775), or 'biased, inaccurate and bad' NBC News (#817). Trump here describes specific media as being economically unsuccessful (which carries the undertone that they just criticise him in order to increase their audience ratings), being of low quality and acting immorally. Trump implies that economic, journalistic and moral failure results in mainstream media opposing him. He rarely says or acknowledges that critical journalism may simply oppose him because of his politics, but rather constructs an image of the press that is biased when it is critical of him and objective when it gives him space for self-presentation without critique. Consider the following examples:

Wow, it is unbelievable how distorted, one-sided and biased the media is against us. The failing @nytimes is a joke. @CNN is laughable! (#208)

Crooked Hillary Clinton is being protected by the media. She is not a talented person or politician. The dishonest media refuses to expose! (#347)

It is not 'freedom of the press' when newspapers and others are allowed to say and write whatever they want even if it is completely false! (#349)

The reporting at the failing @nytimes gets worse and worse by the day. Fortunately, it is a dying newspaper. (#377)

If the press would cover me accurately & honorably, I would have far less reason to 'tweet.' Sadly, I don't know if that will ever happen! (#1,540)

In these examples Trump argues that media critical of him are of low quality and struggle economically. In addition, he says that they only criticise him and not his opponent Hillary Clinton. He claims that fake news is being invented about him, that the media abuses the freedom of the press in their coverage of him and that they act immorally. He ridicules them by saying they are 'laughable' and 'a joke'.

TRUMP'S FAKE FAKE NEWS

In a news conference in January 2017, Trump (2017a) refused to allow a CNN journalist to ask a question by arguing: 'Your organisation is terrible. [...] Quiet! Quiet! [...] I'm not gonna give you a question. You are fake news.' In another news conference, in February 2017, he said: 'But I am not ok when it is fake. When I watch CNN, it's so much anger and hatred. [...] If a guest comes out and says something positive about me, it's brutal. [...] You're dishonest people. [...] Story after story after story is bad. [...] They're fake. They're not true. [...] [T]he false, horrible, fake reporting' (Trump 2017b).

In his speech at the Conservative Political Action Conference 2017, Trump said:

> A few days ago I called the fake news the enemy of the people, and they are. They are the enemy of the people. Because they have no sources, they just make them up when there are none. [...] I'm against the people that make up stories and make up sources. They shouldn't be allowed to use sources unless they use somebody's name. Let their name be put out there. Let their name be put out. [...] But there are some terrible, dishonest people that do a tremendous disservice to our country, and to our people. They are very dishonest people, and they shouldn't use sources. They should put the name of the person. [...] So when they make it up and they make up something else, and you saw that before the election – polls, polls. [...] Well, you have a lot of them. The Clinton News Network is one. [...] Look at how inaccurate. Look at CBS, look at ABC also. Look at NBC. [...] They have a professional obligation as members of the press to report honestly, but as you saw throughout the entire campaign and even now, the fake news doesn't tell the truth. Doesn't tell the truth. So just in finishing, I say it doesn't represent the people, it never will represent the people, and we're going to do something about it because we have to go out and we have to speak our minds and we have to be honest. (Trump 2017c)

Polls can never perfectly predict results and can do nothing against individuals who do not answer in a truthful manner or refuse to participate.

The polling crisis has to do with the 'shy Tory effect' (Skibba 2016): Conservative voters tend to hide their views in artificial interview situations or refuse to participate in surveys. However, Trump claims, without having any proof, that the liberal media deliberately falsify polls, and he announces that 'we're going to do something about it', which can easily create the fear that freedom of speech and the press could be limited.

Observers have voiced the fear that Trump's portrayal of the liberal media as fake news could manipulate communication in the public sphere:

> Trump's real nemesis is the truth. By attacking the media, he opens up a new line of attack against facts, his true target. He is, after all, the Gaslighter in Chief.[7] He is trying to confuse the public so that they will not believe inconvenient truths. What he wants is to manufacture his own pseudo-truth; to create a reality where he always wins. Where the only polls that count are the ones where he's doing great. Where the only comments about him are compliments, and where anything negative is false, the work of an out-of-control media. Where when things go wrong it is someone else's fault. [...] Trump wants America to think that it is the media that is out of control, because he wants to control what people view as true and false. [...] Trump's tactic may work for dictatorships. It won't work in the United States. (Ghitis 2017)

It remains to be seen whether Trump will, in practical media-policymaking terms, tolerate criticism of himself voiced in the media. On 17 February 2017, he posted the following tweet: 'The FAKE NEWS media (failing @nytimes, @NBCNews, @ABC, @CBS, @CNN) is not my enemy, it is the enemy of the American People!' (Twitter, @RealDonaldTrump, 17 February 2017, 1.48 pm). In a speech given on 18 February 2017, Trump said to his supporters: 'When the media lies to the people, I will never let them get away with it. I will do whatever I can so they don't get away with it. They have their own agenda and their agenda is not your agenda' (Merica 2017).

Among the media listed, Trump includes those that have most criticised him and about which he has most complained on Twitter, especially

---

7. 'Gaslighter in Chief' here refers to an authoritarian personality who tries to manipulate the public.

CNN and the *New York Times*. Trump has also described NBC News as '[t]otally biased' (#1,784) and NBC's *Saturday Night Live* as 'totally one-sided, biased' (#1,459) and 'the worst of NBC' (#1,766). Not only does Trump question the credibility of those media organisations that are among his strongest critics by calling them the 'fake news media', he also identifies himself with the American people, calls his critics the 'enemy of the American People' and argues that the media's interest 'is not your [the American people's] agenda'. Here he works with a combination of the topos of the national interest and the topos of danger (Reisigl and Wodak 2001, 77) and a combination of a relatonym and a militarionym (51–2): the American nation is opposed to the liberal media that is presented as its enemy. The problem is the war-like rhetoric that the friend/enemy scheme takes on: speaking of an enemy of the nation often implies combating and getting rid of this adversary. In authoritarian politics, as conceived by the legal theorist Carl Schmitt, the 'foe is in the last resort anyone who must be exterminated physically' (Neumann 1944/2009, 45). Trump's tweets can easily be understood as a threat to the media that they either stop criticising him or may have to face the consequences.

There is a history of authoritarian political leaders' attacks on and threats to liberal and socialist media that use the right-wing argument that these media are lying to and threatening the nation. In a very different context, Hitler argued that liberal and socialist media were lying and that their reporting damaged the German nation and people. He spoke of the 'papers of lies', a term very similar to the one of 'fake news' that Trump uses today for characterising media who oppose him:

> The activity of the so-called liberal press was the work of gravedig-gers for the German people and the German Reich. One can pass by in silence the Marxist papers of lies; to them lying is as necessary to their life as catching mice is to the cat; but its task is only to break the people's folkish and national spine, in order to make it ripe for the yoke of slavery of international capital and its masters, the Jews. (Hitler 1941, 331)

TRUMP'S BIOPOLITICAL IDEOLOGY ON TWITTER

On 29 June 2017, Donald Trump tweeted about Joe Scarborough and Mika Brzezinski, the two moderators of MSNBC's show *Morning Joe*:

'I heard poorly rated @Morning_Joe speaks badly of me (don't watch anymore). Then how come low I.Q. Crazy Mika, along with Psycho Joe, came. ... to Mar-a-Lago 3 nights in a row around New Year's Eve, and insisted on joining me. She was bleeding badly from a face-lift. I said no!' (Twitter, @RealDonaldTrump, 29 June 2017 5.52 am and 5.58 am)

In this tweet Trump uses biopolitical ideology by ridiculing the bodies and minds of journalists and portraying them as mentally and bodily abnormal. In respect to thought, Trump describes one of the journalists as mentally ill and the other as silly. In respect to the body, he claims that one journalist had been undergoing cosmetic surgery and had open wounds while wanting to conduct an interview with him. MSNBC said in a statement that it is 'a sad day for America when the president spends his time bullying, lying and spewing petty personal attacks instead of doing his job'. On 2 July, Trump posted a video from Wrestle Mania XXIII that shows him taking another person down with a clothesline move. The head of that person was substituted by a CNN logo and Trump used the hashtags #FraudNewsCNN and #FNN. CNN reacted with a statement that said that it 'is a sad day when the President of the United States encourages violence against reporters' (Disis 2017). The meme originated in postings on the 'alt-right' reddit forum The_Donald. The postings were by a user known for racist and anti-Semitic contributions.

TRUMP'S MEDIA FRIENDS: FOX AND CO.

Fox, the media organisation owned by Rupert Murdoch that is generally said to be fairly right-wing, is the group with the highest number of positive mentions in Trump's tweets. Trump for example tweeted: 'Wow, @CNN is so negative. Their panel is a joke, biased and very dumb. I'm turning to @FoxNews where we get a fair shake!' (#810). In August 2017, Trump followed just 45 accounts on Twitter, among them Tucker Carlson (host of *Tucker Carlson Tonight* on Fox News), Jesse Watters (host of *The Five* and *Watters' World* on Fox News), Laura Ingraham (Fox News host, founder and chief editor of the website LifeZette), Bill O'Reilly (Fox News), Eric Bolling (Fox News), Sean Hannity (Fox News), *Fox & Friends* (morning show on Fox News), Fox Nation, Greta Van Susteren (MSNBC), Piers Morgan (ITV), the news aggregation site Drudge Report, and the vloggers Diamond and Silk (who describe themselves on their Twitter profile as 'Trump's Most Outspoken & Loyal

Supporters'). In terms of media organisations and journalists whom Trump considers his Twitter friends, there is a clear domination by Fox. Also some web-based media such as Drudge Report, LifeZette and video blogs are included. Trump's media relations are highly polarised: there is a small group of right-wing supporters that he counts as friends, as well as a number of media organisations who are critical of him and whom he tends to present as enemies.

TRUMP ON IMMIGRANTS AND REFUGEES

Immigrants and refugees are among the groups that Trump most frequently mentioned negatively in the dataset. Consider the following example:

> http://twitter.com/realDonaldTrump/statuses/788930678255517696
>
> ISIS has infiltrated countries all over Europe by posing as refugees, and @HillaryClinton will allow it to happen here too! #BigLeagueTruth https://t.co/MmeW2qsTQh
>
> [Embedded video, text in the video:]
>
> [Spoken] Donald Trump: If she did nothing, we'd be in much better shape. And this is what has caused the Great Migration, where she is taking in tens of thousands of Syrian refugees, who probably in many cases, not probably, who are definitely in many cases ISIS-aligned. And we now have them in our country. And wait until you see that this is going to be the great Trojan Horse. And wait until you see what happens in the coming years. Lots of luck, Hillary. Thanks a lot for doing a great job
>
> [Written] TRUMP PENCE MAKE AMERICA GREAT AGAIN! 2016
>
> [Written] PAID FOR BY DONALD J. TRUMP FOR PRESIDENT, INC. (#1,152)

A synecdoche is a linguistic construct in which a part refers to a whole or a whole to a part. The generalising synecdoche is a specific form of synecdoche in which the whole stands for a part (*totum pro parte*) (Reisigl and Wodak 2001, 57). A stereotype is 'the logical form of a judgement that attributes or denies in an oversimplified and generalizing manner, and with an emotionally slanted tendency, particular qualities or behavioural patterns to a certain class of persons' (19). Generalising stereotypes take single events, behaviours or individuals and conclude inductively that the totality of individuals, events or behaviours has the same characteristics. The problem is that inductive generalisation is a form of logical argumentation that tends to be incorrect.

An example of a generalising synecdoche is the following argument: 'There are ISIS terrorists in Syria. There are Syrian refugees. Refugees are ISIS terrorists. Clinton wants to be open for refugees on humanitarian grounds. She therefore supports letting in terrorists.' It is a logically false inference to assume that Syrian refugees are terrorists because there are terrorists in Syria. Demagogues often mention minorities such as immigrants, refugees and people of colour in combination with references to crime and terror, which can easily create the impression that all immigrants, refugees and people of colour are criminals or terrorists.

TRUMP'S TRAVEL EXECUTIVE ORDER

On 27 January 2017, Trump signed the executive order Protecting the Nation from Foreign Terrorist Entry into the United States. Its intention was temporarily to ban citizens from Iran, Iraq, Libya, Somalia, Sudan, Syria and Yemen from entering the United States and to prevent Syrian refugees from coming to the USA. The order says, for example, that it wants

> to ensure that adequate standards are established to prevent infiltration by foreign terrorists or criminals, pursuant to section 212(f) of the INA [Immigration and Nationality Act], 8 U.S.C. 1182(f), I hereby proclaim that the immigrant and nonimmigrant entry into the United States of aliens from countries referred to in section 217(a)(12) of the INA, 8 U.S.C. [United States Code] 1187(a)(12), would be detrimental to the interests of the United States, and I hereby suspend entry into the United States, as immigrants and nonimmigrants, of such persons for 90 days from the date of this order.[8]

The INA's section 217(a)(12) refers to 'Iraq, Syria, or any other country or other area of concern'. The executive order also states: 'Numerous foreign-born individuals have been convicted or implicated in terrorism-

---

8. www.federalregister.gov/documents/2017/02/01/2017-02281/protecting-the-nation-from-foreign-terrorist-entry-into-the-united-states, accessed on 21 February 2017.

related crimes since September 11, 2001, including foreign nationals who entered the United States after receiving visitor, student, or employment visas, or who entered through the United States refugee resettlement program.'

The formulation that foreigners have been implicated in terrorism and that therefore 'entry into the United States of aliens' from specific countries is 'detrimental to the interests of the United States' is a generalising argument that draws conclusions from single cases to all nationals of specific countries. It puts citizens of seven countries under the categorical suspicion of being terrorists. The problem is that it reverses the presumption of innocence that is formulated in paragraph eleven of the Universal Declaration of Human Rights. On 3 February 2017, the United States District Court for the Western District of Washington temporarily blocked key parts of Trump's executive order. On 9 February, the United States Court of Appeals for the Ninth Circuit denied Trump's appeal. The ruling argued: 'Two States challenged the Executive Order as unconstitutional and violative of federal law, and a federal district court preliminarily ruled in their favor and temporarily enjoined enforcement of the Executive Order. [...] We [...] hold that the States have standing.'[9] In June 2017, the US Supreme Court ruled that citizens of the countries in question could be barred from entering the USA, except if they have a 'bona fide relationship with a person or entity in the United States'. Since Donald Trump appointed Neil Gorsuch as member of the Supreme Court, the judges put into office by Republican presidents hold a majority.

Trump announced in his election campaign that he would introduce what some termed a 'Muslim ban': 'When I am elected, I will suspend immigration from areas of the world when there is a proven history of terrorism against the United States, Europe or our allies, until we understand how to end these threats' (Trump 2016i). In the '100-Day Plan to Make America Great Again', Trump announced his intention to 'suspend immigration from terror-prone regions where vetting cannot safely occur' (Trump 2016i). He tweeted: 'Everybody is arguing whether or not it is a BAN. Call it what you want, it is about keeping bad people (with bad intentions) out of country!' (Twitter, @RealDonaldTrump,

---

9. State of Washington v. Trump, No. 17-35105; 9 February 2017, www.leagle.com/decision/In%20FCO%2020170209142/STATE%20OF%20WASHINGTON%20v.%20TRUMP, accessed 14 October 2017.

1 February 2017). 'We must keep "evil" out of our country!' (Twitter, @RealDonaldTrump, 3 February 2017). The basic argument is that everyone from certain countries could pose a terrorism risk and should therefore be kept out. Trump uses generalising logic for ideologically justifying the ban.

THE FRIEND/ENEMY SCHEME AS IDEOLOGY

Leo Löwenthal explains the ideological and psychological dimensions of the friend/enemy scheme: 'The agitator dehumanizes the enemy on several levels: The enemy seems to the agitator to be a foreigner who comes from suspect geographical regions; he is a criminal who inhabits reprehensible moral regions; and he is a degenerate who derives from disgusting biological regions' (Löwenthal 2016, 64). The agitator 'warns against the dangers of foreign entanglements' (54). For citizens who feel alienated, the ideological imagination that all evil comes from refugees and immigrants poses the illusionary hope that their own lives will get better by repression against foreigners. 'The refugee's homeless-ness becomes the psychological equivalent of the audience's repressed instincts' (57). The hatred against the refugee is a release of the hatred felt about one's own alienation and one's feelings or fears of homelessness and suppression.

DONALD TRUMP AND HILLARY CLINTON

Given that Hillary Clinton was Trump's opponent in the presidential election, it is not a surprise that she is the individual whom he attacked most in the analysed set of tweets. She was negatively mentioned in 507 out of 1,815 Trump tweets (27.9 per cent), which was the largest number of negative references in the entire dataset.

In his tweets about Hillary Clinton, Trump referred with particular frequency to the issue concerning leaked emails from her private server. Clinton and her aides during her time as US secretary of state used her private email server for official communications. The FBI and the State Department started investigations into whether classified information was stored on or sent via the private server and whether the use of a private server violated rules of government record-keeping. WikiLeaks published a searchable archive of 30,068 emails from Clinton's private server that had been released by the State Department as a result of a

Freedom of Information Act request.[10] On 5 July 2016, FBI Director James B. Comey said in a statement that out of the 30,000 emails, 110 contained

> classified information at the time they were sent or received. [...] Although we did not find clear evidence that Secretary Clinton or her colleagues intended to violate laws governing the handling of classified information, there is evidence that they were extremely careless in their handling of very sensitive, highly classified information. [...] [w]e assess it is possible that hostile actors gained access to Secretary Clinton's personal e-mail account. [...] Although there is evidence of potential violations of the statutes regarding the handling of classified information, our judgment is that no reasonable prosecutor would bring such a case. (Comey 2016)

TRUMP'S PINOCCHIO/CLINTON VIDEO

Clinton repeatedly said publicly that she had not sent or received emails marked classified. Trump posted a video on Twitter that contained excerpts from Comey's statement and from interviews with Clinton. The video communicated that Clinton was a liar and depicted her as Pinocchio with a nose growing in length:

> http://twitter.com/realDonaldTrump/statuses/760420894271471620: The Washington Post calls out #CrookedHillary for what she REALLY is. A PATHOLOGICAL LIAR! Watch that nose grow! https://t.co/FsrUGByuuD
>
> [Embedded video, the video features at the bottom a cartoon Hillary Clinton with a Pinocchio nose that grows in size during the video and at the end of it explodes into flames; text in the video:]
>
> [Written] The Washington Post CALLS OUT CROOKED HILLARY'S LIES
>
> [Spoken] Hillary Clinton: I did not email any classified material
>
> [Written] She did ...
>
> [Spoken] Hillary Clinton: to anyone on my email. There is no classified material

---

10. wikileaks.org/clinton-emails/, accessed 14 October 2017.

[Written] … there is. She did …

[Spoken] Hillary Clinton: I am confident that I never sent nor received any information that was classified. Hillary Clinton: I had not sent classified material nor received anything marked classified.

[Spoken] Fox News host Chris Wallace: James Comey said none of those things that you told the American public were true.

[Written] CLASSIFIED EMAILS: 110

[Spoken] James Comey: 110 emails in 52 email chains have been determined by the owning agency to contain classified information.

[Written] TOP SECRET EMAIL CHAINS: 7

[Spoken] James Comey: seven email chains concerned matters that were classified at the top secret special access programme at the time. They were sent and received.

[Written] SO MANY LIES!

[The Hillary Clinton cartoon and its long nose burst into flames]

[Written] TRUMP PENCE MAKE AMERICA GREAT AGAIN! 2016. (#234)

Trump's video builds on material broadcast by Fox News as part of an interview Chris Wallace conducted with Hillary Clinton.[11] It accuses Clinton of lying about her emails. The video says: 'SO MANY LIES!' And Trump tweeted that Clinton is 'A PATHOLOGICAL LIAR!' According to the *Cambridge English Dictionary*, a lie is 'something you say that you know is not true'.[12] So the question is whether Clinton knew that the material in the emails was classified or not. She repeatedly said that it was a mistake to use a personal server and that she felt sorry about it. In an interview, Clinton commented:

Classified material has a header which says 'top secret', 'secret', 'confidential'. Nothing – and I will repeat this, and this is verified in the report by the Department of Justice – none of the emails sent or received by me had such a header. […] And what we have here is the use of an unclassified system by hundreds of people in our government

11.   www.youtube.com/watch?v=r55U-T8_KSs, accessed 14 October 2017.
12.   dictionary.cambridge.org/dictionary/english/lie, accessed 14 October 2017.

to send information that was not marked, there were no headers, there was no statement, top secret, secret, or confidential. (Beckwith 2016)

Clinton can only be said to have lied if she knew that the material was classified and knew that she was breaking rules. Trump's video does not present her side of the story, but simply claims that she lied. The fact-checking organisation PolitiFact that won the Pulitzer Prize in 2009 checked these facts and concluded:

> For information to be considered properly marked classified, it must contain a header. Clinton is correct that nothing in her email had a header signifying its classification status. Three email chains had a '(C)' indicating 'confidential' information, but that is not enough to consider the emails properly marked classified. But that doesn't mean there wasn't any classified information in her email. If someone has determined information to be classified, it is still technically classified even if someone neglects to label it down the line. The FBI found 81 email chains that contained information determined to be classified, though none of the information was appropriately labeled, so it wasn't necessarily obvious to the recipients. (Carroll 2016)

Trump's video depicts Clinton as Pinocchio with a growing nose that at the end of the clip explodes, which symbolises that Trump uncovers lies and that only voting for him will save the truth. Visual depictions of a political opponent as physically unattractive, disabled or ill are an old political strategy that aims at steering negative feelings. Depicting Clinton as Pinocchio with a long nose is a visual somatonym, a visual 'construction of social actors by synecdochisingly picking out a part or characteristic of their body' (Reisigl and Wodak 2001, 53). Somatonyms aim at ridiculing and thereby weakening the enemy.

TRUMP AND THE JOURNALIST SERGE KOVALESKI

Serge Kovaleski is a reporter who works for the *New York Times*. He suffers from arthrogryposis, a disease that results in a curving of the joints. In 2015, Trump referred to a 2001 article by Kovaleski that, he claimed, argued that Muslims publicly celebrated the 2001 attacks on the World Trade Centre. Kovaleski said that he did not remember anyone saying that hundreds or thousands celebrated. In a speech, Trump imitated Kovaleski, jerking his arms and saying: 'Now, the poor guy, you ought to see this guy, "Ah, I don't know what I said, I don't remember, I don't remember, maybe that's what I said"' (Kessler 2016). Observers argued that Trump was 'clearly imitating Kovaleski's disability – the reporter has arthrogryposis, which visibly limits the functioning of his joints' (Kessler 2016). If this is true, then it is another example of the use of somatonyms in the context of the friend/enemy logic. Meryl Streep in a Golden Globe award speech criticised Trump, saying:

There was one performance this year that stunned me. It sank its hooks in my heart. Not because it was good – there was nothing good about it, but it was effective and it did its job. It made its intended audience laugh, and show their teeth. It was that moment, when the person asking to sit in the most respected seat in our country imitated a disabled reporter, someone he outranked in privilege, power and the capacity to fight back. It kind of broke my heart when I saw it. And I still can't get it out of my head because it wasn't in a movie – it was real life. And this instinct to humiliate when it's modelled by someone in the public platform, by someone powerful, it filters down into every-body's life, 'cause it kind of gives permission for other people to do the same thing. Disrespect invites disrespect. Violence incites violence. When the powerful use their position to bully others, we all lose.[13]

TRUMP AND MERYL STREEP

Trump argued that he 'was merely mocking the fact that the reporter was trying to pull away from a story that he wrote 14 years ago'.[14] On Twitter he started attacking yet another person who had criticised him – Meryl Streep:

Meryl Streep, one of the most over-rated actresses in Hollywood, doesn't know me but attacked last night at the Golden Globes. She is a. ... Hillary flunky who lost big. For the 100th time, I never 'mocked' a disabled reporter (would never do that) but simply showed him. ...

13. www.youtube.com/watch?v=EV8tsnRFUZw, accessed 14 October 2017.
14. www.donaldjtrump.com/press-releases/donald-j.-trump-demands-an-apology-from-new-york-times, accessed 14 October 2017.

'groveling' when he totally changed a 16 year old story that he had written in order to make me look bad. Just more very dishonest media! (#1,725, #1,726, #1,727)

RIDICULE ON TWITTER

In the analysed dataset, forms of ridicule that operate by prefixing negative words to names and organisations were found. Trump for example spoke of '"Little" Michael Bloomberg' (#164), the 'clown Chuck Schumer' (#1,691), 'Elizabeth Warren, often referred to as Pocahontas' (#100), 'disgusting (check out sex tape and past) Alicia M' (#779), '#failing@ nytimes' (#793), 'failing @CNN' (#323). By far the most frequent slur was that Trump called Hillary Clinton 'Crooked Hillary' (83 times) or referred to her with the hashtag #CrookedHillary (29 times). 'Crooked Hillary' is a criminonym, a linguistic construct that tries to portray someone as criminal and a social problem (Reisigl and Wodak 2001, 52). Investigations left no doubt that Clinton's private email server was insecure, but that a criminal investigation would remain without success.

TRUMP AND WIKILEAKS

The dataset contained 21 positive references by Trump to WikiLeaks' publication of emails from Clinton's private server. Trump for example tweeted: 'I hope people are looking at the disgraceful behavior of Hillary Clinton as exposed by WikiLeaks. She is unfit to run' (#975). There were speculations that Julian Assange started the searchable Clinton email archive as revenge for Clinton's threats against WikiLeaks and because he expected to be pardoned by Trump. Asked about whether he had helped Trump, Assange responded in an interview: 'If in the end, the American people decided they preferred Mr. Trump to her, then that's their business' (Assange 2017). Although Trump positively referenced WikiLeaks, one can have strong doubts that he has more sympathies for Assange than Clinton. In 2010, Trump said about Assange and WikiLeaks: 'I think it's disgraceful, I think there should be like death penalty or something' (Kaczyński 2017).

TRUMP AND BERNIE SANDERS

It is not a surprise that Trump's candidate for the vice presidency (Mike Pence) and members of his family, such as his children Eric and

Ivanka and his wife Melania, are among the most frequently positively mentioned individuals in the analysed Twitter dataset. It is more surprising that Bernie Sanders was the person whom Trump mentioned second most frequently in a positive manner. There were 25 positive and eleven negative mentions of Sanders in the dataset. Consider the following two examples:

Clinton betrayed Bernie voters. Kaine supports TPP, is in pocket of Wall Street, and backed Iraq War. (#94)

http://twitter.com/realDonaldTrump/statuses/759084522705068032: What Bernie Sanders really thinks of Crooked Hillary Clinton. https://t.co/VgMaAsZBep

[Embedded video, text in the video:]

[Video excerpt 1] Bernie Sanders: I don't think you're qualified

[Video excerpt 2] Bernie Sanders: I do not know any progressive who has a Super Pac, and takes 15 million dollars from Wall Street.

[Repetition of video excerpt 1, longer version] Bernie Sanders: I don't think you're qualified, if you have supported virtually every disastrous trade agreement, which has cost us millions of decent paying jobs.

[Video excerpt 3] Bernie Sanders: I do question her judgement. I question a judgement which voted for the war in Iraq.

[Repetition of video excerpt 1] Bernie Sanders: I don't think you're qualified

[Video excerpt 4] Bernie Sanders: I have shown a lot better judgement than she has on foreign policy.

[Repetition of video excerpt 1] Bernie Sanders: I don't think you're qualified

[Video excerpt 5] Hillary Clinton: You know. Bernie Sanders: Excuse me, I am talking. (#172)

These two examples provide indications that Trump hoped to convince Bernie Sanders supporters to vote for him. He sets up a binary between Clinton and Sanders in respect to trade agreements, financial support by Wall Street and foreign policy. There are certainly large political differences between Clinton and Sanders in these respects. Trump tries to communicate that on these issues he holds positions that are comparable to Bernie Sanders. In another tweet, this motivation is directly communicated: 'While Bernie has totally given up on his fight for the people, we welcome all voters who want a better future for our workers' (#95).

The friend/enemy logic in such tweets takes on a particular form, namely the argument 'The enemy of my enemy is my friend'. Trump communicates that Sanders' supporters should act according to this logic. In order to underline this point, the video four times repeats the short passage in which Sanders says about Clinton, 'I don't think you're qualified'. Sanders himself is very clear that he does not abide by the friend/enemy logic, that he sees much more fundamental differences between him and Trump than between him and Clinton, and that he radically opposes Trump's political agenda:

It is no secret that Hillary Clinton and I disagree on a number of issues. [...] In these stressful times for our country, this election must be about bringing our people together, not dividing us up. While Donald Trump is busy insulting one group after another, Hillary Clinton understands that our diversity is one of our greatest strengths. (Sanders 2016c)

In Trump's view people should ignore all the news except what comes directly from him. That is what totalitarianism is all about. (Twitter, @SenSanders, 18 February 2017)

Trump said he would take on Wall Street guys. It turns out that 'taking them on' means filling up his cabinet with them.

[Video showing an interview with Sanders] Bernie Sanders: We talked about Trump being a liar. You will recall, Trump went before the American people in the campaign. He said: 'I'm gonna take on Wall Street! We are gonna clean the swamp!' Well, the swamp has now overrun Washington, DC. Because you got all these guys from Goldman Sachs, the same old crew of Wall Street people, the people whose greed and recklessness and illegal behaviour that nearly destroyed our economy. These are the guys in Trump's administration after he told people that he would take them on. So I think that's what you're seeing with Mnuchin [Steve Mnuchin: secretary of the Treasury in Trump's administration, worked for Goldman Sachs from 1985 until 2002, also worked as a hedge fund manager] – not any different from Gary Cohn, former president of Goldman Sachs [Gary Cohn: the Trump administration's chief economic advisor,

Goldman Sachs' president and co-chief operating officer, 2006–16]. Received 250 million dollars severance package in order to come into the government. Boy, that is really taking on the establishment and draining the swamp. (Twitter, @SenSanders, 14 February 2017)

FAKE NEWS

Kali Holloway (2017), an associate editor at the progressive news site Alternet, argues that 'Trump has put thousands of fake news stories out there' and that he is 'a fake news factory' and 'a curator of untruths'. She argues that such stories include: 'Obama is a Kenyan Muslim who never attended Columbia University', 'Hillary Clinton was too ill to serve as president', '"Thousands and thousands of [Muslims] were cheering" on 9/11', 'Millions of people in the U.S. voted illegally on November 8'. Consider the following tweets by Trump:

#WheresHillary? Sleeping!!!!! (#381, 20 August 2016)

I think that both candidates, Crooked Hillary and myself, should release detailed medical records. I have no problem in doing so! Hillary? (#467, 28 August 2016)

Hillary Clinton didn't go to Louisiana, and now she didn't go to Mexico. She doesn't have the drive or stamina to MAKE AMERICA GREAT AGAIN! (#491, 1 September 2016)

Hillary Clinton is taking the day off again, she needs the rest. Sleep well Hillary – see you at the debate! (#669, 20 September 2016)

Trump on the one hand complained, as we have seen, about unnamed sources in the liberal media ('They shouldn't be allowed to use sources unless they use somebody's name'). But on the other hand doubts have arisen about double standards and the sources of tweets such as the following: 'How low has President Obama gone to tapp [sic] my phones during the very sacred election process. This is Nixon/Watergate. Bad (or sick) guy!' (Twitter, @RealDonaldTrump, 4 March 2017)

FAKE NEWS ABOUT HILLARY CLINTON

On 5 September 2016, Hillary Clinton was coughing at a rally in Cleveland, Ohio. At a 11 September memorial service, she was stumbling and her aides had to help her get into her car. She was diagnosed with pneumonia and had to take a break from campaigning. Trump described his opponent as 'sleeping Hillary' who does not have 'drive or stamina'. These descriptions are health-oriented somatonyms that try to make references 'in terms of the state of health' (Reisigl and Wodak 2001, 49). They thereby construct a dichotomy between activity/passivity, health/illness, awake/asleep, stamina/frailty, movement/standstill, and drive/lethargy. The intention seems to be that potential voters identify Trump with the active side of the dichotomy and Clinton with the passive one. There is also a gender dimension: patriarchal ideology often constructs men as active and women as passive. It postulates a fundamental biological and social difference between men and women. Trump plays with such distinctions in order to present himself as strong and Clinton as weak.

The claim that Hillary Clinton is very ill turned into a fake news story. 'Fox News's Sean Hannity dedicated a week of coverage to "investigating" Clinton's health, bringing on a panel of medical experts – "Fox News Medical A-Team" – to diagnose Clinton's possible ailments. None of these experts had ever examined Clinton personally and were going off photos and allegations surfaced on the web' (Golshan 2016). Fake medical reports about Clinton circulated on the Internet: 'One letter purporting to be from Dr. Bardack, Clinton's doctor, and dated 5 February 2014, says Clinton suffers from seizures and dementia that both are getting worse. Dr. Bardack released a statement Aug. 16, 2016, saying the document is a fraud' (Emery 2016). The same Twitter user who posted the fake medical report 'later posted what was purported to be a magnetic resonance angiogram of Clinton's brain showing a significant "abnormality" in the brain tissue. This is also a bogus image' (Farley 2016). In July 2015,[15] Clinton's doctor released a letter about her health status that was more detailed than a letter by Trump's doctor published in December 2015.[16]

BREITBART

The right-wing online site Breitbart ran multiple stories about Clinton's alleged health problems with titles such as 'Physician: Mainstream Media

---

15. assets.documentcloud.org/documents/2188570/letter.pdf, accessed 14 October 2017.
16. www.donaldjtrump.com/images/uploads/trump_health_record.pdf, accessed 14 October 2017.

"Strangely Silent" About Hillary Clinton's Health' (10 August 2016), 'Google Hides Popular Hillary Clinton Health Searches' (30 August 2016), 'Doctors Weigh In on Hillary's Health' (12 September 2016), 'Stealth Over Health: Hillary Clinton Was Headed to ER But Diverted to Avoid Bad Optics' (12 September 2016), 'Hillary Clinton "Health Conspiracy" Turns Out to Be Real' (14 September 2016), 'Doctors Debate Hillary Clinton's Mysterious Health Status' (19 September 2016), 'Six Times Hillary Clinton's Team Emails About Naps, Sleep and Health' (19 October 2016), 'How Hillary Clinton's Inner Circle Tiptoes Around Her Health Issues' (24 October 2016). Repeating one issue over and over aims at creating the impression that there is some truth to it. Another fake news story about Hillary Clinton circulated on social media on 5 November 2016. A fake newspaper called the *Denver Guardian* circulated a story under the headline 'FBI Agent Suspected in Hillary EMail Leaks Found Dead in Apparent Murder-Suicide' (Lubbers 2016).

Breitbart is a right-wing news website that was created in 2007. Its founder, Andrew Breitbart, died in 2012. Following his death, Steve Bannon took over the role of the website's executive chairman until 2016, when he became the CEO of Donald Trump's campaign. After Trump had won the election, he appointed Bannon as White House chief strategist. In February 2017, Breitbart was the world's 243rd most accessed website and the twenty-ninth most read in the USA.[17] Its number of monthly views increased from 2.7 million in March 2009 to eighty-two million in February 2016.[18] Since May 2016, the growth of users became particularly rapid, which is also the time when the links between Trump's campaign and Breitbart became ever closer. In the analysed dataset, we identified 13 links to Breitbart articles, which indicates that Trump sees the right-wing news site as a credible medium that provides friendly coverage of him. Breitbart News Network LLC is a for-profit company. It uses a capital accumulation model that is based on targeted advertising. Breitbart's financial supporters and investors are largely unknown. It is believed that Robert Mercer, a co-CEO of the Renaissance Technologies hedge fund, is one of them (Byers 2015, Cadwalladr 2017). Mercer was a major financial supporter of Donald Trump's presidential campaign.

---

17.   www.alexa.com/siteinfo/breitbart.com, accessed on 20 February 2017, accessed 14 October 2017.
18.   www.rank2traffic.com/breitbart.com, accessed on 28 February 2017, accessed 14 October 2017.

FAKE NEWS IN THE 2016 US PRESIDENTIAL ELECTION

Allcott and Gentzkow (2017) conducted a study that focused on fake news in the 2016 US presidential election. They estimated that there were three times more fake news stories supporting Trump than Clinton. The 41 fake pro-Clinton stories identified were shared 7.6 million times on social media, the 115 fake pro-Trump stories 30.3 million times, which means that fake news items supporting Trump were four times more visible than those supporting Clinton. The empirical data confirm the assumption that fake online news, in the contemporary political moment, is a predominantly far-right phenomenon. Allcott and Gentzkow also conducted a survey with 1,208 participants: 15.3 per cent indicated that they remembered a fake news story they were confronted with in the survey, 7.9 per cent said that at the time of seeing the fake news story they believed it was true. In another survey, in which 3,015 Americans participated, 75 per cent of the presented fake news stories were considered to be very or somewhat accurate (Silverman and Singer-Vine 2016). The data in both surveys indicate that a significant share of those confronted with fake news believe the stories are true. The second survey also found indications that Republicans are more likely to believe fake news than Democrats: 'The survey found that those who identify as Republican are more likely to view fake election news stories as very or somewhat accurate. Roughly 84% of the time, Republicans rated fake news headlines as accurate (among those they recognized), compared to a rate of 71% among Democrats' (Silverman and Singer-Vine 2016).

Silverman (2016) presents the results of another empirical study of fake news: 'During these critical months of the campaign, 20 top-performing false election stories from hoax sites and hyperpartisan blogs generated 8,711,000 shares, reactions, and comments on Facebook. Within the same time period, the 20 best-performing election stories from 19 major news websites generated a total of 7,367,000 shares, reactions, and comments on Facebook.' Seventeen out of 20 of these false news stories were pro-Donald Trump, which seems to confirm that contemporary fake news tends to be predominantly right-wing in character.

POLITICAL BOTS IN THE 2016 US PRESIDENTIAL ELECTION

A study estimates that in the third US presidential election debate, political bots posted 36.1 per cent of the pro-Trump tweets and 23.5 per cent of the pro-Clinton tweets (Kollanyi, Howard and Woolley 2016). Another study analysed 17 million tweets associated with Trump and Clinton (Woolley and Guilbeault 2017). Bots made up around 10 per cent of the analysed sample of unique user accounts. The bot networks (botnets) supporting Trump were up to four times larger than those supporting Clinton. One result was that 'pro-Trump bots garnered the most attention and influence among human users' (22). Bots 'played a much more prominent role in boosting the salience of Trump' (21).

The problem is that in semi-automated politics, it can be difficult to discern whether humans or machines create information, visibility and attention. Secret algorithms determine the Facebook newsfeed and Google results. Social media bots are algorithms that try to intervene in these algorithms and create artificial attention. The problem is therefore not just that attention and visibility are semi-automatic, but that communication power-asymmetries can be enforced. Post-truth politics on social media does not democratise politics away from experts towards citizens, but rather enforces giving attention power to a minority.

Algorithms do not have morals, ethics, consciousness, identity or anticipatory thinking like humans. They can easily be programmed to insult and threaten humans and to communicate fascism and ideological violence. In (semi-)automated politics, it becomes difficult to discern between what is communicated by humans and by machines. Algorithms can manipulate the public perception of politics and thereby undermine the validity claims of truth, truthfulness, rightness and understandability of political communication in the public sphere.

FAKE NEWS AND CAPITALIST MEDIA

Fake news is at least as old as tabloid media. Stories that are invented in order to increase audience ratings are an integral part of the capitalist media spectacle. We could even say that fake news – that is, news that deliberately manipulates, neglects, distorts or only partially reports factual reality (society and the world as it really is) – is the very essence of tabloid media. Conspiracy theories have a similar role to fake news. They are fake news aggregated into theory format. What has changed in the age of social media is that fake news can be user-generated, compressed into short tweets, messages, memes, images and video, and can circulate at high speed through the globally networked communication environment of social media such as Twitter and Facebook, which increasingly acts as an important source of news for many. Victor Pickard (2016) warns that Trump's rise should not be reduced to fake news circulating on social media, but that at the same time one should not simply dismiss the role of Twitter, Facebook and algorithms. The 'proliferation of fake news is symptomatic of an unregulated news monopoly, one that is governed solely by profit imperatives' (Pickard 2016, 119). In a way, all journalism is political because the choice of what topics to cover, the length of a news piece, whom to interview for it, how prominently it is placed, etc. is a question of power. Journalism as activism was already known in the eighteenth century (Dorf and Tarrow 2017) and has a long history in the form of alternative and investigative journalism. However, an aspect that is new to the political moment we live in is the proliferation of right-wing nationalist news that makes use of the networked online and social media environment for spreading politically motivated fake news stories, which aim at supporting a nationalist agenda and delegitimising those who are considered as enemies.

The proliferation of contemporary fake news is an indication of a high level of political polarisation. Fake news is a form of ideological and psychological warfare that aims at the symbolic domination and defeat of perceived enemies. It is the online expression of the friend/enemy scheme in the time of new nationalisms, Brexit and Trump. Some speak of the emergence of post-truth politics, which is intended to indicate that what is true is, for many, no longer defined by factual reporting, but by emotions, ideology, what is popular and what one 'likes' on social media. We mentioned earlier that the former Tory secretary of state for justice, Michael Gove – one of the main 'Leave' campaigners in the Brexit referendum – declared in a television interview: 'I think that people in this country have had enough of experts […] from organisations with acronyms, saying that they know what is best and get it consistently wrong.' In times of crisis, extreme political polarisation and a general shift towards the right of the political spectrum, ideology becomes more than facts and discussion and, compared to other phases, a more important influencing factor in politics. The term post-truth is imprecise because it implies that there are ages of enlightenment and truth that may be followed by a post-truth age dominated by ideology and lies. Ideology and the distortion of reality are key features of capitalism and capitalist media as such. The opportunities for presenting non-ideological and critical information in liberal democratic capitalism are, however, certainly better than in authoritarian capitalism. The danger of the Trump era is that it has the potential to contribute to a transition towards authoritarian capitalism (see Chapters 3 and 4).

FACT-CHECKING ORGANISATIONS: A CURE FOR FAKE NEWS?

What can be done against fake news? One suggestion is to develop and use fake news filters (O'Malley and Levin 2017). Just like spam filters in email communication, an equivalent is sought for social media. The problem is that there is no technological fix to political problems. Algorithms are also fallible and can never perfectly discern between what is true and what is false. So what about using human intelligence for combating fake news? In the time of fake online news, fact checking has become an important profession.

For fact checking to work, fact-checking organisations need significant funding in order to pay their employees and professional fact checkers, who have a research background, are well paid and not precarious click-workers. Fact-checking organisations include, for example, PolitiFact, FactCheck.org, Full Fact and Africa Check. After Facebook had come under criticism for allowing its algorithms to post fake news stories in users' news feeds, it announced that it would introduce a reporting mechanism. If a significant number of users report a posting as being fake, fact checkers are alerted and investigate how truthful the posted content is. Facebook hired ABC News, Snopes, PolitiFact and FactCheck.org.

That Facebook hires fact-checking organisations is certainly a decision that should be welcomed, because this move brings a bit of human control back into algorithmic politics. But there are limits. First, ABC News is not a fact-checking organisation, but a primary news production organisation that is for-profit and part of the Walt Disney Company. It is, like any news producing organisation, prone to produce fake news itself. News organisations are not professional fact checkers, but producers of news that correspond more or less to reality. It is an important matter of media power and of checks and balances that those who fact check are not those who produce the news. If that is not the case, conflicts of interest may arise. Second, fact checking cannot solve the underlying class conflicts, social problems and political and ideological contradictions that cause fake news. Fact checking cannot replace the need to solve the societal problems causing social and political polarisation. Third, given a highly polarised political system, fact checking may not be able to challenge the behaviours that create falseness. In the Facebook case, fake news activists may turn into fake reporting activists, who strategically report truthful and progressive content as being false and thereby impose limits on fact checking or bring it to a collapse. In a society that is full of political contradictions, fundamental political change that weakens polarisation is required in order to strengthen the public sphere.

We saw that Fromm (1936) sees a polarised relation between individuals and groups as an important feature of authoritarianism. The analysis of Trump's tweets shows that he has a very positive relationship with specific groups and individuals, whereas there are other groups and individuals whom he radically rejects and opposes. Negative references to groups and individuals by far outweigh the positive ones (see Table 6.4). It seems like Trump feels an urge to hit back at those who criticise him. We mentioned earlier that one of his mottos is: 'When somebody screws you, screw them back in spades. [...] When someone attacks you publicly, always strike back. [...] Go for the jugular so that people watching will not want to mess with you' (Trump and Zanker 2007, 199). Trump uses Twitter as a communication tool for this purpose.

Patriarchy and Militarism

KLAUS THEWELEIT ON PATRIARCHY

The leadership principle and the friend/enemy scheme need ideological justification. Patriarchy is not just a political-economic system of gender domination and exploitation, but also one of the ideologies that fulfils the role of justifying the leadership principle and the friend/enemy scheme. Patriarchal ideology makes a distinction between 'typical' and 'adequate' characteristics and behaviours for men and women. Women are thereby often reduced to sexuality, biology and housework. Klaus Theweleit (1987, 272) argues in this context: 'Under patriarchy, the productive force of women has been effectively excluded from participating in male public and social productions.' Leaders are typically conceived of as being male. The friend/enemy logic in the final instance implies warfare. Militarism and the glorification of the male soldier as the ideal human are part of patriarchal ideology. The glorification of the soldier aims at instilling discipline and hierarchy as fundamental organisational principles in society. The goal is to destroy the opposition and perceived enemies by repressive means. In order to do so, war and law-and-order policies are often used, which explains why authoritarian societies are often both imperialistic and control societies. They enforce militancy and repression both outside and inside of society. The soldier is also inherently linked to nationalist ideology. He is the figure who is said to defend the nation's interests against foreign enemies. The policeman is the principle of the soldier applied to the nation's internal system of defence.

Right-wing authoritarian thought is often based on the idea that the leader turns a mass into a nation and puts life into it (Theweleit 1989, 94). 'The leader attains potency by desexualizing and devivifying "the mass"' (97). The soldier repeats the leadership principle by erecting his ego in the act of killing, by turning something human into nothing and creating the psychological feeling of victory and superiority: 'The act of killing is itself the most absolute form of this dedifferentiation and devivification of living life. It is the core of the white terror, the act by which the soldier male guarantees his own survival, his self-preservation and self-regeneration' (221). Authoritarians 'destroy others to create themselves; they destroy things in the alien object-world and metamorphose into killing-machines and their components: a "baptism of fire." *Wreaking revenge* is their way of becoming one with themselves' (382).

TRUMP AND CHILDCARE IN THE USA

Trump's childcare plan aims to 'rewrite the tax code to allow working parents to deduct from their income taxes child care expenses for up to four children and elderly dependents' (Trump 2016i). The deductions would be available for an individual annual income of up to US$250,000. Furthermore, Trump wants to 'guarantee six weeks of paid maternity leave' (Trump 2016i):

> http://twitter.com/realDonaldTrump/statuses/782020266771812352:
> I believe in #AmericaFirst and that means FAMILY FIRST! My childcare plan reflects the needs of modern working-class families. #ImWithYou https://t.co/RCnZZtTk4c

[Embedded video, text in the video:]
[Spoken text:]
Ivanka Trump: The most important job that any woman can have is being a mother. And it shouldn't mean taking a pay cut. I'm Ivanka Trump – a mother, a wife and an entrepreneur. Donald Trump understands the needs of the modern workforce. My father will change outdated labour laws so that they support women and American families. He will provide tax credits for childcare, paid maternity leave, and dependent care savings accounts. This will allow women to support their families and further their careers.

Donald Trump: I'm Donald Trump and I approve this message

[Written text:] TRUMP PENCE MAKE AMERICA GREAT AGAIN! 2016

[Written text:] PAID FOR BY DONALD J. TRUMP FOR PRESIDENT, INC. APPROVED BY DONALD J. TRUMP. (#787)

In the video associated with tweet #787, motherhood is defined as the most important 'job' of a woman. Men are not mentioned, which creates the impression that the Trump campaign sees care work as a domain for women only. Ivanka Trump is introduced as being 'a mother, a wife and an entrepreneur', which communicates that it is easily possible to combine professional life with motherhood and family life. Right at the moment when Ivanka Trump says 'entrepreneur' in the video, there is a cut and one sees Donald Trump. This juxtaposition reminds us on the one hand that Ivanka Trump comes from a privileged billionaire background. On the other hand she says that 'Donald Trump understands the needs of the modern workforce', which communicates a unity between the billionaire class, to whom she and her father belong, and the everyday worker. The simultaneous referencing of entrepreneurs and the workforce creates the impression of a classless society. It fetishises hard labour as an alleged joint feature of the capitalist and the worker. The video leaves out aspects of class that make it much harder for everyday workers in the USA to raise children and much easier for the rich, who can afford private care.

Childcare is in the USA not offered or supported by the state. There is no paid parental leave. Trump's idea to make childcare deductible from income tax would predominantly benefit those with higher incomes and does not tackle the problem that childcare is expensive in the USA: it costs on average US$18,000 per year (Martin 2016). Terry O'Neill (2016), president of the National Organization for Women, commented that 'the Trump plan gives the wealthiest families big tax deductions for childcare, while leaving little or nothing for the women and their families who need the most help'. The USA is the only developed country without paid parental leave (OECD 2016). Whereas Trump suggested six weeks of paid leave, Hillary Clinton's plan was to '[g]uarantee up to 12 weeks of paid family and medical leave to care for a new child or a seriously ill family member'.[19]

The average paid maternity, parental and home care leave in OECD countries is 54.1 weeks, out of which on average 17.7 weeks is paid maternity leave (OECD 2016). Neither Clinton's nor Trump's suggestion comes anywhere near the OECD average. The International Labour Organization (ILO) Maternity Protection Convention says that a 'woman to whom this Convention applies shall be entitled to a period of maternity leave of not less than 14 weeks' (ILO 2000). Trump's suggestion of six weeks' maternity leave is not even half of what the ILO prescribes as the absolute acceptable minimum in its international labour regulations. The United States is not among the countries that have ratified the ILO convention. Given that Trump's plan does not adhere to international labour standards, it is hard to see how it 'reflects the needs of modern working-class families'. A progressive agenda would subscribe to ILO conventions and update legislation at least to OECD averages.

IVANKA TRUMP AND THE 'WOMEN WHO WORK' CAMPAIGN

Ivanka Trump started the campaign #WomenWhoWork in order to celebrate women who work. She said in a campaign video: 'The women who I know, who are working today, are working hard to create and build the lives they want to live.'[20] On another occasion, she commented: 'It's sometimes easy for women who are working hard at all aspects of their life to go through things without showing a level of vulnerability because you have to keep moving forward and you're always in motion'

---

19. www.hillaryclinton.com/issues/paid-leave/, accessed on 22 February 2017, accessed 14 October 2017.

20. ivankatrump.com/womenwhowork/, accessed on 22 February 2017, accessed 14 October 2017.

(ABC News 2016). In this worldview, it is a woman's individual task and responsibility to manage the life of herself, her family and her children. Aspects of collective responsibility guaranteed by public services are missing in this worldview. The implication is that if there is failure, then the cause of it must be that the mother has not worked hard enough. The message is that you can do what you love and be successful when you work hard enough. The campaign communicates that hard labour is the key that makes it easily possible for women to combine career, family and children. The message conveyed is highly individualistic and labour-fetishistic. It leaves out saying anything about women and men who work hard, but struggle to combine labour and family because their salaries are low, their working conditions are precarious and there is not enough financial and organisational state support for childcare in the United States.

DONALD TRUMP AND THE LEAKED TAPE

In October 2016, a tape emerged that was recorded in 2005, in which Donald Trump said: 'You know I'm automatically attracted to beautiful – I just start kissing them. It's like a magnet. Just kiss. I don't even wait. And when you're a star, they let you do it. You can do anything. Grab them by the pussy. You can do anything.'[21] Trump was confronted with major criticism. He responded with a video statement that he also posted on Twitter (#885). In it, he argues that he has 'said and done things I regret, and the words released today on this more than a decade old video, are one of them' (#885). He immediately in the same video started a counter-offensive, saying: 'Bill Clinton has actually abused women and Hillary has bullied, attacked, shamed and intimidated his victims' (#885).

On 9 October, Trump organised a press conference ahead of the second presidential debate between him and Hillary Clinton that took place on the same day. Paula Jones, Kathleen Willey and Juanita Broaddrick, who had alleged that Bill Clinton sexually harassed them, gave individual statements that supported Trump. Also Kathy Shelton, who had been raped at the age of twelve by a man whom Hillary Clinton defended, also expressed her support. Trump live broadcast the press conference on Facebook and posted a link to it on Twitter (#902). Two hours later,

---

21. www.youtube.com/watch?v=8wM248Wo54U, accessed 14 October 2017, accessed 14 October 2017.

he tweeted: 'There's never been anyone more abusive to women in politics than Bill Clinton. My words were unfortunate – the Clintons' actions were far worse' (#909). Trump combined two elements of the ideological square model (van Dijk 2011): he and four women stressed positive things about him and at the same time said negative things about his political opponents, the Clintons. The goal was to distract attention from negative reporting and news about Trump.

Sexism and misogyny have repeatedly played a role in Trump's universe of attacks on opponents: he said about comedian Rosie O'Donnell, who had criticised him, that she has a 'fat, ugly face' (Oppenheim 2016), eats 'like a pig' (Zaru 2016) and 'is an unattractive person both inside and out' (Trump and Zanker 2007, 187–8). Trump reduces humans to their looks and uses somatonyms ('fat', 'ugly') and animal metaphors ('pig') for attacking his enemies. Twitter has become one of his preferred means of communicative attack.

DONALD TRUMP AND ALICIA MACHADO

In the first presidential debate, Hillary Clinton said that one of the worst things Trump said 'was about a woman in a beauty contest. He loves beauty contests, supporting them and hanging around them. And he called this woman 'Miss Piggy'. Then he called her 'Miss Housekeeping', because she was Latina. Donald, she has a name. [...] Her name is Alicia Machado. [...] And she has become a US citizen, and you can bet she's going to vote this November' (Clinton and Trump 2016a). Alicia Machado was Miss Universe 1996. At that time, Trump was the owner of Miss Universe Inc. She worked for this organisation during her reign as Miss Universe. She gained some weight. Trump arranged a series of reporters to watch Machado starting a workout programme in order to lose weight. He called her 'somebody who likes to eat' (Graves, Turbin and Delaney 2016) and commented on her weight:

And some people, when they have pressure, they eat too much, like me, like Alicia. And what she is going to do now is she has got one of the great trainers of the world, [...] and he's been working with her for the last few days. And I think she is gonna show up at that contest actually being probably a little bit heaver than what she wanted, but you think that is actually better.[22]

In 2016, Machado said in an interview: 'he [Trump] started to use me. To expose me. To bully me. [...] I was sick for almost five years, anorexic and bulimic. [...] I know what he can do. [...] And we don't need to have somebody like him as our president' (Graves, Turbin and Delaney 2016). In a Fox interview after the presidential debate with Clinton, Trump commented on Machado that she 'was the worst [Miss Universe] we ever had, the worst, the absolutely worst, she was impossible. [...] She gained a massive amount of weight, and it was a real problem' (Morrison 2016). He continued on Twitter, writing: 'Did Crooked Hillary help disgusting (check out sex tape and past) Alicia M become a U.S. citizen so she could use her in the debate?' (#779). It is not proven that Trump called Machado 'Miss Piggy', but he used somatonyms in respect to her body's weight ('massive amount of weight'), and heavily affective speech ('disgusting', 'the worst', 'the absolutely worst') for characterising her.

TRUMP, THE ARMY AND THE POLICE

Trump often likes to invoke positive references to the army and the police. The police was the third most frequently positively referenced group, the military the fourth most (see Table 6.5). Here are two examples:

http://twitter.com/realDonaldTrump/statuses/776842647294009344: I am truly honored and grateful for receiving SO much support from our American heroes ... https://t.co/S9bvbysiOr https://t.co/JJQncd3zhf.

[Embedded image showing the shadow of a saluting soldier in front of the American flag, the text at the bottom of the image reads '164 MILITARY LEADERS SUPPORT DONALD TRUMP'.] (#633)

http://twitter.com/realDonaldTrump/statuses/796797436752707585: Happy 241st birthday to the U.S. Marine Corps! Thank you for your service!! https://t.co/Lz2dhrXzo4.

---

22. www.youtube.com/watch?v=PpXsAoXZIMg, accessed 14 October 2017, accessed 14 October 2017.

[Embedded image showing two US Marine Corps veterans in front of the Marine Corps War Memorial. The Memorial portrays six Marines raising the US flag; the image contains the following text:
THE UNITED STATES MARINE CORPS

SEMPER * FIDELIS

SINCE NOVEMBER 10, 1775]. (#1,422)

In July 2016, Trump tweeted: 'Shooting deaths of police officers up 78% this year. We must restore law and order and protect our great law enforcement officers!' (#133). He tends to tweet about the shooting of police officers, but never about police shootings of black people, an issue that has become highly controversial during recent years in the USA. In 2015, 41 US law enforcement officers were shot and killed (Grinberg 2016). According to statistics, US police killed 346 black people in the year 2015, of which 31 per cent were allegedly armed and violent.[23] In 97 per cent of the cases, no charges were raised against the officers firing the bullets.[24] Angela Davis argues that there is 'an unbroken line of police violence in the United States that takes us all the way back to the days of slavery, the aftermath of slavery, the development of the Ku Klux Klan' (Davis 2014). In November 2014, a grand jury decided not to raise charges against the white police officer who had shot Michael Brown. Brown was an unarmed, eighteen-year-old black man, who was shot to death in August 2014 after he had stolen cigarillos from a store in Ferguson, Missouri. Unrest broke out in Ferguson. Donald Trump tweeted: 'There is no excuse for riots in Ferguson regardless of the grand jury outcome' (24 November 2014). Noting that Trump had never said something about police shootings of black people on Twitter, a user asked in response to Trump: 'I'd love to hear what the excuse is for killing unarmed, young black males though. @RealDonaldTrump'.

Trump's fondness of the military and police fits in with his overall patriotic and nationalist ideology. This attitude also indicates that he considers military conflict an appropriate way of solving conflicts. He leaves no doubt that he sees nuclear weapons as an important military means: 'The United States must greatly strengthen and expand its nuclear capability until such time as the world comes to its senses regarding

---

23.   Data source: mappingpoliceviolence.org/, accessed on 23 February 2017.
24.   Data source: mappingpoliceviolence.org/, accessed on 23 February 2017.

nukes' (#1,625). The problem is that nuclear armament on one side enforces the fear of being annihilated on other sides, which can result in more armament, more fear, more armament, etc. A vicious cycle of armament and fear can also turn from quantity into the new quality of a nuclear war that could easily wipe out human life on Earth.

GUN OWNERSHIP

Trumps seems to see war, violence, weapons and guns as a generally appropriate means of handling conflicts. Trump is a strong supporter of the unrestricted right of gun ownership:

> http://twitter.com/realDonaldTrump/statuses/788912156234227712: #SecondAmendment #2A #Debates https://t.co/QbOaf8Dlhs.
>
> [Embedded greyscale image showing Donald Trump speaking in front of a crowd plus the following printed text:
> The Second Amendment to our Constitution is clear. The right of the people to keep and bear Arms shall not be infringed upon. Period. DONALD J. TRUMP.] (#1,102)

Trump announced that he would appoint Supreme Court justices who are committed to not limiting gun ownership. He argued that 'Hillary wants to take your guns away. She wants to leave you unprotected in your home' (Trump 2016j). He sees gun ownership as a legitimate means of protection. The problem is that guns in homes can also go wrong, especially in unexpected, extraordinary situations. Studies have shown that guns in the home increase the probability of homicide, accidental shooting deaths among children and suicide.[25] In February 2017, Trump appointed Neil Gorsuch as a Supreme Court judge. Gorsuch is generally viewed as supporting private gun ownership. For example, he wrote as legal opinion that the 'Second Amendment protects an individual's right to own firearms and may not be infringed lightly' (McBride 2017). In a debate in February 2016, Trump said: 'I would bring back waterboarding, and I'd bring back a hell of a lot worse than waterboarding.'[26]

---

25. smartgunlaws.org/guns-in-the-homesafe-storage-statistics/, accessed on 22 February 2017.
26. www.democracynow.org/2016/2/8/trump_leads_gop_charge_embracing_torture, accessed on 23 February 2017.

LAW AND ORDER

In line with military, police and gun fetishism, Trump also stands for law-and-order politics. He stresses that under his presidency, 'we will once again be a country of law and order' and that he will 'Make America Safe Again' (Trump 2016i). The Trump campaign also introduced the hashtag #MakeAmericaSafeAgain. The problem is that heavy sentencing does not necessarily or automatically prevent crime because the underlying social problems are often to do with inequality, class, asymmetric power, alienation and domination, and do not disappear by making laws tougher and more threatening. In March 2016, Trump was asked in an interview if he 'believes in punishment for abortion'. 'Trump: The answer is that there has to be some form of punishment. Interviewer: For the woman? Trump: Yeah. There has to be some form' (Glenza 2016). The idea of making abortion more difficult is a link between patriarchal ideology and law-and-order politics.

PROSECUTING HILLARY CLINTON?

In the second presidential debate, Trump talked about appointing a special prosecutor to investigate Hillary Clinton:

> Donald Trump: And I tell you what, I didn't think I would say this, but I'm going to and I hate to say it. But if I win, I am going to instruct my attorney general to get a special prosecutor to look into your situation. Because there has never been so many lies, so much deception. There has never been anything like it. And we're gonna have a special prosecutor. When I speak, I go out and speak, the people of this country are furious. In my opinion, the people that have been long time workers at the FBI are furious. There has never been anything like this where e-mails, and you get a subpoena. You get a subpoena, and after getting the subpoena you delete 33,000 e-mails and then you acid wash them or bleach them, as you would say. Very expensive process. So we're gonna get a special prosecutor and we're gonna look into it. Hillary Clinton: Everything he just said is absolutely false, but I'm not surprised [...] it's just awfully good that someone with the temperament of Donald Trump is not in charge of the law in our country. Trump: Because you would be in jail. (Clinton and Trump 2016b)

After this debate, Trump repeated his threat twice on Twitter: 'If I win – I am going to instruct my AG to get a special prosecutor to look into your situation bc there's never been anything like your lies' (#912). 'Hillary Clinton should have been prosecuted and should be in jail. Instead she is running for president in what looks like a rigged election' (#1,010). Audiences at Trump's campaign events frequently cheered 'Lock her up'. In an interview after the election, Trump said such an investigation is 'not something that I feel very strongly about' (Trump 2016k). But the fear many observers have is that someone who announces a special prosecutor against a political opponent and says that the same opponent 'should be in jail' may be capable of jailing or outlawing political opponents and critics. The fear that many have in this context is that an authoritarian political system may replace liberal democracy.

The discussion shows that Trump stands for family politics that favour the wealthy and those on high incomes, made highly problematic comments about women, favours law-and-order politics that use repressive means and disregard crime's causes, worships the police and the military, and seems to consider jails, waterboarding, warfare, guns and nuclear weapons as appropriate responses to conflicts. His comments about political opponents, the media and artists have worried many and created the fear that he might be capable of jailing his critics or using other tactics to shut them down. The analysed Twitter dataset provides indications of a patriarchal and militaristic worldview.

CONCLUSION

Trump on Twitter

The analysis of 1,815 tweets searched for traces of an authoritarian personality in Donald Trump's online behaviour. Trump uses Twitter to present himself as a boss, strong leader and authority. The language used is very self-centred and narcissistic. He uses the first-person singular ('I', 'me') much more frequently on Twitter than the first-person plural. Twitter's brevity, speed, individualism and its structure for the accumulation of acclamation (via 'likes' and 'retweets') supports Trump's use of it as a communication tool for authoritarian leadership. Trump uses Twitter for continuously repeating nationalist slogans, above all that he will 'make America great again', which is supported by the use of hashtags such #MAGA, #AmericaFirst or #MakeAmericaSafeAgain. Trump constructs average Americans as an in-group who are under constant threat from immigrants, refugees, criminals, terrorists, foreign forces and the political elite. He uses Twitter for communicating that there is a conspiracy against America that aims at destroying it. Trump's ideological discourse presents a national community of US Americans that are under attack and who have to struggle for existence. His nationalism constructs a joint political interest of capital and labour and thereby deflects attention from class structures being at the heart of social problems. Trump's Twitter communication postulates political dualisms between friends and enemies. Negative references to individuals and groups strongly outweigh positive ones. His main scapegoats, whom he frequently attacks on Twitter, are the liberal media, Democratic politicians, immigrants, refugees, criminals and Islam. Among his main positive references on Twitter are Mike Pence, his family, Fox, the American people, the police and the military. Trump counts right-wing journalists and media, especially those associated with Rupert Murdoch's Fox, among his friends, whom he follows on Twitter. He draws a clear distinction between friendly media and enemy media, and uses Twitter to constantly characterise his enemies in a negative manner as 'crooks', 'disgusting', 'failing', 'dishonest', 'biased', 'bad', 'terrible', 'fake', etc. Twitter's structure of 140-character messages does not allow for arguments. Trump welcomes this circumstance as it allows his friend/enemy propaganda to work through negative affects instead of arguments. He uses generalising synecdoches for presenting his enemies as unitary groups of bad people. Trump also makes use of cartoons, derogatory imitation, short video excerpts, repetition and symbols (the US flag, Ronald Reagan, military, police, etc.) for communicating agreement with the national community of US Americans and disagreement with what he considers to be his and the USA's enemies. Trump uses Twitter for overall patriarchal and militaristic political communication that postulates a conservative view of society, calls for law-and-order politics, glorifies the military, the police, guns and weapons, and sees violence as an appropriate response to social problems.

Trump is a post-truth politician, who accuses media that are critical towards him as being 'fake' and often questions empirical evidence. His political strategy puts ideology over facts, illusion over reality, and ficti-tiousness over facticity. Right-wing online media such as Breitbart and the Drudge Report supported his campaign. Fake news stories circulating on social media have predominantly taken a pro-Trump position. According to studies, conservatives are more likely to believe fake news than progressives and fake news predominantly has a right-wing character. Social media bots that automatically liked and reposted content that favoured him also supported Trump's campaign to a certain degree.

The analysis overall found strong evidence for the online communication of authoritarian leadership, nationalism, the friend/enemy scheme, patriarchy and militarism in the analysed dataset. The ideological belief in authoritarian leadership, nationalism, the friend/enemy scheme, patriarchy and militarism together form key elements of right-wing authoritarianism. The conducted analysis found indications that Trump has an authoritarian personality structure that shapes the way he uses Twitter as a tool of political communication. Brian Ott (2017, 62) argues that Twitter suits Trump's political communication because 'Twitter's lack of formality and intimacy undermines the social norms that uphold civility and predisposes users to engage in both divisive and derisive communication'. Twitter's 140-character limit affords keeping messages simple. Its dominant use implies spatio-temporal distance and the invisibility of communication partners, which encourages impulsivity and affectivity. As a consequence, humans are more likely to engage in uncivil communication on Twitter than when sitting in the same room. The conducted CDA shows that Trump uses Twitter as a tool for authoritarian political communication.

Twitter's Great Little Man

Frankfurt School critical theory allows us to interpret and understand Trump's authoritarian use of Twitter. Trump's populist, aggressive, attack-oriented, offensive, proletarian language and style make him appear as a great little man, who is on top but at the same time an ordinary person. The great little man is, according to Adorno, 'a person who suggests both omnipotence and the idea that he is just one of the folks' (Adorno 1951a, 142). The leader often presents himself as a lone wolf fighting against political elites. This behaviour comes along with 'aversion to the professional politician and perhaps to any kind of expertness' (Adorno 1975, 21). Trump constructs himself as the great little man on Twitter. Neumann (1957/2017, 618) argues that in authoritarianism, '[h]atred, resentment, dread, created by great upheavals, are concentrated on certain persons who are denounced as devilish conspirators'. In such situations, the 'fear of social degradation [...] creates for itself "a target for the discharge of the resentments arsing from damaged self-esteem"' (624). Trump allows individuals who are afraid of social degradation to channel their fears into hatred against scapegoats. He uses Twitter as a medium that helps to construct scapegoats and enemies and to offer his followers material for channelling their aggressions into hatred.

Twitter's Affective Politics

Wilhelm Reich (1972, 83) argued that authoritarian politicians are convinced that one cannot 'get at the masses with arguments, proofs, and knowledge, but only with feelings and beliefs'. Twitter is a medium that supports politics that are based on feelings, beliefs and irrationality instead of arguments, proofs and knowledge. Donald Trump has made emotionally laden ideological Twitter politics a key element of his political strategy. He uses Twitter's brevity of 140 characters for a politics that does not rely on arguments, but on negative emotions that he communicates and tries to stir among his followers. Twitter is the best-suited medium for the emotional and ideological politics of outrage, scapegoating, hatred and attack because its ephemerality, brevity and speed support spectacles and sensationalism. It leaves no time and no space for substantial debates. 'Twitter is perfect for General Trump who can blast out his opinions and order his followers what to think' (Kellner 2016, 9).

Is Trump a fascist? In posting this question, one needs to again bear the distinction between the micro, meso and macro level of the far right in mind, as well as the distinction between right-wing authoritarianism and fascism. The Twitter analysis conducted here provides indications of all four aspects of right-wing authoritarian consciousness, personality and ideology (hierarchic leadership, nationalism, the friend/enemy scheme, patriarchy/militarism). Trump is certainly guided by these principles in politics and aims at building an authoritarian-capitalist society. This does not imply that the USA is today a fascist society. US courts blocked Trump's executive order that aimed at restricting the travel of citizens from seven predominantly Muslim countries into the USA. This circumstance shows that constitutional mechanisms can protect democracy. Although Trump certainly works at establishing an authoritarian-capitalist society, there is no guarantee that at some point this project will not turn into a fascist project that eliminates democracy and the rule of law. Political awareness and vivid oppositional movements are the best means for trying to forestall such developments.

The question arises of how to best challenge authoritarianism in general and online authoritarianism in particular. The *New York Times* saw its paid subscriptions increase by 132,000 during a three-week period in November 2016, a growth rate ten times higher than during the same period in 2015 (Belvedere and Newberg 2016). The first television debate between Trump and Clinton reached a total of 84 million US viewers, the largest audience ever in 60 years of televised US presidential debates (Stelter 2016). In the world of the capitalist spectacle, the capitalist media need Trump just like Trump needs the media. The mainstream media helped make Trump, both economically and politically.

Ignoring Trump

The mainstream media's Trump spectacle also continues after the election. It has now become common that they devote front pages and entire articles to Trump tweets. Either they report what Trump tweets, or in a Kafkaesque manner discuss whether it is good or not that the media report about Trump's tweets. The point is that they give constant attention to Trump and provide free propaganda for the Trump brand. The continuous attention on Trump is itself the message. Trump makes strategic use of the fact that he helps to sell attention.

A truly critical strategy would be to provide no free promotion to Trump by ignoring him. To say nothing, report nothing and comment on nothing that is right-wing populist in character has to be part of breaking the right-wing spectacle's spell. According to a report, NBC, CBS and ABC gave 23.4 times more coverage to Trump than to Sanders (Boehlert 2015). An alternative strategy also requires changing the balance of forces in media coverage.

Trump's tweets are the ultimate expression of populist and ideological communication in a capitalism that is based on high velocity, high one-dimensionality and high superficiality. The only practical hope for political communication is the struggle for dialectical forms of political communication that provide space and time for reporting and debating the world's complexity.

Satire, Parody and Humour as Political Strategies

Right-wing ideology is a rational form of irrationality. It mobilises emotions, insecurities, fears and political anxiety in an instrumental manner. Irrationality can only to a certain degree be countered by rational arguments. This does not mean that the response to nationalism should be similar forms of scapegoating and simplistic affective hatred. But satire, parody and humour can work for constructing counter narratives.

Comedian John Oliver in the HBO show *Last Week Tonight* created the satirical name 'Donald Drumpf':

> The very name Trump is the cornerstone of his brand. If only there were a way to uncouple that magical word from the man he really is. Well guess what? There is. Because it turns out the name 'Trump' was not always his family's name. One biographer found that a prescient ancestor had changed it from – and this is true – 'Drumpf'. [...] And Drumpf is much less magical. It is the sound produced when a morbidly obese pigeon flies into the window in a foreclosed old navy. Drump![27]

The hashtags #MakeDonaldDrumpfAgain and #Drumpf have been used for satirical campaigning. The Twitter account @RealDonalDrumpf posts parodistic tweets about Trump, for example: 'I have asked Andy Puzder to withdraw as Secretary of Labor, but he's definitely first in line to be Secretary of Labor Camps' (Twitter, @RealDonalDrumpf, 15 February 2017, 11.38 am). In August 2017 it had about 80,000 followers. There are Drumpf jokes, songs and memes.

The question is whether comedians such as John Oliver reach Trump voters, or if the reception of their jokes remains limited to liberal and progressive voters. At the same time, left-wing politics is often too sterile, humourless and deadly serious. Left-wing activists should aim at taking comedians such as Oliver as a starting point for thinking about what left-wing satirical responses to right-wing propaganda could look like,

---

27.   www.youtube.com/watch?v=DnpO_RTSNmQ, accessed on 24 February 2017.

and how it could be used for trying to on the one hand mobilise progressive activists and on the other hand trying to advance more reflection among supporters of right-wing politicians. This requires the radicalisation of liberal comedy into socialist comedy that mocks right-wing politicians as well as the ruling class and shows how they are connected.

The Ambiguity of Laughter

Horkheimer and Adorno (2002, 60) spoke about the 'ambiguity of laughter': 'If laughter up to now has been a sign of violence, an outbreak of blind, obdurate nature, it nevertheless contains the opposite element, in that through laughter blind nature becomes aware of itself as such and thus abjures its destructive violence.' Humour is part of oppression itself, but may also be turned into challenging oppression. Anti-fascism can be simultaneously enlightening, humorous and serious. Charlie Chaplin's *The Great Dictator* is the masterpiece of an enlightening satirical parody. Anti-fascism 2.0 requires *The Great Dictator* 2.0, an update of Chaplin for the social media age. Chaplin commented on the strategy of his movie: 'Pessimists say I may fail – that dictators aren't funny any more, that the evil is too serious. That is wrong. If there is one thing I know it is that power can always be made ridiculous. The bigger that fellow gets the harder my laughter will hit him' (Van Gelder 1940). Anti-fascism 2.0 needs a political strategy that is multidimensional. Satire, parody and humour form one dimension that requires people, time, space and resources in order to be an effective praxis.

Critical Data Visualisation

Part of the problem of the Left is that it has more difficulties in appealing to the psyche, emotions, affects and desires than the Right. It would be wrong simply to imitate the communication strategies and elements of right-wing authoritarianism. But the Left should also not leave psychology to the Right, but rather practice critical political psychology. Those who feel politically anxious and disenfranchised want to express their desires for love and hate. How can one turn a disenfranchised group's love for nationalism and authoritarian leaders into the love for socialism and participatory democracy, and its hatred of immigrants and foreigners into the hatred of capitalism and inequality? Rational arguments and statistical data can often counter prejudices. Prejudices operate at the psychological level of hopes and fears that form the inner dimension of post-truth politics. Progressive should not give up the use of well thought-out arguments and debates. The point is to understand the complexity of the world and come up with proper responses that are supported by critical visualisations of data.

Brecht 2.0, *Verfremdung* 2.0

Critical data visualisation is a way of popularising progressive thought so that it challenges right-wing authoritarianism. Political humour, satire and parody form an important way of challenging and responding to right-wing authoritarianism. In the age of big data and social media, the Left 2.0 requires Charlie Chaplin 2.0 and Brecht 2.0. Authoritarian spectacles that are staged via social media and reality TV need to be challenged by the Brechtian dialectical theatre 2.0 and the Boalian theatre of the oppressed 2.0.

Brecht opposes *Verfremdung* to society's *Entfremdung* (estrangement, alienation). *Verfremdung* forms a principle of the dialectical theatre: '*Verfremdung* estranges an incident or character simply by taking from the incident or character what is self-evident, familiar, obvious in order to produce wonder and curiosity. [...] The V-effect consists in turning the object of which it is to be made aware, to which one's attention is to be drawn, from something ordinary, familiar, immediately accessible, into something peculiar, striking and unexpected' (Brecht 2015, 143, 192). *Verfremdung* negates the negation. It aims at producing emotions, feelings and effects of surprise and curiosity. *Verfremdung* is the alienated alienation and estranged estrangement. It is a negated negative that turns into a determinate negation. *Verfremdung* 2.0 is the strategy of creating equivalents of the principles of Brecht's dialectical theatre in the digital age and on social media.

Smart ways of challenging Trump's ideology are, however, not enough. They must feed into political movements. And alternative communication strategies alone may also not suffice. We require a shift in political communication away from speed, ephemerality, brevity, superficiality and tabloidisation towards slow media that provide enough time and space for outlining and discussing the complexity of political phenomena in an enlightening manner.

7

Conclusion: Authoritarian Communicative Capitalism and its Alternatives

MAIN FINDINGS

This book has analysed authoritarian capitalism's objective and subjective conditions. It has looked at right-wing authoritarian consciousness, psychology, ideology, movements, organisations and society. Right-wing authoritarian thought and right-wing authoritarian society interact dialectically. Thought and consciousness are part of and produced in society, and society shapes and is shaped by consciousness and human practices. Human practice and communication are the processes that mediate the dialectic of consciousness and society (Fuchs 2016b, 2015). The key aspect of consciousness and society is that humans bring about both in social production processes mediated by communication (Fuchs 2016b). When we analyse right-wing authoritarian society and its consciousness, we therefore also have to look at right-wing authoritarian practices, including communicative practices.

Chapters 2 and 3 outlined the theoretical foundations of ideology, nationalism, right-wing authoritarianism, authoritarian capitalism and fascism. Chapters 4 and 5 analysed the objective conditions of right-wing authoritarianism, Chapter 6 its subjectivity. The theoretical approach employed is grounded in a combination of Frankfurt School theory, especially works by Neumann, Adorno and Fromm, and critical political economy.

Right-Wing Authoritarianism

There is a micro (individuals), a meso (groups and institutions) and a macro level (society) of right-wing authoritarianism. Right-wing authoritarianism can take on the form of character structure, consciousness, ideology, movement, group, organisation, institution and society. All forms and levels of right-wing authoritarianism involve four elements, namely the belief in (a) hierarchic leadership, (b) nationalism, (c) the friend/enemy scheme and (d) patriarchy and militarism. Its social role is to distract attention from class and social contradictions that underlie class society's structure, stratification patterns and problems. Right-wing extremism and fascism are an intensification of right-wing authoritarianism such that an increase in quantity turns into a new quality: fascists favour terror and violence for achieving their goals (hierarchic leadership, nationalism, opposing perceived enemies, patriarchy, militarisation). Fascism's final factor 'is the reliance upon terror, i.e., the use of non-calculable violence as a permanent threat against the individual' (Neumann 1957, 245). A right-wing authoritarian individual, group, institution or society does not necessarily favour terror and a police state that represses all opposition, but right-wing authoritarianism can turn into fascism. The difference between right-wing extremism and fascism is that the use of violence is more latent among right-wing extremists and fascists, while in fascist society it is a concrete practice. Right-wing extremism is an ideology and movement, whereas fascism can exist on all levels of organisation, including fascist societies. It is important to draw a distinction between right-wing authoritarianism on the one hand and right-wing extremism and fascism on the other hand.

Chapters 4 and 5: Donald Trump

Chapters 4 and 5 analysed the economic, political and ideological aspects of Donald Trump and asked how the US state could change under Trump's rule. A key feature of Trump's presidency is that it means an overlap of the billionaire class and the political elite. Via Trump, factions of US capital rule directly. Trump is likely to favour the interests of specific factions of capital such as the oil/gas/coal industry, the healthcare and pharmaceutical industry, private education, construction or real estate. He argues in favour of private–public partnerships in infrastructure projects featuring socialised financial risk and private ownership. This could result in a 'neoliberal Keynesianism', where the state invests in infrastructure projects that are carried out by private corporations, which own the results as private property that is viewed according to commodity logic. Trump favours law-and-order politics, nationalist economic policies, anti-immigration ideology and policies, armament and hierarchic leadership. The key question is to what extent such elements remain just a publicly communicated ideology under Trump's rule, or whether and how the US state puts them (or is able to put them) into practice, which is also a question of power dynamics and conflicts (as, for example, in the case of Trump's executive order travel ban that was blocked by US courts). The more right-wing authoritarian ideology becomes the US state's legal and political practice, the more we will experience a shift towards authoritarian capitalism.

Based on the study of right-wing authoritarianism's societal conditions outlined in Chapters 2 and 3, Chapters 4 and 5 presented the results of case studies that analysed aspects of subjectivity. They used the methods of empirical ideology critique and critical social media discourse analysis, and it is hoped make a contribution to the methodology of studying ideology by giving examples of how to study ideology on social media (see also Fuchs 2016c and 2016d for further case studies).

Chapter 6: Donald Trump and Twitter

Chapter 6 analysed 1,815 tweets that Donald Trump posted between his nomination as Republican candidate and his inauguration as the forty-fifth president of the USA. The chapter reconstructed the Frankfurt School's theory of the authoritarian personality and used this approach as the foundation for a critical social media discourse analysis. The study confirmed the presence of all the features of the authoritarian personality in the analysed dataset: leadership ideology, nationalism, the friend/enemy logic, patriarchal ideology and elements of militaristic ideology. Trump's me-centred personality and Twitter's structure, characterised by brevity, speed, individualism and accumulation of acclamation, fit each other perfectly. Trump presents himself as a great little man on Twitter, a strong leader who is one of the people. Trump's ideological discourse presents a national community of US Americans that are under attack and who have to struggle for existence. His nationalism constructs a joint political interest of capital and labour that is directed against perceived enemies. Trump's main Twitter scapegoats, whom he frequently attacks, are the liberal media, Democratic politicians, immigrants, refugees, criminals and Islam. Trump also makes use of cartoons, imitation, short

Conclusion

video excerpts, repetition and symbols for communicating nationalism on Twitter. Fake news stories circulating on social media during the 2016 US presidential campaigns predominantly took a pro-Trump position.

AUTHORITARIAN CAPITALISM TODAY

Capitalism's Dialectic of Enlightenment

Horkheimer and Adorno (2002) describe capitalist development as the dialectic of enlightenment. Capitalism entails the tendency of the 'self-destruction of enlightenment' (Horkheimer and Adorno 2002, xvi). Capitalism is ruled by the logic of 'calculability and utility' (3), it reduces qualities to 'abstract quantities' (4). It is inherently positivist: 'For the Enlightenment, anything which cannot be resolved into numbers, and ultimately into one, is illusion' (4). Positivism is not just a mode of knowledge production, but the mode of capitalist production: capitalism's logic of accumulation requires the measurement of time, quantities of labour, commodities, money, capital and profits in order to exist. In capitalism mathematics becomes an omnipotent political-economic force that also shapes culture and everyday life. Where commodity logic enters, measurability and positivist knowledge come along. In the 'identification of the thoroughly mathematized world with truth, enlightenment believes itself safe from the return of the mythical' (18). Capitalist enlightenment separates subjects from objects and reduces the former to the latter. The same can be said about qualities and quantities, relations and things, emotionality and rationality, mind and body, culture and nature, metaphysics and physics, transcendence and immanence, etc. But this reduction, separation and ignorance backfires so that enlightenment 'regresses to the mythology it has never been able to escape' (20). By becoming a machine, enlightenment 'mutilates people' (29), although it set out to liberate them. Historically, liberalism emerged as the emancipation from feudalism, the rule of the church, aristocracy and emperors. However, it constituted the rule of capital and monopoly capital, backfired and turned against itself, which not only brought inequality, but also war and Auschwitz. Capitalism's negative dialectic is not over because it is an inherently crisis-ridden and inequality producing system.

The New Dialectic of Enlightenment

It looks like we are experiencing a new dialectic of enlightenment, in which neoliberal capitalism could turn over into authoritarian capitalism if it cannot be stopped by a progressive socialist agenda. Neoliberal capitalism's dialectic of enlightenment advanced freedom of the market and freedom of private ownership by dismantling the welfare systems of social protections. But neoliberal freedom can backfire and turn into tyranny, unfreedom and authoritarianism.

The neoliberal age emerged along with liberal values such as favouring multiculturalism, cosmopolitanism, feminism, LGBT rights, environmental protection, secularism, humanitarianism, cultural diversity, animal rights, vegetarianism and veganism. Political and cultural agendas, including the one of social democracy that shifted towards the right and imitated and developed neo-conservative politics, ignored and downplayed the continued existence of class conflicts and class structures. In academia, postmodern thought that ignored political economy became fashionable. The problem is that in the course of the simultaneity of the ignorance and continued existence of class and capitalism, a new negative dialectic of enlightenment emerged. Neoliberalism backfired against liberal values. Social freedom and the freedom of the market and of private ownership came into conflict. Neoliberalism's politics of market freedom and commodification increased the exploitation of labour and income and wealth inequalities, which resulted in an economic and social crisis. These crises turned into a political crisis and a legitimacy crisis, in which civil liberties have come under attack and capitalism has become authoritarian. With a weak Left and a social democracy that is no longer social, the new negative dialectic of enlightenment tends to give rise to authoritarian capitalism.

Neoliberalism = The Big Data Machine of Commodification

Neoliberalism is a huge machine of calculation and accumulation that tries to turn everything into a commodity. Lost in the depth of data and quantification, neoliberalism loses ground to the emotionally laden populism of right-wing extremism. Many then find the qualitative emotionality of prejudices and stereotypes more appealing than an argument or tweet that an algorithm predicts is the most likely candidate for winning over the largest number of people. Given that the world is not a machine, treating it like a machine will often have negative, unintended consequences.

Neoliberal capitalism created a monster that is based on the logic of a constant quantitative increase of profits, profit rates, shareholder values, bonuses and key performance indicators. It is based on the logic of not just commodifying, but also measuring and ranking everything. The emergence of big data stands in the context of neoliberalism's fetishism of quantification. Neoliberalism is big data capitalism, a capitalism that in an ever-expanding number of realms within society ranks the logic of quantification and commodification above people. Big data is part of the monster that was unleashed a long time ago and that has lashed out without restraint for decades. *The Apprentice*'s ruthless and fierce celebration of possessive individualism, competition, entrepreneurship, managerialism and neoliberalism gives an impression of Donald Trump's ideal model of society. It is a society that does not challenge, but instead deepens the dominant model.

The capitalist fetishism of quantification has as its negative downside an increase in inequality and precarious labour, a drop of the wage share, increasing debt levels of everyday people, low levels of corporate taxation and as a consequence a fiscal and austerity crisis of the state. Inequality and disrespect breed anger that can easily be channelled into barbarism as a political project. Neoliberalism is experiencing its own negative dialectic. Not only can we learn from the US elections that the logic of big data is mistaken and should be replaced, we can also learn that raising the logic of quantification to the point where its model dominates society is a failed political project. There might still be a slim chance of overcoming this project and replacing it with one that is oriented towards commonality and humanity.

Capitalism and Fascism

This book has stressed that it is important to see that authoritarian capitalism is not the same as capitalism. There is a dialectic of capitalism and fascism: fascism is capitalist, but because of its institutionalised terrorism it is also more than capitalism. Capitalism contains fascist potentials, which is why fascism can exist as long as capitalism exists and produces crises. Geoff Eley speaks in this context of the possibility of a 'fascism-producing crisis' (Eley 2015, 112). It is a mistake to say that Trump is creating a fascist society. But it is also a mistake to argue that the conditions for fascism do not exist in modern democracies and that fascism is impossible today, because the economic, social, political and cultural crises that can evolve into fascism continue to haunt capitalism.

Eley (2016) argues that one must ask today: 'So what kind of political crisis produces fascism?' He provides an analysis of US politics today:

Now when these two crises occur together – crisis of representation, crisis of consent; government paralysis, democratic impasse – we are in deep trouble. That's what makes sense of the Trump rhetoric. Then we need to add some other aspects. We need to talk about fundamental capitalist restructuring – deindustrialization and neoliberal globalization. We need to talk about drastic class recomposition, including the reorganization of work and labor markets, the rewriting of the labor contract. We need to talk about the global environmental catastrophe, climate change in particular, which now challenges effective and accountable governance at every possible level. Competition among nations for basic resources; struggles to contain economic migrancy and refugee populations fleeing shortages, droughts, and floods; rivalries over resources for energy – these will all reshape the language of national security ever more divisively. Fortress mentalities, idioms of politics organized by anxiety, gatedness as the emergent social paradigm – these increasingly drive the authoritarian and violent tendencies of contemporary governmentality. If we put all of this together, then we have the kind of crisis that can enable a politics that looks like fascism to coalesce. And this is where Trump has prospered. [...] Indeed, it seems more useful to think about this question structurally or perhaps typologically. That is, are there aspects of the crises in 1917–22 or 1930–33 (or for that matter 1933–36 in France & Spain, etc) we can theorize in order to help us make sense of the present? [...]

We can readily acknowledge (as I've done often elsewhere) the fundamental differences between now and then, without rendering the above questions nugatory. What are those differences? Well, for starters: no World War I and its outcomes; no total war; no Bolshevism; no revolutionary insurgency across most of Europe; no ascendant mass trade unionism; no mass Communist and social democratic parties; no great pan-European wave of democratization (1918–19). (Eley 2016)

So Eley ascertains that there are both structural commonalities and differences between the 1920s/1930s and today. It is a mistake to define fascism as restricted to its historical forms in Mussolini's Italy and Hitler's Germany or other past regimes. Capitalism has inherent potentials for creating crises and inequalities and has an inherent fetishistic character that can take on the form of repressive political fetishisation of the nation in the form of nationalism, xenophobia, racism and anti-Semitism. As long as capitalism exists, there is an inherent fascist potential.

Progressive and Right-Wing Movements

At present Europe is in a deep economic, political and social crisis. The 2008 economic crisis turned into a political crisis, governments bailed out banks and they have protected the rich and transnational corporations. At the same time the mass of people has suffered from hyper-neoliberalism and austerity. Europe has refused a haircut of Greece's debt. It has abandoned its weakest link. No end to Greece's social and economic crisis is in sight. Even the International Monetary Fund has argued for debt relief. Furthermore, the refugee crisis and the way it was mismanaged by European governments has cast doubt on the existence of solidarity in Europe. Although progressive left-wing movements and protests such as Occupy, the Indignant Citizens Movement in Greece, the Spanish 15-M movement, the Nuit debout movement in France, Syriza, Podemos, the movements supporting Jeremy Corbyn and Bernie Sanders, etc. have emerged, the crisis has produced a lot more far-right elements than leftism.

Far-right forces such as Donald Trump's movement, the Freedom Party of Austria, the Front National in France, the Alternative for Germany, the Dutch Party for Freedom, the Sweden Democrats, UKIP, the Finns Party in Finland, the Danish People's Party, Jobbik in Hungary, Golden Dawn in Greece, or the Slovak National Party have been strengthened. As one of the impacts of this crisis, right-wing populism has been expanding during recent years. At the same time, the media landscape has seen the rise of user-generated content and so-called social media (Fuchs 2017d).

Ruth Wodak argues that contemporary right-wing populism uses a broad range of media, including social media, for its 'performance strategies' (Wodak 2015, 21) in order to provoke and cause scandals and to obtain public attention. Social media would be a way for right-wing populists to brand and commodify themselves in a multimodal and interactive manner (134–40). Wodak argues that '[n]ew media-savvy leaders instrumentalize such disenchantment in text, image and talk, via many discursive and material practices' (182). She speaks in this context of a combination of the Haiderisation and the Berluconisation of Europe (Wodak 2013): the political rise of Jörg Haider, the former chairman of the Austrian Freedom Party (FPÖ), in the 1980s and 1990s, marked a turning point after which right-wing populism in Europe has been rapidly expanding. Silvio Berlusconi stands for the mediatisation of Haiderisation.

Studying online expressions of right-wing authoritarianism, right-wing extremism, fascism, Nazism, racism, anti-Semitism and nationalism is an important aspect of the role critical media and communication studies can play in the crisis. This book is a contribution to the critical study of right-wing authoritarianism 2.0, i.e. the expression and practice of elements of right-wing authoritarianism on social media.

Erich Fromm: Sadomasochism and Right-Wing Authoritarianism

According to Erich Fromm (1942/2001), masochism (hating and destroying oneself), sadism (hating and destroying others) and sadomasochism (a synthesis of masochism and sadism) are reactions to feelings and fears of aloneness, powerlessness and alienation. The masochistic reaction to such fear can involve attempting 'to become a part of a bigger and more powerful whole outside of oneself' (Fromm 1942/2001, 133). The sadistic reaction is to become a master, who dominates, uses and exploits others. A third, very different reaction that Fromm terms positive freedom, is to help others develop themselves, care for them and show solidarity (120–1, 141–2). The basic distinction is the one between power as domination (power over others) and power as potency and empowerment as reactions to fear, crisis and alienation (139). Fromm argues that authoritarian societies and fascism give a dominant role to authority 'in its social and political structure' (141). 'By the term "authoritarian character", we imply that it represents the personality structure which is the human basis of Fascism' (141). Right-wing authoritarianism is a generalised reaction to fear, crisis and alienation that fetishises negative power.

Alienation's Complexity

The human psyche is the totality of one's conscious and unconscious experiences. One's identity is the outcome of one's own personal history that is intertwined with the history of interpersonal relations, groups and social systems that one is, was or has been part of. How one reacts to alienation is not really calculable in advance, but the outcome of the intersection of the many experiences one has, including personal relations, economic life, political life, cultural life, sexual life and emotional life, and how key events and experiences have shaped one's personality and worldview. Generalising the works of Marx, Georg Lukács and Axel Honneth on alienation, one can distinguish between economic, political and cultural alienation that takes place at the level of the subject, social relations and society (see Table 7.1).

Table 7.1   Forms of alienation in society's three realms

Forms of alienation	Subject (experiences, emotions, attitudes)	Intersubjective (social relations and communication)	Object (structures, products)
Economic alienation	Work dissatisfaction	Lack of control/alienation of labour-power: exploitation	Lack of control/alienation of the means of production and output: propertylessness
Political alienation	Political dissatisfaction	Lack of control/alienation of political power: disempowerment and exclusion	Lack of control/alienation of decisions: centralisation of power
Cultural alienation	Cultural discontent	Lack of control/alienation of influential communication: insignificance of voice, disrespect, malrecognition	Lack of control/alienation of public ideas, meanings and values: centralisation of information

Source: Fuchs (2016b, 167)

Alienation refers to the objective conditions in which humans lack control over their lives, but it can also mean being treated with disrespect and in an alienating manner by others in social relations that take place in specific realms and social systems within society. At the subjective level it can also mean that one feels alienated, discontent and dissatisfied. One of these three dimensions does not causally lead to or invoke the others. For example, one can work in a company that makes large profits and has a high rate of exploitation, which constitutes objective alienation, but it may be the case that in the same company managers treat employees with respect, unions are integrated into decisions and the wages are relatively good and well above the industry and social average. As a consequence, workers may not feel alienated despite there being objective alienation. Conditions, relations and feelings of alienation form a complex whole that shapes social systems and society. Those who experience alienation can either accept this situation or try to overcome it. In such situations strategies of empowerment or domination – power as potency and social freedom or power as social violence – are two options. If others share the same feelings, then the formation of new social groups may be the response. In this situation, existing social groups that offer a social identity can play an important role. The difference is whether they have a vision of changing the social system through the liberation of oneself and others or through the domination of others.

Capitalism, Class, Alienation

Capitalism is inherently built on structures of economic alienation (class society), political alienation (power inequality between the rulers and the ruled) and cultural alienation (asymmetric education, skills, reputation and status). It is therefore not just a source of potential agency that strives towards a fair and just society, but also always a potential source of fascism, especially in situations of deep crisis.

Fromm (1942/2001) argues that at the time of the rise of the Nazis the lower middle class, consisting largely of small shopkeepers, white-collar workers and artisans, would have had a higher level of 'the isolation of the individual and the suppression of individual expansiveness' so that 'the destructiveness of the lower middle class' was 'an important factor in the rise of Nazism' (158). He argues that the lower middle class felt threatened by the improvement of the living conditions of manual workers because they could no longer look down on them (185).

But we have seen in this book that a significant proportion of blue-collar workers also supported the Nazis (and indeed were members of the Nazi Party). Fromm cannot explain this phenomenon. Post-First World War Germany was a society with many sources of anxiety: German capital feared socialism, especially in the course of revolutionary uprising such as in 1918/19. Workers faced a general fear of economic precarity. The middle class faced the fear of social decline to the status of the proletariat. The unemployed lived in constant social fear. Some considered the Versailles Treaty and the imposed reparations as a political anxiety. The defeat of the Left in the 1918/19 uprisings that culminated in the assassination of Rosa Luxemburg and Karl Liebknecht constituted disappointments for progressive forces. Right-wing coup attempts, such as the Kapp Putsch in 1920 or the Nazis Munich Putsch in 1923, constituted another political anxiety. When the Great Recession hit Germany, economic downturn, unemployment, precarity, hyperinflation, etc. affected the lives of many. The Nazis managed to speak successfully to and be heard and followed by parts of those who had such anxieties and feelings of alienation. 'The dismissed employee, the jilted lover, the disgruntled soldier deprived of a promotion, the student who fails an examination, the small grocer driven out of business by a chain competitor – any of these may be inclined to blame mysterious persecutors motivated by obscure grudges' (Löwenthal 2016, 27).

The Importance of Neumann's Approach Today: 'Anxiety and Politics'

Based on Freud, Neumann (1957/2017) in his essay 'Anxiety and Politics' argues that fear can take on the role of warning, protection or destruction. When in a society of societal anxiety, a larger amount of individuals identify with a caesaristic leader and project their anger and aggressions on an imagined enemy who has been constructed by a conspiracy theory, then the danger of dictatorship or even fascist dictatorship becomes real.

Destructive collective anxiety can emerge when one or several of the following factors are present (Neumann 1957/2017, 624–8):

(a) The alienation of labour;
(b) Destructive competition;
(c) Social alienation: a group fears or is threatened by the decline of 'its prestige, income, or even its existence' and 'does not understand the historical process or is prevented from understanding it' (626);
(d) Political alienation with respect to the political system;

(e) The institutionalisation of anxiety (for example, in the form of a totalitarian movement, propaganda or terror); and
(f) Destructive psychological alienation and persecutory anxiety.

Factors (a) and (b) are aspects of economic alienation with respect to wealth and resources, factor (d) means political alienation with respect to political influence, and factor (c) cultural alienation with respect to status and reputation. Dimensions (e) and (f) point to the presence of right-wing movements that want to mobilise anxieties in politically destructive ways.

Neumann gives the following summary of these six dimensions:

> Neurotic, persecutory anxiety can lead to ego-surrender in the mass through affective identification with a leader. This caesaristic identification is always regressive, historically and psychologically. An important clue for the regressive character is the notion of false concreteness, the conspiracy theory of history. [...] The intensification of anxiety into persecutory anxiety is successful when a group (class, religion, race) is threatened by loss of status, without understanding the process which leads to its degradation. Generally, this leads to political alienation, i.e., the conscious rejection of the rules of the game of a political system. The regressive mass movement, once it has come to power must, in order to maintain the leader-identification, institutionalize anxiety. The three methods are: terror, propaganda, and, for the followers of the leader, the crime committed in common. (Neumann 1957/2017, 628)

Neumann points out that situations of crisis in society that intensify anxieties are particularly dangerous when right-wing authoritarian or fascist movements gain ground and try to mobilise fear by nationalism and hatred. Neumann (1957/2017, 618) at the same time points out that an alternative to persecutory anxiety in a crisis situation is cooperative identification, in which 'many equals identify co-operatively with one another'. He here points towards the importance of socialist alternatives. If they are missing, then the risk of right-wing authoritarian movements succeeding grows.

In the Weimar Republic, the communists and social democrats did not unite against the Nazi threat, but opposed each other, which weakened socialist alternatives and strengthened the fascist threat. Fromm (1942/2001) characterises the Nazis and Hitler as sadomasochistic. Their ideology was based on 'craving for submission' and 'lust for power' (183), 'sadistic craving for power' (191), the 'projection of social inferiority to national inferiority' (186), sadistic hatred against constructed enemies (194), 'the wish to have power over helpless beings' (200) and the masochistic proclamation that 'the individual is nothing and does not count' (200). By submitting and sacrificing itself to the power of the leader and the national, the individual dies and is reborn as *Volk*. Nazism's sadistic side is 'the craving for power over men', its masochistic side is 'the longing for submission to an overwhelmingly strong outside power' (204).

'Anxiety and Politics' Today

Neumann's and Fromm's analyses are so topical today because many of Neumann's six factors are present in various parts of the world, and right-wing movements partly take on the sadomasochistic characteristics that Fromm analysed. Neoliberal capitalism has intensified the alienation of labour, destructive competition, large-scale fear of social decline, political apathy and a lack of trust in the political system, political parties, politicians and democracy, the institutionalisation of anxiety in the form of demagogic, nationalist, xenophobic far-right movements and the large-scale psychological desires not just for social change, but for destructive social change. Contemporary societies may thereby be at a tipping point, where quantity turns into a new quality. Neumann argues that persecutory anxiety can take on three methods: 'terror, propaganda, and, for the followers of the leader, the crime committed in common' (Neumann 1957/2017, 628). In many parts of the world, anxiety has taken on at least one of these elements, namely right-wing propaganda. In some, it has already taken on others too.

The Alternative: Socialism

The question arises regarding how best to fight a far-right demagoguery – one that propagates nationalist politics and constructs a contradiction between a national ethnic community and foreign forces as the cause of social problems, and thereby diverts attention from how social problems and discontent are grounded in capitalism, class, social inequalities and power inequalities. Nationalist propaganda is to a certain extent irrational, and operates on the psychological level of fears and hopes that can be resistant to rational arguments that operate with statistics and logical reasoning in order to deconstruct far-right ideology. The point is to bring about structural changes, i.e. to change the social foundations that enable authoritarianism, nationalism, xenophobia and support for far-right politics. It requires a strengthening of the welfare state and public services, decent housing, educational opportunities and health care services, increasing equality, a new deal that reinvigorates deindustrialised areas through economic activities that provide decent jobs so that unemployment and low wages can be overcome, etc. Fighting nationalism and far-right ideology requires socialist politics that challenge neoliberalism. The key challenge in questioning the politics of nationalism is to make visible the fact that society is divided by class and power inequalities, and that these asymmetries are at the heart of social problems.

To create socialist alternatives means to create structures in our social systems that enable humans to develop as real human beings who can realise their potentialities, that value and foster creativity, solidarity and critical thought, the 'spontaneous affirmation of others'[1] (Fromm 1942/2001, 225):

We must replace manipulation of men by active and intelligent co-operation, and expand the principle of government of the people, by the people, for the people, from the formal political to the economic sphere. [...] Democracy is a system that creates the economic, political and cultural conditions for the full development of the individual. Fascism is a system that, regardless under which name, makes the individual subordinate to extraneous purposes and weakens the development of genuine individuality. (Fromm 1942/2001, 235–6)

A factor that should not be underestimated is political communication. Nationalist ideology can only be successful if it is heard on a constant basis

---

1. Whether this process should be called love, as Fromm (1942/2001, 225) does, or rather solidarity or cooperation is a question of interest, but that we cannot discuss here in any detail because it requires theorising love, which must certainly be part of a theory of socialism (see Badiou 2012; Fromm 1956).

and not adequately challenged. Tabloid media often follow a strategy of focusing on superficial and one-dimensional news that simplifies reality and does not adequately engage with social problem's causes. New ways of communicating the complexity of society and politics are urgently needed.

The problem today is that neoliberal capitalism has undermined social rights so much that civil and political rights have become endangered by a negative dialectic that has advanced destructive political forces. The only feasible alternative is a democratic front that defends social, political and cultural rights against the threat of authoritarianism.

Neumann's article 'Anxiety and Politics' reminds us that in such a situation, the role of academics should be that they act as critical public intellectuals more than ever:

> Hence there remains for us as citizens of the university and of the state the dual offensive on anxiety and for liberty: that of education and that of politics.
>
> Politics, again, should be a dual thing for us: the penetration of the subject matter of our academic discipline with the problems of politics – naturally, not day-to-day politics – and the taking of positions on political questions. If we are serious about the humanization of politics; if we wish to prevent a demagogue from using anxiety and apathy, then we – as teachers and students – must not be silent. We must suppress our arrogance, inertia, and our revulsion from the alleged dirt of day-to-day politics. We must speak and write. [...] Only through our own responsible educational and political activity can the words of idealism become history. (Neumann 1957/2017, 629)

The Commodification of Almost Everything and Society's Commons

Society is an integrated realm of human activity oriented towards the economic production of resources (economy), the political production of collective decisions (politics) and the cultural production of shared meanings (culture) (Fuchs 2008b). Society also stands in an intimate relationship with nature. Technologies mediate the physical relationship between society and nature and the social relationship between humans in society. The latter are also called communication technologies. Given that neoliberal capitalism has brought about the commodification of almost everything (Harvey 2005), Toni Negri (2017, 50) speaks of the 'process of real subsumption of society under capital'.

What humans own, share and create in common has increasingly become private property: humans' outer nature, humans' inner nature (the body, their genetic heritage), technologies, common economic resources, public services and culture (knowledge, traditions, etc.). Parts of the natural commons, the technological commons and the social commons have been privatised. The social commons entail the economic commons, the political commons and the cultural commons. The strengthening of right-wing extremism is neoliberal capitalism's negative dialectic of the enlightenment: the commodification of almost everything, including the commons, turns against liberalism's political enlightenment ideals and advances anti-democratic forces.

The Radical Right's Politics

In respect to nature, technology and the social, radical right-wing parties, leaders and movements take reactionary positions:

- With respect to nature, radical right-wing forces fetishise national identity and interests, and family and conservative traditions against immigrants, transnational and global identity, people of colour, Jews, Muslims, etc. They naturalise society and often present immigration and multiculturalism as an environmental problem.
- With respect to technology and communications, radical right-wing forces on the one hand advance a conservative techno-pessimism that sees traditional values under threat on the Internet and argues in favour of limitation and law-and-order control of the Internet and other new technologies. On the other hand, they show a neoliberal techno-capitalist ideology that celebrates capitalist technologies and the corporate Internet.
- With respect to the social, radical right-wing forces combine with a neoliberal ideology that propagates survival of the fittest, commodification and a national 'socialist' rhetoric that reserves welfare for the autochthonous national population and frames international trade as a struggle between nations.

Social Democracy 2.0: An Internationalist Movement-Party for the Commons, Socialist Democracy and Democratic Socialism

As the commons experience a dialectic of subsumption and subversion, they become simultaneously commodified and socialised. When cooperation, language and common relations form 'the new basis on which exploitation operates' (Negri 2017, 38), then not only do new relations of exploitation emerge, but also new potentials for living and working alternatively. We can see such new demands for a different life beyond capitalism and domination in the environmental movement, new socialist movements, the free software/peer-to-peer/open access/ creative commons, feminist movements, etc. What they put on the political agenda are demands for the defence and strengthening of the natural, social and technological commons. The only way to fight the radical right is to advance a new deal that aims at the 'creation of new rights of social ownership of common goods' (Negri 2017, 31). The best anti-fascist strategy is the convergence of movements for the environmental commons, the social commons and the technological commons into an international movement and party for the commons (see Figure 7.1). Such a movement-party is built on the insight that the commons sustain our life, which means the life of all humans on the planet, which requires a humanist, socialist and internationalist approach for solving society's problems.

Michael Hardt and Sandro Mezzadra (2016) argue that Trump and other right-wing leaders 'promise a combination of neoliberalism and nationalism as the solution to economic and social malaise'. They argue that facing these developments requires 'wide coalitional ties among diverse movements', avoidance of a 'return to centralized party structures that dictate a unitary line of struggle', a transformation of the 'party-form itself [...] if left parties are to play a positive role in such coalitional politics', 'building connections beyond the national frame' and 'transnational coalition politics' because 'the dynamics of neoliberalism along with racist right-wing forces cannot be contested effectively within the bounds of the nation-state', as well as 'perspectives and practices that combine the most local concerns with broad connections and consciousness that extend well beyond the national frame'.

An internationalist movement for the commons would renew social democracy not in the understanding of Tony Blair's New Labour, but

Figure 7.1 The convergence of progressive forces into an international movement-party for the commons as a defence mechanism against the rise of fascism

Rosa Luxemburg's understanding of social democracy: twenty-first-century social democracy needs to reboot social democracy. Social democracy 2.0 is socialist democracy and democratic socialism that builds society's commons. Social democracy 2.0 – socialist democracy and democratic socialism – is the only feasible democratic front against the rise of fascism. This requires a political agenda that breaks with neo-liberalism.

In the UK, the Labour Party's 2017 election campaign and manifesto showed how democratic socialism can gain broad support today. The party increased its share of the vote by 9.6 per cent to 40.0 per cent and increased their number of parliamentary seats by 30. The *Labour Party Manifesto* called for increasing the taxation of corporations and high-income earners; clamping down on tax avoidance; nationalising the railways, utilities and postal service; investing in infrastructure, education, research and the National Health Service; strengthening the cooperative sector and workers' rights (increasing the minimum wage, abolishing zero-hour contracts, an excessive pay levy for companies with staff on very high pay, making employees the buyer of first refusal when a company is sold, etc.); abolishing university tuition fees; introducing free care for children aged two to four; creating four new public holidays, etc. Jeremy Corbyn and the Labour Party advanced a vision of a society 'that works for the many, not the few' (Labour Party 2017, 5). When Tony Blair came to power in 1997, his neoliberal 'Third Way' politics influenced social democracy around the world. Such a domino effect can happen again, shifting social democracies on to the path of socialist democracy and democratic socialism. A socialist vision opposed to neo-liberalism is the best strategy with which to oppose the strengthening of right-wing authoritarianism, authoritarian capitalism and fascism.

THE ACCELERATION OF THE PUBLIC SPHERE AND THE NEED FOR SLOW MEDIA

Society consists of dialectically interacting and mutually encroaching subsystems: the economy, the political system and culture (Fuchs 2016f). In modern society, these systems take on the character of systems of accumulation (Fuchs 2008b). Modern society is a capitalist society. The public sphere is a realm of public communication that mediates between the other subsystems. In its ideal-type model, the public sphere is a realm that allows society to become engaged in 'critical public debate' (Habermas 1991, 52). The public sphere is a mediated space of political interaction, where humans encounter each other as citizens, who discuss and form opinions.

Public communication is fundamental to the existence of humans and society. In modern society, public communication has taken on the form of the media system (Fuchs 2016f). The media system produces public information that citizens use as sources of information and opportunities for communication. In a complex society, social roles and systems are differentiated. In a class society, this differentiation takes on the form of a division of labour and power. As an effect of such divisions, various social groups (communities of interest, consumer groups, activist and political groups, economic interest groups, etc.) try to lobby the media system's organisations, i.e. they try to shape the form of information production and to influence the content of information.

In his book *The Structural Transformation of the Public Sphere* (1991), Habermas analyses how the dialectic of enlightenment shapes the realm of public communication: the freedom to communicate publicly

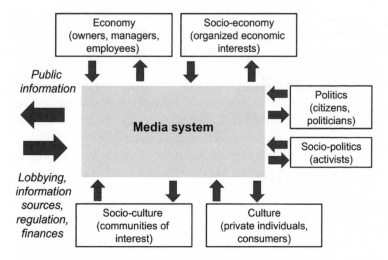

Figure 7.2 The media system (source: Fuchs [2016f]). Acknowledgement: this image has been reproduced with kind permission by the journal *tripleC: Communication, Capitalism & Critique* (www.triple-c.at)

without being controlled by the church or an emperor turned into a new unfreedom as capitalist control of the media advanced. The more the monopoly character of media capital increases, the more this dialectic expresses itself. With the increasing role of profit orientation, commodity logic, advertising and entertainment in the media, the public sphere according to Habermas becomes colonised and refeudalised (there are new dominant powers and media barons): 'Reporting facts as human-interest stories, mixing information with entertainment, arranging material episodically, and breaking down complex relationships into smaller fragments – all of this comes together to form a syndrome that works to depoliticize public communication' (Habermas 1996, 377).

The communicative network of a public made up of rationally debating private citizens has collapsed, the public opinion once emergent from it has partly decomposed into the informal opinions of private citizens without a public and partly become concentrated into formal opinions of publicistically effective institutions. Caught in the vortex of *publicity that is staged for show or manipulation* the public of nonorganized private people is laid claim to not by public communication but by the communication of publicly manifested opinions. (Habermas 1991, 248)

There is also a negative dialectic of the Internet and social media, a dialectic of online enlightenment: promising to free humans from centralised communication power controlled by broadcasters and newspapers, decentralised online communication envisioned a new age of democratic communication, where everyone is a producer and the means of democratic production are in the hands of the consumers. The reality is that online it is indeed easy to produce information. It is today much harder to erect monopolies of production. But there are new monopolies and power structures that constitute an attention and visibility economy, in which the freedom of online communication backfires and regresses into the freedom of some to be heard and seen and the unfreedom of many to communicate without responses and respondents (Fuchs 2017d). Further dimensions of the negative dialectic of online communication's enlightenment are, for example, online surveillance, the exploitation of digital labour or online hatred and online fascism (Fuchs 2017d, 2008b).

Capitalism's Acceleration

Hartmut Rosa (2013) has created a critical theory of acceleration that argues that modernity is acceleration. Modernity's sources of acceleration are for Rosa capital accumulation, functional differentiation and cultural survival. The development of technology, social change and life changes would be the three expressions of modern acceleration. Rosa's theory sees three relatively independent sources of modern acceleration. However, acceleration is inherently connected to the principle of accumulation that is the social foundation of capitalism. Acceleration is about accumulating more power in less time: more commodities are produced and consumed, more decisions are made and more experiences are organised and offered ever faster. Capitalist society's accumulation structures are driving acceleration (Fuchs 2015).

Figure 7.3 shows a model of capitalist acceleration: economic accumulation results in acceleration because it is based on the logic that 'time is money'. Political accumulation results in acceleration because it is based on the logic that 'time is strength and power'. Cultural accumulation results in acceleration because it is based on the logic that 'life/time' is short.

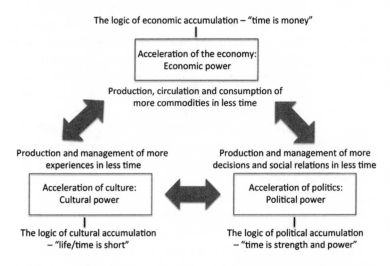

Figure 7.3 The logics of accumulation and acceleration (source: Fuchs [2015])

In neoliberal capitalism, the constant commodification and profit orientation of (almost) everything has increased. Media organisations are increasingly driven to accumulate ever more profits, to sell more advertisements, to attract larger audiences, etc. Entertainment-oriented formats such as commercial television include drama series, movies and reality TV. Such formats tend to sell advertising space and to accumulate audiences easier than public service content, which contains news and public affairs, features and documentaries, education, arts and music, children's programmes and plays (Williams 1974). As a result of commercialisation and commodification, public service media have come under increased pressure to turn into advertising-funded media, to adopt profit and accumulation principles, or to imitate private competitors' strategies that foreground entertainment, advertisement and the acceleration of experiences.

The acceleration of the media's logic is the search for higher ratings or larger profits. There are several negative effects of the media's acceleration on political communication that one can observe. The first tendency in political communication is that there is a *lack of time* for discussion.

Political Communication's Lack of Time for Debate

ITV's Brexit debate on 9 June 2016 featured three 'Remain' and three 'Leave' politicians (Angela Eagle/Amber Rudd/Nicola Sturgeon; Boris Johnson/Gisela Stuart/Andrea Leadsom). Each contributor was allowed to make a one-minute opening and closing statement. Julie Etchingham was the moderator. Audience members asked questions, to which each discussant answered for 40 seconds before a free-floating debate started.

The second 2016 presidential debate between Hillary Clinton and Donald Trump took place on 9 October. ABC's Martha Raddatz and CNN's Anderson Cooper moderated the discussion. The audience was made up of undecided voters. Audience members asked some of the questions. Other questions were submitted online in advanced by voters and chosen by the moderators, who also posed follow-up questions. Raddatz explained: 'Both candidates will have two minutes to answer each audience and online question. We hope to get to as many questions as we can. We've asked the audience here not to slow things down with any applause.'

In such debates, all aspects are planned and timed in detail. Answering time is short and strictly limited. Raddatz's explanation that the presidential debates focus on 'as many questions as we can' and that things should not be 'slowed down' shows that political communication in accelerated capitalism is high-speed debate that lacks time for developing an argument. When information flow and communication takes place at high speed, the result is accelerated standstill. In the case of television debates, the consequence of the logics of acceleration and accumulation are many short questions with many short and superficial sound bites as answers. Such formats invite populism that lives through stoking fears and prejudices and keeps things simple, entertaining and spectacular. High-speed debates lack time for developing arguments. Society and its problems are complex. Complexity cannot be properly analysed in 40 seconds, one minute or two minutes. High-speed debate formats invite and support the populist style of right-wing politicians such as Donald Trump, Nigel Farage or Jörg Haider.

The lack of time in political communication is manifold: there is (a) lack of time for discussion, (b) lack of attention time and (c) lack of time for preparation, interviewing and production.

Political Communication's Lack of Space for Debate: Reality TV as Unreality TV

The second tendency in political communication is that there is a *lack of space* for debate.

Steven Barnett (2011, 169) observes a tendency towards tabloidisation of the media in general and political communication in particular. 'Tabloidization is the progressive displacement of citizen-enhancing material with material which has *no other purpose* than to shock, provoke, entertain or retain viewers'. It involves 'sensationalism, distortion, misrepresentation and dramatization of the trivial'.

There is a tendency that media spaces are more spaces for entertainment, sensationalism, advertising and consumerism instead of spaces for political discussion and education. Barnett (2011) shows that between 1975 and 1999, the share of tabloid news in BBC news increased from 18.4 per cent to 28.9. In the ITN-produced early evening news, the share increased from 15.4 per cent to 33 per cent.

Reality TV started to take off in the late 1990s and early 2000s. Ever since, thousands of reality TV formats have been developed. Reality TV is an expression of the colonisation of television spaces and television time by the logic of the spectacle. *Survivor, Big Brother, The Apprentice, The Great British Bake Off, Next Top Model*, or *Dancing With the Stars* are among the most well-known reality TV shows. Format types include, for example, competing for prizes (e.g. *Survivor, Big Brother*), talent competitions (e.g. *America's Next Top Model, Project Runway, American Idol*), dating and love (e.g. *The Bachelor, Temptation Island*), family (e.g. *The Osbournes*), autobiographical shows (e.g. *The Anna Nicole Show*), ridiculous people (e.g. *The Simple Life, Obsessive Compulsive Cleaners*), life improvement (e.g. *Extreme Makeover*), business and careers (e.g. *The Apprentice*), or hidden camera and trickery (e.g. *The Secret Millionaire*) (see Yahr, Moore and Chow 2015). No format seems to be too spectacular, too dangerous or too ridiculous. Candidates will do (almost) anything to realise the idea that reality TV can make you famous. Such fame is, however, often very limited in time and scope. The idea of reality TV as an opportunity for fame that is democratic and open to everyone reflects the ideology of the American Dream that everyone can become rich and famous. Reality TV as the televised land of opportunities is an ideology. Reality TV fame is often short and is limited to the few. Reality

TV is an artificial reality that does not reflect everyday life. Reality TV is unreality TV. Guy Debord argues in this context that the society of the spectacle de-realises society: 'Understood in its totality, the spectacle is both the result and the goal of the dominant mode of production. It is not a mere decoration added to the real world. It is the very heart of this real society's unreality' (Debord 1970, §6).

Reality TV often reflects the logic of neoliberalism in everyday life. Consider the following elimination scene from *The Apprentice*:

Donald Trump: And what did you do, Tom? Did you bring money in?

Tom: No, I was organising everything.

Donald Trump: You didn't organise very well. You had a lousy looking store. You had no control over Denis. Not that anyone can control Denis because I am not sure he can be controlled. But you had no control over Denis. And you didn't bring any money in. Wait a minute! You couldn't control him. You brought in no money. And you had a lousy looking store. You were not much of a team leader.

Tom: When you say I am a bad leader, you have to understand ...

Donald Trump: Well, you are not a good leader I tell you right now. First of all, you could have been fired last week. You didn't get along with your team. This week you are worse. And you're the project manager. And you had a guy who didn't even show up.

Tom: That's a misunderstanding of what happened there. A lot ...

Donald Trump: Frankly, you wanna know the truth. I think Jesse is in. I think I should fire maybe both of 'em. Clint, if you were me, whom would you fire?

Clint: I'd fire both of them.

Donald Trump: Brian?

Brian: I think when Tom didn't show up this morning. That showed that he wasn't ready to ...

Donald Trump: Whom would you fire between the two of them?

Brian: Tom. Period.

Donald Trump: You'd fire Tom because he was a lousy project manager. And frankly, you were lousy last week, Tom. Tom, you are fired! Go! You were lousy last week, lousy this week. We have to do it. Go! (*The Apprentice*, Season 8, Episode 3)

Neoliberal subjectivity here means that the whole show focuses on rewarding individualism, egoism and entrepreneurialism, while discouraging solidarity. *The Apprentice* uses the logic of accumulation and possessive individualism. It is based on the principle of the 'survival of the fittest' and encourages cut-throat competition. There is a top-down elimination process of contestants executed by Donald Trump. The entire show, just like reality TV itself, is artificial reality and based on the ideology of the American Dream of individuals becoming rich and famous.

Insiders argue that reality TV is not spontaneous at all, but scripted and planned. Whether it is scripted or spontaneous, or a bit of both, Donald Trump is being portrayed as a tough leader who is in control and executes neoliberal logic. He also uses this image of the tough leader that he embodies on reality TV as a politician. Organising politics and society based on principles practiced in the artificial environment of reality TV can create a form of politics where strict hierarchy, command and control, the friend/enemy scheme and the fierce struggle against opponents dominate. The result can be an uncompromising politics of constant battle and war. Douglas Kellner (2016, 5) argues in this context: 'Trump is empowered and enabled to run for the presidency in part because media spectacle has become a major force in US politics, helping to determine elections, government, and, more broadly, the ethos and nature of our culture and political sphere, and Trump is a successful creator and manipulator of the spectacle.'

Political Communication's Short Attention Span: Social Media as Unsocial Media

A third tendency in political communication that has to do with the proliferation of the logics of accumulation and acceleration is that there are *short attention spans*. Given that society is complex, adequately understanding it takes time, and yet the attention time given to information tends to be very short.

The average Internet use per day has increased from 59.6 minutes per day in 2010 to 144.8 minutes in 2017. Average television-watching time has decreased during the same period from 195.6 minutes to 175.4 minutes (ZenithOptimedia 2015). According to a study by Ofcom (2016), in 2016 adults watched on average 18 minutes of TV news per day, those aged 16–24 just four minutes; 91 per cent in this age group said they used social media at least once weekly, whereas the share was just 68 per cent in the general population. The data indicate that in the future, online media will become, besides television, the main information and communication technology among all age groups. It is therefore important to think about political online communication's potential, and desirable and undesirable futures.

The highly accelerated online world of searching and clicking supports this tendency. How many users click beyond the first page of search results on Google? According to a study, 36.4 per cent of users only clicked on the first Google result and less than 3 per cent clicked on results beyond the first page (Optify 2011). Most users only click on the top results on the first page. The attention span given to search results is short, which results in the fact that online visibility is a key aspect of communication power.

On 21 June 2016, the BBC broadcast *The Great Debate* on the EU referendum. The hashtag #BBCDebate was used on Twitter for allowing users to comment. Two archives of tweets referring to two time periods during the debate are available online[2] (archive 1: 20.09.54–20.12.37 [163 seconds], archive 2: 21.11.27–21.12.44 [77 seconds]). In the first dataset, there were on average 17.5 tweets per second, in the second one 37.5 per second. This makes an average of 27.5 tweets per second. If one projects this amount of tweets to the full duration of the programme (120 minutes), then one can estimate that there must have been around 198,000 tweets posted over two hours. Such a high volume of information communicated at high velocity is impossible to follow. The result is that the acceleration of information results in a standstill: nobody can follow this amount of information, and communication is reduced or stopped altogether. The high speed of information flow results in the disablement of communication. Social media's logics of acceleration and accumulation turn it into unsocial media.

Analysis of three larger datasets (N_1 = 985,667, N_2 = 73,395, N_3 = 32,298) of political tweets focused on different themes (WikiLeaks, the 2011 Egyptian protests, Jeremy Corbyn) showed that on average there were 49.9 per cent retweets, 30.7 per cent info-tweets without comments

2. epriego.wordpress.com/2016/06/22/bbcdebate-on-twitter-a-first-look-into-an-archive-of-bbcdebate-tweets/, accessed 14 October 2017.

and 15.3 per cent of tweets that resulted in comments by others (Fuchs 2017d, tables 8.5 and 8.6). The level of direct communication on Twitter therefore seems to be fairly low. Twitter is a medium whose speed and brevity discourages communication and debate.

When using YouTube, 64 per cent of the users in 2016 watched music videos, whereas only 27 per cent watched news (Ofcom 2016). In the age group 16–24, 81 per cent watched music videos and 27 per cent news. This shows that the engagement with news and politics is on YouTube significantly lower than with entertainment. Also, attention spans with regard to news videos seems to be fairly low online: a study of online news videos found that 'most successful off-site and social videos tend to be short (under one minute), are designed to work with no sound (with subtitles), focus on soft news, and have a strong emotional element' (Kalogeropoulos, Newman and Cherubini 2016, 5). An analysis of Facebook news videos showed that the average length was 75 seconds, only 8 per cent were longer than 120 seconds, and 56 per cent were shorter than a minute (16). The study analysed a particular news event, namely the Paris terrorist attacks in November 2015. In extreme situations, there is a particularly high level of attention from audiences towards the news. The average length of event-related videos posted on Facebook, YouTube and the BBC website was three minutes. On Facebook, users on average just watched for 25 seconds (21). Recently, so-called long-form journalism has developed online. This category covers articles that have a typical length of between 1,000 and 20,000 words. Platforms that have experimented with it include Medium.com, Buzzfeed, and the *New York Times*' online site. An analysis conducted by the PewResearchCenter (2016) found that users on average engaged for 123 seconds with a long-form online article and 57 seconds with a short-form online article. The data indicate that even if there is longer content, the engagement time with it seems to be quite short.

Taken together, such data indicate that news and politics in the contemporary online landscape follow the logic of acceleration: online reports and news tend to be short. Users spend little time engaging with them. In a society where time is precious because capitalism compels us to do a lot in little available time, there is often not enough time for political information and communication. The logic of acceleration and short-termness can be found on both the side of the producers and of the consumers of online information.

Further Trends in Political Communication

Lifestyle politics has strongly influenced political communication. As a result, politics has become personalised politics – a show and circus, where you increasingly need to be an entertainer in order to win elections and supporters. Engagement with arguments is replaced by a focus on personal characteristics, lifestyles, scandals, looks, etc. Donald Trump is a me-centred politician, who uses politics just like reality TV and Twitter, for living out his personal philosophy that a 'big ego is a positive thing' (Trump and Zanker 2007, 280). Right-wing populists tend to make use of celebrity culture and the personalisation and commodification of politics: they 'oscillate between self-presentations as *Robin Hood* (i.e. saviour of "the man and woman in the street") and self-presentations as "rich, famous and/or attractive" (i.e. an "idol"), frequently leading to a "softer" image' (Wodak 2013, 28).

Another aspect of political communication that has come along with tabloidisation is the focus on one-dimensional, superficial messages that simplify, distort or manipulate the facts. Some speak of the emergence of post-truth politics, where facts and knowledge do not count, but rather emotions, ideology and popularity (e.g. the number of 'likes' or followers on social media) define what is seen as the truth. In contemporary politics and election campaigns, fake news stories play a significant role. Fake news stories tend to be more right-wing than progressive in character (Allcott and Gentzkow 2017; Silverman 2016). Fact checking can pose certain limits on fake news, but at the same time do not solve underlying societal problems. Fake news is not something new, but is as old as the tabloid media that try to attract attention through sensationalism and spectacle. A study estimates that in the third US presidential election debate, political bots posted 36.1 per cent of the pro-Trump tweets and 23.5 per cent of the pro-Clinton tweets (Kollanyi, Howard and Woolley 2016). The problem is that in semi-automated politics, it can be difficult to discern whether humans or machines create information, visibility and attention. Algorithms do not have morals, ethics, consciousness, identity or anticipatory thinking. Bots can be programmed to act in a scrupulous manner. Such bots will always act nastily when an opportunity arises, where the programme tells them to act in such a manner. In the world of bots and automated politics, it becomes difficult to discern what is communicated by humans and what by machines. Algorithms can manipulate the public perception of politics. Post-truth politics on social media does not democratise politics away from experts towards citizens, but rather enforces the attention power possessed by a minority.

Online publics tend to be fragmented, isolated small-publics. In addition, the online world tends to be dominated by the selected few, who are often celebrities, entertainers or companies (Fuchs 2017d, chapter 5). A study by Pablo Barberá (2015) analysed 15 million tweets mentioning Obama and Romney during the 2012 US presidential election: 85 per cent of the interactions were among users who held the same ideological position. The study confirmed the existence of social media echo chambers and filter bubbles on the contemporary Internet.

The overall effect of these tendencies is that political information and communication become anti-dialectical and one-dimensional. The world is not seen as a complex and contradictory whole, but is reduced to single aspects and linear cause–effect relations. As a result, 'ideas, aspirations, and objectives that, by their content, transcend the established universe of discourse and action are either repelled or reduced to terms of this universe' (Marcuse 1964, 12). Communication in the public sphere becomes manipulated, one-dimensional and fragmented. The colonised, accelerated, accumulative Internet poses the danger of the 'fragmentation of large but politically focused mass audience into a huge number of isolated issue publics' (Habermas 2006, 423).

Summary of the Main Tendencies in Political Communication

We can summarise some of the main tendencies of how commodification, accumulation and acceleration have shaped the public sphere:

- Lack of time: politics of short sound bites
- Lack of space: spectacles colonise public communication
- Unreal reality TV
- Unsocial social media
- Short online attention span
- Personalised politics instead of issue-based politics
- One-dimensional, superficial, tabloid and 'post-truth' politics
- Automated, algorithmic politics
- Fragmented publics

The colonised public sphere and its commercialised, entertainment-oriented media form the communicative context of a broader societal environment, in which phenomena such as Donald Trump flourish. There are many causes of right-wing authoritarianism, and a fragmented, colonised, commercialised, commodified, accelerated public sphere is just one of the influencing factors.

The question arises as to whether there can be alternatives to accelerated, colonised, feudalised, spectacularised, idiotised, capitalist media.

Slow Media: *Club 2* and *After Dark*

Dominant media are high-speed spectacles focused on superficiality and lack of time. They erode the public sphere and political debate. They leave no time and space for exploring the complexity of society or engaging in debate and political controversy. We require the combination of the decommodification and the deceleration of the media. We require slow media.

Slow media and slow political communication is not new. *Club 2* in Austria and *After Dark* in Britain were prototypical examples of slow media. The journalists Kuno Knöbl and Franz Kreuzer conceptualised the format of *Club 2* for the Austrian Broadcasting Corporation (ORF). It was a debate programme that was usually broadcast on Tuesday and Thursday evenings. The first episode was broadcast on 5 October 1976, on ORF's second channel. The final episode was broadcast on 28 February 1995. The programme was aired around 1,400 times (*Der Standard* 2001). *Club 2* returned between 2007 and 2012, but used a different concept that did not adhere to the original ground rules. In the United Kingdom, the media production company Open Media created a similar format called *After Dark* that was based on *Club 2*. *After Dark* was broadcast once a week between 1987 and 1991, and thereafter occasionally until 1997, on Channel 4. In 2003, *After Dark* made a short comeback on the BBC.

Sebastian Cody, who founded and produced *After Dark*, describes the *Club 2/After Dark* concept in the following way:

> You might remember the red sofas, leather Chesterfields recovered in quieter fabric. You might remember that the talking didn't end at any specific time, unique in an era when all television channels closed

down at night. You might remember Oliver Reed getting drunk, although he was hardly the only disruptive guest. [...] This seemingly innocent idea, which we imported to the UK under the name *After Dark*, depended on strict adherence to a short list of unshakeable principles. Namely, the number of participants in these intimate debates (always conducted in agreeable surroundings and without an audience) was never less than four, never more than eight (like, as it happens, group therapy); the discussion should be hosted by a non-expert, whose job rotates, thus eliminating the cult of personality otherwise attaching to presenters; the participants should be a diverse assortment, all directly involved in the subject under discussion that week; and, most importantly, the programme was to be transmitted live and be open-ended. The conversation finishes when the guests decide, not when TV people make them stop. [...] *After Dark* broke all these rules [of existing power structures] from the beginning, built as it was by the Viennese to reflect the polygon of views that is real life, rather than the binary fallacy of yes/no, pro/contra stylised debates. [...] *After Dark's* ground rules – absolutely live broadcasting (no editing or delay) and open-ended intimate discussion – meant that what the guests said was uncensorable. (Cody 2008)

Whatever one's feelings about individual guests or programmes, *After Dark* offered a precious space in the schedule, uniquely intimate, unpredictable and spontaneous. Perhaps this is why the *Listener* magazine, before it too disappeared, described *After Dark* as a 'necessary safety valve in a climate of increased pressure on the media'. (Cody 2003)
The concept of *Club 2/After Dark* seems rather unusual for us today because we are so used to short formats, high speed and lack of time in the media and our everyday lives. Open-ended, uncensored, controversial, engaging live debate differs from accelerated media in terms of space and time: *Club 2* and *After Dark* provided a public space for guests to meet and discuss, where they had unlimited time available for public communication about topics that were important for society. Space and time are two important dimensions of the public sphere's political economy. But a social space with ample time does not guarantee an engaging, dialectical discussion that transcends one-dimensionality and gives focus to arguments and the exploration of commonalities and dif-

ferences. The public sphere's space and time needs to be organised and managed in a smart way so that the right kind of people are present, the atmosphere is suitable, the moderator asks the right kind of questions and makes sure that the guests all listen and speak, the debate can go on in an uninterrupted manner, etc. Unlimited time, dialectically controversial and engaging space, and smart organisation are three important characteristics of a public sphere. They are preconditions for slow media, non-commercial media, decolonised media and public interest media.

Slow Media 2.0

We need slow media. Offline and online. Slow media. And slow media 2.0. Is a new version of *Club 2* possible today? What would Club 2.0 look like? Speaking of a second version may on the one hand mean that the *Club 2* concept could be revived in order to help strengthen the public sphere in times of authoritarian capitalism. On the other hand, one has to take into account the fact that society does not stand still, develops dynamically and has created new realities such as the Internet that have become key aspects of public communication. Club 2.0 therefore also means a somewhat updated concept of *Club 2* that sticks to its ground rules, but also extends the concept. If Club 2.0 can turn from a possibility into a reality is not simply a technical question, it is a question of political economy. It is a political question because it requires the decision to break with the logic of commercial, entertainment-oriented TV that is dominated by reality TV and comparable formats. Club 2.0 requires a political choice in favour of public service media and public interest media. Club 2.0 is also an economic question because realising it requires breaking with the principles that shape the media today, such as high speed, superficiality, brevity, the algorithmisation and automation of human communication, post-truth, the spectacle, etc. Club 2.0 is a question of resources and changing the media system's power relations.

Figure 7.4 visualises a possible concept of Club 2.0. This model is a basic idea that can certainly be varied in many ways and so is just one of many possible versions. They key aspects are the following:

- *Club 2/After Dark's* ground rules: Club 2.0 uses and extends the traditional principles of *Club 2/After Dark*. The live television part requires all of the traditional principles of *Club 2/After Dark*. These

CLUB 2.0

Audience, users

No use of existing online platforms (Twitter, Facebook, Internet-based discussion and video platform C2-Tube
1) Viewers (online, TV)
2) Discussion inputs
Video platform C2-Tube
Registered users (real/full names; registration requires e.g. licence fee number or utility bill)

Programme transmission (TV, online)

Studio
- Open-ended discussion
- Live broadcast
- Uncensored
- Controversial topics
- 4-8 participants
- Diversity of guests (incl. non-experts)
- One rotating host
- Leather couches & coffee table
- Floor lamps & dark studio
- No studio audience
- TV broadcast
- Online broadcast on videoplatform C2-Tube

User videos as discussion inputs at 2 points of time; Selection (can be varied):
- Club 2.0 team
- Random
- One registered user is randomly chosen to make the selection
- Invited users/ audience members

Number of active/registered users can be limited
1 discussion input video per registered user can be uploaded throughout the whole debate:
- at least 3 minutes long
- maximum of 5 minutes
- opinion & discussion question
- Uploaded as online video to C2-Tube
3) Audience/User discussion:
Two selected videos are open for discussion:
- Discussion on the C2-Tube platform
- Video- and text-based comments:
limited to x times per registered user
Video comments: exactly 5 minutes long [shorter not possible]
Text-based comments: at least 500 words, no upper limit [e.g. 10,000 words => will not be read]

Figure 7.4   Concept of Club 2.0

ground rules are key for the format's success. Club 2.0's broadcasts need to be open-ended, live and uncensored.

- Cross-medium: Club 2.0 is a cross-medium format that brings together live television and the Internet.

- Online video: Club 2.0 live broadcasts are available online via a video platform.

- Autonomous social media, no traditional social media: existing commercial social media platforms (YouTube, Twitter, Facebook, etc.) are not suited because they are not based on the principles of slow media and public interest. Broadcasting Club 2.0 over YouTube would, for example, result in frequent advertising breaks that would disrupt and disable discussion.

- Autonomous video platform C2Tube: Club 2.0 requires its own video platform that we can provisionally call C2Tube. C2Tube poses the possibility for viewers to watch the debate online via a diversity of technical devices.

- Interactivity: C2Tube also allows interactive features.

- User-generated discussion inputs: there is the possibility for discussion inputs generated by users. Such a feature requires that users are non-anonymous and register on the platform. Anonymity encourages Godwin's law that says that 'as an anonymous online discussion grows longer, the probability of a comparison involving Hitler approaches 1'. Setting an upper limit of registrations or activating only a certain number of users during a specific debate allows limiting the number of registered and active users. The selection of active users can for example be made randomly. Or all users can be allowed to participate. User-generated discussion inputs should ideally use a video format. The number of user-generated discussion inputs that can be made should best be limited (ideally to just one per active user). User-generated discussion inputs can be uploaded to the C2 platform.

- Interfacing the studio debate with user-generated videos: at certain points during the live broadcast, a user-generated video input is chosen and broadcast and informs the studio debate. Users in such videos formulate their own views and can also provide a question for discussion. Ideally, during a two- to three-hour debate, about two user-generated videos could be broadcast. Inevitably a selection mechanism is needed for deciding which user-generated videos are broadcast. There are several principles, such as random selection, selection by the Club 2.0 production team, random choice of a registered user who is enabled to choose the video, special guests who make the selection, etc.

- User discussion: Club 2.0 also enables discussion between users. Discussion could take place simultaneously with the live broadcast and/or after it. The two selected user-generated C2 videos can be opened up for discussion on the C2 platform. Ideally, video- and text-based comments should be possible. There should be a minimum length for text-based comments and maybe a maximum length for video comments. In order to stick with the principle of slow media and to avoid the Twitter effect of accelerated standstill, the number of video and text comments a single user can post per debate should be limited.

- Forgetting data: videos are fairly large and storage-intensive. Therefore the question is what should happen to all those videos that were uploaded, but not broadcast and not opened for discussion? Given that they have no practical use, they could be deleted. This means that the users must be aware of the fact that uploading a video means loss of data. Contemporary social media store all data and metadata forever. Forgetting data can therefore be used as a counter-principle. The online debates that feature text and video comments could either be preserved or deleted after a certain period of time.

- Privacy-friendliness: contemporary social media use data and user surveillance for economic and political purposes, i.e. for making monetary profits by selling targeted advertisements and for implementing a political surveillance society that promises more security, but undermines privacy and installs a regime of categorical suspicion. Club 2.0's way of dealing with data should be privacy friendly, only store the minimum amount of data necessary for operating the platform, not sell user data, and in general use good practices of data protection and privacy protection. This principle is also called privacy-by-design, which means that privacy is designed into the platform and the format. This does not, however, mean that users, who debate publicly, are anonymous. Privacy rather relates to the way user data is stored and handled.
- Social production: contemporary social media are highly individualistic. The production of user-generated Club 2.0 input videos could in contrast take on the form of social production that transcends individualism and creates truly social media content by integrating Club 2.0 into educational institutions, in which individuals together learn by co-creating video content as inputs for discussions. For doing so, the topic of a specific Club 2.0 evening needs to be known in advance, which can be achieved by publishing a description. Groups of individuals can get together and prepare videos that they can upload to C2Tube on the evening of the broadcast once the uploading possibility is enabled.

Club 2.0 alone would not bring about a better world. In times of authoritarian, high-speed capitalism, complexity and critique are largely missing from the news and political information and communication. Club 2.0 could contribute to strengthening the public sphere. Public sphere communication is part of society's critical capacities. With the rise of authoritarian capitalism, we have witnessed intensifying attacks on critical capacities. Imagine Donald Trump sitting on the Club 2.0 leather couch together with some of his hardest critics. There is no Twitter that allows short sound bites from a distance thrown into the anonymous virtual space. There is only face-to-face live discussion without escape, where claims and counter-claims are explored, ideologies are questioned, opposite opinions are given time to meet, etc. Club 2.0 would bring back a bit of dialectics into a one-dimensional world, in which the public sphere is under attack by authoritarian capitalism.

AUTHORITARIAN CAPITALISM'S INFLUENCING FACTORS AND THE QUEST FOR SOCIALIST HUMANISM

Authoritarianism's Influencing Factors

There is an academic debate about whether cultural and/or socio-economic factors are more important in shaping voting behaviour for the far right. The first position argues that conservative cultural values and a cultural backlash, a generational gap in moral values between the older and the younger generations, form the causes of right-wing authoritarian's support among citizens. The socio-economic hypothesis says that right-wing authoritarianism's support has to do with economic inequality, class, de-classification and fears of social degradation. The losers of capitalist development take their revenge by voting for right-wing parties.

Roland Inglehart and Pippa Norris: Post-Materialism

Inglehart and Norris (2016) analysed data from the European Social Survey and the Chapel Hill Expert Survey that classified 268 political parties in 31 European countries on the left–right spectrum. They analysed who voted for populist parties. The basic explanation Inglehart and Norris give is that we live in a post-material age, in which younger people's new cultural values question the morals and traditions of their parents and grandparents. 'Populist support is greatest among the older generation, men, the less educated, ethnic majority populations, and the religious' (Inglehart and Norris 2016, 26). The 'combination of several standard demographic and social controls (age, sex, education, religiosity and ethnic minority status) with cultural values can provide the most useful explanation for European support for populist parties. Their greatest support is concentrated among the older generation, men, the religious, majority populations, and the less educated – sectors generally left behind by progressive tides of cultural value change' (Inglehart and Norris 2016, 28).

The cultural values tested included attitudes towards immigration, mistrust in global and national governance, authoritarian thought and right-wing self-placement. Testing empirically whether those who hold anti-immigration, nationalist, authoritarian and right-wing views support far-right parties is a tautological and cyclical approach: such ideological worldviews are definition criteria of far-right parties and politicians. Voters support parties with whom they agree more than with other parties. So inevitably the voters of right-wing parties will hold and share at least parts of the views of these parties. It is logical that the cultural values correlate highly with voting for right-wing parties because right-wing ideology is defined by these ideological values. The argument is therefore circular and tautological: cultural values are important predictors of right-wing party voting because right-wing parties are defined by these values. Inglehart and Norris don't present a model that takes economic inequality as a predictor for right-wing voting into account. One would have to look at which cultural values are present among which socio-economic groups, an aspect that was also left out. In addition, managers and professionals were not included as groups in the model.

Economy, politics and culture are different features of society, but also have joint qualities. They are humans' social products. Humans' social production is mediated through communication. Any social system is produced and reproduced. Right-wing authoritarian individuals, groups, institutions and systems are produced and reproduced by humans within economic, political and cultural contexts. Economy, politics and culture interact just like the individual, groups, social systems, institutions and society at large interact. One cannot divorce the dialectics of all these factors and reduce a complex phenomenon such as right-wing authoritarianism to culture. The culturalist hypothesis is contested by a number of studies.

Empirical Studies Beyond Post-Materialism

Lubbers, Gijsberts and Scheepers (2002) analysed voting behaviour in 16 Western European countries based on cross-national survey data from N = 49,801 individuals. An expert judgement survey classified the level of right-wing extremism that right-wing political parties in the 16 countries (EU15 countries and Norway) took on specific political issues such as immigration. The study found that factors influencing the electoral success of far-right parties included unemployment, economic malaise, fear of social downgrading, low education level, being young, non-religious and male, dissatisfaction with democracy and party characteristics (charismatic leadership, etc.). 'Manual workers, the self-employed, routine non-manual workers and the unemployed are more likely to vote for extreme right-wing parties (compared to the service class), but this also holds true for housewives and retired people' (Lubbers, Gijsberts and Scheepers 2002, 364).

Socio-Economic, Political and Cultural Factors

Oesch (2008) analysed data from the European Social Survey 2002/2003 for Austria, Belgium, France, Norway and Switzerland. He found that:

> proletarianization of the right-wing populist parties' electorate clearly seems correct for the five countries on which this study focuses. Hence, production workers (for example, assemblers, mechanics, and bricklayers) are the class showing the highest level of support for the FPÖ in Austria, the VlB in Belgium, and FrP [Progress Party] in Norway. In France, another working-class category is even more strongly over-represented among the FN [Front National] electorate than production workers: service workers (for example, cooks, shop assistants, and nursing aides). In Switzerland, the SVP [Swiss People's Party] receives its largest support from small business owners, but production workers are also strongly overrepresented among RPP [right-wing populist parties] voters. Production workers' support for an RPP exceeds average support by a factor of 1.3 in Switzerland, 1.4 in France, 1.6 in Austria, 1.7 in Belgium, and 1.9 in Norway. Second, alongside the two little-privileged classes of production and service workers, a third category is over-represented among RPP followers, namely, small- business owners. As noted, this class provides the SVP in Switzerland with its strongest support, but it also offers above-average support for the respective RPP in Austria, Belgium, and (very slightly so) France. This somewhat unlikely alliance between the *petite*

bourgeoisie and the working class in right-wing populist support has received extensive attention in the literature. (Oesch 2008, 356)

The study showed that for blue-collar workers, economic fear of welfare competition and wage dumping is an important factor for their support of far-right parties. For the 'middle class', the largest factor was the fear that immigrants undermine the country's culture. Political dissatisfaction with democracy played a general role.

Werts, Scheepers and Lubbers (2012) analysed data for 18 countries taken from four waves of the European Social Survey conducted between 2002 and 2009:

> Lower-educated people, manual workers, the unemployed, non-religious people, people who hardly go to church, singles (divorced), young people, men, as well as people who feel deprived about their present socio-economic situation turned out to be more likely to vote for a radical right-wing party. Moreover, we found that self-employed people (with and without employees) and people working on farms are more likely than higher controllers to cast a radical right-wing vote. (Werts, Scheepers and Lubbers 2012, 193)

Political attitudes that influenced voting for far-right parties were perceived ethnic threat, political distrust and Euroscepticism.

Bornschier and Kriesi (2012) analysed data from 14 countries included in the European Social Survey 2008/2009:

> While income has no effect, three classes stand out in terms of their propensity to vote for the extreme right: both skilled and unskilled workers are overrepresented in this electorate, while social-cultural specialists are significantly under-represented. Contrary to what earlier analyses revealed, small business owners no longer form a core constituency of the extreme right, and neither do any of the other lower classes. (Bornschier and Kriesi 2012, 19)

Rooduijn (2016) analysed data from the European Social Survey for the year from 2002 until 2012. He found that 'the differences in education and class between the mainstream electorate and the radical right-wing populist electorate did not decrease over the years' (65).

Interpreting the Empirical Results: Tendencies and Factors Shaping Right-Wing Authoritarianism

Taken together, these studies provide indications of the following tendencies:

- Blue-collar workers are prone to voting for radical right-wing parties.
- The unemployed, routine service workers and small business-owners show a certain tendency to vote for such parties.
- Given that socio-economic groups, who feel the pressures of capitalist change most directly, are among the main constituency of radical right-wing parties, Inglehart and Norris' hypothesis that socio-economic factors hardly play a role in the rise of right-wing authoritarianism cannot be confirmed. There are doubts that the aversion to 'post-material' values and a generational conflict between younger and older people are the decisive factors. The causes of the far-right's success are very material. They have to do with economic, political and cultural power inequalities that stem from the inherent features of capitalist society, i.e. a society based on the logic of accumulation of economic, political and cultural capital, exploitation and domination.
- There is also a tendency that voters of radical right-wing parties are male and have a low level of education.
- Typically, voters of radical right-wing parties show a combination of economic fears (welfare competition, wage dumping and job loss because of immigration), political fears (dissatisfaction with the government, democracy, political institutions – e.g. the EU – and the political system) and cultural fears (loss of national identity because of immigration).
- These motivations play different roles for different groups. Economic fears are, for example, an important factor among blue-collar and routine workers.

Anxiety and Politics

Neumann (1957/2017, 288–93) argues that the alienation of labour, destructive competition, social alienation, political alienation, the institutionalisation of anxiety and persecutory anxiety play an important role in the rise of right-wing authoritarian movements in society. Empirical studies confirm the relevance of these factors today: socio-economic factors (automation, unemployment, deindustrialisation, globalisation, transnational capital, the rise of a tertiary service and information economy) play a particular role among blue-collar workers, who are declining in numbers. Small capital feels threatened by big transnational capital. Political alienation takes on the form of dissatisfaction with the government, democracy and political institutions. Social alienation is expressed as cultural nationalism and fear of multiculturalism and heterogeneity.

These economic, political and cultural anxieties and fears are ideologically intensified when radical right-wing parties are present that have the resources and skills to institutionalise anxiety, stoke fear and construct scapegoats. The far right can especially thrive when the political left is weak, split or occupied with internal struggles.

Socialist Humanism: The Recipe Against and the Antidote to Fascism

Right-wing authoritarianism and authoritarian capitalism have political-economic, ideological and psychological dimensions. The latter level has to do with the dialectics of love/hate, hope/fear, life/death, destruction/construction. To what extent an individual's personality and behaviour is shaped by progressive love, reactionary love, progressive hate or reactionary hate depends on the sum-total of his/her life-experiences. In this context, the broader political, economic and cultural/ideological contexts in which the individual acts play a key role. The presence of authoritarian forces, starting with the parents, but also taking on the form of teachers, bosses and politicians, can play a role in shaping either of these dispositions. The broader task for society in order to avoid authoritarianism is a question of the choice between humanism and inhumanity and between socialism and capitalism. It is a question of socialist humanism. For the development of non-authoritarian personalities, all 'that is really essential is that children be genuinely loved and treated as individual humans' (Adorno et al. 1950, 975). Adorno's insight can be generalised: for society to flourish and avoid authoritarianism and fascism, it is essential that humans treat each other in a social and humane manner. Socialist humanism is the recipe and weapon against and the antidote to fascism.

References

ABC News. 2016. Ivanka Trump Describes 'Chaos' of Her Life, Initiative to Support Women. *ABC News Online*, 21 September 2016.

Adorno, Theodor W. 1991. *The Culture Industry*. Abingdon: Routledge.

Adorno, Theodor W. 1981. *Prisms*. Cambridge, MA: MIT Press.

Adorno, Theodor W. 1975. The Psychological Technique of Martin Luther Thomas' Radio Addresses. In *Soziologische Schriften II.1*, 11–141. Frankfurt am Main: Suhrkamp.

Adorno, Theodor W. 1973. *Studien zum autoritären Charakter*. Frankfurt am Main: Suhrkamp.

Adorno, Theodor W. 1972. *Soziologische Schriften I*. Frankfurt am Main: Suhrkamp.

Adorno, Theodor W. 1971. *Erziehung zur Mündigkeit*. Frankfurt am Main: Suhrkamp.

Adorno, Theodor W. 1962. Aberglaube aus zweiter Hand. In *Soziologische Schriften I*, 146–76. Frankfurt am Main: Suhrkamp.

Adorno, Theodor W. 1956. The Stars Down to Earth. In *Soziologische Schriften II.2*, 7–120. Frankfurt am Main: Suhrkamp.

Adorno, Theodor W. 1955. Schuld und Abwehr: Eine qualitative Analyse zum *Gruppenexperiment*. In *Soziologische Schriften II.2*, 121–324. Frankfurt am Main: Suhrkamp.

Adorno, Theodor W. 1954. Ideology. In *Aspects of Sociology*, ed. Frankfurt Institute for Social Research, 182–205. Boston: Beacon Press.

Adorno, Theodor W. 1951a. Freudian Theory and the Pattern of Fascist Propaganda. In *The Culture Industry*, 132–57. Abingdon: Routledge.

Adorno, Theodor W. 1951b. *Minima Moralia*. Frankfurt am Main: Suhrkamp.

Adorno, Theodor W., Else Frenkel-Brunswik, Daniel J. Levinson and R. Nevitt Sanford. 1950. *The Authoritarian Personality*. New York: Harper & Brothers.

Allcott, Hunt and Matthew Gentzkow. 2017. Social Media and Fake News in the 2016 Election. https://web.stanford.edu/~gentzkow/research/fakenews.pdf.

Altemeyer, Bob. 2016. Donald Trump and Authoritarian Followers. *Daily Kos*, 5 August 2016.

Altemeyer, Bob. 1996. *The Authoritarian Specter*. Cambridge, MA: Harvard University Press.

Anders, Günther. 1956. *Die Antiquiertheit des Menschen. Band 1: Über die Seele im Zeitalter der zweiten industriellen Revolution*. Munich: C. H. Beck.

Althusser, Louis. 2005. *For Marx*. London: Verso.

American Immigration Council. 2015. The Criminalization of Immigration in the United States. www.americanimmigrationcouncil.org/sites/default/files/research/the_criminalization_of_immigration_in_the_united_states.pdf.

Amnesty International. 2017. *Amnesty International Report 2016/17: The State of the World's Human Rights*. London: Amnesty International.

Anderson, Benedict. 1991. *Imagined Communities. Reflections on the Origin and Spread of Nationalism*. London: Verso, 2nd edition.

Ashcroft, Michael. 2016. How the United Kingdom Voted on Thursday ... And Why. http://lordashcroftpolls.com/2016/06/how-the-united-kingdom-voted-and-why/.

Assange, Julian. 2017. Interview on ITV's Preston on Sunday. 29 January 2017. www.youtube.com/watch?v=MmRooKhmRSA.

Associated Press. 2016. Trump to Nominate Retired Gen. James Mattis to Lead Pentagon. *Associated Press Online*, 2 December 2016.

Badiou, Alain. 2012. *In Praise of Love*. London: Serpent's Tail.

Bailer-Galanda, Brigitte and Wolfgang Neugebauer. 1997. *Haider und die Freiheitlichen in Österreich*. Berlin: Elefanten Press.

Balibar, Étienne. 2007. *The Philosophy of Marx*. London: Verso.

Balibar, Étienne. 1994. *Masses, Classes, Ideas*. New York: Routledge.

Balibar, Étienne and Immanuel Wallerstein. 1991. *Race, Nation, Class*. London: Verso.

Barberá, Pablo. 2015. Birds of the Same Feather Tweet Together: Bayesian Ideal Point Estimation Using Twitter Data. *Political Analysis* 23 (1): 76–91.

Barnett, Steven. 2011. *The Rise and Fall of Television Journalism. Just Wires and Lights in a Box?* London: Bloomsbury.

Bartlett, Evan. 2016. People are Calling Out Ukip's New Anti-EU Poster for Resembling 'Outright Nazi Propaganda'. *The Independent Online*, 16 June 2016.

Bauer, Otto. 1938. Fascism. In *Austro-Marxism*, ed. Tom Bottomore and Patrick Goode, 167–86. Oxford: Clarendon Press.

Bauer, Otto. 1924/2012. The Nation. In *Mapping the Nation*, ed. Gopal Balakrishnan, 39–77. London: Verso.

Baxter, Anthony. 2011. *You've Been Trumped*. Documentary. Montrose: Montrose Pictures.

Bay Area Study Group. 1979. *On the Roots of Revisionism: A Political Analysis of the International Communist Movement and the CPUSA 1919–1945*. San Francisco, CA: Revolutionary Road Publications.

BBC. 2017a. North Korea 'Ready for Nuclear Attack' Amid Show of Force. *BBC Online*, 15 April 2017.

BBC. 2017b. North Korea 'Will Test Missiles Weekly', Senior Official Tells BBC. *BBC Online*, 17 April 2017.

Beckwith, Ryan Teague. 2016. Read Hillary Clinton and Donald Trump's Remarks at a Military Forum. *Time Magazine Online*, 8 September 2016. http://time.com/4483355/commander-chief-forum-clinton-trump-intrepid/.

Belvedere, Matthew J. and Michael Newberg. 2016. New York Times Subscription Growth Soars Tenfold, Adding 132,000, after Trump's Win. *CNBC Online*, 29 November 2016.

Benjamin, Walter. 1930. Theorien des deutschen Faschismus. In *Walter Benjamin Gesammelte Schriften III*, ed. Hella Tiedemann-Bartels, 238–50. Frankfurt am Main: Suhrkamp.

Billig, Michael. 1995. *Banal Nationalism*. London: Sage.

Boccara, Paul. 1982. *Studien über 'Das Kapital'*. Frankfurt am Main: VMB.

Boehlert, Eric. 2015. ABC *World News Tonight* Has Devoted Less than One Minute to Bernie Sanders' Campaign This Year. *MediaMatters*, 11 December 2015. http://mediamatters.org/blog/2015/12/11/abc-world-news-tonight-has-devoted-less-than-on/207428.

Booth, Robert et al. 2016. Breitbart: How 'Trump Pravda' Muddied the Waters and Surfed Wave. *Guardian Online*, 14 November 2016.

Borger, Julian and Alec Luhn. 2017. US-Relations with Russia May Be at All-Time Low, Says Donald Trump. *Guardian Online*, 12 April 2017.

Bornschier, Simon and Hanspeter Kriesi, ed. 2012. The Populist Right, the Working Class, and the Changing Face of Class Politics. In *Class Politics and the Radical Right*, ed. Jens Rydgren, 10–29. Abingdon: New York.

BPS (British Psychological Society). 2009. *Code of Ethics and Conduct*. Leicester: BPS.

Brecht, Bertolt. 2015. *Brecht on Theatre*, ed. Marc Silberman, Steve Giles and Tom Kuhn. London: Bloomsbury, 3rd edition.

Brustein, William. 2003. *Roots of Hate: Anti-Semitism in Europe before the Holocaust*. Cambridge: Cambridge University Press.

Brustein, William. 1996. Blue-Collar Nazism: The German Working Class and the Nazi Party. In *The Rise of National Socialism and the Working Classes in Weimar Germany*, ed. Conan Fischer, 137–61. Providence, RI: Berghahn.

Byers, Dylan. 2015. Hedge-Fund, Magnate Backing Cruz is Major Investor in Breitbart News Network. *Politico*, 13 April 2015.

Cadwalladr, Carole. 2017. Robert Mercer: The Big Data Billionaire Waging War on Mainstream Media. *Guardian Online*, 26 February 2017.

Carrell, Severin. 2009. Donald Trump Issues Abusive Statement Against Golf Course Opponent. *Guardian Online*, 24 November 2009.

Carrell, Severin. 2016. Donald Trump Faces Wall of Opposition as He Returns to Scotland. *Guardian Online*, 23 June 2016.

Carroll, Lauren. 2016. Hillary Clinton Says None of Her EMails Had Classification Headers. *PolitiFact Online*, 7 September 2016, www.politifact.com/truth-o-meter/statements/2016/sep/07/hillary-clinton/clinton-says-none-her-emails-were-labeled-top-secr/.

Carter, Bill. 2004. 'The Apprentice' Scores Ratings Near Top for the Season. *New York Times Online*, 17 April 2004.

Chomsky, Noam. 2016a. Interview. *Al Jazeera Online*, 22 January 2016. www.aljazeera.com/programmes/upfront/2016/01/noam-chomsky-war-isil-160122112145301.html.

Chomsky, Noam. 2016b. Trump in the White House: An Interview. *Truth Out*, 14 November 2016. www.truth-out.org/opinion/item/38360-trump-in-the-white-house-an-interview-with-noam-chomsky.

Clarke, Harold D., Matthew Goodwin and Paul Whiteley. 2016. *Why Britain Voted for Brexit: An Individual-Level Analysis of the 2016 Referendum Vote*.

https://blogs.kent.ac.uk/epop/files/2016/07/Clarke-Goodwin-and-Whiteley.pdf.

Clinton, Hillary and Donald Trump. 2016a. First Presidential Debate. 26 September 2016. www.youtube.com/watch?v=855Am6ovK7s.

Clinton, Hillary and Donald Trump. 2016b. Second Presidential Debate. 9 October 2016. www.youtube.com/watch?v=FRlI2SQoUeg.

Clinton, Hillary and Donald Trump. 2016c. Third Presidential Debate. 19 October 2016. www.youtube.com/watch?v=smkyorC5qwc.

Cody, Sebastian. 2008. *After Kelly*: After Dark, David Kelly and Lessons Learned. *Lobster* 55.

Cody, Sebastian. 2003. Light After Dark. *Guardian Online*, 28 January 2003.

Comey, James B. 2017. James Comey's Prepared Testimony. *CNN Online*, 7 June 2017.

Comey, James B. 2016. *Statement by FBI Director James B. Comey on the Investigation of Secretary Hillary Clinton's Use of a Personal E-Mail System*. 5 July 2016. www.fbi.gov/news/pressrel/press-releases/statement- by-fbi-director-james-b-comey-on-the-investigation-of-secretary-hillary-clinton2019s-use-of-a-personal-e-mail-system.

Cook, Lynn. 2015. What Will the U.S. Energy Industry Look Like Over the Next Five Years? *Wall Street Journal Online*, 15 November 2015.

Couldry, Nick and Jo Littler. 2011. Work, Power and Performance: Analysing the 'Reality' Game of *The Apprentice*. *Cultural Sociology* 5 (2): 263–79.

Courtois, Stéphane et al. 1999. *The Black Book of Communism*. Cambridge, MA: Harvard University Press.

Davenport, Coral and Eric Lipton. 2016. Trump Picks Scott Pruitt, Climate Change Dissenter, to Lead E.P.A. *New York Times Online*, 7 December 2016.

Davis, Angela. 2014. Interview. *Guardian Online*, 14 December 2014.

Debord, Guy. 1970. *The Society of the Spectacle*. London: Rebel Press.

DeNavas-Walt, Carmen and Bernadette D. Proctor. 2015. *Income and Poverty in the United States: 2014*. Washington, DC: US Census Bureau.

Der Standard. 2001. Der 'Club 2' ging vor 25 Jahren erstmals auf Sendung. *Der Standard Online*, 5 October 2001.

Dimsdale, Nicholas, Nicholas Horsewood and Arthur Van Riel. 2004. Unemployment and Real Wages in Weimar Germany. *Discussion Papers in Economic and Social History* 56. Oxford: University of Oxford.

Disis, Jill. 2017. CNN: Trump's Latest Tweet 'Encourages Violence Against Reporters'. *CNN Online*, 2 July 2017.

Dmitrov, Georgi. 1935. *The Fascist Offensive and the Tasks of the Communist International in the Struggle of the Working Class Against Fascism*. www.marxists.org/reference/archive/dimitrov/works/1935/08_02.htm.

Dockray, Heather. 2017. Trump Just Added 4 Million New Soldiers to His Twitter Bot Army, and We Didn't Even Notice. *Mashable Online*, 30 May 2017.

Dorf, Michael C. and Sidney Tarrow. 2017. Stings and Scams: 'Fake News', the First Amendment, and the New Activist Journalism. Cornell Law School Research Paper No. 17–2. Ithaca, NY: Cornell Law School.

References

Dorocki, Sławomir and Paweł Brzegowy. 2014. The Maquiladora Industry Impact. on the Social and Economic Situation in Mexico in the Era of Globalization. In *Environmental and Socio-Economic Transformations in Developing Areas as the Effect of Globalization*, ed. Mirosław Wójtowicz and Anna Winiarczyk-Raźniak, 93–110. Kraków: Wydawnictwo Naukowe.

Duckitt, John et al. 2010. A Tripartite Approach to Right-Wing Authoritarianism: The Authoritarianism-Conservatism-Traditionalism Model. *Political Psychology* 31 (5): 685–715.

Dunwoody, Philip T. and Friedrich Funke. 2016. The Aggression-Submission-Conventionalism Scale: Testing a New Three Factor Measure of Authoritarianism. *Journal of Social and Political Psychology* 4 (2): 571–600.

Eagleton, Terry. 1991. *Ideology: An Introduction*. London: Verso.

Edkins, Brett. 2016. Donald Trump's Election Delivers Massive Ratings For Cable News. *Forbes Online*, 1 December 2016.

Eichenwald, Kurt. 2016. How Donald Trump Ditched U.S. Steel Workers in Favor of China. *Newsweek Online*, 3 October 2016.

Eley, Geoff. 2016. *Is Trump A Fascist?* https://hate2pointo.com/2016/11/21/is-trump-a-fascist/.

Eley, Geoff. 2015. Fascism Then and Now. *Socialist Register* 52: 91–117.

Emery, C. Eugene Jr. 2016. What We Know About the Health of Donald Trump and Hillary Clinton. *PolitiFact*, 16 August 2016.

Fairclough, Norman. 2015. *Language and Power*. New York: Routledge, 3rd edition.

Fairclough, Norman. 2010. *Critical Discourse Analysis: The Critical Study of Language*. Harlow: Pearson Education.

Fairclough, Norman. 2009. A Dialectical-Relational Approach to Critical Discourse Analysis in Social Research. In *Methods of Critical Discourse Analysis*, ed. Ruth Wodak and Michael Meyer, 162–86. London: Sage.

Falter, Jürgen W., ed. 2016. *Junge Kämpfer, alte Opportunisten: Die Mitglieder der NSDAP 1919–1945*. Frankfurt: Campus.

Falter, Jürgen W. 2013. Die 'Märzgefallenen' von 1933: neue Forschungsergebnisse zum sozialen Wandel innerhalb der NSDAP-Mitgliedschaft während der Machtergreifungsphase. *Historical Social Research* (Supplement) 25: 280–302.

Falter, Jürgen W. 1996. How Likely Were Workers to Vote for the NSDAP? In *The Rise of National Socialism and the Working Classes in Weimar Germany*, ed. Conan Fischer, 9–45. Providence, RI: Berghahn.

Falter, Jürgen W. 1987. Warum die deutschen Arbeiter während des 'Dritten Reiches' zu Hitler standen. *Geschichte und Gesellschaft* 13 (2): 217–231.

Falter, Jürgen W. and Dirk Hänisch. 1986. Die Anfälligkeit von Arbeitern gegenüber der NSDAP bei den Reichstagswahlen 1928–1933. *Archiv für Sozialgeschichte* 26: 179–216.

Farley, Robert. 2016. Fake Clinton Medical Records. *FactCheck.org*, 16 August 2016.

Faulkner, Neil. 2017. *Creeping Fascism: Brexit, Trump, and the Rise of the Far Right*. Public Reading Rooms.

FBI. 2016. 2015 Crime in the United States, https://ucr.fbi.gov/crime-in-the-u.s/2015/crime-in-the-u.s.-2015/tables/table-1 (accessed on 15 February 2017).

Foster, John Bellamy. 2017. Neofascism in the White House. *Monthly Review* 68 (11), https://monthlyreview.org/2017/04/01/neofascism-in-the-white-house/.

Foster, John Bellamy. 2010. The Age of Monopoly-Finance Capital. *Monthly Review* 61 (9): 1–13.

Foster, John Bellamy. 2006. Monopoly-Finance Capital. *Monthly Review* 58 (7): 1–14.

Foster, John Bellamy and Robert W. McChesney. 2012. *The Endless Crisis: How Monopoly-Finance Capitalism Produces Stagnation and Upheaval from the USA to China.* New York: Monthly Review Press.

Fraenkel, Ernst. 1941. *The Dual State.* Clark, NJ: Lawbook Exchange.

Franko, Elizabeth. 2006. Democracy at Work? The Lessons of Donald Trump and *The Apprentice.* In *How Real is Reality TV? Essays on Representation and Truth,* ed. David S. Escoffery, 247–58. Jefferson, NC: McFarland & Company.

Friedersdorf, Conor. 2016. The Radical Anti-Conservatism of Stephen Bannon. *The Atlantic Online,* 25 August 2016.

Fromm, Erich. 1997. *To Have or to Be?* New York: Continuum.

Fromm, Erich. 1984. *The Working Class in Weimar Germany.* Leamington Spa: Berg.

Fromm, Erich. 1956. *The Art of Loving: An Inquiry Into the Nature of Love.* New York: Harper.

Fromm, Erich. 1942/2001. *The Fear of Freedom.* Abingdon: Routledge.

Fromm, Erich. 1936. Sozialpsychologischer Teil. In *Studien über Autorität und Familie,* 77–135. Lüneburg: zu Klampen.

Fromm, Erich. 1933. Rezension von Wilhelm Reich: Der Einbruch der Sexualmoral: Zur Geschichte der sexuellen Ökonomie. *Zeitschrift für Sozialforschung* 2 (1): 119–122.

Fuchs, Christian. 2017a. Marx's *Capital* in the Information Age. *Capital & Class* 41 (1): 51–67.

Fuchs, Christian. 2017b. From Digital Positivism and Administrative Big Data Analytics towards Critical Digital and Social Media Research! *European Journal of Communication* 32 (1): 37–49.

Fuchs, Christian. 2017c. Günther Anders' Undiscovered Critical Theory of Technology in the Age of Big Data Capitalism. *tripleC: Communication, Capitalism & Critique* 15 (2): 584–613.

Fuchs, Christian. 2017d. *Social Media: A Critical Introduction.* London: Sage, 2nd edition.

Fuchs, Christian. 2016a. Capitalism Today: The Austrian Presidential Election and the State of the Right and the Left in Europe. *LSE Euro Crisis in the Press-blog:* http://blogs.lse.ac.uk/eurocrisispress/2016/06/16/capitalism-today-the-austrian-presidential-election-and-the-state-of-the-right-and-the-left-in-europe/.

Fuchs, Christian. 2016b. *Critical Theory of Communication: New Readings of Lukács, Adorno, Marcuse, Honneth and Habermas in the Age of the Internet*. London: University of Westminster Press.

Fuchs, Christian. 2016c. Neoliberalism in Britain: From Thatcherism to Cameronism. *tripleC: Communication, Capitalism & Critique* 14 (1): 163–88.

Fuchs, Christian. 2016d. Racism, Nationalism and Right-Wing Extremism Online: The Austrian Presidential Election 2016 on Facebook. *Momentum Quarterly – Zeitschrift für sozialen Fortschritt (Journal for Societal Progress)* 5 (3): 172–96.

Fuchs, Christian. 2016e. Red Scare 2.0: User-Generated Ideology in the Age of Jeremy Corbyn and Social Media. *Journal of Language and Politics* 15 (4): 369–398.

Fuchs, Christian. 2016f. Social Media and the Public Sphere. *tripleC: Communication, Capitalism & Critique* 12 (1): 57–101.

Fuchs, Christian. 2015. *Culture and Economy in the Age of Social Media*. New York: Routledge.

Fuchs, Christian. 2014. *Digital Labour and Karl Marx*. New York: Routledge.

Fuchs, Christian. 2008a. Foundations and Two Models of Guaranteed Basic Income. In *Perspectives on Work: Perspectives of Social Ethics Volume 1*, ed. Otto Neumaier, Gottfried Schweiger and Clemens Sedmak, 235–48. Vienna: LIT.

Fuchs, Christian. 2008b. *Internet and Society: Social Theory in the Information Age*. New York: Routledge.

Gambino, Lauren and Alan Yuhas. 2016. Rex Tillerson Named as Donald Trump's Secretary of State. *Guardian Online*, 13 December 2016.

Ghitis, Frida. 2017. Why Trump Wants You to Hate the Media. *CNN Online*, 18 February 2017.

Glenza, Jessica. 2016. Donald Trump Retracts Call for Women Who Have Abortions to be 'Punished'. *Guardian Online*, 31 March 2016.

Golshan, Tara. 2016. Here's How We Know the Bonkers Conspiracy Theory About Hillary Clinton's Health is Catching On. *Vox*, 23 August 2016. www.vox.com/2016/8/18/12505078/hillary-clinton-health-stroke-conspiracy-fake.

Goodwin, Matthew and Oliver Heath. 2016. Brexit Vote Explained: Poverty, Low Skills and Lack of Opportunities. www.jrf.org.uk/report/brexit-vote-explained-poverty-low-skills-and-lack-opportunities.

Gramsci, Antonio. 1988. *The Antonio Gramsci Reader: Selected Writings 1916–1935*, ed. David Forgacs. London: Lawrence and Wishart.

Gramsci, Antonio. 1971. *Selections from the Prison Notebooks*. New York: International Publishers.

Graves, Lucia, Sarah Turbin and Carmen Delaney. 2016. Former Miss Universe Alicia Machado on Trump: 'I Know What He Can Do' – Video. *Guardian Online*, 27 September 2016.

Green, Joshua. 2017. *Devil's Bargain: Steve Bannon, Donald Trump, and the Storming of the Presidency*. New York: Penguin.

Griffin, Drew, David Fitzpatrick and Curt Devine. 2016. The Truth About Hillary Clinton's Wall Street Speeches. *CNN Online*, 20 April 2016. http://money.cnn.com/2016/04/20/news/economy/hillary-clinton-goldman-sachs/.

Griffin, Robert, John Halpin and Ruy Teixeira. 2017. Democrats Need to Be the Party of and for Working People – of All Races. *American Prospect Online*, 1 June 2017.

Griffin, Roger. 1993. *The Nature of Fascism*. Abingdon: Routledge.

Grinberg, Emanuella. 2016. Police Officer Deaths from Guns up 78%, from July Last Year. *CNN Online*, 28 July 2016.

Gross, Bertram. 1980. *Friendly Fascism*. Boston, MA: South End Press.

Guardian. 2016. Hungarian Prime Minister Says Migrants are 'Poison' and 'Not Needed'. *Guardian Online*, 27 July 2016.

Haberman, Maggie, Julie Hirschfeld Davis and Eric Lipton. 2017. Sons to Run Trump Business via Trust; Ethicists Still See Conflict. *New York Times Online*, 11 January 2017.

Habermas, Jürgen. 2006. Political Communication in Media Society: Does Democracy Still Enjoy an Epistemic Dimension? The Impact of Normative Theory on Empirical Research. *Communication Theory* 16 (4): 411–26.

Habermas, Jürgen. 1996. *Between Facts and Norms: Contributions to a Discourse Theory of Law and Democracy*. Cambridge, MA: MIT Press.

Habermas, Jürgen. 1991. *The Structural Transformation of the Public Sphere: An Inquiry into a Category of Bourgeois Society*. Cambridge, MA: MIT Press.

Habermas, Jürgen. 1989. *The New Conservatism*. Cambridge: Polity.

Hall, Stuart. 1993. Culture, Community, Nation. *Cultural Studies* 7 (3): 349–63.

Hall, Stuart. 1986/1996. The Problem of Ideology: Marxism Without Guarantees. In *Stuart Hall: Critical Dialogues in Cultural Studies*, ed. David Morley and Juan-Hsing Chen, 25–46. London: Routledge.

Hall, Stuart. 1982. The Rediscovery of 'Ideology': Return of the Repressed in Media Studies. In *Culture, Society and the Media*, ed. Michael Gurevitch, Tony Bennett, James Curran and Janet Woollacott, 56–90. London: Methuen.

Handros, Libby. 1991. *Trump: What's the Deal?* Documentary Film. New York: The Orchard.

Hardt, Michael and Sandro Mezzadra. 2016. The Power of the Movements Facing Trump. *Roar Magazine Online*, 16 November 2016.

Harvey, David. 2005. *A Brief History of Neoliberalism*. Oxford: Oxford University Press.

Harwell, Drew. 2017. Trump Outlines Plan to Shift Assets, Give Up Management of His Company. *Washington Post Online*, 11 January 2017.

Hiltzik, Michael. 2016. Does Andy Puzder Really Want to Replace his Carl's Jr. Workers with Robots? No, but ... *Los Angeles Times Online*, 30 March 2016.

Hirsch, Joachim, John Kannankulam and Jens Wissel. 2015. Die Staatstheorie des 'westlichen Marxismus'. Gramsci, Althusser, Poulantzas und die so genannte Staatsableitung. In *Der Staat der bürgerlichen Gesellschaft*, 93–119. Baden-Baden: Nomos, 2nd edition.

Hitler, Adolf. 1992. *Hitler: Reden, Schriften, Anordnungen. Februar 1925 bis Januar 1933. 12 Bände*. München: Saur.

Hitler, Adolf. 1941 [1925/6]. *Mein Kampf: Volume 1 and 2*. New York: Reynal & Hitchcock.

Hobsbawm, Eric. 1994. *The Age of Extremes: The Short Twentieth Century 1914–1991*. London: Abacus.

Hobsbawm, Eric. 1992. *Nations and Nationalism Since 1780: Programme, Myth, Reality*. Cambridge: Cambridge University Press, 2nd edition.

Hobsbawm, Eric and Terence Ranger, eds. 1983. *The Invention of Tradition*. Cambridge: Cambridge University Press.

Holloway, Kali. 2017. 14 Fake News Stories Created or Publicized by Donald Trump. *Alternet*, 12 January 2017. www.alternet.org/media/14-fake-news-stories-created-or-publicized-donald-trump.

Holmes, Oliver. 2016. Rodrigo Duterte Vows to Kill 3 Million Drug Addicts and Likens Himself to Hitler. *Guardian Online*, 1 October 2016.

Holzer, Willibald I. 1993. Rechtsextremismus – Konturen, Definitionsmerkmale und Erklärungsansätze. In *Handbuch des österreichischen Rechtsextremismus*, ed. Dokumentationsarchiv des österreichischen Widerstandes , 11–96. Wien: Deuticke, 2nd edition.

Horkheimer, Max. 1972. *Sozialphilosophische Studien*. Frankfurt am Main: Fischer.

Horkheimer, Max. 1941. The End of Reason. *Studies in Philosophy and Social Science* 9 (3): 366–88.

Horkheimer, Max. 1940. The Authoritarian State. In *The Essential Frankfurt School Reader*, ed. Andrew Arato and Eike Gebhardt, 95–117. New York: Continuum.

Horkheimer, Max. 1936a. Allgemeiner Teil. In *Studien über Autorität und Familie*, 3–76. Lüneburg: zu Klampen.

Horkheimer, Max. 1936b. Authority and the Family. In *Critical Theory: Selected Essays*, 47–128. New York: Continuum.

Horkheimer, Max and Theodor W. Adorno. 2002. *Dialectic of the Enlightenment*. Stanford, CA: Stanford University Press.

Huang, Jon et al. 2016. Election 2016: Exit Polls. *New York Times Online*, 8 November 2016. www.nytimes.com/interactive/2016/11/08/us/politics/election-exit-polls.html?_r=0.

Huffschmid, Jörg. 2010. *Kapitalismuskritik heute. Zeitdiagnosen: Vom staatsmonopolistischen zum finanzmarktgetriebenen Kapitalismus*. Hamburg: VSA.

Huffschmid, Jörg. 1990. Staatsmonopolistischer Kapitalismus. In *Europäische Enzyklopâdoe zu Philosophie und Wissenschaften, Band 2: F-K*, ed. Hans Jörg Sandkühler, 758–61. Hamburg: Meiner.

Human Rights Watch. 2017. *World Report 2017*. New York: Human Rights Watch.

ILO (International Labour Organization). 2000. Maternity Protection Convention, 2000 (No. 183). Convention Concerning the Revision of the Maternity Protection Convention (Revised), 1952 (Entry into force: 07 Feb 2002). www.ilo.org/dyn/normlex/en/f?p=NORMLEXPUB:12100:0::NO::P12100_ILO_CODE:C183.

IMSF (Institut für Marxistische Studien und Forschungen). 1981. *Der Staat im staatsmonopolistischen Kapitalismus der Bundesrepublik. Staatsdiskussion und Staatstheorie*. Frankfurt am Main: Institut für Marxistische Studien und Forschungen.

Inglehart, Roland and Pippa Norris. 2016. Trump, Brexit, and the Rise of Populism: Economic Have-Nots and Cultural Backlash. Harvard Kennedy School Faculty Research Working Paper Series RWP16–026. Cambridge, MA: Harvard University.

Jessop, Bob. 2016. *The State: Past, Present, Future.* Cambridge: Polity.

Jessop, Bob. 1990. *State Theory: Putting the State in its Place.* Cambridge: Polity.

Jopson, Murphy and Demetri Sevastopolu. 2016. New Trump Hire Pledges Tax and Regulation Shake-Up. *Financial Times Online*, 30 November 2016. www.ft.com/content/4e3eb306-b6f7-11e6-961e-a1acd97f622d.

Justia. 1991. *Diduck v. Kaszycki & Sons Contractors, Inc., 774 F. Supp. 802 (S.D.N.Y. 1991). U.S. District Court for the Southern District of New York - 774 F. Supp. 802 (S.D.N.Y. 1991), April 30, 1991.* http://law.justia.com/cases/federal/district-courts/FSupp/774/802/1425921/.

Kaczyński, Andrew. 2017. Trump in 2010: Wikileaks 'Disgraceful', There 'Should Be Like Death Penalty or Something'. *CNN Online*, 4 January 2017.

Kagan, Robert. 2016. This is how Fascism Comes to America. *Washington Post Online*, 18 May 2016.

Kalogeropoulos, Antonis, Nic Newman and Federica Cherubini. 2016. *The Future of Online News Video.* Oxford: Reuters Institute for the Study of Journalism.

Kautsky, Karl. 1932. *Communism and Socialism.* www.marxists.org/archive/kautsky/1932/commsoc/index.htm.

Kellner, Douglas. 2016. *American Nightmare: Donald Trump, Media Spectacles, and Authoritarian Populism.* Rotterdam: Sense Publishers.

Kershaw, Ian. 2008. *Hitler: A Biography.* New York: W.W. Norton & Company.

Kershaw, Ian. 2004. Hitler and the Uniqueness of Nazism. *Journal of Contemporary History* 39 (2): 239–54.

Kessler, Glenn. 2016. Donald Trump's Revisionist History of Mocking a Disabled Reporter. *Washington Post Online*, 2 August 2016.

Khalid, Saif. 2016. Kanhaiya Kumar on Sedition and 'Freedom' in India. *Al Jazeera Online*, 7 March 2016.

Khosravinik, Majid. 2013. Critical Discourse Analysis, Power, and New Media Discourse. *In Why Discourse Matters: Negotiating Identity in the Mediatized World*, ed. Yusuf Kalyango Jr and Monika Weronika Kopytowska, 287–305. New York: Peter Lang.

Kim, Jong-un. 2017. *2017 New Year's Address.* www.ncnk.org/resources/news-items/kim-jong-uns-speeches-and-public-statements-1/kim-jong-uns-2017-new-years-address.

Kitchen, Martin. 1976. *Fascism.* Basingstoke: Macmillan.

Klein, Naomi. 2017. *No is Not Enough: Defeating the New Shock Politics.* London: Allen Lane.

Kollanyi, Bence, Philip N. Howard and Samuel C. Woolley. 2016. Bots and Automation over Twitter during the Third U.S. Presidential Debate. http://politicalbots.org/wp-content/uploads/2016/10/Data-Memo-Third-Presidential-Debate.pdf.

Kranish, Michael and Marc Fisher. 2016. *Trump Revealed: An American Journey of Ambition, Ego, Money and Power.* London: Simon & Schuster.

Kühnl, Reinhard. 1998. *Der Faschismus: Ursachen und Herrschaftsstruktur. Eine Einführung.* Heilbronn: Distel.

Kühnl, Reinhard. 1990. *Faschismustheorien: Ein Leitfaden.* Heilbronn: Distel.

Kurlantzick, Joshua. 2016. *State Capitalism: How the Return of Statism is Transforming the World.* Oxford: Oxford University Press.

Labour Party. 2017. *For the Many, Not the Few: The Labour Party Manifesto 2017.* London: Labour Party.

Landauer, Karl. 1934. Rezension von Wilhelm Reich: Masenpsychologie des Faschismus and Charakteranalyse. *Zeitschrift für Sozialforschung* 3 (1): 106–7.

Laskos, Christos and Euclid Tsakalotos. 2013. *Crucible of Resistance: Greece, the Eurozone and the World Economic Crisis.* London: Pluto.

Lazare, Sarah. 2016. Trump's Disastrous Education Pick: A Billionaire Heir of Right-Wing Dynasty and Champion of Privatization Efforts. *Alternet,* 23 November 2016.

Lenin, Vladimir I. 1917. The State and Revolution. In *Lenin Collected Works, Volume 25,* 385–497. Moscow: Progress.

Levine, Daniel S. 2016. Wilbur Ross: 5 Fast Facts You Need to Know. http://heavy.com/news/2016/11/wilbur-ross-jr-donald-trump-cabinet-treasury-net-worth-bio-who-is-wl-secretary-wife-commerce/.

Li, Xiaokun. 2017. Korean Peninsula Restraint Urged. *China Daily Online,* 15 April 2017.

Löwenthal, Leo. 2016. *False Prophets: Studies on Authoritarianism.* New Brunswick, NJ: Transaction.

Lubbers, Eric. 2016. There is No Such Thing as the Denver Guardian, Despite that Facebook Post You Saw. *Denver Post Online,* 5 November 2016.

Lubbers, Marcel, Mérove Gijsberts and Peer Scheepers. 2002. Extreme Right-Wing Voting in Western Europe. *European Journal of Political Research* 41 (3): 345–78.

Lukács, Georg. 1986. *Werke. Band 14: Zur Ontologie des gesellschaftlichen Seins. 2. Halbband.* Darmstadt: Luchterhand.

Luxemburg, Rosa. 2013. *The Letters of Rosa Luxemburg,* ed. Georg Adler, Peter Hudis and Annelies Laschitza. London: Verso.

Luxemburg, Rosa. 1976. *The National Question: Selected Writings.* New York: Monthly Review Press.

Luxemburg, Rosa. 1970. *Rosa Luxemburg Speaks.* New York: Pathfinder.

Marcos, Subcomandante. 2002. *Our Word Is Our Weapon: Selected Writings.* New York: Seven Stories Press.

Marcuse, Herbert. 1998. *Technology, War and Fascism: Collected Papers of Herbert Marcuse, Volume One.* London: Routledge.

Marcuse, Herbert. 1964. *One-Dimensional Man: Studies in the Ideology of Advanced Industrial Society.* London: Routledge.

Marcuse, Herbert. 1955. *Eros and Civilization: An Inquiry into Freud.* Boston, MA: Beacon Press.

Marcuse, Herbert. 1936. Ideengeschichtlicher Teil. In *Studien über Autorität und Familie,* 136–228. Lüneburg: zu Klampen.

Marcuse, Herbert. 1934. The Struggle Against Liberalism in the Totalitarian View of the State. In *Negations: Essays in Critical Theory*, 3–42. London: Free Association.

Martin, Carmel. 2016. Trump's Childcare Plan is Good for the Rich. But What About the Rest of Us? *Guardian Online*, 15 September 2017.

Marx, Karl. 1871. The Civil War in France. In *Marx and Engels Collected Works (MECW), Volume 22*, 307–59. New York: International Publishers.

Marx, Karl. 1852. The Eighteenth Brumaire of Louis Bonaparte. In *Marx and Engels Collected Works (MECW), Volume 11*, 99–197. New York: International Publishers.

Marx, Karl and Friedrich Engels. 1975–2005. *Marx and Engels Collected Works (MECW)*. New York: International Publishers.

Marx, Karl and Friedrich Engels. 1845. *The German Ideology*. Amherst, NY: Prometheus Books.

Mason, Tim. 1995. *Nazism, Fascism and the Working Class*. Cambridge: Cambridge University Press.

Matthews, Dylan. 2016. I Asked 5 Fascism Experts Whether Donald Trump Is a Fascist. Here's What They Say. *Vox Online*, 19 May 2016.

Mayer, Nonna. 2013. From Jean-Marie to Marine Le Pen: Electoral Change on the Far Right. *Parliamentary Affairs* 66 (1): 160–78.

McBride, Jessica. 2017. Neil Gorsuch, Guns and the Second Amendment: 5 Fast Facts You Need to Know. Heavy.com, 31 January 2017. http://heavy.com/news/2017/01/neil-gorsuch-second-amendment-guns-gun-control-nra-concealed-carry-gun-issues-supreme-court-nominee/.

McGuigan, Jim. 2008. Apprentices to Cool Capitalism. *Social Semiotics* 18 (3): 309–19.

Merica, Dan. Trump Gets What He Wants in Florida: Campaign-Level Adulation. *CNN Online*, 19 February 2017.

Moore, Michael. 2007. *Sicko*. Documentary. New York: Dog Eat Dog Films.

Morrison, Sara. 2016. Woman Trump Called 'Miss Piggy' Is a Post-Debate Star. *Vocativ*, 27 September 2016.

Mühlberger, Detlef. 1996. A 'Workers Party' or a 'Party Without Workers'? The Extent and Nature of the Working-Class Membership of the NSDAP, 1919–1933. *The Rise of National Socialism and the Working Classes in Weimar Germany*, ed. Conan Fischer, 47–77. Providence, RI: Berghahn.

National Bureau of Statistics of China. 2016. *Statistical Communiqué of the People's Republic of China on the 2015 National Economic and Social Development*. www.stats.gov.cn/english/PressRelease/201602/t20160229_1324019.html.

Negri, Antonio. 2017. *Marx and Foucault*. Cambridge: Polity.

Neumann, Franz. 1957/2017. Anxiety and Politics. *tripleC: Communication, Capitalism & Critique* 15 (2): 612–36.

Neumann, Franz. 1957. *The Democratic and the Authoritarian State*. Glencoe, IL: The Free Press.

Neumann, Franz. 1944/2009. *Behemoth: The Structure and Practice of National Socialism, 1933–1944*. Chicago, IL: Ivan R. Dee.

Neumann, Franz L. 1943. Anti-Semitism: Spearhead of Universal Terror. In *Secret Reports on Nazi Germany: The Frankfurt School Contributes to the War Effort*, ed. Raffaele Laudani, 27–30. Princeton, NJ: Princeton University Press.

Neumann, Franz L. 1936a. *European Trade Unionism and Politics*. New York: League for Industrial Democracy.

Neumann, Franz L. 1936b. *The Governance of the Rule of Law: An Investigation into the Relationship Between the Political Theories, the Legal System; and the Social Background in the Competitive Society*. Dissertation. London: London School of Economics.

Neumann, Franz L., Herbert Marcuse and Otto Kirchheimer. 2013. *Secret Reports on Nazi Germany: The Frankfurt School and the War Effort*. Princeton, NJ: Princeton University Press.

Nolte, Ernst. 1980/1993. Between Historical Legend and Revisionism? The Third Reich in the Perspective of 1980. In *Forever in the Shadow of Hitler?*, ed. James Knowlton and Truett Cates, 1–15. Atlantic Highlands, NJ: Humanities Press.

NSDAP (Nationalsozialistische Deutsche Arbeiterpartei). 1932. Emergency Economic Programme of the NSDAP. http://research.calvin.edu/german-propaganda-archive/sofortprogramm.htm.

Nunns, Jim, Len Burman, Ben Page, Jeff Rohaly and Joe Rosenberg. 2016. *An Analysis of Donald Trump's Revised Tax Plan*. 18 October 2016. Washington, DC: Tax Policy Center.

O'Brien, Timothy L. 2016. Trump's Financial Report? That's Rich. *Bloomberg View*, 20 May 2016.

O'Malley, Martin J. and Peter L. Levin. 2017. How to Counter Fake News. *Foreign Affairs*, 20 February 2017. www.foreignaffairs.com/articles/americas/2017–01–05/how-counter-fake-news.

O'Neill, Terry. 2016. When It Comes to Child Care, Donald Trump Is a Blockhead. *Huffington Post*, 18 August 2016.

ODNI (Office of the Director of National Intelligence). 2017. *Background to 'Assessing Russian Activities and Intentions in Recent US Elections': The Analytic Process and Cyber Incident Attribution*. https://upload.wikimedia.org/wikipedia/commons/0/0a/ODNI_Statement_on_Declassified_Intelligence_Community_Assessment_of_Russian_Activities_and_Intentions_in_Recent_U.S._Elections.pdf.

OECD. 2016. *Key Characteristics of Parental Leave Systems*. www.oecd.org/els/soc/PF2_1_Parental_leave_systems.pdf.

Oesch, Daniel. 2008. Explaining Workers' Support for Right-Wing Populist Parties in Western Europe: Evidence from Austria, Belgium, France, Norway, and Switzerland. *International Political Science Review* 29 (3): 349–73.

Ofcom. 2016. *Adults' Media Use and Attitudes*. London: Ofcom.

Oppenheim, Maya. 2016. Rosie O'Donnell Hits Back at Donald Trump After He Stands By 'Fat Pig' Comments. *Independent Online*, 27 September 2016.

Optify. 2011. The Changing Face of SERPs. www.my.epokhe.com/wp-content/uploads/2011/05/Changing-Face-of-SERPS-Organic-CTR.pdf.

Osborne, Samuel. 2017. Donald Trump's 'Armada' Steams On as North Korea Warns of Nuclear Strike on US. *Independent Online*, 12 April 2017.

Ott, Brian L. 2017. The Age of Twitter: Donald J. Trump and the Politics of Debasement. *Critical Studies in Media Communication* 34 (1): 59–68.

Özkirimli, Umut. 2010. *Theories of Nationalism: A Critical Introduction.* Basingstoke: Palgrave Macmillan, 2nd edition.

Paquette, Danielle. 2017. The Vast Majority of these Counties Voted for Donald Trump – Even if they had Backed Democrats for Years. *Washington Post Online*, 11 January 2017.

Paxton, Robert O. 2016. Is Fascism Back? *Project Syndicate*, 7 January 2016. www.project-syndicate.org/onpoint/is-fascism-back-by-robert-o--paxton-2016-01?barrier=accessreg.

Paxton, Robert O. 2004. *The Anatomy of Fascism.* New York: Knopf.

PewResearchCenter. 2016. *Long-Form Reading Shows Signs of Life in Our Mobile News World.* www.journalism.org/2016/05/05/long-form-reading-shows-signs-of-life-in-our-mobile-news-world/.

Pickard, Victor. 2016. Media Failure in the Age of Trump. *The Political Economy of Communication* 4 (2): 118–22.

Pollock, Friedrich. 1975. *Stadien des Kapitalismus.* Munich: C.H. Beck.

Pollock, Friedrich. 1941a. Is National Socialism a New Order? *Studies in Philosophy and Social Science* 9 (3): 440–55.

Pollock, Friedrich. 1941b. State Capitalism. *Studies in Philosophy and Social Science* 9 (2): 200–25.

Pollock, Friedrich and Theodor W. Adorno. 2011. *Group Experiment and Other Writings.* Cambridge, MA: Harvard University Press.

Postone, Moishe. 2003. The Holocaust and the Trajectory of the Twentieth Century. In *Catastrophe and Meaning: The Holocaust and the Twentieth Century*, ed. Moishe Postone and Eric Santner, 81–114. Chicago, IL: University of Chicago Press.

Postone, Moishe. 1993. *Time, Labor, and Social Domination: A Reinterpretation of Marx's Critical Theory.* Cambridge: Cambridge University Press.

Postone, Moishe. 1980. Anti-Semitism and National Socialism: Notes on the German Reaction to 'Holocaust'. *New German Critique* 19 (1): 97–115.

Poulantzas, Nicos. 1980/2000. *State, Power, Socialism.* London: Verso, new edition.

Poulantzas, Nicos. 1974. *Fascism and Dictatorship: The Third International and the Problem of Fascism.* London: NLB.

Pruitt, Scott and Luther Strange. 2016. The Climate-Change Gang. *National Review Online*, 17 May 2016.

Puzder, Andy. 2014. Minimum Wage, Maximum Politics. *Wall Street Journal Online*, 5 October 2014.

Qiu, Jack L. 2016. *Goodbye iSlave: A Manifesto for Digital Abolition.* Urbana, IL: University of Illinois Press.

Rehmann, Jan. 2013. *Theories of Ideology.* Leiden: Brill.

Reagan, Ronald. 1986. *Address to the Nation on National Security.* February 26, 1986. http://reagan2020.us/speeches/address_on_national_security.asp.

Reich, Wilhelm. 1972. *The Mass Psychology of Fascism.* London: Souvenir Press.

Reich, Wilhelm. 1932. *Der Einbruch der Sexualmoral*. Berlin: Verlag für Sexualpolitik.

Reisigl, Martin and Ruth Wodak. 2009. The Discourse-Historical Approach. In *Methods of Critical Discourse Analysis*, ed. Ruth Wodak and Michael Meyer, 87–121. London: Sage.

Reisigl, Martin and Ruth Wodak. 2001. *Discourse and Discrimination. Rhetorics of Racism and Antisemitism*. London: Routledge.

Renton, David. 1999. *Fascism: Theory and Practice*. London: Pluto.

Ritsert, Jürgen. 1972. *Inhaltsanalyse und Idelogiekritik: Ein Versuch über kritische Sozialforschung*. Frankfurt am Main: Fischer.

Robbins, Tom. 1999. Deal Sealed in Trump Tower Suit. *New York Daily News*, 8 March 1999.

Rooduijn, Matthijs. 2016. Closing the Gap? A Comparison of Voters for Radical Right-Wing Populist Parties and Mainstream Parties Over Time. In *Radical Right-Wing Populist Parties in Western Europe*, ed. Tjitske Akkerman, Sarah de Lange and Matthijs Rooduijn, 53–69. New York: Routledge.

Rosa, Hartmut. 2013. *Social Acceleration: A New Theory of Modernity*. New York: Columbia University Press.

Rothwell, Jonathan. 2016. Explaining Nationalist Political Communication: The Case of Donald Trump. www.umass.edu/preferen/You%20Must%20Read%20This/Rothwell-Gallup.pdf.

RT. 2017a. 'America 1st Doesn't Mean Europe Last' – EU Lashes Out at US Sanctions Against Russia. *Russia Today Online*, 26 July 2017.

RT. 2017b. New US Sanctions Against Russia 'Defy Common Sense', Will Cause Retaliation – Moscow. *Russia Today Online*, 26 July 2017.

RT. 2011. I Want to Free France from EU Straitjacket – Far-Right Party Leader. *Russia Today Online*, 27 April 2011.

Sanders, Bernie. 2016a. Carrier Just Showed Corporations How to Beat Donald Trump. *Washington Post Online*, 1 December 2016.

Sanders, Bernie. 2016b. *Our Revolution: A Future To Believe In*. London: Profile.

Sanders, Bernie. 2016c. Speech at the Democratic National Convention. 26 July 2016. http://time.com/4421574/democratic-convention-bernie-sanders-speech-transcript/.

Schiedel, Heribert. 2007. *Der rechte Rand: Extremistische Gesinnungen in unserer Gesellschaft*. Wien: Edition Steinbauer.

Schmitt, Carl. 1932/1996. *The Concept of the Political*. Chicago, IL: University of Chicago Press.

Sciutto, Jim et al. 2017. Trump promises North Korea 'fire and fury' over nuke threat. *CNN Online*, 3 August 2017.

Scott, Eugene. 2016. Donald Trump: Fidel Castro is Dead! *CNN Online*, 26 November 2016.

Scott, Robert E. 2011. *Heading South: U.S.-Mexico Trade and Job Displacement after NAFTA*. Washington, DC: Economic Policy Institute.

Senate Intelligence Committee. 2017. Full Transcript and Video: James Comey's Testimony on Capitol Hill. *New York Times Online*, 8 June 2017.

Shear, Michael D. and Eric Lipton. 2016. Trump Vows Steps to Avoid Appearance of Business Conflicts. *New York Times Online*, 30 November 2016.

Silver, Nate. 2016. The Mythology of Trump's 'Working Class' Support. *FivtyThirtyEight*, 3 May 2016.

Silverman, Craig. 2016. This Analysis Shows How Viral Fake Election News Stories Outperformed Real News on Facebook. *BuzzFeed*, 16 November 2016.

Silverman, Craig and Jeremy Singer-Vine. 2016. Most Americans Who See Fake News Believe It, New Survey Says. *BuzzFeed*, 7 December 2016.

Skibba, Ramin. 2016. The Polling Crisis: How to Tell What People Really Think. *Nature* 538: 304–6.

Smith, Anthony D. 1991. *National Identity*. London: Penguin.

Spiering, Charlie. 2017. Donald Trump on Charlottesville: 'Fake News Media Will Never Be Satisfied'. *Breitbart*, 14 August 2017.

Stalin, Joseph I. 1924. Concerning the International Situation. In *Stalin Works, Volume 6*, 292–314. Moscow: Foreign Languages Publishing House.

Steen, Michael. 2010. Intolerant Kingmaker Defies Dutch Clichés. *Financial Times Online*, 26 February 2010.

Stelter, Brian. 2016. Debate Breaks Records as Most-Watched in U.S. History. *CNN Online*, 27 September 2016.

Stephenson, Jill. 2001. *Women in Nazi Germany*. London: Routledge.

Sullivan, Tim. 2017. North Korea Flaunts Long-Range Missiles in Massive Parade. *Associated Press Online*, 15 April 2017.

Sum, Ngai-Ling and Bob Jessop. 2013. *Towards a Cultural Political Economy: Putting Culture in its Place in Political Economy*. Cheltenham: Edward Elgar.

Sundaram, Rangarajan K. 2012. Derivatives in Financial Market Development. Working Paper. London: International Growth Centre.

Tamás, Gáspár Miklós. 2000. On Post-Fascism. *Boston Review*, 1 June 2000.

Taguieff, Pierre-André. 2001. *The Force of Prejudice: On Racism and its Doubles*. Minneapolis, MN: University of Minnesota Press.

Thalheimer, August. 1932. The Struggle for the United Front in Germany, 1920–23. www.marxists.org/archive/thalheimer/works/ufront20–23.html.

Thalheimer, August. 1930. *On Fascism*. www.marxists.org/archive/thalheimer/works/fascism.htm.

Theweleit, Klaus. 1989. *Male Fantasies. Volume 2: Male Bodies: Psychoanalyzing the White Terror*. Minneapolis, MN: University of Minnesota Press.

Theweleit, Klaus. 1987. *Male Fantasies. Volume 1: Women, Floods, Bodies, History*. Minneapolis, MN: University of Minnesota Press.

Todd, Chuck, Sally Bronston and Matt Rivera. 2017. Rep. John Lewis: 'I Don't See Trump as a Legitimate President'. *NBC News Online*, 14 January 2017.

Townsend, Leanne et al. 2016. *Social Media Research: A Guide to Ethics*. Output from the ESRC project 'Social Media, Privacy and Risk: Towards More Ethical Research Methodologies'. www.gla.ac.uk/media/media_487729_en.pdf.

Trotsky, Leon. 1968. *Fascism: What It Is and How To Fight It*. www.marxists.org/archive/trotsky/works/1944/1944-fas.htm.

Trotsky, Leon. 1934. *Bonapartism and Fascism*. www.marxists.org/archive/trotsky/germany/1934/340715.htm.

Trotsky, Leon. 1931. *Germany, the Key to the International Situation*. www.marxists.org/archive/trotsky/germany/1931/311126.htm.

Trump, Donald. 2017a. News conference, 11 January 2017. www.youtube.com/watch?v=SUyAkobYpso.

Trump, Donald. 2017b. News conference, 16 February 2017. www.youtube.com/watch?v=KaYRi6pPDXI.

Trump, Donald. 2017c. *Speech at CPAC*, 24 February 2017. www.vox.com/policy-and-politics/2017/2/24/14726584/transcript-donald-trump-cpac-speech.

Trump, Donald. 2016a. Address on Immigration. Phoenix, Arizona. 31 August 2016. www.donaldjtrump.com/press-releases/donald-j.-trump-address-on-immigration.

Trump, Donald J. 2016b. *An America First Economic Plan: Winning the Global Competition.* 8 August 2016. www.donaldjtrump.com/press-releases/an-america-first-economic-plan-winning-the-global-competition.

Trump, Donald J. 2016c. *Contract for the American Voter: 100-Day Plan to Make America Great Again – For Everyone.* www.donaldjtrump.com/press-releases/donald-j.-trump-delivers-groundbreaking-contract-for-the-american-vote1.

Trump, Donald J. 2016d. *Fact Sheet: Donald J. Trump's New Child Care Plan.* www.donaldjtrump.com/press-releases/fact-sheet-donald-j.-trumps-new-child-care-plan.

Trump, Donald. 2016e. Full Transcript of an Interview with the *New York Times.* *New York Times Online,* 23 November 2016. www.nytimes.com/2016/11/23/us/politics/trump-new-york-times-interview-transcript.html.

Trump, Donald. 2016f. *Law & Order Speech (Transcript).* 16 August 2016. http://heavy.com/news/2016/08/read-full-transcript-donald-trump-transcript-law-and-order-speech-west-bend-wisconsin.

Trump, Donald. 2016g. Let Me Ask America a Question. *Wall Street Journal Online,* 14 April 2016.

Trump, Donald J. 2016h. *Military Readiness Remarks.* 7 September 2016. www.donaldjtrump.com/press-releases/donald-j.-trump-military-readiness-remarks.

Trump, Donald J. 2016i. *National Security Speech.* 13 June 2016. www.politico.com/story/2016/06/transcript-donald-trump-national-security-speech-224273.

Trump, Donald J. 2016j. *Second Amendment Rights.* www.donaldjtrump.com/press-releases/donald-trump-discusses-second-amendment-rights-on-hannity.

Trump, Donald. 2016k. Transcript of an Interview with the *New York Times. New York Times Online,* 23 November 2016. www.nytimes.com/2016/11/23/us/politics/trump-new-york-times-interview-transcript.html.

Trump, Donald. 2016l. Trump to Ohio: I Will Campaign for Every Vote. www.donaldjtrump.com/press-releases/trump-to-ohio-i-will-campaign-for-every-vote.

Trump, Donald. 2015a. *Crippled America: How To Make America Great Again.* New York: Threshold Editions.

Trump, Donald. 2015b. Donald J. Trump Statement on Preventing Muslim Immigration. www.donaldjtrump.com/press-releases/donald-j.-trump-statement-on-preventing-muslim-immigration.

Trump, Donald. 2015c. Trump on Healthcare, Trade, Climate, and Gay Marriage. *CNN Online*, 28 June 2015. http://edition.cnn.com/videos/politics/2015/06/28/sotu-tapper-trump-on-healthcare-trade-climate-abortion-and-same-sex-marriage.cnn.

Trump, Donald. 2007. *Trump 101: The Way to Success*. Hoboken, NJ: John Wiley & Sons.

Trump, Donald and Bill Zanker. 2007. *Think Big: Make It Happen in Business and Life*. New York: Harper.

Tsur, Oren, Katherine Ognyanova and David Lazer. 2016. The Data Behind Trump's Twitter Takeover. *Politico Magazine*, 29 April 2016. www.politico.com/magazine/story/2016/04/donald-trump-2016-twitter-takeover-213861.

Unger, Johann W., Ruth Wodak and Majid Khosravinik. 2016. Critical Discourse Studies and Social Media Data. In *Qualitative Research*, ed. David Silverman, 277–93. London: Sage.

Uz, Irem. 2014. Individualism and First Person Pronoun Use in Written Texts Across Languages. *Journal of Cross-Cultural Psychology* 45 (10): 1671–8.

van Dijk, Teun. 2011. Discourse and Ideology. In *Discourse Studies: A Multidisciplinary Introduction*, ed. Teun van Dijk, 379–407. London: Sage.

van Dijk, Teun. 1998. *Ideology: A Multidisciplinary Approach*. London: Sage.

Van Gelder, Robert. 1940. Chaplin Draws a Keen Weapon. *New York Times*, 8 September 1940.

Washington Post. 2017. Full Transcript: FBI Director James Comey Testifies on Russian Interference in 2016 Election. *Washington Post Online*, 20 March 2017.

Weaver, Matthew. 2016. Chomsky Hits Back at Erdoğan, Accusing Him of Double Standards on Terrorism. *Guardian Online*, 14 January 2016.

Weber, Max. 1978. *Economy and Society*. Berkeley, CA: University of California Press.

Weisbrot, Mark, Stephan Lefebvre and Joseph Sammut. 2014. *Did NAFTA Help Mexico? An Assessment After 20 Years*. Washington, DC: Center for Economic and Policy Research.

Werts, Han, Peer Scheepers and Marcel Lubbers. 2012. Euro-Scepticism and Radical Right-Wing Voting in Europe, 2002–2008: Social Cleavages, Socio-Political Attitudes and Contextual Characteristics Determining Voting for the Radical Right. *European Union Politics* 14 (2): 183–205.

West, Cornel. 2017. Pity the Sad Legacy of Barack Obama. *Guardian Online*, 9 January 2017.

Williams, Raymond. 1983a. *Keywords*. New York: Oxford University Press, revised edition.

Williams, Raymond. 1983b. *Towards 2000*. London: Chatto & Windus.

Williams, Raymond. 1974. *Television: Technology and Cultural Form*. London: Routledge.

Wodak, Ruth. 2015. *The Politics of Fear: What Right-Wing Populist Discourses Mean*. London: Sage.

Wodak, Ruth. 2013. 'Anything Goes!' – The Haiderization of Europe. In *Right-Wing Populism in Europe: Politics and Discourse*, ed. Ruth Wodak, Majid KosraviNik and Brigitte Mral, 23–37. London: Bloomsburg.

Wodak, Ruth. 2009. *The Discourse of Politics in Action*. Basingstoke: Palgrave Macmillan.

Wodak, Ruth and Michael Meyer. 2009. *Methods of Critical Discourse Analysis*. London: Sage, 2nd edition.

Woodley, Daniel. 2010. *Fascism and Political Theory: Critical Perspectives on Fascist Ideology*. Abingdon: Routledge.

Woolley, Samuel C. and Douglas Guilbeault. 2017. Computational Propaganda in the United States of America: Manufacturing Consensus Online. Working Paper 2017.5. Oxford: Project on Computational Propaganda.

Wright, Joshua. 2017. Rust Belt Counties Dependent on Blue-Collar Jobs Nearly All Voted for Trump. www.economicmodeling.com/2017/01/11/rust-belt-counties-dependent-on-blue-collar-jobs-nearly-all-voted-for-trump/.

Yahr, Emily, Caitlin Moore and Emily Chow. 2015. How We Went from 'Survivor' to More than 300 Reality Shows: A Complete Guide. *Washington Post Online*, 29 May 2015.

Zaru, Deena. 2016. Rosie O'Donnell Responds to Donald Trump Debate Attak. *CNN Online*, 27 September 2016.

ZenithOptimedia. 2015. *Media Consumption Forecasts 2015*. London: ZenithOptimedia.

Žižek, Slavoj. 2017. *The Courage of Hopelessness: Chronicles of a Year of Acting Dangerously*. London: Allen Lane, ebook version.

Žižek, Slavoj. 2000/2006. Why We All Love to Hate Haider. In *The Universal Exception*, 33–41. London: Continuum.

Žižek, Slavoj, ed. 1994. *Mapping Ideology*. London: Verso.

Index

Index

Index

Index